The Power of Economic Ideas

ALEX MILLMOW

ANU
THE AUSTRALIAN NATIONAL UNIVERSITY

E PRESS

The Power of Economic Ideas

The origins of macroeconomic management
in Australia 1929–39

ALEX MILLMOW

THE AUSTRALIAN NATIONAL UNIVERSITY

E PRESS

![ANU E PRESS]

Published by ANU E Press
The Australian National University
Canberra ACT 0200, Australia
Email: anuepress@anu.edu.au
This title is also available online at: http://epress.anu.edu.au/keynes_citation.html

National Library of Australia
Cataloguing-in-Publication entry

Author: Millmow, A. J. (Alex J.)

Title: The power of economic ideas : the origins of Keynesian macroeconomic
               management in interwar Australia, 1929-1939 / Alex Millmow.

ISBN: 9781921666261 (pbk.) 9781921666278 (ebook)

Notes: Includes bibliographical references.

Subjects: Keynesian economics.
               Macroeconomics--Australia.
               Australia--Economic conditions--1929-1939

Dewey Number: 994.042

Cover design and layout by ANU E Press

Cover image: Courtesy of Caroline de Maistre Walker

Frontispiece: Courtesy of the Art Gallery of NSW

Contents

Acknowledgments ix

Lists of abbreviations xi

A word on the artwork xiii

Preface xv

1. The triumph of the economists? 1

Part I.
Backing into the Limelight: the Interwar Australian Economics Profession

2. Economic ideas and an assessment of Australian
   economists in the 1930s 13

3. The Australian economy during the Depression decade 31

4. The interwar Australian economics profession 43

Part II.
Triumph and Tribulation

5. The Premiers' Plan and the economists 79

6. The agonistes of the economists, 1931–1932 117

7. The Australian recovery, 1933–1936 149

Part III.
The March of Keynesian Ideas

8. The Royal Commission on Monetary and Banking Systems . . 193

9. Australia, 1936–1938: the nascent Keynesian state? 225

10. The economics of near-war 249

Dramatis personae 269

Bibliography 277

Acknowledgments

This book, stemming from doctoral studies undertaken at The Australian National University, has been long in the making. First and foremost, I wish to thank my doctoral supervisor, Selwyn Cornish, for providing the leadership and inspiration for this path-breaking study. We have had countless meetings going through the ambition and rationale of this study. No-one could ask for a better, more considerate and, I must add, patient supervisor. When we first agreed on the scope of this study, I circulated an exploratory chapter to those with some expertise in the area: Tim Battin, William Coleman, John King, Peter Groenewegen, Evan Jones, Marjorie Harper, Sean Turnell and the late Heinz Arndt. My thanks to all of them, especially Heinz Arndt, who took a particular interest in this project and showed me his fine collection of economic literature pertaining to that period.

I owe a debt of gratitude to the following archivists for consulting their collections: first, the staff at the University of Melbourne Archives. I was lucky to have unrestricted access to their collection, on D.B. Copland and L.F. Giblin and the Faculty of Commerce and Economics for the period 1925-1940. In Melbourne, too, I consulted the oft-overlooked Sir Robert Gibson Papers held at the State Library of Victoria. I would also like to thank the stockbroking firm J. B. Were and Son for giving me the privileged access to consult the business diary of Staniforth Ricketson. I also wish to thank the archivists of the ANZ collection who hold the collection on the Bank of Australasia. My gratitude extends also to the National Bank Archive that contains the L. J. McConnan collection. By far the most powerful and most interesting banker in the interwar era was Alfred Davidson and his papers and those of the Bank of New South Wales remain with the Westpac Archive. I wish to thank the Westpac archivist, Julie Gleaves, for giving me unrestricted access to the general manager's files for the 1930s. To consult the records of the Commonwealth Bank, including its senior personnel during the interwar era, I visited the archives of the Reserve Bank of Australia in Sydney. I thank Virginia McDonald for being especially helpful in trawling through their files. I would also like to thank her counterpart at the Bank of England for guiding me through their collection on material relevant to Australia. At Cambridge University, I consulted, of course, the Keynes Papers and I wish to thank the archivist and the fellows of King's College for the right to quote from their collection. I have made much use of the archival materials at the National Library of Australia and I would like to thank the chief archivist for his advice in uncovering troves of literary treasure. Within the parliamentary vicinity there is the National Archives of Australia, where I trawled through the

Federal Treasury files. I would also like to thank the archivists at the University of Tasmania, the University of Sydney and the University of Queensland for allowing me to read the archives of certain economists of the interwar era. I would also like to thank Tony Endres, Geoff Harcourt and Sean Turnell for their comments, encouragement and advice on this study.

Lastly, I would like to thank my parents, David and Nancy, for putting up with their son who never really left university. I dedicate this book to them and to my beautiful wife, Amanda, with much love and appreciation.

List of abbreviations

AA	National Archives of Australia
BE	Bank of England Archives
BNSW	Bank of New South Wales, now Westpac, Archive
CPD	*Commonwealth Parliamentary Debates*
KPKC	Keynes Papers, King's College, Modern Archives Centre
NLA	Manuscript collection, National Library of Australia
PRO	Public Records Office, London
RBA	Papers of governors and senior personnel at the Reserve Bank of Australia
SMH	*Sydney Morning Herald*
UMA FECC	Faculty of Economics and Commerce, University of Melbourne Archives
UT	University of Tasmania

A word on the artwork

Thematic to this book, both the sketch and the watercolour of J. M. Keynes were undertaken by the Australian-born artist Roy de Maistre. He spent a good part of his career working in London. The sketch appears courtesy of the Art Gallery of New South Wales. The watercolour, inspired by the sketch, appears courtesy of Caroline de Maistre Walker and the Castlemaine Art Gallery. In 1964 Roy De Maistre was commissioned by the National Mutual Life Assurance Society to undertake a posthumous portrait of Keynes to commemorate the economist's stint as chairman during the interwar years. De Maistre used the famous David Low cartoon of Keynes reclining in an armchair as well as photographs to recapture Keynes in a characteristic impish mood. The artist was 'happy' with his rendering of Keynes (Johnson 1995).

Preface

This book focuses on the transformation in Australian economists' thought and ideas during the period 1929–39. In a decade marked by depression, recovery and international political turbulence, Australian economists moved from a classical orthodox economic position to that of a cautious Keynesianism by 1939. In the international literature on the diffusion of Keynesian economics, there has been little recognition of just how extensive the prewar conversion of Australian economists actually was. That advance in theoretical insight was channelled into policy.

Since its inception, the Australian economic profession has always been a publicly focused one. This book looks at how economists tried to influence policymaking in the 1930s. Having devised a unique macroeconomic stabilisation package in 1931, economists felt obliged to seek changes to the parameters as economic conditions altered but, more importantly, as their insights about economic management changed. This aspect requires an insight of the interplay between economic ideas, players and policy. This approach aids our primary thesis by teasing out the growing divide between the perspectives of economists and that of policymakers.

There are three related themes that underscore this study. First, the professionalisation of Australian economics took a gigantic leap in this period, aided in part by the adverse circumstances confronting the economy but also by the aspirations economists held for their discipline. This necessitates looking at the activities of the economists through the 1930s as they tried to enlighten preconceived economic ideas and conventions among policymakers.

A second theme relates to the rather unflattering reputation foisted on interwar economists after 1945. A consensus was formed that their anti-depression advice was unfortunate, inappropriate and mistimed. This view will be strongly contested by showing how, in fact, Australian economists moved quickly and radically away from the analytical framework that underpinned their earlier advice.

That transition underlies a third theme of this book—namely, that Australian economists were emboldened by John Maynard Keynes's *General Theory* to confidently push for greater management of economic activity than hitherto. By 1939, and perhaps earlier, Australian economists conceptualised from a new theoretical framework, from which they advanced comment and policy advice. When the committee that advised P. C. Spender was first appointed in 1939, it drew one economist, E. R. Walker, to proclaim that '[t]he value of economic science was at last recognised' (cited in Brown 1994:93). This book therefore will rehabilitate the works of Australian interwar economists, arguing that they not only had an enviable international reputation but facilitated the acceptance of Keynes's *General Theory* among policymakers before most of their counterparts in the northern hemisphere.

1. The triumph of the economists?

In 1981, Colin Clark wrote to the Cambridge economist Joan Robinson suggesting that he had found a telling insight into J. M. Keynes and the evolution of some of his thought that was later embedded in *The General Theory*.[1] In 1932, Keynes had written an appraisal of the economic response by Australian authorities to the Depression. Somewhat uniquely guided by economics expertise, the authorities had responded with an orchestrated mix of cost-cutting, fiscal austerity and a modest form of monetary expansion. Asked to review Australian economic policy, Keynes demurred on the idea of further wage cuts or indeed devaluation, suggesting that Australia wait for an internationally coordinated response to revive economic activity. He suggested greater recourse to public works. That advice, as we shall see, did not entirely please Australian economists.

Keynes once remarked that there had been 'few passages in the history of controversy more valuable...than that which took place among economists in the ten years...before the war'.[2] This study directs attention to Australia and her economic profession. By the eve of World War II, Australia's small community of academic economists had been swept along by the Keynesian tide. A new vista of managing the economy was at hand. Aside from the intellectual activity Keynes's *General Theory* stirred among Australia's economists, they had long been articulating the need for greater control over the economy before World War II broke out. During the 1930s, relations between Australian economists and the federal government had wavered between considerable relevance and quiet neglect. In 1931, economists and politicians came together to frame a cohesive and unique policy response to the Depression within Australia. That outcome, the 'Premiers' Plan', was an attempt at economic experimentation that its prime architect, Douglas Copland (1937a:409), billed as 'constructive deflation'. This plan was hurriedly designed to meet the country's need for financial rehabilitation and structural readjustment. At that point, the Premiers' Plan led the world in economic experimentation against the slump; it elicited intellectual curiosity and scholarship from afar (MacLaurin 1936; Dow 1938:Hawtrey 1934; Garnett 1949). It was acknowledged that Australia was one of the first countries to appoint a 'brains trust' of economists, with some degree of executive authority to help guide the nation out of its difficulties (Goodwin 1974:235).

---

1   C. Clark to J. Robinson, 14 May 1981, Colin Clark Papers, University of Queensland.
2   J. M. Keynes to E. Durbin, 1942, Keynes Papers, King's College, Cambridge (hereafter, KPKC).

Only a short time before, economists had neither the plan nor the authority to deal with Australia's peculiar economic difficulties. The Premiers' Plan was, by necessity, a politically inspired one with events pushing economists to the forefront. In private, Copland referred to it, with good reason, as 'the economists' plan', but it was politicians who had to implement it. It was not long before economists grew concerned that economic policy settings were too deflationary and preoccupied with the external account. It was also the case, though, that as the economy slowly recovered the less inclined were the authorities prepared to turn, again, to economists. On the whole, Australian economists did, however, make inroads into the world of policy advice during the 1930s. By 1938, for instance, Australia's central bank, with economists in the backrooms, dealt effectively with the threat of an internationally transmitted downturn known as the Roosevelt recession. The year after, economists—with some now serving in a semi-official capacity—had further success with a plan to facilitate Australia's war preparations without causing undue economic disruption. Why was it, then, that Australian economists were becoming more influential with policymakers? The answer was not just they had always been a policy-focused profession but, more importantly, their advice sprang from new economic ideas.

This gulf between economists and politicians is, of course, hardly a unique occurrence. Policymaking is renowned for being an intramural, opaque process with many divergent interests impinging on it. Politicians rarely look to economists to tell them what to do; rather economists, as with the Premiers' Plan, usually provide rationales for action or inaction (Harcourt 1986). The predominant new paradigm of economic thought in the 1930s was the birth of macroeconomics. Keynes's *General Theory*, once understood, made economists energetic in calling for greater ambition in managing an economy. The failure of Keynes to win much policy ground in Britain during the late 1930s has been well documented (Peden 1988; Middleton 1985; Tomlinson 1984; Skidelsky 1992). Even Keynes despaired of it. Treasury officials in Britain would prove too sceptical, by nature and training, to be swept along by a 'revolution' in economic theory until the outbreak of war changed this (Peden 1988:120).

When policymaking institutions in Britain did display an acceptance of Keynes's *General Theory* it was usually muddled, ambivalent or incomplete (Bridges 1964). While Keynes's ideas and theories might have swept through the cloisters, the corridors of power proved a harder nut to crack. The diffusion process was held back by circumstances, bureaucratic inertia, the climate of opinion and, not least, the nature of the ideas themselves. It was only when Keynes entered and worked at the British Treasury during World War II that his ideas found application in policy. Even then, a little known memoir of him recalls that Treasury officials still felt that Keynes did not seem fully aware of the recalcitrance and intractability of the political process (Le Pan 1979:83).

The transmission of Keynes's ideas into the Australian political mainstream, in contrast, was smoother and innovative—attributable to the useful start economists had made in establishing a rapport and credibility with government leaders in the 1930s. Australia seemed fertile ground for authentic Keynesian economics to take root, though not necessarily in officialdom (Markwell 1985; Smyth 1994; Turnell 1999). One commentator described Australia as 'the utopia of practical economists' (cited in Goodwin 1974:236). Apart from the avowedly public orientation of their profession, economists also owed their influence to the fact that economic policy was not entirely within the Australian government's ambit. Four extra-parliamentary agencies—namely, the Arbitration Court, the Tariff Board, the Commonwealth Bank and the Australian Loan Council—exercised a 'quadripartite control of industrial and financial circumstances' (cited in Brown 1994:91).

As the Commonwealth assumed greater executive command over the shaping of monetary and budgetary policy, academic economists were replaced, to some extent, with 'inside economists' (Corden 1968). They were, however, still cut from the same cloth. In international forums, too, Australian economists had gained pre-eminence by adopting a proto-Keynesian stance for restoring balance to the global economy (Turnell 1999). More importantly for our purposes, Australian economists were freshly apprised of the latest developments in economic theory and practice.

Against what would become the dazzling light of economic reason stood a federal government comfortable with the recovery achieved by economic readjustment and fiscal consolidation. Notorious for its 'let business alone' stance, the three Lyons governments that ruled from 1932 until 1939 were prone to intellectual torpor (Hart 1967). Throughout the 1930s, academic economists, in a bid to change the climate of opinion, made representations to politicians directly and via the press. On balance, as many overseas commentators noted, Australian economists were quite influential with policymaking authorities relative to their overseas counterparts. How they achieved that profile had to do with the circumstances facing Australia, together with axioms and conventions that underpinned the economics profession.

The groundwork was already in place, then, which would spearhead Australia's acceptance of Keynesianism. It did not come, alas, with an accommodating 'explicitly altered economic vision' among political leaders (Heilbroner and Milberg 1995:43). The first threads of comprehensive economic management in Australia came with the 1939/40 budget, which put into circulation the Keynesian technique of estimating the inflationary gap (Cornish 1993a; Markwell 1985). The war-finance approach that Keynes (1940) outlined in *How to Pay for the War*—that is, how to shift resources from civilian to war purposes without incurring inflation—was acted on by Australian economists (Walker 1939b).

The ambit of this book

This book intends to show how the ideas and theoretical thinking of Australian economists, seen through the prism of their policy advice, underwent a major transformation through the 1930s. It will be argued that Australia's small nucleus of economists was emboldened, as the 1930s wore on, to push for a more informed and more expansionist line on economic activity than hitherto. Economists would have a fundamentally different theoretical and policy outlook in 1939 from that which they had in 1929. The marked change in the theorising and policy advice of the economists during that period was in stark contrast with that of Australian politicians, though there were exceptions. This divergence of opinion between the two groups will be set against the peculiarities of Australian economic experience in the 1930s. This includes not just the slump and protracted recovery but the precariousness of the external account, together with fears of another boom–bust cycle. It will also be set against the economic events that punctuated the period, such as the Royal Commission on Banking Systems and the Treasury bills and funding debates, together with preparations for war.

This book will reveal the process by which Australian economists came to achieve a superior command of Keynesian statecraft arguably earlier than most of their overseas counterparts. It does so by tracing the development in their thought through the years 1929–39. While the study is set within the province of the history of ideas, it is also a study in political economy. That is, it focuses on the complex interaction between economic ideas, events, personalities and policy in interwar Australia. It will closely examine the process Australian economists endured in coming to terms with new ideas on economic philosophy in the 1930s and whether or not they shaped economic policy. The activities and input of economists, expressed through numerous committees, meetings, correspondence and memoranda, will be traced to reveal a conceptual gap between economists and politicians. It will be argued that after being uncommonly influential in 1931, the new conceptual vision of economists, expressly to do with economic management, was frustrated by political inertia, vested interests and complacency. The publication of Keynes's *General Theory* in 1936, once understood, fortified the intellectual shift towards economic management. It will examine how, as the first to be liberated from old ways of economic thought, Australian economists went about propagating that new wisdom. Usually their advice fell on deaf ears; the new economic thinking articulating a coherent form of macroeconomic management more distinct and concrete than longings for 'planning' raced ahead of political convention and attitudes. This was to become apparent when examining the appropriate economic policy settings for Australia in the late 1930s.

This philosophical shift took some time, of course, to materialise at the official policy level. Some agencies, such as the Federal Treasury—like its British counterpart—remained unmoved by the 'new economics' of Keynes. That is, a body of economics with its central focus on the principle of effective demand with policies such as public works, budget deficits and cheap money as the appropriate responses for an economy in slump. Simply put, the new economics of Keynes brought a physical resources perspective to economics. Demand could be safely expanded as long as there was generalised idle capacity in the economy. A commitment to counter-cyclical management of overall demand is too indiscriminate. At a more sophisticated level, it translated not just to the manipulation of aggregate demand but to eschew reliance on market forces to deliver an economy from the slump. While the term 'macroeconomic policy' came into circulation only in 1941, Keynes's emphasis on the aggregate dimension in the *General Theory* marked the effective start of macroeconomics (Clarke 1996:68–9). This study closes by examining the propitious preconditions that underpinned the early acceptance of the Keynesian economic policy in wartime Australia.

The appeal of this book

The hiatus in Australian economic history from the Depression to World War II—a period of recovery and reconstruction—has been well explored by economic historians (Cain 1980, 1982, 1983, 1984, 1985, 1987a, 1987b, 1988a, 1988b; Schedvin 1970; Sinclair 1974; Clark 1976; Gregory and Butlin 1988). In a series of papers, Neville Cain made a pioneering study of the players, including economists, officials and politicians, behind the formation of Commonwealth economic policy from the Depression through to 1936. No work until now, though, has cogently and systematically looked at how Australian economists moved towards a new constellation of economic ideas in the years leading up to 1939.

Most of the literature on the arrival of Keynesian economics usually dates it from World War II. As the British economist Ian Little (1957:35) put it, 'Thanks to Keynesian ideas (and the war) the economist has found his way in to government.' In Australia, it was somewhat different. There was, seemingly, a 'revelatory' adoption of Keynes's *General Theory* by Australian economists (King 1997). Turnell (1999:13) posits that the rapid propagation of Keynesian economics in Australia was because economists had adopted a proto-Keynesian line in the various international forums, together with their unpublished writings, all of which focused on their advocacy for international reflation. In contrast, domestic economic policy was—given the adverse circumstances confronting the economy—more orthodox and deflationary. The Premiers'

Plan became the leitmotiv of Australian economic policy in the 1930s (Turnell 1999:23). This discontinuity between domestic and international strands of Australian economic thought and policy detracts, however, from reaching a true picture of the receptivity of Australian economists to Keynes's *General Theory*.

This account complements and adds to Sean Turnell's (1999) unpublished work by showing how Australian economists urged a more expansionist line to domestic policy settings from 1932 onwards. They were not prepared to wait for an upturn in export prices to bring about recovery; nor did the weight of Australia's external obligations totally circumscribe domestic attempts to reflate. Indeed, the failure of the two major international trade and monetary conferences held in 1932 and 1933 to engineer a global economic stimulus that would lift the export incomes of countries such as Australia forced reliance on domestic expedients. This approach was encouraged and theoretically informed by Keynes, not just with the publication of the *General Theory*, but earlier in 1932 with his incisive review of the policy thinking of Australian economists. For the most part, the federal authorities rejected this expansionist line by Australian economists. The economists did have some success, however, in preventing monetary policy from becoming even more contractionary than it was. There was further recognition of the value of economics expertise when the federal government established a committee in 1938 to expedite the transition to a war economy (Coombs 1981:7).

There are other compelling reasons for this study. In the literature on the spread of Keynesianism across nations, only a handful of studies have touched—and touched lightly—on the reception of the *General Theory* in Australia (Coleman et al. 2006; Cain 1983; Cornish 1993; Markwell 1985; Turnell 1999; Smyth 1994; Whitwell 1994). Cain (1983:21) urged others to investigate the 'antipodean impact of the *General Theory*' on Australian economists and policymakers before 1939. There has been little work, too, on how economists shaped Australian domestic economic policy during the 1930s other than the contributions of Cain and works by Copland (1934), Walker (1933a) and Schedvin (1970). There is little literature examining the deliberations and scope of Australian economic policy from 1936 through to 1939. In that regard, it has been claimed that all Australian economists were basically Keynesian—in theory and policy—by the advent of World War II.[3] Certainly, Richard Downing (1972), a young Australian economist at the time, recalled that this was the case. Given this, it might be said that Australia, bar Sweden, led the way in terms of adopting Keynesianism (Winch 1966). One historian goes so far as to claim that Australian monetary authorities or the central bank practised Keynesian-inspired policy in 1938 to quarantine the nation from the impact of the Roosevelt recession (Gilbert 1973:219). The accepted assessment of Australian economic policy during the

---

3   Melville, TRC 182, 1971, NLA, p. 158.

1930s is, however, usually much bleaker; both the efficacy of economic policy in the 1930s and the theoretical and public contributions of economists were called into question and judged to be comparatively poor against efforts made overseas (Schedvin 1970).[4] This view will be re-examined and found wanting.

In much of the literature for this period there has been little examination of the factors that helped shape Australian public policy, particularly the interplay between economic ideas and economic policy. Peter Hall's (1989) edited study of the diffusion of Keynesian ideas across nations found that the influence of Keynes's ideas could not be divorced from particular national circumstances. Hall pioneered three analytical approaches in the study of the way this new economic wisdom percolated down to policy. A 'state-centred' approach focuses on the role of policymaking bureaucracies as the creators or, more likely, inhibitors to the diffusion of new economic ideas (Hall 1989:10–12). In this regard, it might be argued that Australia was philosophically attuned in its institutions and prevailing culture for a ready embrace of Keynesianism (Smyth 1994). Institutionally, Australia had an extensive public sector and publically minded economists, who, up to a point, supported tariff protection and public investment projects on economic development grounds (Whitwell 1986:57). Australia also had a small but active core of university economists all predisposed and well versed in the art of giving practical, level-headed advice to governments (Green 1960:29–32; Cain 1973; Copland 1951). Partly by design and partly by accident, Australia's central bank financed budgetary deficits using Treasury bills during the Depression and thereby kept the banking system liquid (Copland 1932a). Lastly, Australia possessed a centralised wage-fixing system—'another form of economic control'—that gave an independent but trusted body, the Arbitration Court, a direct lever over wage levels (Reddaway:1938) Administratively, therefore, Australia had more than the rudiments of the institutional apparatus necessary for economic management. An embryonic Keynesianism was there but without the philosophical and intellectual conviction among the policy elite.

A second approach of Hall's is a 'coalition-centred' one in which economic policy depends on the interplay between politically mobilised interest groups (1989:12). Here, the emphasis is on politics serving as the clearing house of pressures for different groups with divergent interests (Hall 1989:13). The last approach is the 'economist-centred approach'. Here, economists and intellectuals play a leading role in not just the dissemination of new economic ideas, but their shaping into policy (Hall 1989:9). As Whitwell (1994:123–4) notes, the

---

4   Boris Schedvin's work *Australia and the Great Depression* (1970) derives from his Sydney University dissertation, which was entitled 'Economic policy in depression and recovery in Australia 1927–1935' (1964). The doctorate, in itself, had some standing being the first PhD awarded by the Faculty of Economics at the University of Sydney (Groenewegen 2009:81). As Schedvin's study effectively concludes in 1935, it concords with Hancock's observation that Schedvin pays relatively little attention to the years 1935–39. Dyster and Meredith (1990:146) corroborate this.

economist-centred approach tends to exaggerate the influence economists and new ideas actually have on policy formation. While Hall has argued that for a new paradigm to take hold a nation must have favourable conditions for all three dimensions, we will focus primarily on the latter approach because it draws 'attention to the qualities of Keynesian ideas themselves. It suggests that these ideas may have a persuasiveness and a political dynamism of their own; and it forces us to ask which ideas make for persuasiveness and which detracts from it' (Hall 1989:9–10). One must be wary, of course, of taking a 'delightfully simple' view of visualising 'economic theory as the main force behind policy' (Booth 1983:104). Other factors and variables, besides politics, enter into the process. We adopt this approach, however, because it allows us to focus on how economists underwent a sea change in their thinking and whether that bore any imprint on official economic policy.

The order of this book

This study comprises 10 chapters broken into three thematic parts. The first part, entitled 'Backing into the limelight: the interwar Australian economics profession', sets the scene. Chapter 2 reviews the literature on economic ideas and policy together with an early, equivocal assessment of the early Australian economists. Chapter 3 provides some background on the monumental problems confronting the Australian economy in the Great Depression and the economic institutions and conventions policymakers relied on. The last chapter of Part I uncovers the capstone of this study—namely, the Australian economics profession and its theoretical and practical grounding.

Part II, entitled 'Triumph and tribulation', recounts how Australian economists seized the opportunity in 1931 to present an economic stabilisation plan adapted and moulded, with some improvisation, from existing economic theory. Chapter 5 discusses the theoretical origins and rationale of the Premiers' Plan and the measures that preceded it, together with how it was then regarded as a towering achievement for the economics profession. The years that followed, however, were marked by disappointment for the profession with subsequent and quite innovative economic thinking rejected by official authorities. These setbacks to enlightened economic policy form the basis of Chapters 6 and 7. One reason why this professional advice went unheeded was because economic recovery was by then well grounded and the political and monetary authorities were reluctant to do anything to jeopardise it. This could not be said of the bleak years—1932 until 1934—when monetary authorities rejected expansionary economic policy advice prepared by a committee of economists.

The last part of the book, entitled 'The march of Keynesian ideas', consists of Chapters 8, 9 and 10, followed by a short conclusion. As monetary reformers, Australian economists had the fortunate opportunity to be able to present their latest views on economic policy—especially the choice between price stability and exchange rate stability—to an official inquiry. This Royal Commission on Banking and Monetary Systems sprang from community dissatisfaction with the conduct of trading banks and the central bank during the Depression. Chapter 8 discusses the commission's findings—a great part of which was shaped by the evidence submitted by economists. Since some of that evidence cited Keynes's *General Theory*, its early reception among Australian economists will also be examined. It was a case, as Chapter 9 shows, of the new wisdom finding fertile ground with Australian economists applying this new theoretical insight to dealing, first, with an imbalanced economy, and then with the risk of being affected by an international recession. The first exigency was met by economists recommending a real wage increase while the second was addressed by the central bank taking pre-emptive monetary action to insulate or fireproof the economy from fluctuations in Australia's trade account. The final chapter briefly discusses how economists played a critical part in shaping Australia's war finance. Before the advice of economists penetrated into the upper reaches of official policy, the federal government endured a difficult time reconciling greater defence spending with more social spending. Besides dealing with an economic slowdown, it also had to contend with the states reluctant to restrict their borrowings. The judicious advice from economists, together with an enlightened Treasurer, would lighten the government's woes.

Part I.
Backing into the Limelight: the Interwar Australian Economics Profession

2. Economic ideas and an assessment of Australian economists in the 1930s

Introduction

This chapter briefly reviews the existing literature on two areas central to the ambit of this book. First, we briefly examine, in the form of a backdrop, the problematic issue of the relationship between economic ideas and policy. While Keynes's oft-quoted and noble peroration about the power of economic ideas marks the start of this discussion, there is no simple, linear relationship between ideas and policy. Indeed, the whole gamut of policymaking is enveloped by a fog of disparate influences, interests and entanglements, many of which could detract from the ambition of this thesis. If anything, we might say that the ideas and thinking of economists rarely immediately shape economic policy. In the Australian case, there were instances, however, when the ideas of economists did have some bearing on official policy but only after they had established themselves in positions of some influence and when their views were palatable to politicians. The passage of time and the review of past performance also carried some weight.

The second field of study in this chapter is more straightforward. It provides a self-contained historiography of how Australian economists—then and in the post-World War II period—assessed the policy contribution of their predecessors in dealing with the economic problems of the 1930s. The subsequent literature, it will be found, is largely a negative one, with Australian interwar economists largely criticised for rendering incorrect economic advice in 1931 and then failing to engage intellectually with new paradigms of economic thought then unfolding.

Ideas and economic policy

It is agreed that the process by which ideas come to influence economic policy is not completely understood, even from a historical perspective. In a famous quote, Keynes suggested that

[t]he ideas of economists...are more powerful than is commonly understood. Indeed the world is ruled by little else. Practical men, who believe themselves to be quite exempt from any intellectual influences, are usually the slaves of some defunct economist. Madmen in authority, who hear voices in the air, are distilling their frenzy from some academic scribbler of a few years back. I am sure that the power of vested interest is vastly exaggerated compared with the gradual encroachment of ideas. Not, indeed, immediately, but after a certain interval, for in the field of economic and political philosophy there are not many who are influenced by new theories after they are twenty-five or thirty years of age, so that the ideas which civil servants and politicians and even agitators apply to current events are not likely to be the newest. But, soon or late, it is ideas, not vested interests, which are dangerous for good or evil. (Keynes 1936:383–4)

While this passage adorned the end of the *General Theory*, Keynes was astute to know that it was not entirely true, at least in the short run. There is a vast difference, first, between new ideas or views and them being implemented. In a letter to George Bernard Shaw in which Keynes spoke about writing a book that would revolutionise the way the world would think about economic problems, he qualified it by adding 'when my new theory has been duly assimilated and mixed with politics and feelings and passions, I can't predict what the final upshot will be [of] its effect on action and affairs' (cited in Clarke 1988:309). Those trying to prove when a Keynesian revolution in policy took place often overlook the important rider on theory being immersed into the milieu of 'politics and feelings and passions'. In other words, Keynes knew that particular circumstances and real situations were far more telling than the ideas themselves in shaping official policy (Cornish 1993). The word 'revolution' was an inappropriate one, therefore, to describe any change in economic policy by the fact that the policymaking process is usually incremental, responding tentatively to a number of different processes and strains (Cornish 1992). Keynes's stricture was that economic models must always be relevant to the contemporary world; if the context in which economic activity took place changed then a new rationalisation and explanation were needed to overcome dogma. Keynes (1973:122) reminded his audience that his own economic remedies 'are on a different plane from my diagnosis...they are not meant to be definitive, but subject to all sorts of special assumptions and are necessarily related to the particular conditions of the time'.

Some have inferred the mistaken view that ideas do, in fact, conquer political and social obstacles, even in the short run—this, as Winch (1969:24) puts it, fans the 'rationalist fallacy that ideas alone are powerful enough to determine the course of history'. According to Austin Robinson, Keynes observed that it took more than 50 years for Adam Smith's ideas to make an impact in the political sphere (cited in Leeson 1996:45). For his own theory, Keynes predicted—correctly as it turned out—a 10-year lag for his vision to be taken up at the political level (Keynes 1973:492–3). It confirmed Sayers' observation that 'views from academic sources always reach Whitehall sooner or later' (cited in Moggridge 1986:365). One of Keynes's contemporaries, Lionel Robbins (1932:199), agreed that '[i]n the short run, it is true ideas are unimportant and ineffective, but in the long run they can rule the world'. He later felt that the interpretation of Keynes's oft-quoted peroration overlooked, too, the role of political philosophers; it is the conjunction of the two—namely, ideas and intellectuals—that, in the right circumstances, makes for irresistible force.

The misinterpretation of Keynes's famous quote mirrors another, but less familiar tale closer to our study. It relates to E. R. Walker's tale of how a copy of Keynes's *General Theory* in the Commonwealth Parliamentary Library in Canberra was apparently dog-eared in the last 80-odd pages, where it was hoped the practical application of Keynes's theory of income determination was to be found (cited in Cairncross 1996:255). Australian politicians' assimilation of Keynes's new framework was to prove just as protracted as elsewhere and the last 80 pages of the *General Theory*, in any case, were hardly a handbook on economic policy.

Economic ideas are not always powerful enough to change the course of events or shape economic policy. The Cambridge economist Arthur Pigou (1927:280) would have found favour with Keynes in saying that '[e]conomic analysis can provide data for statesmen; but the attitude of public opinion and the current political and diplomatic situation are dominant factors in determining what on the whole it is best to do; and these lie beyond our range'. William Barber supports Pigou's position, arguing that there is an element of exaggeration in the claims made for, or by, academic scribblers. In other words, 'the process through which new ideas are generated and ultimately translated into policies and programs that shape the flow of history may be too complex to be reduced to a simple and unidirectional schema' (Barber 1993:119). In that light, one might say that all economic policies evolve within a context, characterised by a mosaic of norms, beliefs, goals, interests and pressures different from those enshrouding academia. Economists and ideas, in any case, exert only one influence in the composition of economic policy (Arndt 1996:97). In short, economic policy derives from the confluence of ideas, politics, circumstances and ideology (Winch 1969:20–1).

Garside's (1993:16) comparative study of the pattern of various countries' responses to depression boiled it down to 'an amalgam of circumstance, historical legacy and expediency'. Ideas for solving economic problems are plentiful, but it is only the ideas that attract support from those in political power that ultimately matter. Ideas taken in isolation from individuals, circumstances and interests are unlikely to provide an adequate explanation of policy changes (Battin 1997). Seldon (1996:289) puts it plainly that '[i]deas, to be successfully taken up, need advocates (individuals or interests), they need to square with the facts, to have a dominant idea or interest benign or positive, and to be launched into positive circumstances'. Seldon pointedly reminds us that if internal interests are set against a change in policy, no change is likely to occur even if the ideas, circumstances and intellectual leadership are quite favourable. In short, ideas matter but not in isolation. An opponent of this view, Nigel Ashford (1997:25), believes that ideas reign supreme and shape economic policy far more than supposedly independent factors such as interests and circumstances. Ashford plausibly argues that circumstances and problems are, in themselves, the consequence of old and changing ideas.

The political theorist David Marquand cleverly inverts Keynes's words:

> Madmen in authority may distil the frenzy of academic scribblers, but academic scribblers respond to the pressures of the society around them, and their scribbles resonate only when allied with social forces. If practical men are to be enslaved by defunct economists, living economists inhabit a world managed by practical men. (Marquand 1996:6)

Practical men, perhaps as politicians, are quite capable of fashioning ideas as weapons to promote their interests and support their policies (Skidelsky 1996:44).

As intellectuals, academic economists can exercise influence, but wield little direct power (Etzioni-Halevy 1985:11). In the transmission of ideas it is ultimately political forces that drive economic policy, not vice versa—that is, economists propose but politicians dispose. New economic theory can become effective only when it is politically accepted (McKibbin 1990). Nonetheless, economists can exert some indirect input into policy decisions by shaping the climate of ideas and shading the perspective in which policy decisions are made (Etzioni-Halevy 1985:27). Their input can even prove decisive in fostering policy that is considerably different from what it would have been without their involvement. Failing that, the academic economist's first duty, when solicited for advice, is to 'furnish knowledge-based advice on the available options for policy decisions. This, in itself, is an important contribution to policy formation' (Etzioni-Halevy 1985:25).

In illuminating the political context in which economic debates take place, it is important to examine how the ideas of economists percolate down to policy. This is particularly so in a setting in which the political process is diffuse, with the key players not renowned for their perspicacity in matters of economic thought. There has been a rich vein of research on this topic, especially how the Depression and economists' response to it resulted in the birth of macroeconomics and, more importantly for our purposes, the idea of demand management (Battin 1997; Hall 1989). Economic policy has never really been the simple translation of theory into action. Seldon's straightforward model of how ideas in fact result in significant policy change dissects the process into four dimensions. These determinants are: first, the ideas themselves; second, the individuals who carry them forth; third, the circumstances of the period; and, last, the events that punctuated the period (Seldon 1996:263). His study can be compared with Hall's schema mentioned above. Economists, if listened to, have to be theoretically and rhetorically persuasive but also politically attuned with their advice. The audience economists catered to had to be convinced of the plausibility and applicability of theory to policy questions (Moggridge 1986). The British economic mandarin Alec Cairncross, in a definitive chapter on economists and policymakers, details the non-economic sources of resistance to the spread of new economic ideas and especially their imprint on policy. Policy might be under the influence of non-economic considerations, even the views of non-economists or an economic dogma that is out of date. Ideas might not translate into policy because they are insufficiently precise or built on inappropriate assumptions. In the prism of the policymaking process, planners and politicians are 'as a rule…slightly deaf, there is too much noise' (Cairncross 1986:21).

Economic policy is governed by 'the general climate' of economic ideas and by the direct advice given to government by its economic advisers (Tomlinson 1995:78). There could be some symmetry in the process whereby, as we shall see in the Australian case, economists spend much time in public affairs and the process is, therefore, 'policy intensive'. Equally, policymaking can, at times, become 'economist intensive' (Sandelin et al. 1997:1). Pigou (1933:v) reminds us that economists are more likely to clarify issues than formulate solutions; they are 'engineers, not engine-drivers'. The conditions for a revolution in policy go beyond a mere mental leap in the minds of policymakers (Tomlinson 1984:261). Moreover, as Winch (1969:19) notes, even to pose a connection between economic ideas and policy is both an optimistic 'conception of technocratic status of economics, and a naive view of the processes of political decision-making'. In Keynes's case, and for some countries, the link was reversed: the *General Theory* was written to give theoretical support to the expansionist economic proposals already being put forward in the 1930s (Beaud and Dostaler 1995:45)—that is, the political or intuitive vision preceded the theoretical one.

The diffusion of ideas, in short, is a complex process. Solow (1993:81–2) suggests that the demands of the political process are such that there is a bias for theories or ideas that are simple and uncomplicated and therefore capable of a high guarantee of success. Cairncross (1996:255) points out that policy is 'intrinsically political' whereas economists have a fixation on the scientific and the apolitical. This raises the issue not just of the political acceptability of new ideas but of their facility of being comprehended by politicians. Apart from political and other groups' resistance to new thinking, there had to be a public clamour for change. Keynes alluded to this problem when he confessed that with reference to the new ideas contained within the *General Theory* 'even if economists and technicians knew the secret remedy, they could not apply it until they had persuaded the politicians; and the politicians, who have ears but no eyes, will not attend to the persuasion until it reverberates back to them as an echo from the great public' (cited in Cornish 1993a;44).

Ideas could, therefore, be the 'ultimate reality', as Australian economic historian Edward Shann once put it, but a fundamental reorientation of them within society is 'a protracted affair' (Copland 1945:4). Copland believed it took a decade for people to recast their ideas about economic policy. Policymakers were, therefore, frequently to be seen fighting the last war. This response lag, as it were, squares with politicians taking up 'the Keynesian crusade' with relish in the 1940s so as to put behind them the experience of mass unemployment (Tange 1996). Ten years earlier, informed opinion was fixated on resisting the spectre of inflationism and the boom–bust cycle. The weight of the past, therefore, together with economic dogma, made bankers, Treasury officials and politicians 'prisoners of doctrine'—a doctrine that had little relevance to the problems of the 1930s (Butlin 1961:389). As we shall see, these artefacts could not be shed overnight. In Australia, during the 1930s, a coalition of political and financial interests opposed calls for economic expansion premised on proto-Keynesian and then Keynesian lines. As Australian economists discovered in 1931, public opinion mattered as much as the machinations of the political elite. As Keynes had predicted, 'these new ideas, this new wisdom must have a solid foundation in the motives which govern the evolution of political society' (cited in Clarke 1988:309). Keynes added that ideas only resonate when they fit the conditions of the time.[1] More pointedly, Keynes's ideas would be potent only when reinforced by group interests or when they touched some deep-seated emotion in the community. As late as 1939, Keynes acknowledged that in Britain, at least, the resistance to his new theoretical framework meant that the import of the *General Theory* would have to wait: 'A change in mental atmosphere was a necessary condition for the bold experiment in achieving full employment by the methods I advocate' (cited in Harrod 1951:446). Only the prosecution of total war would allow the grand experiment to begin.

---

1 Skidelsky, Keynes's biographer, puts it sublimely: 'The rise or fall of ideas in economics is as much connected with attendant circumstances, including ideological and political circumstances, as with their logical properties or their power of passing any test of prediction' (Skidelsky 1996:xviii). One dissident to this generous view was Leon Keyserling, a Washington official, who felt that the New Deal initiatives 'would have been enacted in just the form it was, if there had never been a Lord Keynes' (Colander and Landreth 1996:224).

In Australia, what was missing was not just the enabling vision from politicians to close the gap between them and economists but public opinion in favour of reflation; as we shall see, the 'boom and borrow' policies of the 1920s cut deeply into the Australian psyche. Escape from this mind-set could be alleviated only by intellectual input, by ideas and the propagation of those ideas. In Australia's case, obstructionist financial interests, mediocre political leadership and the pressing force of circumstances kept the new ideas of economists at bay. The marked increase in economic intervention or 'planning' that did take place in Australia during this time lacked therefore, for the most part, a considered political philosophy or coherent strategy. Within academe, however, '[i]nstructed opinion was already far in advance of public policy' (Keynes 1977:427). That previous sentence might serve as the leitmotiv for this book focusing on the theorising of interwar Australian economists and their subsequent policy advice.

Australian economists and the Depression: a historiography

The key issue in contention within the literature on Australian interwar economics has been the appropriateness of anti-depression policy. Much of that issue crystallises around the two leading protagonists—Douglas Copland (1934) and, two generations later, Boris Schedvin (1970)—and their respective and considered views of the role economists played in the 1930s.[2] It was only in the post-World War II era that intellectual recrimination and revisionism about the worth of interwar economic policy, especially the Premiers' Plan, really began (Clark 1958:222). Even some of the players peripherally involved in the 1930s, such as H. C. 'Nugget' Coombs and Colin Clark, were critical, in part, of the advice emanating from their older colleagues. Coombs (1981:107–8) remarked that the 1930s showed 'evidence of economic mismanagement' and that the confrontation between the Commonwealth Bank and the Scullin government intensified and prolonged the impact of the Depression. Colin Clark (1958:222–3) was blunter, accusing Australian economists of lamely following public opinion in opting for balanced budgets, regardless of the state of the economy. Spearritt (1981) picks up on this theme, saying that economists used the cloak of scientific respectability to recommend conservative economic policies.

In the heyday of postwar Keynesianism, Copland (1951:21–3), looking back over the early 1930s, issued an apologia, noting that 'the mistake was made of not recognizing clearly enough that government activities needed to expand tremendously to offset the fall in private spending' and that there had not been

---

2   A fuller version of this section is in Millmow (2003a).

enough deviation 'from the deflationist line'. Copland (1951:21–2) also ceded errors in the conduct of economic policy—first, in the authorities opposing monetary expansion, and second, and perhaps more forgivably, in seeing the Depression purely in monetary terms. In a tribute to a fellow economist, Copland (1950:107) lamented that had Edward Dyason's expansionist prescriptions been followed in 1931 'the impact of the depression on the public mind might have been much less severe'. Copland (1934:145) apparently reached this conclusion in his Marshall Lectures given at Cambridge University, commenting that the lack of a stronger stimulus, in the form of public works, was a grievous error. He remained adamant, however, that the emphasis on an adjustment in relative costs 'was a mistake in degree rather than principle' (Copland 1951:23). Along with his colleagues, Copland (1951:21) insisted that the circumstances at the time dictated fiscal balance to help restore business confidence. There was also Australia's external debt commitment to uphold. Much later, an Australian Federal Treasurer, R. G. Casey, could claim that his country was 'at the forefront of the world's most trustworthy borrowers'.[3] In his last retrospective on the Premiers' Plan, Lyndhurst Giblin (1951:81) proffered that 'heavy unemployment was the inevitable price of national solvency'.[4] He went on to defend the Premiers' Plan, stating 'that it was not far from the very best that was possible with a public inexperienced as it was at the time in violent economic vicissitudes and their remedies' (Giblin 1951:81).

Before and even after World War II, it was accepted that Australian economists were not only instrumental but quite correct, if not heroic, in putting forward the Premiers' Plan because it enabled Australia to not default on her foreign debts (Goodwin 1974:231–2; Hall 1938; Dow 1938 Garnett 1949 Mandle 1978). Copland (1934) declared in his 1933 Marshall Lectures that the deliberate policies put in place by the Commonwealth Government and, inferentially, by the economists, were also responsible for Australia's economic recovery (Hawtrey 1934). Copland emphasised that university economists had, from May 1930 onwards, played a bold and prominent part in framing remedial policies. This was some achievement in a country said to 'despise scientific economists' (Hancock 1930:86). Copland's theme in his Marshall Lectures was that in facing a difficult price–cost problem, Australia's institutions—namely, the Arbitration Court, the Loan Council, the Commonwealth Bank and the Tariff Board—allowed the economy to respond flexibly to the crisis. A unique 'middle road' was hewn out, encompassing cost cutting with a modest expansionary monetary element (Copland 1934). In a later commentary, Copland (1936:11) was adamant that too much had been made of the orthodox or 'sound' features of the Premiers' Plan and not enough of its more expansionary aspects.

---

3   R. G. Casey to Sir M. Norman, 7 March 1938, Bank of England (hereafter BE), G1/288.
4   A view candidly shared by Sir Leslie Melville, one of the economists directly involved in the making of the Premiers' Plan, in personal communication with the author.

Corden (1968:58) attributes the influence of academic economists, besides there being few economists within the Australian public service, to the need for expert guidance in the crisis besetting the country. More importantly, economists had begun to be employed in some key advisory posts or, at least, were having their opinions sought via the media or committee work (Cain:1984). A few years earlier, economists had advised the Bruce government on the economic rationale for the Australian tariff—a practice Jacob Viner felt worthy of imitation by other nations. Economists also had input into the Development and Migration Commission and other committees of inquiry (Cain 1980:14–18; Harcourt 1986). The growing sense of professionalisation was marked, too, by the later placement of economists within the Commonwealth Public Service, particularly in wartime, which would strengthen the 'technocratic application of economic ideas' (Winch 1969; Petridis 1981).

Australian economists were uncommonly influential in the 1930s since the policymaking process was accessible, shaped in part by four extra-parliamentary agencies—some of which occasionally called on the services of economists (Dow 1938). There was also the Commonwealth Grants Commission, established in 1933, which inquired into matters of economic equity between the states and the Commonwealth in a federal political system. Australia's centralised wage-setting process, too, afforded a clear advantage in that the Arbitration Court could facilitate an enviable degree of money wage flexibility in times of both economic duress and prosperity (Reddaway 1938:335). The interaction, moreover, between the Australian Loan Council and the Commonwealth Bank was a 'guarantee' that a moderate policy outcome would be forthcoming (Copland 1937a:422). Meanwhile, Prime Minister Joseph Lyons, who dominated the period under review, enjoyed a certain rapport with economists and solicited counsel from those considered not too unorthodox (Hart 1967:12; Cain 1983). Ultimately, however, Lyons was forced by a trenchantly conservative cabinet to reject the advice of economists.

Economists were influential not just because the general public had lost faith in its politicians but because they were a small cohesive group with a fair degree of authority. Second, and just as importantly, the public statements made by economists struck a chord with the Australian electorate.[5] Non-partisan 'experts' would deliver Australia from the crisis better than any meddling politicians (Nicholls 1992). That they did cemented the standing and prestige of interwar Australian economics (Goodwin 1966:638). The whole interwar period has been suggested as something of 'a golden age for Australian economics' in the sense that national problems were met by national economic expertise (Groenewegen and McFarlane 1990).

---

5   D. B. Copland to B. Ruml, 15 December 1936, University of Melbourne Archives, Faculty of Economics and Commerce (hereafter UMA FECC), Box 50.

The overriding impression, then, was of how a small core of economists had saved their country from defaulting on its loans (Shann and Copland 1933). At the time, Australian economists were hailed for the role they played in the crisis and thereafter. At the Ottawa Imperial Trade Talks in 1932, for instance, the Australian economist Edward Shann reported: 'On all sides we are greeted by the remark that Australia has made the best stab of all at keeping her economy liquid and active.'[6] D. H. Robertson (1940:122), the Cambridge economist, had Sweden and Australia distinctly in mind when he wrote, 'There are said to be, in the far north and far south, lands where economists all give the same advice, where the Government listens to it, where the public understands why the Government has listened.' An Australian economist at Oxford, Robert Hall (1938:120), believed the Premiers' Plan set a marvellous example of what cohesive economic advice could achieve. Ralph Hawtrey (1934:1) stated that Australia had anticipated the United States in having an economics brains trust at its disposal. One American historian called the Premiers' Plan 'the most remarkable exercise in planned economy that had been carried through by any democracy up to that time' (Garnett 1949:96). Keynes told one of his abler students, W. Brian Reddaway, to spend some time in far-off Australia because its governments heeded the advice of its economists (Tribe 1997:77).

An American observer, Rupert MacLaurin (1936), writing on Australia's economic recovery policies, agreed with Copland's premise that, together with some ration of luck, a small, open commodity-based economy could take measures to escape the clutches of the slump. More intriguing, however, was MacLaurin's view, later developed further by Boris Schedvin, that Australian economists had, at times, played only a spasmodic part in formulating recovery policy:

> The economists were used only in a haphazard fashion. That is to say, they were called on only on special tasks and with a particular problem to report on. When economists tried to broaden the bases of their inquiries in order to make their work more effective, governments not infrequently were resentful. Economists never had an opportunity to make a report on an entire economic programme. (MacLaurin 1936:257).[7]

---

6   E. O. G. Shann to A. C. Davidson, 21 July 1933, Bank of New South Wales Archive (hereafter BNSW), A-53-409.

7   MacLaurin, in his lengthy study tour of Australia, was chaperoned and greatly assisted by Copland, who wrote letters of introduction for him to the key figures involved in 1931. MacLaurin (1936:255) noted that economists 'agreed in the beginning of the depression, that to be effective they must refrain from public controversy and concentrate on pushing the measures on which they concurred'. This was a slightly different experience to that of Britain, where the Economic Advisory Council (EAC) was beset by disagreement among the serving economists (Howson and Winch 1977:72). In his history of the British Treasury, Lord Bridges (1964:90) felt that the EAC was 'rather remote from the active centre of things'.

In other words, economists were never allowed full latitude in the policy advice they could convey to the Commonwealth. Despite this finding, the public perception endured that economists played a significant part in composing an economic plan that helped rehabilitate the Australian economy. One reviewer of MacLaurin's work—a newspaperman—suggested that 'Australia's recovery was not quite the neat and ordered thing that Mr MacLaurin and other economic authors have pictured it to be. The rules were not written round a study table and pinned on a University notice board. They had a more exciting, more dangerous birth and infancy' (Adam 1937:278).[8]

Schedvin's book *Australia and the Great Depression*, stemming from a doctoral thesis, was not just a detailed narrative of the origins and impact of that event but, more importantly for our purposes, a study of the role of economists in the making of economic policy at the time. While it was ostensibly a work in economic history, the focus on economic policy necessitates some inquiry into the public activities and ideas of economists. Schedvin, however, undertook only a cursory examination of this aspect. This can be related to his key finding that, for the most part, economic policy was essentially shadowing the market. Schedvin took the view, therefore, that anti-depression economic policy was not the product of 'expert' opinion but rather responses that were either accidental or mirrored what would have been, in any case, market outcomes. This view was first suggested by University of Sydney economist E. R. Walker (Cain 1983). The Schedvin view has, however, been questioned by Gregory and Butlin (1988) in a symposium held to re-examine the experience of the Australian economy during the 1930s. They found that economic policy did matter to some extent though its benefit was belated.

In contrast, the central thesis of Schedvin's (1970:372) book was that 'deliberate policy measures were comparatively unimportant in influencing the nature of the contraction or the speed of recovery'. Consequently, economists had not played a decisive role in rescuing Australia from the slump. The germ for this idea came from his doctoral supervisor, S. J. Butlin. In his history of the *Australia and New Zealand Bank*, Butlin suggested that the measures that emerged from the famous 'battle of the plans' episode in Australian history were in fact the 'traditional responses of the free market'. He went on to state that the 'planning' of 1930–32 'was directed not to novel policies but to traditional ones dictated by inherited ways of thought; it represented rather the inevitable political process by which conflicting interests were finally brought to compromise, not a resolution of significant differences in policy' (Butlin 1961:390). In short, the Premiers' Plan

---

8   As editor of the *Economic Record*, Copland interestingly elected not to have one of his colleagues review MacLaurin's book, opting instead for an outside independent voice that might do, as Copland put it, 'a little debunking' of reputations won in the drama. For his part, Copland felt that MacLaurin's work was 'a little tinged' by the author's reluctance to bless the 'heresies' Australian economists had resorted to (D. B. Copland to H. Adam, 6 October 1937, UMA FECC, Box 141).

was really a cosmetic exercise disguising primal political forces at play. Butlin had earlier summed up the economists' handiwork contained within the plan as merely the extension of the welfare economics drawn from Edwin Cannan's text *Wealth* but watered down to everyday discourse (Butlin 1948:40).

Apart from not bringing about recovery, the Premiers' Plan, Schedvin contended, was also needlessly deflationary. Policy was too cautious and more—though he rarely says what—could have been done to alleviate the slump (Arndt 1971:123). To argue the counterfactual aspect, as Schedvin does, is, however, fraught with difficulty. In the psychological and economic setting Australia was placed in, there could be little recourse to massive reflation of the economy. As a loyal member of the Empire, Australian authorities felt it paramount that the nation honour its debts to London and steer clear of default. Devaluation of the currency, too, could not be overplayed. Schedvin (1992:50) believes that not allowing the exchange rate to find its natural and much lower rate was probably the cardinal policy error of the 1930s—a view shared by economists at the time.

Schedvin bemoaned that even if economists had heterodox notions in their head, they were, in any case, quite powerless since strong external and internal pressures prevailed over the economic parameters. Recurrent deficit budgets, whether accidental or deliberate, were equated with the spectre of default. Australia's foreign exchange reserves—or London balances—together with the repayment of overseas debt, precluded policy expansionism. Hart's (1967) definitive account of the Lyons government concurred, noting how subterranean influences, mostly financial ones, underpinned the administration. The Board of the Commonwealth Bank, in ideological league with the other trading banks, together with a pliant Loan Council, presided over monetary policy (Butlin and Boyce 1988; Gilbert 1973). Exchange rate policy was one area, though, where economists' advice, to some extent, bore some influence, but they always encompassed it as part of the Premiers' Plan (Markwell 1985:22–3). In contrast, Schedvin (1970:156) saw the 1931 devaluation of the Australian pound as an isolated market-driven event, 'not part of any plan or policy'. According to Tom Valentine (1987a:67), the devaluation was more a 'passive reaction to balance of payments pressures than a deliberate policy measure aimed at improving matters'.

In sum, Schedvin's argument that anti-depression policy was, in fact, largely market generated rather than considered policy meant that the Premiers' Plan hardly deserved the effusive praise Copland had showered on it, particularly its 'institutional and theoretical novelty' (Schedvin 1970:252). To Schedvin's eye:

> The Premiers' Plan was merely the embodiment of a series of expedients designed to maintain external solvency. The plan was not conceived as a means to promote recovery, nor did it in any tangible way. The view

that the Premiers' Plan was the foundation of Australia's recovery, that it
represented a judicious and deliberate mixture of deflation and inflation
is a figment of Sir Douglas Copland's imagination. (Schedvin 1970:7)[9]

Since the Premiers' Plan policies were essentially reactive and market driven,
Schedvin (1970:9) argued that economists were ciphers in the policymaking
process—their primary function being to knit the fabric of the 1931 Premiers' Plan
into a 'shroud of technical competence and expertise'. That is, the economists'
policymaking activities in 1931 and thereafter were designed 'to embellish
the [federal] government–bank compromise with a veneer of impartiality'
(Hancock 1972:77). Schedvin's reassessment of the federal authorities' policy
during the Depression is, however, on face value, tendentious, for it is difficult
to distinguish at times between the effects of policy and those of market forces,
with each interacting on the other (Forsyth 1972:376).

Since the publication of Schedvin's book there has been renewed debate about
the genesis and economic soundness of the Premiers' Plan in dealing with
Australia's debt and budgetary imbalance problem. Moreover, in a point lost in
the subsequent literature, Schedvin admitted that 'serious work on the interwar
period is still in its infancy and this study bears the mark of that uncertain
exploration' (cited in Clark 1981b:192). The Premiers' Plan, politically at least,
might have been partly accidental but whether the policies that flowed from it
were ineffective, as Schedvin alleges, is highly debatable.

Despite the severity of the Premiers' Plan, the business and financial
communities drew enormous psychological relief from the plan in the belief
that it would deliver Australia from liquidation. Leaving it to market forces to
engineer the same adjustments would not have triggered the same response,
but, more likely, would have drawn militant resistance. There was, in fact, great
community compliance with the plan as demonstrated by the successful and
irreversible internal debt-conversion process—something NSW Premier Jack
Lang thought would never succeed (Dow 1938:96). Higher tariff protection
gave the Commonwealth government some latitude in the deployment of public
works without putting pressure on the exchange rate (Arndt 1971). Sinclair
admits that this response, partly at the behest of Australian economists, was
in some defiance of 'the rules of the game' permitted by the gold standard.
The Bank of England's advice that Australia deflate its internal level of income

---

9 Schedvin (1970:373) is of the opinion that Australian authorities lacked the know-how to mount a
reflationary policy. A full-bodied economic reflation for Australia or any other country for that matter in the
1930s would have required 'extensive state supervision of the economy', which itself implied drastic political
action (McKibbin 1990:227). Germany under Hitler proved one exception. There was, in any case, an absence
of 'a mature reflationary economics'. The alternatives open to Australia were not deflation or reflation but, in
fact, drift or deflation (McKibbin 1990:217, 224–5).

to maintain the Australian pound's parity with sterling was rejected outright by Australian economists who elected for devaluation coupled with tariffs and monetary stimulus (Sinclair 1974:57).

Of even greater interest to this book is Schedvin's attack on interwar Australian economists for failing miserably

> to work towards the building of a positive policy in the later depression years, when this task was the preoccupation of overseas economists. When they should have been questioning traditional modes of thought, they clung to the myth of the efficacy of the Premiers' Plan and implicitly condoned thereafter the inept policies of the Lyons Government. There was nothing remotely comparable in Australia to the vigour of the New Deal or the Cambridge intellectual revolution. (Schedvin 1970:225)

Schedvin (1970:374) also did not discern any evidence of an intellectual hunger for experimentation within academe: 'There is nothing in Australia which even approximates the widespread intellectual reconsideration of traditional doctrines which occurred overseas.' These are strong charges and they find some corroboration in Tim Harcourt's (1986:87) survey of Australian economists' theoretical views on unemployment at that time.

This minimalist view of the role economic ideas and indeed economists played in 1931 and beyond will be strongly contended. For the moment, Schedvin's thesis can be questioned by listing some of its more telling omissions. First and foremost, Schedvin's study extends only until 1935, meaning that the economists' evidence—verbal and written—on the conduct of economic policy put before the Royal Commission on Monetary and Banking Systems was not covered. By the same token, Schedvin's study does not discuss how the *General Theory* was received and adapted by Australian economists. There are, moreover, more telling sins of omission that apply before 1935. These are covered in forthcoming chapters, but we can briefly mention some of them. Schedvin completely overlooks, for instance, Copland and Giblin's advice of following Keynes's stricture of seeking price-level stabilisation in the face of deflationary pressure by resorting to cheap money and devaluation (Cain 1987a; Clark 1974b:50). Schedvin also does not acknowledge Keynes's qualified approval of the Premiers' Plan contained in his *Report of the Australian Experts* (Keynes 1982b). It was devaluation and Treasury bill finance that Copland and Shann (1933:87) felt were the really 'heretical' parts of the Premiers' Plan. Alfred Davidson, the powerful head of the Bank of New South Wales, who was instrumental in forcing the devaluation, first opposed it until economists persuaded him of its merits (Holder 1970). Even when the Premiers' Plan was put into operation, the authorities were not wholly conscious that some of its measures would impart some mildly expansionary effect on the economy; the economists, however, knew better. Moreover, some economists had begun to relax their strictures on fiscal consolidation when they saw that the economy was in need of further stimulus by the end of 1931 (Copland 1951:22). This view gathered strength as the recovery in export prices failed to materialise. In 1933, for instance, Giblin found support for his own position in Keynes's pamphlet *The Means to Prosperity*, with its message that an increase in expenditure would expand income, rather than prices. Meanwhile, Davidson's bank, with its own economics department, put out a circular in 1933 declaring that 'Deflation in Australia has reached a point at which it may be dangerous to continue'.[10] It went on to urge the economic benefit of public works rather than the stimulus from trade. Again in 1934, a group of Sydney University economists, led by E. R. Walker, composed a proto-Keynesian plan for the NSW Premier to take to the Australian Loan Council.

In a retrospective interview, Leslie Melville strongly contested the Schedvin thesis of the impotency of interwar economists' ideas. He defended his colleagues and the advice they gave to the Commonwealth government. Their advice not only prevented breakdown of the monetary system, it played an important part in the recovery process (Cornish 1993b:17, 1999:132–3). Melville recalled that '[t]he fact is that measures taken on wages, on the exchange rate, on budgets were the result of deliberate policy and were decisive in preventing the flight of capital and external default'.[11] In a review of Schedvin's book, Melville expressed wonderment about how an ensemble of measures including tariffs, devaluation, wage cuts and easy money—all of which were ultimately sanctioned by authorities—could not but have had a conscious and beneficial economic effect. This view was supported by Alford (1994) in her reappraisal of interwar economic policy, especially in giving an impetus to Australia's manufacturing sector. Melville did concede that more could have been done in 1932 to aid economic recovery but only by further devaluation—something that was articulated by economists in a commissioned report to the government. Despite being at the time the last surviving member of the four key economists behind the Premiers' Plan, Melville's categorical rebuttal of Schedvin has not changed the prevailing view that Australian economists did perform poorly in the Depression and thereafter. Only Arndt (1971), Boehm (1973), Butlin and Boyce (1988) and Foster (1986) offer a sympathetic account of the advice the economists tendered. In contrast, the contributions by Catley and McFarlane (1983), Clark (1974b, 1981a, 1981b), Hancock (1972), Sinclair (1974) and Spearritt (1981) were unforgiving in their assessment of the role Australian economists played during this period.

---

10   'Towards recovery', *BNSW Circular*, May 1933, p. 8.
11   Melville, TRC 182, NLA, p. 145.

In a commentary on the events of 1931, Sinclair (1974:58) argued that 'Australian governments had some freedom of action and failed to choose the fiscal action appropriate to the highest attainable level of employment'. He concluded that the timing of the Premiers' Plan proved abysmal in that the moment of external crisis had passed when the elected policy of making sharp reductions to governmental expenditure began to take effect. Put simply, public policy exacerbated the slump.[12] Consequently, the economists involved in formulating the plan should be apportioned some blame for unleashing this deflationary impulse on the economy. This view was shared by David Clark (1981b:190–1) and Keith Hancock (1972), both of whom argued that the economists' advice in 1931 and again in 1932 was inept in the circumstances. Hancock (1972:78) judged that the interwar economists, in terms of their assumptions and advice, and without having recourse to Keynesian preconceptions, 'performed badly'.

The concerns of external balance and business confidence that economists then regarded as crucial were overlooked by David Clark (1974b:50), who, in one account, revisits the episode through the eyes of R. F. Irvine. In their study of the history of Australian economic thought, Groenewegen and McFarlane (1990:128) offered only lukewarm support for the Premiers' Plan. They noted how the enshrined 'principle of equal sacrifice' or wage cuts across the board inadvertently delivered recovery only by improving international competitiveness and allowing greater import replacement. Catley and McFarlane (1983:58–9) denounced the Premiers' Plan as solely deflationary, concocted by 'the most reactionary' of Australian economists. They admonish the interwar economists for being preoccupied with external balance to the detriment of internal balance. In addition, the economists presented their advice as being objective and impartial when it was quite political (Foster 1986:128). Spearritt (1981:5) presents Copland and Giblin as tendering advice intentionally injurious to the working class. Holder considers this view as beyond the pale especially with the idiosyncratic Giblin whose 'views were then tending more liberal, even radical' (cited in Foster 1986:128).

Certainly it was true that the authorities' reluctance to question deflationary policy or contemplate a further devaluation in 1932 proved tragic. Australia, consequently, endured an unemployment rate of 20 per cent for four years. Australian economists had, however, long pushed for another devaluation to ease the external constraint. They would have readily agreed, therefore, with their modern-day critics that another devaluation would have allowed more policy-induced domestic expansion to have been attempted (Butlin and Boyce 1988:205; Gregory and Butlin 1988:14–16; Arndt 1971). Gregory and Butlin (1988) found that Australia was not alone in being reluctant to devalue. Only in Australia, however, were economists successful in not only persuading that

---

12 A view incidentally shared by a current first-year Australian economics textbook (McTaggart et al. 1992).

step to be first taken but persuasive, too, in preventing the reversal of that measure by the central bank (Eichengreen 1988:57). It is true the advice of the economists was mostly rejected in 1932–33 as the conservative forces behind the Lyons government exerted influence. The steadfast reluctance to experiment, to authorise even modest public sector stimulus, even when pressure on Australia's foreign exchange had eased, appalled the economists. While Australia did suffer significantly high unemployment rates through the early 1930s, an incipient economic recovery quelled the official need for any major revisions to policy. The critical absence of a Keynesian conceptual framework in the late 1930s gave the Lyons government a difficult time reconciling the competing resources between war and civilian needs (Ross 1995).

The Schedvin–Copland debate about how effective economists and economic policy really were in combating the depression is a critical point. If one adopts the Schedvin view that economists were, despite their public profile, really only minor players in formulating Australian economic policy during the early 1930s, it lends support to the view that the ideas of economists made little impact except when their advice was congruent with prevailing political currents. Political advocacy for a new economic approach was obviously unlikely to gain support if public opinion, supreme politics and high finance railed against it.[13] This book will, however, show that Australian economists were influential in this period and far more than Schedvin gave them credit for. The economists then showed, moreover, a fine appreciation of Australia's place in the international economy and the possibility of staging a multilateral effort at coordinated expansion led by the industrialised countries (Turnell 1999). When that avenue failed, they continued their quest within the bounds of national economic policy. This meant lobbying and arguing for greater ambition with economic policy. Economists were also intent on fostering a greater manufacturing capacity for Australia. Apart from Foster's (1986), Melville's (1971; Cornish 1993b) and Arndt's (1971) rebuttals, this rather belittling view of Australian economists during the 1930s has been allowed to fester. Rejecting the Schedvin judgment and rehabilitating the reputation of Australian economists during the 1930s are two of the desired ambitions of this book.

---

13   To Keynes's mind, popular opinion came a long way first. As he told a correspondent: 'The mistake… is in thinking that the difficulty lies in conceiving a plan; in truth there is not much difficulty in that. The difficulty is to think of a plan which can be dressed up in such a form that there is the slightest likelihood of its being adopted. It is not so much a question of discovering the truth, as of adapting to one's ideas the common opinion which it would take years to modify' (J. M. Keynes to A. S. Darroch, 6 June 1934, KPKC, L/32/128).

A restatement of this book

In Australian economic history, the 1930s is often presented as the interregnum between depression and war, a lacuna of nine years in which supply-side economic policies were in place—a period of readjustment and resolution, but not of experiment. The 'grin and bear it' believers in natural forces and in 'the healing virtues of time', as Keynes termed it, took root in the Australian psyche (cited in Leeson 1996:50). The period was, however, punctuated by events and circumstances that, it will be argued, propelled the case for greater management of the economy. It was, in fact, a period of immense mental activity and excitement—and frustration—within the small, but not inconsequential, economics profession. Much of the change in their thinking was conveyed in the policy suggestions they put forward in various national and international forums. Economists had begun to slacken in their support for the Premiers' Plan and urged more ambition in economic policy. This process was aided by the penchant Australian economists had for a practical view of matters—the end result, Copland (1951:16) suggests, of being called in to advise on matters of economic management. A theoretical framework, nonetheless, still underpinned their advice. Critically, that outlook would shift during the 1930s.

While ideas about demand management had begun circulating among Australian economists after the publication of the *General Theory*, Keynes's new theoretical framework attracted little attention from policymakers until 1939. For Australia, the juncture, when Keynes's new theory translated into policy, came only with the preparation for and prosecution of war. This, as we shall see, was earlier than either Britain or the United States though it has never been explicitly recognised. Keynes, for instance, rejoiced at the initiative of US President Franklin Roosevelt's New Deal and regarded Washington, DC, as 'the economic laboratory of the world' (cited in Skidelsky 1996:97). In the literature, 'the Keynesian revolution', in policy terms, became a transatlantic phenomenon. Yet the Australian economy, with its institutional framework, its milieu of state-led development and tradition of egalitarianism, together with the influence of its economists, was more amenable to the ready adaptation of Keynesian ideas. The Australian historian W. K. Hancock (1930), who had noted his countrymen's disdain for economists, also observed the tendency of social and political developments in Britain to follow a course already mapped out in his own country—that is, the periphery could sometimes lead the metropole, and to the Empire's benefit. All these preconditions suggested an early official adoption of Keynesian ideas within Australia with economists leading the crusade.

3. The Australian economy during the Depression decade

Introduction

The Australian-based Douglas Copland, who assumes a key role in this story, once noted '[r]arely, if ever, has the economy of a country been subject to such penetrating scrutiny as was the Australian economy in the years 1927 to 1939' (Palmer 1940:224–5). The same could not be said, however, of Australian economists, particularly of their advice to combat the Depression and promote economic recovery in the 1930s. The purpose of this chapter is to undertake a survey of the Australian economy during the 1930s, using contemporaneous and revisionist accounts of the traverse from slump to recovery. This will entail highlighting the marked peculiarities of Australia's economic experience through that decade. This background is useful to understand the economic environment Australian economists had to contend with and, in some cases, were held accountable for. There are, moreover, differing accounts of the causes behind the slump and the recovery within Australia and, germane to this account, the role professional economic advice played in driving those processes.

The second part of this chapter is a review of the existing economic policy machinery and the dogma and conventions that underpinned it. Largely to do with monetary matters, it was an area where the ideas of academic economists did not, at first, intrude. The advice of 'academic gentlemen' on monetary management was usually dismissed by bankers and policymakers, but the events of 1931 altered this.

What caused the Depression in Australia?

With the notable exception of Schedvin (1970), most of the literature on the causes of Australia's depression cites external influences as the leading factors. These were the calamitous fall in export prices coupled with the closing of the international capital market to Australian borrowing. There has, in brief, been considerable debate about the competing strengths of these two factors. Some emphasise the worsening terms-of-trade in reducing Australian incomes while

Valentine (1987a) argues that the fall in export prices was the cardinal factor behind Australia's woes rather than the cessation of borrowing. In an exhaustive study of the causes, Schedvin (1970) identified long-run internal factors that greatly contributed to the severity of Australia's depression. For instance, apart from private investment reaching its peak in 1924, there had also been cutbacks to public sector projects due to disillusionment with the benefit of rural development programs (Sinclair 1974:56). There had been overexpansion in too compressed a period. In contrast, Valentine (1987) and Siriwardena (1995) downplay the role of internal factors in Australia's depression, which they believe to be somewhat exaggerated. In his account, Copland (1934), too, ascribed the Depression entirely to the drop in export prices, the cessation of overseas borrowing and the concomitant lack of confidence in the country's political and economic stability.

In a nutshell, then, it was export prices that proved an infallible index to Australian prosperity. Its corollary—the external account—preoccupied policymakers' minds in the sense that there had to be a sufficient level of external reserves ready to meet the exigency of poor seasons or low prices. It was that factor that dominated all other considerations and to which we now turn.

The Australian economic predicament

In 1929, Australia was basically a small, open economy specialising in exporting primary goods within the British imperial trading circuit. Nearly 50 per cent of Australia's exports went to Britain (Ross 1995:186). It was an asymmetrical relationship; Australia needed Britain more than Britain needed Australia. The dependence was not just for trade access for Australia's primary products, but for foreign capital. Economists estimated that roughly 25 per cent of Australia's national income was generated by exports with another 25 per cent from tariff-protected industries (Copland 1937a:412). The other half of national income was generated by sheltered industries. These ratios changed with the attendant structural change that ensued in the 1930s. Australia's role in the imperial circuit was to absorb British capital and migrants recruited for ambitious rural development schemes, which would, in turn, generate exports to the mother country. An oversupply of primary commodities in the global economy drove down prices, spelling embarrassment for Australia (Schedvin 1970:21–34). Her greatest economic booms were attributable to capital inflow and favourable export prices (Walker 1933a:209). Australia's exports were predominantly wool, wheat, hides, metals, dairy and fruit produce, while her imports, mostly manufactures, were drawn from Britain. About 40 per cent of Australia's exports consisted of wool, while wheat made up another 20 per cent. Foreign investment—mostly in the form of loans—was, apart from export prices, the principal cause of Australia's prosperity. The prices of Australia's export staples were volatile and highly susceptible to economic fluctuations. At the peak of her pre-depression prosperity in 1927–28, Australia had managed to disperse her exports to many markets other than Britain. This she was compelled to do to maintain the debt-servicing costs on loans recruited from London.

In the blind rush to development, the overseas debt of Australian governments by June 1929 stood at just more than £631 million. The capital was sunk into public utilities and infrastructure necessary for the expansion of primary and secondary industries. While the borrowing created a form of hothouse prosperity, normal unemployment remained high. Copland, among others, defended the subsequent expansion in industrial and agricultural capacity, positing that it would bear fruit in the future. It would eventually allow Australia to raise the volume of its primary exports by one-third by 1932. This increase in volume came, however, with the crumbling of commodity prices, meaning that Australia earned only two-thirds of the income it had earned in the 1920s (Dyster and Meredith 1990:132).

Since 1919, foreign debt had grown by 73 per cent, with the most rapid build-up in the late 1920s, averaging £47 million per annum. Consequently, Australia faced a rising external interest bill equivalent to 40 per cent of her export receipts. This impost—the legacy of large-scale borrowing from London—was to linger through the 1930s, meaning that, even in very good years, Australia could still not easily trade her way out of difficulties. During the Depression, Australia's foreign exchange reserves—then known as the London funds—fell from about £108 million in 1928 to £27 million in 1931, when usually £70 million was regarded as the absolute minimum to service Australia's needs. This conundrum afflicted policymakers and economists with a preoccupation with the external balance and 'a brooding pessimism' about its prospects (Corden 1968:15).

Australia's terms of trade did not improve much during the 1930s, except for a brief period after the adverse movement between 1928/29 and 1932/33.

The *annus horibilis* for Australia was surely 1929. In the middle of that year, export prices plunged 30 per cent—equivalent to a 9 per cent fall in real gross domestic product (GDP)—while investors began to sell Australian securities on the London market, making it more difficult for Australia to raise capital. Australian governments were forced to take out overdrafts with London banks. By October, the London balances were depleted and the Scullin government agreed to a Commonwealth Bank request to requisition gold and control its export. In 1929/30, Australia shipped 25 million pounds worth of gold to London, which effectively took her off the gold standard. The initial fall in export prices was a reflection of a decline in global demand caused by the slump in the United States and the transmission effects stemming from it. It raised Australia's current account deficit to 11 per cent of GDP compared with the four-year average of 7 per cent. The bind Australia was in marked the onset of acute financial diplomacy between Canberra and London. As subsequent chapters recall, the Bank of England was prepared to assist but only under the most austere conditions. The City and the English press had been alarmed at the scale of Australian borrowing in the 1920s. There had been forebodings expressed locally about the reliance on the huge build-up of capital inflow but the warnings were lost in the euphoria and the mantra of 'men, money and markets'.

The trade account

Australia enjoyed a surge in imports, allied with the huge scale of capital inflow until 1929/30. Following that dramatic year was the inverted story of a famine of imports and capital outflow from Australia. Capital left Australia when there was market concern about the country's exchange rate and, related to that, the overall degree of political and economic stability. The subsequent reversal in Australia's trade performance, spearheaded by a massive dose of relative cost adjustment together with deflationary economic policy, brought forth a huge expansion in the tradeables sector of the economy. It was aided by a run of good agricultural seasons. For instance, in 1931/32, the volume of Australia' exports had risen by 25 per cent since 1928/29. The devaluation of the Australian pound in 1931, along with the ensuing elasticity of domestic costs, underpinned this performance. It was made all the more remarkable given the adverse international trading environment. Following trade concessions won at the 1932 Ottawa Imperial Trade Conference, Britain took a marked increase in Australian produce (Rooth 2000). Japan and China compensated for depressed markets elsewhere (Dyster and Meredith 1990:133). Meanwhile, imports from Britain shrank dramatically. Apart from the dramatic impact of deflation, Australia's relative cost adjustment lay behind the plunge in import volumes falling from £143 million in 1928/29 to £44 million in 1932/33. With import consumption falling faster than national income, opportunities arose for domestic manufacturers to capture more of the domestic market (Dyster and Meredith 1990:135).

High tariff barriers, in tandem with the devaluation of 1931 and the measures taken on relative costs, were extremely conducive for a marked rise in import-replacing manufacturing. Imports as a proportion of GDP fell from an average of 18 per cent in the 1920s to 12 per cent by the early 1930s (Schedvin 1970:303). In this respect, Schedvin (1970:148) asserts that the mild expansion in manufacturing that occurred in 1933 was 'sufficient to initiate more general recovery'. It became the conventional wisdom in the postwar years to ascribe recovery largely to this development—much of it financed by British capital (Schedvin 1970:295). That is, Australia was forced to turn to 'new and untried factors to initiate the recovery' (Walker 1933a:209). In the recovery years, imports recovered some lost ground while export prices rose intermittently, meaning renewed pressure was placed on the balance of payments.

Australia had to endure one of the worst unemployment experiences resulting from the effect of the Depression and structural adjustment policies put in place to deal with it. At one stage, the unemployment rate hovered near 30 per cent of the available workforce (Valentine 1987:63). The blow to employment came from the adverse movement in the terms of trade together with the termination of public works financed by overseas capital. Added to this was the near collapse in business and consumer confidence in the country's immediate economic future. Private capital investment expenditure plunged from 1929 through to mid-1933 (Valentine 1987a:64). After the nadir of 1932, the unemployment rate began to improve and fell in 1937/38 to pre-depression levels. This, as we shall see, was enough for economists to proclaim that full employment had been reached. There was a slight relapse in 1938/39 as the fallout from an international recession hit Australia. By the outbreak of war, unemployment was again at 10 per cent.

Public spending and public borrowing

Australia had extensive experience with public works programs through the 1920s; indeed public sector investment played a significant part in Australia's economic development. During the 1930s, the Lyons government's fiscal stance was to achieve budgetary surpluses and dissipate them by tax remissions. 'Sound finance' was regarded as proper and honest (Groenewegen and McFarlane 1990:162–3). Balanced budgets were, therefore, de rigueur, while deficits were regarded as inflationary and perversely affecting business confidence. This had added force with the weight and the guilt of the reckless expenditure that had been incurred in the 1920s. Consequently, public investment spending fell in the period between 1929 and 1932 (Valentine 1987a:64). Capital markets here and in London blessed the fiscal consolidation strategy and rewarded Canberra by usually subscribing to loans or facilitating loan conversion operations. After subtracting for external payments, the combined net government surplus rose from £7 million in 1930/31 to £25 million in 1932/33, and remained there until defence preparations spelt greater federal outlays.

Most states subscribed to the same dogma, but not all. The Loan Council and the Commonwealth Bank monitored public sector borrowing but could not prevent some states engaging in borrowing for public works using the channel of semi-governmental authorities. Business and financial groups were steadfast in warning of the inflationary dangers that would ensue from tampering with money supply or running deficit budgets. Federal budget deficits were regarded as equivalent to creating credit. On that note, the Lyons government strongly adhered to the Treasury–Commonwealth Bank line that using credit to hasten economic activity would lead to inflationary repercussions (Ross 1995:117). This issue is discussed more fully in Chapters 5 and 6.

Economic policy and the recovery

Australia's national income fell from £650 million in 1928/29 to £450 million in 1931/32—a fall of nearly one-third, making it one of the largest contractions suffered by any Western economy. There was a swift reaction to this in official and unofficial policy terms. Apart from increasing tariffs and a market-led devaluation, another response was the Arbitration Court's decision to attempt to reduce real wages by 10 per cent (Copland 1934). Further, given the widespread deflation, wages were indexed downwards, resulting in an overall money wage cut of 20 per cent. Since interest and rental income receivers increased their share of national income between 1929 and 1931, it became necessary, in the name of burden sharing, that their allocation of income fell proportionately. This was executed with the successful bond conversion operation of 1931, which was an integral part of the federal government's policy response to the crisis. There was also retrenchment of public expenditures and tax increases to repair budgetary imbalances for both tiers of government.

MacLaurin (1936) dates the first green shoots of recovery from the last months of 1932. It was there perhaps that the economy's generators of income were close to 'bedrock levels' (Sinclair 1974). The recovery, initially weak, grew in strength and continued until a slight relapse in 1938/39. Real GDP began to rise from 1933/34 and increased steadily to 1937/38 when it was 20 per cent higher than 1928/29. Commentators at the time attributed the upturn to the return of business confidence along with the tonic of public spending and cheap money (Copland 1936; MacLaurin 1936). The overall tone of economic policy was, however, a supply-sided one. It was export prices—particularly wool and wheat—that were still the ultimate determinants of prosperity. There was a spasmodic recovery in export prices from 1933.

While there were considerable laxity and resistance in implementing the fiscal austerity of the Premiers' Plan, the removal of the Scullin Labor government reduced the risk of psychological crowding-out (Walker 1933a). Public works were resorted to as a palliative, not for achieving a permanently higher level of activity. Apart from fears of crowding-out private investment, it was held that greater public sector spending would inflate the domestic price level and put an added burden on the export sector (Plumptre 1935). It also seemed the electorate was not ready for more bold measures such as reflation (Nairn 1986:235). Any commissioned public works had to be—given the waste of the 1920s—'reproductive', yielding, within a reasonable period, a revenue at least equal to the debt (Robinson 1986:84). As the 1930s wore on, some could dispute whether there was, in fact, a need for public sector-led stimulus since the economy showed signs of overexpansion from 1935 onwards. This came with concomitant fears over the external account and the level of foreign exchange reserves. Consequently, policymaking authorities wanted to continue to scale back public and private debt, unaware that debt sometimes engendered productive enterprise. Indeed, as will be shown below, the recovery was interpreted as conditional on the authorities not doing anything rash in economic policy and thereby affecting business confidence. There was little recognition by the Commonwealth of manipulating policy levers to achieve a higher level of output and employment, except the traditional faith in counter-cyclical monetary management. From 1932 onwards, remissions of taxation were made from the Commonwealth's budget even when it compelled commensurate retrenchment in government expenditure. The fact that these tax cuts came from consolidated and improved budgetary outcomes was well advertised so as to placate community concerns about future debt levels (Ross 1995:109–10).

Until export prices recovered, the Commonwealth sought to reduce the costs of primary production by bearing down on cost levels. Cheap money was the other policy fundamental the Lyons government upheld throughout the 1930s (Mills and Walker 1952). The low interest rates were the fruit of the money market's confidence that the high inflationary road would not be taken; more materially, they were the end result of Treasury bill finance used to cover government budget deficits. This supply-side economic strategy was rigorously upheld until the threat of war intruded (Ross 1995:110). This condition was also in part externally imposed since the London capital markets remained closed to Australian borrowers. The financial year 1937/38 would be an *annus mirabilis* for Australia with the recovery continuing, to the astonishment of economists, when, as exports faltered, domestic expansion and import replacement took up the slack.[1] Fortune, too, played some part in the recovery. Australia enjoyed seven successive good agricultural seasons during the 1930s.

---

1 'Australian business on continued upswing', *The Financial Times Banking Supplement*, 2 May 1938.

Following Schedvin (1970), the new conventional wisdom of the recovery process was attributed to the rise of the manufacturing sector and the employment it generated. Apart from making a greater show at import replacement, the plasticity of local wage rates meant that Australia enjoyed a real devaluation in 1931. Economic historians have contested the alleged structural pre-eminence of manufacturing in driving recovery. Schedvin does not fully document, for instance, how developed the manufacturing sector really was before 1929 (Alford 1994:10). Manufacturing, for instance, already employed more of the labour force than the rural sector by 1926. Schedvin also does not take into account how manufacturing employment in fact suffered more than any sector as a consequence of the Depression (Boehm 1973). Whatever the relative magnitude of manufacturing's contribution to recovery, it did generate more employment than the huge lift in rural output, which, in itself, accounted for one-third of the improvement in GDP (Dyster and Meredith 1990:147).

Gregory and Butlin argue that Schedvin also overlooked the huge increase in primary sector production that took place in the 1930s. They also visualise the rise in manufacturing as taking place within the broader scheme of things. That is, the recovery process in Australia, as elsewhere, exhibited 'a rubber band effect' in that the upswing was 'a mirror image of the downswing' (Gregory and Butlin 1988:25); the vigour of the recovery corresponded with the severity of the preceding recession. They agree with Schedvin only in the sense that market forces, not government policy per se, largely engineered the traverse. They do not, however, totally dismiss the intent of the federal government's recovery policies as Schedvin does. Following Eichengreen (1988), Gregory and Butlin (1988) insist that had there been a devaluation earlier than 1931 Australia might have escaped the worst of the slump—a finding similar to the advice Australian economists stated before a major inquiry into banking and monetary policy in 1936. The nature of the response by the authorities suggests a brief appraisal of the policy apparatus at their command.

Economic institutions and monetary arrangements

Colin White has interestingly argued that there was a delay or 'policy vacuum' within Australia in coming to terms with the colossal external shocks of falling export prices and the near cessation of capital inflow. This was due to the absence of a 'central economic authority' (White 1992:190). This is debatable but there was undoubtedly dithering and inaction in responding to the problem largely because the Scullin government had been elected on a non-economic platform.

The Bruce government (1923–29) was chided for its complacency by observers who detected the emerging economic problems and conveyed warnings to those in power (Osmond 1985:148). Shaping a meaningful response to the gathering storm was hampered, not just by an antipathy to economists, but by adversarial politics complicated further by the federal–state divide. For instance, while the Commonwealth and the states were regarded as equal partners in economic enterprise, it was still an era when citizens attended more to their own state government than the federal government. One upshot of this was that premiers' conferences had to deliver unanimous agreement before any national policy could be put into place. Another was that expenditure on public works and the relief of unemployment were the responsibility of the states.

As to the 'absence of a central authority', it was true that the Commonwealth Treasury, as a central coordinating agency, was then quite insignificant. This was because the Commonwealth played only a minor part in the economy; taxing and spending powers, together with borrowing rights, rested with the states. At the time, New South Wales wielded as much economic weight as the Commonwealth. Federal outlays, even in the mid to late 1930s, represented only a modest fraction of total national income. The Federal Treasury performed not much more than an auditing role (Whitwell 1986:54). While the Treasury was ably staffed, none of its senior officers had formal training in economics—nor would things progress much by the mid-1930s. The political scientist Fin Crisp gave some inkling of the Treasury's role during the 1930s:

> The establishment still saw government and Treasury as sideline aids to a substantially autonomous and preferably self-acting national economy…the level of loan raisings, London funds, tax revenues were indicators of the economy's health and not instruments for its regulation or stimulation. One gathered that the general level of economic activity had an effect on budget totals, but hardly the reverse. It was essentially old world, pre-Keynesian stuff. Neither the Treasurer nor his senior officers of those days had a training such as would make them quickly aware of or eagerly responsive to new economic ideas. (Cited in Hudson 1986:98)

The Federal Treasury also did not employ economists until L. F. Giblin's arrival as Acting Commonwealth Statistician in 1931.[2] The Treasury's standing within

---

2 Roland Wilson arrived at Treasury in 1931 inauspiciously disguised as an assistant to the Commonwealth Statistician, L. F. Giblin (Wilson Transcript, NLA). Wilson recalled that he was truly a 'backroom boy at Treasury working in statistics to keep me out of sight of Treasury officers' (Wilson, TRC 1612, NLA). He was, nevertheless, considered to be the first professionally trained economist to serve with the Commonwealth government. Giblin, like Keynes, was a mathematician by training.

the economy was elevated, however, when the Australian Loan Council was established as a statutory body by the Bruce government's *Financial Agreement Act* of 1927; the Federal Treasury was to act thereon as the council's secretariat and it was from there that it started to gain some influence on the setting of monetary policy through the vehicle of the Australian Loan Council (Schedvin 1970; Gilbert 1973). Against the Loan Council stood Australia's then central bank, the Commonwealth Bank, which exercised an intimidating presence over monetary matters under its chairman, Sir Robert Gibson.

The Board of the Commonwealth Bank, dominated by Gibson, closely monitored the note issue and Australia's capital borrowings. In truth, however, the Commonwealth Bank did not truly function as a central bank partly because the trading banks need not keep reserves with it and, in fact, regarded it as a competitor; nor was Australia strictly on the gold standard (Coleman 1999:163). Moreover, the bank's board did not possess the expertise and knowledge needed for the art of central banking. The Bruce government had made amendments to the *Commonwealth Bank Act*, one of which made the board of directors free from political interference but, alas, unaware of the science of central banking (Schedvin 1992:50). This antagonised the Labor Party, which felt that proper central banking was negated if it was free from political persuasion. There were other obstacles to the bank operating as a central bank. It was, for instance, unable to exert control over the exchange rate or even gauge the depth of Australia's external reserves or 'London funds', held by Australian trading banks. The latter aspect was remedied by the Mobilisation Agreement of August 1930.

The mechanics of Australia's banking system was that a fall in London funds caused by a rise in imports or a fall in Australia's export receipts meant that the advances to deposit ratio rose. The decline in bankers' cash would lead to stringency in the money market, which could be relieved only by central bank action. Throughout the 1930s, then, Australia had an underdeveloped money market and an immature central bank presiding over the country's financial affairs. Gibson and his board, together with the Secretary of the Treasury, did, however, exert authority over interest rates, though here, again, the more powerful banks could usurp this power. On matters of monetary doctrine, the Commonwealth Bank Board rigorously upheld parity with sterling and was paranoid about 'monetary credit' abuse (Schedvin 1992:50; Coleman 1999). Parity with sterling was enshrined until 1930 when the official rate came under severe market pressure. To the board, 'inflation' translated into any expansion of the note issue whatever the circumstance. This stance helped explain the Commonwealth Bank's reluctance to provide Treasury bill finance to cover budget deficits until after June 1931 (Schedvin 1992:50). Confusingly, the bank board also regarded currency devaluation as nothing but another form of inflation and those who supported it as expansionists (Copland 1932a:114). The bank board regarded exchange rate stability, therefore, as the best means to guard against inflation (Schedvin 1992:52–3). Many in the financial world, too, wrongly linked currency inflation with currency devaluation. It was true that currency inflation could lead to a currency devaluation but the 1931 measure, as we shall see, was triggered by a trade imbalance.

Gibson was probably mindful of his lack of central banking expertise but equally wary of letting monetary experts dictate policy to him or, for that matter, anyone else on the board. He did, however, move with the times and appoint a monetary expert to the bank. It came in the form of a cautious one-year appointment of Leslie Melville, who held the chair of economics at Adelaide University. The inspiration for Melville's appointment can be traced to a comment made be Claud Janes at a meeting of the Victorian Branch of the Economic Society in October 1930. Janes encouraged the Bank to appoint an economist to the Commonwealth Bank Board along with the establishment of an Economic Council to advise the Government. Sir Robert Gibson, in attendance, supported the idea. The Bank of New South Wales' matched it by appointing another academic economist, Edward Shann, as its economic adviser in November 1930.[3]

As will be seen, the Commonwealth Bank Board throughout the 1930s remained extremely vigilant about the extent of the short-term federal government borrowing sanctioned by the Loan Council and expedited by Treasury bills. Externally, the bank board monitored, in tandem with the Loan Council, borrowings against the existing London balances. The two institutions orchestrated, therefore, the borrowings of all Australian governments (MacLaurin 1936:24–5). These decentralised and vague monetary arrangements brought the trading banks into almost immediate friction with the Scullin government over the drain on Australia's gold reserves and the cessation of borrowing from London. Given the central bank's refusal to rediscount Treasury bills, falls in the London reserves meant that the trading banks had to, quite properly, restrict their advances (Butlin and Boyce 1988:197). Labor Party politicians saw the subsequent credit squeeze, however, as deliberate sabotage. Later, the conflict between the two parties would escalate as to who had the final say in determining monetary and economic policy.

For all Gibson's intransigence and ignorance of central bank techniques, he was, as Schedvin (1970) and Giblin (1951) state, the most important individual in determining the course of economic policy during the Depression and beyond

---

3   R. Kershaw to L. F. Giblin, 29 May 1947, BE, G1/288.

(Millmow 2006).[4] Sir Montagu Norman and Sir Otto Niemeyer of the Bank of England played on this and acclaimed Gibson as the man 'who is saving Australia' from default.[5] The media, too, conveyed the same message: the dour Scot was the guardian of the people's money.[6] The presence of Gibson at the helm gave the financial and business communities some degree of psychological assurance (Copland 1936:16). It was for this reason alone that Prime Minister James Scullin reappointed him when his term of office came up for renewal in 1930.[7] Gibson soon showed his mettle, informing Scullin before his departure for an 1930 Imperial Conference in London that his government must implement immediate expenditure cuts or face impending bankruptcy with the internal and external loans fast maturing. Scullin pinned his hopes on a sympathetic London and the prospect of assistance.

---

4   Leslie Melville, who served under Sir Robert Gibson as the Commonwealth Bank's resident economist, disagreed with Schedvin's assessment but did admit that the board never voted against Gibson (Melville, TRC 182, NLA, pp. 21–5).

5   Sir O. Niemeyer to A. H. Lewis, 19 October 1932, Gibson Papers, Latrobe State Library of Victoria; E. Shann to Finlayson, 5 May 1931, BNSW, A53/409. Shann reported dinner-party conversation in which Billy Hughes complained about how Gibson was 'consumed with vanity and utterly without foresight or imagination' (E. Shann to A. C. Davidson, 18 April 1933, BNSW, GM 302, p. 590).

6   The opening lines of the *Ballad of Sir Robert Gibson* declared: 'A dour hard-headed gentleman/who guards the treasure hoard/Sir Robert Gibson, he sits light/As Chairman of the Board.'

7   Edmund Godward of the Bank of Australasia found Gibson 'overly susceptible to praise and not adverse to flattery' (E. Godward to Cowan, 15 December 1932, Bank of Australasia, D/O Correspondence, ANZ Group Archives). The sad truth for Labor, too, was that there was no-one else. Dyason's name was mooted but not held to be generally acceptable to the business community—a fair point given his later embrace of fanciful monetary experimentation. Dyason was, however, sounded out in late 1931 as a possible board member for the bank. He demurred, pleading, rather sardonically, an ignorance of monetary affairs (*The Argus*, 28 October 1931, in BNSW, GM 302/221) (Melville, TRC 182, NLA, p. 29).

4. The interwar Australian economics profession

Introduction

The purpose of this chapter is to discuss the development of the Australian economics profession and how the Depression played a part in its elevation. The opening part of the chapter briefly recounts the onset of depression within Australia. How the interwar economists perceived the origins of the Depression and their initial responses to it are discussed later. Australian economists had already made a start in advising state and federal governments on economic matters and this chapter draws out that early relationship. The main part of the chapter deals with the nature of the Australian economics profession at the time, together with some detail of prevailing economic thought and philosophy. The last part of the chapter contains a reassessment of the Niemeyer mission, showing, in particular, how it galvanised local economic expertise in terms of thinking and policy advocacy.

Grim forebodings

In Australia's history, no administration, it has been argued, was more challenged by economic circumstances than the Scullin Labor government (Denning 1982:11). Scullin took office just a week before the Wall Street crash of October 1929. Yet for all the scale of the undertaking Labor was elected into, many, including Scullin, in his earlier guise as Opposition Leader, had foreshadowed that the day of reckoning was coming for Australia. During the federal election campaign of 1929, Scullin warned voters that Australia was incurring an excessive level of foreign debt to finance infrastructure projects at a time when export prices were slipping (Robertson 1970:34). Scullin's warnings had an air of Greek tragedy to them. As Robertson (1974:3), his biographer, remarked, 'It is often the fate of prophets to be ignored; but it does not always follow that the prophet is destroyed by the calamity he has foreseen.' A hapless Scullin, while aware of the economic problems besetting the Commonwealth, shunned until too late the counsel of economists.

A quick recapitulation of the conditions prevailing in the late 1920s illustrates the debt–deflation trap that the Australian economy was falling into. The

Bruce government's development mantra of 'men, money and markets'—much of it underwritten by British capital—fuelled economic activity. The loan proceeds financed a huge appetite for imports, which left, in turn, the federal government awash with customs-duty revenue. In his study of the economic philosophy guiding the Bruce government, Richmond (1971:257) linked the administration's optimism for 'development' schemes with a grand imperial vision. The scale and extent of Commonwealth and state undertakings from the London capital market, however, greatly concerned London. While aware of London's concern about Australia's borrowing, Bruce remained unrepentant; it was a sparse population, not debt, which was Australia's besetting problem (Cumpston 1989:74; Tsokhas 1993:102). The bellwether of success for Bruce's program was judged in terms of per capita income, rather than the aggregative performance of the economy—a view shared by economists (Cain 1974:346). For eight years during the 1920s, the Commonwealth had imports running ahead of exports, with debt-servicing costs met from the proceeds of fresh borrowing (Clark 1981a:23). While there were some institutional checks, the prevailing psychological mood was one of unbridled optimism.

Wrestling free from what the polymath Frederic Eggleston called a 'prosperity complex', Bruce predicted that Australia would take measures to confront the falling exports and loan income otherwise there would be a slump in wealth, employment and the standard of living (Osmond 1985:149). The Scullin government would inherit the inevitable task of economic readjustment, along with the transfer problem of annually paying some £30 million in interest abroad.

Within days of Scullin's coming to power, the paradigm of 'development' came to an abrupt end. The Chairman of the Commonwealth Bank Board, Sir Robert Gibson, informed Scullin that the borrowing of overseas funds could no longer be sustained and that he would veto any further floating of Treasury bills until commitments were given towards achieving budgetary equilibrium (Shann and Copland 1931a).

The Depression in Australia itself was triggered by marked falls in Australia's two major exports—wool and wheat—which merely compounded the deep-seated structural economic problems. The loss in export revenue of some £40 million, together with the cessation of borrowing of some £30 million, translated into a loss in national income of some 10 per cent in one year alone (Copland 1930a:644–5). The cessation of borrowing imparted a huge deflationary impulse through the Australian economy (Schedvin 1970:4).[1] Servicing Australia's huge overseas loan portfolio would now have to be drawn from local resources. On

---

1 Leslie Melville, using Giblin's export multiplier, had come out with a predicted unemployment figure of 500 000 workers (Melville, TRC 182, NLA, p. 19).

the external account, interest and dividend repayments rose 50 per cent during the late 1920s, meaning that the export revenue to servicing costs rose from one-sixth to just more than one-quarter (Schedvin 1970:73).

South Australia had a foretaste of what was soon to become a general occurrence. The economist Leslie Melville recalled:

> We had some sort of recession in South Australia earlier than the rest of the Australia…By 1927 we were in trouble…and we certainly there saw it coming from the consequences of the loan expenditure…The interest bill was climbing very rapidly and we weren't getting revenues to meet the increase in the interest bill that was pressing on us.[2]

He was alluding to not just a fall in export prices but the cutback in public investment spending (Cornish1993b:3). Initially, the economists were, along with many others, not unnerved by the severe fall in export prices.[3] The October stock market crash on Wall Street, however, made the then predicted 'minimal' reduction in living standards look sanguine.[4] Arguably, no corrective action could have checked the colossal and sustained fall in output that marked the Depression's impact on Australia. Deflation had to come.

The Scullin government's first budget responded to falling export prices and loan cutbacks with an austere economic package. Scullin asked the Anglo-Australian financier W. S. Robinson, a *grise eminence* to the Labor Government, to make secret representations to the Bank of England about deferral of an impending loan. Robinson was given short shrift by representatives of the Deputy Governor of the Bank of England, Sir Ernest Harvey: 'Please don't ask for that perforce I must refuse' (Robinson 1967:147). Australia, by dint of some years of negative but, for the most part, accurate reporting, particularly by the *Financial Times*, had become the 'bad boy of the Commonwealth' and an example to be made of (Giblin 1951).[5] L. F. Giblin (1951), the elder statesman of the Australian economics community, felt the bank's action 'very cold. Its attitude was rigid…

---

2 Melville, TRC 182, 1971, NLA, p. 15.

3 The newly elected Prime Minister Scullin heroically took a remarkably benign view of unfolding developments. On 21 November 1929, he publicly intoned: 'We do not view the future with alarm—our troubles will soon be over' (cited in Cook 1979:371).

4 Melville, TRC 182, 1971, NLA, p. 18. According to Valentine, export prices fell by 7.7 per cent in 1928/29 and 22.7 per cent in 1929/30. These adverse movements in Australia's terms of trade were due to a contraction in the world economy. The terms-of-trade movement between 1929 and 1932 delivered a 9 per cent fall in the real GDP (Gregory and Butlin.1988:405). Valentine's empirical research showed that the price falls in wool and wheat mirrored falls in real GDP in 1927/28 and 1928/29, with a more severe fall in 1930/31 (Valentine 1987a:64). The proportion of Australian exports to service the foreign debt grew from 16 per cent in 1919/20 to 28 per cent in 1928/29 (Schedvin 1970:73).

5 D. B. Murdoch, Secretary to the Commonwealth Bank Board, later told Giblin he was astounded at Sir Ernest Harvey's refusal to grant emergency financial assistance to the Scullin government given that he had been 'a good friend' to Australia earlier (D. B. Murdoch to L. F. Giblin, 8 April 1947, RBA, GLG-51-5).

Australia must solve its own trouble for itself.' Before turning to see how his colleagues responded to the crisis, some detail of the local economics profession, including their pre-analytical vision, is required.

The Australian economics profession in 1929

Numbering only a handful of souls, Australian economics in the late 1920s was a fledgling, scattered university discipline with only six chairs extant: Melbourne (established in 1923), Sydney (1913), Hobart (1920), Adelaide (1929), Brisbane (1926) and the isolated post at Perth (1925).[6] Before then, economics was considered a politicised subject, appropriate only for instruction by the Workers' Educational Association (Heaton 1926:235). There were neither qualified instructors nor any body of Australian economic literature to rely on (Heaton 1926:238). Even with the founding of the Economic Society of Australia and New Zealand in 1925, economics was still a cinderella science. The challenges ahead heralded not only opportunity for the profession but national prominence (Bourke 1988:67; Cain 1973). The interwar generation of economists was a remarkable and versatile group even though most had not been formally trained in economics (Butlin 1966:509). Much of the learning of the older generation of economists was done 'on the job' (Cain 1973:2). Perhaps the prime example here was Giblin, who was the Official Statistician for the Tasmanian state government before taking up a position as an academic economist. Given their number and the tasks assigned to them, they were to fulfil Herbert Heaton's description of them as 'economic general practitioners' (cited in Cain 1984:76).

Australia's development strategy of 'men, money and markets' meant demand for economics expertise (Cain 1974). Like their British counterparts, Australian politicians had begun to solicit economists' advice. It gave the local profession a policy-intensive focus (Sandelin et al. 1997). There was something, moreover, within the nature of the Australian economics profession that lent itself to giving practical advice rather than engaging in scientific research. Giblin later reflected on the values and axioms that characterised the local profession:

> In Australia economists are a peculiar tribe. Rarely are they nourished by the pure milk of the word. Mostly they have been advisers to governments for many years—permanently or intermittently, publicly or privately. Governments do not love them but are inclined to believe them honest…They are frequently more practical and realistic than

---

6   Two of these chairs—at the University of Queensland and the University of Western Australia, occupied by Henry Adcock and Edward Shann respectively—were joint chairs in economics and history. While the University of Sydney had a chair in economics and commerce in 1913, which was occupied by R. F. Irvine, the Faculty of Economics there was not established until 1920 (Groenwegen, 2009).

businessmen...They are resented of course by sectional business interests. The word of complaint or abuse is 'academic'; but, in truth, they are the least academic of God's creatures. (Cited in Hytten 1960:154)

Giblin's colleague Douglas Copland, born and educated in New Zealand before emigrating to Australia, said that the distinguishing feature of interwar Australian economists was the habit of 'seeing the economy as a whole, and of realizing the possibility of instituting centrally planned policy to counteract maladjustment within the economy'(Copland,1951:16–17). This bias in the Australian economic establishment towards 'empiricism and pragmatism', as Schedvin (1970:375) puts it, was so entrenched that Melville—who held the foundation chair at Adelaide—felt it was to the detriment of theoretical innovation (Bourke 1988:63). Echoing Giblin, Melville recollected that '[e]ssentially we were all pragmatists dealing with applied economics, applied to practical problems that were developing very rapidly, and there wasn't much development till a good deal later'.[7] This penchant for practicality over theoretical innovation assumes some importance in the telling of our story. It can, however, be oversold. While the attribute paid dividends in pushing economists into the limelight, it did not really mean that they were tardy in acclimatising to new theory or, as we shall see, even pioneering new theoretical innovations. The policies they advocated during the Depression and thereafter sprang from the very latest theoretical and applied research (Copland 1951:17).

At the six universities offering instruction in economics the specific problems of the Australian economy framed the agenda. These were issues such as economic development, economic growth, land settlement, tariffs, price movements and monetary, not fiscal, theories of the trade cycle. Heaton (1926:245–7) told an American audience that the predominant research interests of their Australian counterparts were the economics of federation, wage fixation and banking and currency policy. In terms of ranking, Melbourne had overtaken Hobart in prominence since it had become, in 1925, the newly established home of the Economic Society of Australia and New Zealand. Giblin's arrival in 1928 from Tasmania, moreover, to fill the newly created Ritchie Research Professorship, gave Melbourne a further edge in research profile.[8] Another member of the staff was Gordon Wood, an economic geographer by training.

---

7   Melville, TRC 182, NLA, p. 9.

8   Giblin, then Deputy Commonwealth Government Statistician, won the post almost certainly with Copland's connivance (Millmow 2005). Giblin had acted as a referee for Copland when he applied for the chair in economics at Melbourne. Giblin was elected unanimously despite his lack of academic standing and his 'unorthodox appearance' (D. B. Copland to R. Downing, 25 June 1959, UMA FECC, Box 220A). It was a position Giblin approached with some trepidation. It was only with the encouragement of Brigden—someone Giblin felt should have won the post—that he accepted the challenge. He told his wife, Eilean, 'They have offered me the Ritchie chair and I have not read any of their damn textbooks.' When his wife conveyed this

Before then, Hobart had been the original home of Australian economics with many interwar economists having taught or studied there (Castles 1996; Coleman and Hagger 2003; Roe 1994). In Hobart's heyday, James Brigden and Giblin had made pioneering contributions in multiplier analysis and the optimal degree of tariff protection needed to promote economic development and population growth (Copland 1951:16–17; Cain 1973). For a brief period, then, Hobart resembled the 'Edinburgh of the south' in terms of theoretical innovation (Coleman and Hagger 2003). Roland Wilson was another product of this faculty (Cornish 2003b:9–11). Despite his academic promise, evidenced in his book *Capital Imports and the Terms of Trade*, Wilson dedicated his considerable expertise to the Federal Treasury (Cain 1983:23; Cornish 2003b:19–20). Other eminent scholars who hailed from Hobart were Arthur Smithies (Harcourt 1987:375–6) and Keith Isles. Later, a Federal Treasurer, R. G. Casey, commented on the remarkable profusion of economic talent that sprang from Tasmania.[9] After Giblin took up the Richie Chair, a New Zealand economist remarked that Tasmania had suffered a 'disability...through the drain to the mainland of the best Tasmanian blood'.[10]

The Economic Society, founded by Copland, was made possible by the enthusiastic cooperation between economists and businessmen (Downing 1972:466). As both Scott (1988:3) and Hodgart (1975:2–3) note, it was the business community in Sydney and Melbourne that pushed for the greater edification of economics. The business community sponsored the Economic Society as a means to isolate and suppress the radical outpourings from the economic underworld (McFarlane 1966:17; Clark 1974a, 1975; Roe 1984; Mauldon and Weller 1960). It also marked, as Heaton (1926:235) noted, the first systematic study and teaching of economics within Australia. The society brought, therefore, businessmen, economists and public servants under the one roof. In that regard, Copland, Foundation Dean of the Faculty of Commerce at the University of Melbourne, 'conspicuously identified with the business community' (Harper 1986:43). One instance that caught the attention of the Victorian Trades Hall was when Copland, in formal morning dress, regaled a gathering of conservative luminaries about the dire state of the economy (Spierings 1989:132–3). Copland was regarded as politically safe and 'the proper custodian and expander...of absolute and unbending economic laws' (cited in Spierings 1989:133). Consequently, he was marked out for special attention by Labor politicians, one of whom regarded him as 'one of the most conservative economists in Australia...and whose opinions are not worth much'.[11] Aware of

---

to J. P. Clapham, the English economic historian, he replied: 'Economics is mathematics and common sense. We all know about the first and he has more of the second than anybody I know' (E. Giblin to J. M. Garland, 6 June 1954, Garland Papers, RBA, GJG-59-5).

9   'Export of brains', *The Mercury*, 20 July 1936.
10   A. G. B. Fisher to D. B. Copland, 9 November 1928, UMA FECC, Box 3.
11   N. J. Makin in *Hansard*, 18 October 1931, p. 1356.

an antipathy towards economists within Labor circles, Copland assured Giblin that the Melbourne faculty was, in fact, beholden to no-one.[12] It was ironic that, after the Premiers' Plan, Copland was shunned in certain financial quarters as his political views became more interventionist (Calwell 1960:2).

In his inaugural lecture as dean, Copland looked forward to forging greater links between 'town and gown' (Spierings 1989:128–9; Hodgart 1975:9). In revamping the syllabus of the commerce degree, Copland, as he had done in Hobart, eschewed narrow specialisation in economics for a broad-based education that would suit graduates entering the business world (Selleck 2003:607). The commerce course proved dramatically popular when first launched in 1925, even if many of the students were part-time (Selleck 2003:608). Business houses supplied Copland's department not just with guest lecturers but with tangible support by way of equipment (Spierings 1989:129). Copland invited representatives from business and finance houses and the Trades Hall to be on the faculty board. This included Sir Robert Gibson, then President of the Victorian Chamber of Manufactures and a director on the Commonwealth Bank Board, Edward Dyason, company director and stockbroker, and the Commonwealth Statistician, Charles Wickens.

Neville Cain (1980:2) casts Copland as 'the public relations man of university economics selling its "practical usefulness" to city men…and to politicians'. The Collins House Group of companies, and later the Premier of New South Wales, Bertram Stevens, overlooking the economists at the University of Sydney, hired Copland as an economic adviser. The Canadian economist A. F. W. Plumptre (1934:490) would marvel at Copland's combination of gifts of being an able economic theorist, propagandist and financial expert. Richard Downing later reported on the 'excitement' of being an economics student at Melbourne and having Copland or Giblin give their lectures straight from meetings with businessmen. Students 'were bred to the world of affairs, public policy and applied economics which they brought to the Melbourne school' (cited in Brown 2001:30).

Because of this engagement with public affairs, Cain (1980:3) finds—somewhat unfairly—that Copland's academic output was 'largely derivative…evidencing little theoretical penetration'. While Copland was not 'a pioneer in abstract thought, but rather a man of action and an educator' (Harper 1984:2), he published 11 articles in the *Economic Journal* alone during the interwar period. Keynes told Copland, who was visiting England in 1927 on a survey of economics education, that the training at Canterbury was as good as any other place of the same size.[13] Keynes also told his visitor that classical theory 'had

---

12   D. B. Copland to L. F. Giblin, 6 June 1927, UMA FECC, Box 220.
13   'A professor peregrinates' (extract from Copland's diary of his 1927 trip), *The Margin*, vol. 3, no. 1, p. 7. Visiting London, Copland had lunch with Keynes, who he described as a 'leading British economist' (19 June 1927).

rather worked itself out' and that he was writing a book that would revise it.[14] In his training under James Hight, Professor of History and Political Economy at the University of Canterbury, Copland had been exposed to the tradition of economics developing within the United States concerning monetary theory and practice. When Copland subsequently came to Australia in 1917, he was, as Giblin (1951:6) noted, 'probably the only academic expert on monetary policy in the Commonwealth'.

Copland spent seven years in Tasmania, contributing three articles that appeared in the *Economic Journal* on monetary matters. His first publication was a test of the quantity theory using Australian data, which Keynes rushed into the journal. Copland established a School of Commerce at the University of Tasmania that promised a systematic and thorough study of economics. It heralded a brief but 'golden age' in terms of economics scholarship at Hobart (Coleman and Hagger 2003. Australia needed it, for Copland was mindful of his Australian colleagues' technical competency, particularly when it came to filling a lucrative appointment such as the newly created Ritchie research chair in economics at the University of Melbourne. He remarked to an American economist, Edmund Day, that 'it is true to say that the economists in Australia have a common limitation in respect of their training and interest in pure theory'.[15] Reflecting that, Copland had asked Cannan whether he might like to take the Ritchie Chair.[16] Cannan declined on account of his age. Keynes, who was part of an informal committee to find a British-based economist for the Ritchie Chair, told Copland to appoint an Australian to the position (Millmow 2005).

Copland was, like Giblin, adept in the art of economic policymaking, particularly in devising workable compromises (Harper 1986:43). Copland was, moreover, to draw international fame when he delivered the 1933 Marshall Lectures at the University of Cambridge on how Australia's mix of economic policies and institutions helped Australia emerge from the Depression. Torleiv Hytten (1971:45), who held the chair at Hobart from 1928, found the pugnacious Copland 'an extraordinary person...with little sense of humour and one never knew what he was going to do next'.

Copland co-edited the *Economic Record* along with one of his former Melbourne students, Claude Janes. The early issues of the journal reflected the applied, business-oriented aspect of the Australian economics profession (Scott 1988:14; Fleming 1996:30; Perlman 1977). The special problems of the Australian economy—the tariff, demography, economic development and cyclical fluctuations—formed the main focus of inquiry (Cain 1974). Typically, Copland

---

14 Ibid.
15 D. B. Copland to E. D. Day, 20 April 1928, UMA FECC, Box 5.
16 D. B. Copland to E. Cannan, 24 March 1928, UMA FECC, Box 4.

wrote on monetary and banking matters, while James Brigden specialised in tariffs and population. R. C. Mills, the Dean of the Faculty of Economics at Sydney University, and Giblin wrote on public finance and federalism, while Wickens was the authority on statistical matters (Scott 1988:14). The journal's audience was not just academics but 'responsible men of political and commercial affairs' (Perlman 1977:219). S. J. Butlin (1966:516) attributed the *Record* with having a 'seminal influence on the thought and policy in high places' because its literary style made it accessible to 'men of affairs'. According to Copland, the average reader of the journal was a 'fairly intelligent person but not with a scientific interest in economics and one who would quickly lose his interest if the *Record* became too dull'.[17]

Apart from Giblin and Copland at Melbourne, the other luminaries within the Australian profession at the time were Richard Mills in Sydney, Edward Shann in Perth and Melville at Adelaide University. Mills, who held the chair in economics at Sydney University from 1922, had studied at the London School of Economics and graduated with a DSc in economics. Edwin Cannan was one of his mentors (Groenewegen 2009:9). Interestingly, Shann and Melville soon joined banks in advisory capacities, with the latter making a permanent move to the Commonwealth Bank in 1931. Brigden left the chair at Hobart to become an economist with a shipping concern in Sydney before moving to Queensland to become Director of the Queensland Bureau of Economics and Statistics (Roe 1994). At Sydney University, Mills diligently set about building a 'factory' of local economic expertise (Butlin 1953). Despite Melbourne's prominence, Sydney University would boast that it had Australia's only ensemble of professionally trained economists (Butlin 1978:102). To achieve this, Mills encouraged his staff to further their studies abroad in either England or the United States (Turney et al. 1991:576). There was, therefore, a Melbourne–Sydney rivalry developing, with the latter tending to regard their southern counterparts as too pragmatic and involved in public affairs (Butlin 1978:104). This was a little ungracious in the respect that Copland had been selected to be the Australian representative of the Rockefeller Foundation, which funded fellowships for promising social scientists to study abroad. Ronald Walker was one Sydney economist assisted in this regard during the 1930s. Despite the difference in orientation, there was some commonality in analytical vision among the economists, to which we turn.

The state of Australian economic opinion

Australian economists looked to Britain not just in terms of capital and trade flows but in terms of economic doctrine. By and large, the Australian

---

17   D. B. Copland to H. Belshaw, 20 October 1937, Economic Society of Victoria Branch, UMA FECC, Box 139.

economics fraternity was an outpost of the Cantabridgian tradition, but with an idiosyncratic twist (Cain 1973, 1980; Harper 1986:37). Edwin Cannan of the London School of Economics was also influential with his stress on welfare analysis (Butlin 1966:509). Cannan had personally tutored Brigden, while Mills and Shann had attended his lectures (Roe 1994:73). National income, even the level of real wages, was taken as an index of economic welfare (Cain 1974:74–7). National income became the focal point of policy long before it was officially adopted, as in Britain in 1941 (Whitwell 1994). Apart from the London school, the main influence on Australian economics was Cambridge with its Marshallian–Pigovian tradition. Cambridge became the place, therefore, of higher learning for the crop of young, aspiring Australian economists, although two Rhodes Scholars, Roland Wilson and Arthur Smithies, went to Oxford (Cain 1984:77).

Australian economists were philosophically in favour of competitive markets to harness private interests provided governments were on call to eliminate market distortions and reconcile private and social costs (Harper 1986:37). Limited public works held some appeal to Australian economists since they were predisposed to see the economy as a whole and placed the State before the consumer (Brown 1994:89–92). There was also a role for the State in fostering economic development. That world view had come about due partly to the nation-building paradigm of 'development' and, relatedly, the influence of the Hobart school (Cain 1973). The research on estimating the cost of the tariff assistance, together with Giblin's quantitative export multiplier analysis, bestowed Australian economists with an economy-wide perspective of the costs and benefits of external economic shocks. This would become useful when they adopted the 'spreading the loss' doctrine after Australia's export income plummeted in 1929.

The question that dominated the Australian economics fraternity in the 1920s was determining Australia's optimum population size and the standard of living that could be afforded (Cain 1973). Stemming from Brigden's bleak assessment of Australia's economic future, Hobart was wary that diminishing returns in primary produce would not only skew income distribution to the landowners but drive down welfare levels and restrict the absorption of a growing population (Cain 1974:352; Roe 1994:76). Brigden (1925) had argued, therefore, that tariff assistance was justifiable for Australia's economic development, welfare and population growth. He found, somewhat controversially, that protection had been as 'beneficial' for Australia as free trade had been for Britain (Brigden 1925:45). His finding presaged the more comprehensive *Brigden Report* on the Australian tariff, which stated that the fall in income that would ensue from unimpeded rural development and population growth was prevented because tariffs maintained real wages by redistributing income from landowners to labour. The tariff, moreover, kept the terms of trade favourable by placing a tax on rural exports (Coleman and Hagger 2003:15).

Giblin would later corroborate the Hobart view by calculating the amount of rural production Australia would have had to produce to generate an equivalent standard of living. Such an effort would have driven down produce prices and made Australia acutely vulnerable to world trends (Groenewegen and McFarlane 1990:122). That aside, by the end of the 1920s some economists, particularly Shann and Melville, felt that the economy, especially the labour market, was riddled with too much government intervention. There was also a growing recognition among economists that Australia's high real wage levels were kept up by protection and public works. A technical correction was imminent (Cain 1973:20).

As the Depression descended, money and banking theory assumed the leading research focus. A devotee of the quantity theory, Copland moved with the transatlantic tide of monetary reformers such as Irving Fisher, Ralph Hawtrey and Keynes (Cain 1980, 1987b:3). The reformers held that the way to avoid economic fluctuations was price stability, meaning that monetary policy should make this its overriding goal. Keynes's *Tract* registered a significant impact with Copland, especially the finding that fluctuations in the price level were more likely to be a function of monetary demand than a money supply increase. This revolutionary finding was that, with a variable velocity of circulation, prices and output could change without the real stock of money changing. In short, fluctuations in economic activity were due to price-level instability aggravating the gap between product prices and costs (Turnell 1999:26). Inspired by Keynes's *Tract*, Copland (1930b) was the first among his colleagues to argue that internal price stability should rank as a policy objective before exchange rate stability and that the transmission of large movements in credit, via the external account, be avoided in the name of economic stability. Henceforth, the policy focus in Copland's eyes focused on credit growth as distinct from money supply; it was, however, to be a point hopelessly lost on the Commonwealth Bank Board, which remained fixated on the latter.

In the 1920s, Copland devised a schema that underpinned how to both visualise and manage the Australian economy. The preservation of economic activity in an open economy required insulation against fluctuations being channelled through the trade account. This meant establishing a managed monetary system aimed at stabilising prices and regulating the credit cycle to eliminate short-period fluctuations (Copland 1930b). Since Australia was a small, open, debtor country with its national income determined largely by commodity prices, the economy could achieve price stabilisation by aligning its exchange rate with sterling. Britain—Australia's creditor and largest trading partner—effectively set her monetary policy. This was an optimal arrangement in times of normalcy and also when Australia had an underdeveloped central banking apparatus. Moreover, it kept mischievous hands at bay, for the gold standard was 'knave proof' with banking and monetary policy controlled by mandarins rather than by politicians. The orthodox strictures about quarantining credit and currency matters from political interference found an appreciative audience in Australia (Middleton, 1982). These institutional and banking arrangements were enveloped in an air of anti-intellectualism, which sought to separate the 'sound' views of the real-world financier from the 'academic' opinion of monetary reformers (Winch 1966:92).

Australia's harmonious link with the Bank of England came unstuck, however, with the calamitous fall in her export prices in 1929. The voluntary moratorium on federal and state government borrowing from London compounded Australia's difficulties. Under the traditional rules of the game, Australia could recover external balance only by a severe deflation brought about by a direct reduction in bank credit consistent with the dwindling London funds. Deflation and austerity meant the intensification of unemployment. It also meant pressure on wages that would lead to social unrest, especially where rentiers, benefiting from the deflation, increased their hold over consumption. The financial architecture of the economy would also be placed under great pressure. Copland felt this form of relative cost adjustment too draconian. The more palatable alternative was to break with sterling and implement wage cuts. This would allow Australia to find a more appropriate relationship between her export prices and domestic cost structure. Exchange rate autonomy, Copland held, would give Australia's export trades and unsheltered industries a more favourable price–cost relationship and thereby prevent economic activity from plunging. The markedly lower real wage would improve Australia's cost structure. Copland's analytical framework was strengthened with Giblin's export multiplier—the greatest theoretical innovation of the interwar Australian economists—which showed how a fall in export revenue delivered a direct and amplified effect on output (Cain 1980:10). The concept was especially useful for an open economy dependent on its primary produce for its prosperity (Wilson 1951:194–5). Giblin had stumbled on it while undertaking some applied work on the effect of building a railway as part of a rural development project. Giblin's prototype multiplier, introduced into the public domain in late 1930, had a value of 3, with imports tumbling along with the fall in national income.

Cutting the link with sterling was viewed with horror in financial circles. As we shall see, even Copland's colleagues were initially aghast at his suggestion when he first put it to them in May 1930 (Cain 1987b:5–6). The timing of Copland's apostasy is very interesting. Just two months earlier, Keynes, in evidence before the Macmillan Committee in Britain, outlined seven expedients the Bank of England could turn to to maintain economic activity given pressures on her external account (Booth and Peck 1985:170–4).

Keynes gave a practical demonstration of his new dynamic model of changing equilibria in his evidence before the Macmillan Committee on industry and trade. Keynes's evidence was shaped by the analytical framework from his latest work, the *Treatise on Money*, which would be published in October of that year. Using the interest rate to stimulate activity or, in terms of the framework of the *Treatise*, to align savings and investment was impeded by Britain's need to maintain a high bank rate necessary to keep her on the gold standard. Keynes told the committee that Britain should not apply wage cuts or even consider the heresy of devaluation. One expedient that took the interest of Australian economists was to have an internationally coordinated expansion led by the central banks of the creditor nations. This would deliver an increase in trade and commodity prices for primary-producing export countries such as Australia. Turnell (1999) has written of how this expedient informed and motivated the Australian economists' advocacy for monetary reform at the 1932 Ottawa Imperial Trade Conference.

Among the other more feasible options canvassed by Keynes was his own 'favourite remedy' of public works (Booth and Peck 1985:174). That is, public investment financed from excess savings could be a boon to private enterprise though it would mean rising prices. This option was unthinkable for Australia but she could, within reason, resort to devaluation and wage cuts, or a composite of both, as the best means of making a relative adjustment instead of going through the ritual of deflation (Cain 1987a:3). This expenditure-switching policy—what Copland called his middle course—was later presented to Australian policymaking authorities (Cain 1987a:2). Devaluation and a wage cut would assist the import-competing and export industries besides transmitting a real income loss across all tiers of the community. It was similar to another of Keynes's expedients—namely, a national treaty arrangement in which all economic classes surrendered some income. Once converted to Copland's monetary analysis, economists faced the task of enlightening high opinion away from the Anglo-Saxon fetish that a unit of money—namely, the Australian pound—could be a variable unit and not something immutably fixed (Dyason 1931:236–7). It was to prove a long struggle.

Australian economists and their early contribution to economic policy

Giblin, whom Roland Wilson later called 'the fabulous old man of Australian economics', felt the early 1930s transformed economics from a cinderella science to one of public influence (Wilson 1951:1; Goodwin 1974). Economic circumstances propelled this. The leading political and economic issues in the 1920s all required scientific analysis and input (Cain 1973:2). The various committees of economists that tendered advice to the authorities in the early 1930s were perceived to be remarkably consensual, even innovative, on the direction and content of macroeconomic stabilisation policy (Goodwin 1974). The pioneering spirit of economists carried through to official policy, where, in contrast with British efforts, there was neither a reliance on 'muddling through' nor great division in framing Australia's policy response to the Depression. It marked, then, a 'brief interlude of a genuine Australian economics' with native economic expertise dealing with essentially national economic problems (Groenewegen and McFarlane 1990:115).

The relations between economists and the political elite that unfolded in the 1930s in Australia can be better understood when one considers the antecedents. Starting with Giblin's position as statistical adviser to the Tasmanian government and Mills and Brigden's participation in the 1924 Queensland Basic Wage Commission, Australian high politics had established the precedent in the 1920s of calling on 'experts' to advise on aspects of public policy ranging from child endowment to national insurance (Fleming 1996:29; Cain 1980:80; Clark 1950:2). Calling on a repository of economic wisdom was also in the newly found spirit of 'scientific administration' or 'salvation through science' (Howson and Winch 1977:159). The success economists achieved in tendering advice to Australian authorities was the embodiment of the Marshallian–Pigovian ethic of serving humanity (Fleming 1996:31).

Since the 1920s, Copland had been promoting the idea of placing economists into policy formulation. In 1927, he published the results of investigations made while visiting the United States and Europe, courtesy of the Rockefeller Foundation, to examine developments in the teaching of the social sciences, especially economics (Bourke 1988:58). Copland saw how 'university-trained men' were making inroads in the business world and the public service. Herbert Hoover, then US Secretary of State, informed Copland that the US administration was 'honeycombed with economists'.[18] It moved Copland to declare that 'the economist is king in every country' (cited in Spierings 1989:131). It was not yet the case, however, in Australia. To amend that, Copland felt that the

---

18 'Varsity men in business', *The Herald*, 18 August 1927.

Commonwealth Public Service should have openings for graduates. Consistent with this ambition was the recommendation from Mills that there be chairs of economics established in every Australian university.[19]

Consistent with the acceptance of economics as an academic discipline there was a raft of initiatives aimed at coordinating economic affairs (Cain 1974:356). The Migration and Development Commission established in 1926, for instance, was designed to place the British-Australian '34 million pound agreement' on migration and development on a more scientific footing (Cain 1974:356; Richmond 1971:246–7; Roe 1995:118). Melville felt the commission would tailor development 'in a way which aims at being methodical, consistent and economic and based on sense rather than sensibility' (cited in Cain 1974:356). The businessman Herbert Gepp, equally keen on the potential of economic expertise, headed the commission (Kemp 1964:36).

The issue of business stability concerned policymakers as much as the optimal level of protection. The Development and Migration Commission issued a study written largely by Gepp's offsider, F. J. Murphy, entitled *Unemployment and Business Stability in Australia* (1928). The study was notable for empirically rejecting the popular view that Australia's mounting unemployment was attributable to high wages, excessive British migration and imports. Rather, as Copland's research showed, the problem was pinned on business cycle fluctuations, though the fits and starts of public sector spending, financed by overseas borrowing, did not help matters.[20] As Australia's leading theorist in cyclical fluctuations, Copland wrote an influential adjoining study and apparently had a hand in drafting the commission's recommendations.[21] His findings presaged his later stand in the 1930s on the need for a contra-cyclical policy (Cain 1980). In clear prose, Copland relayed the latest conventional view that experts study the economic picture and give warning of booms and slumps so that policymakers could moderate or, at least, cushion their impact by tapering public works expenditure.[22]

The commission also proposed that the Commonwealth Bank manage the exchange rate, taking action to safeguard the balance of payments, for instance, by reducing imports when export revenue was likely to decline. Adjusting levels of government expenditure spent on development projects could counter cyclical instability. It was a commonplace view in the economics literature that an increase in spending would raise incomes and possibly produce further increases in spending. Long-range planning of public works would allow policymaking bodies time to regulate the level of expenditure thereby securing

---

19   R. C. Mills, 'Economics and social sciences', *SMH*, 12 October 1927.
20   'Causes of unemployment in Australia', *The Commercial*, 9 August 1929.
21   *The Age*, 21 June 1928.
22   'Planning ahead to meet the bad times', *The Herald*, 7 February 1927.

some regularity of employment besides raising funds abroad to protect the exchange rate. Prime Minister Bruce agreed with Gepp that the ideas contained in the report were 'somewhat ahead of the times in which we live'.[23]

Copland's framework was echoed in a memorandum on trade cycles prepared by two Sydney economists, E. R. Walker and Mills.[24] They believed that cyclical fluctuations were made worse by the comparative rigidity of wage costs. This, together with the imperfect mobility of labour, was, they held, the real factor behind unemployment. Both subscribed to the creed that wage regulation should, in time of depression, give way to the capacity-to-pay criterion.[25] Mills and Walker, besides manipulating loan expenditure, argued for a greater 'plasticity of wage rates' to control unemployment. They were, however, hesitant about recommending monetary policy since the economic fluctuations could be externally borne—a factor that Australian policy authorities could do little to address (Cornish 1990:60–1). Walker (1930:39) shared Copland's view that public works be used 'as a counterpoise to the business cycle', but he lamented whether the authorities had the ability to synchronise expenditure with the cycle.

It was, of course, the Brigden Committee's review of the Australian tariff that first made the name of Australian economics (Fleming 1996:29–30). In the foreword to *The Australian Tariff: An economic enquiry*, Bruce hailed it as 'a free gift to the Australian people'. This was a reference not just to the report's clarity and lucidity, but to how economists had laboured without compensation (Davidson 1977:146–7). Charles Wickens, Chairman of the Tariff Committee, reminded his colleagues that they should speak with one voice on the subject. Disunity, he felt, would jeopardise the proposed establishment of a Bureau of Economic Research (Harper 1989:9).[26]

According to Hytten, the committee got off to an impolitic start when Copland wrote 'a learned paper' extolling the merits of free trade. Bruce dispatched his secretary to tell the economists that they must do better.[27] Brigden and Giblin, thereupon, took up the cudgels of drafting. What emerged was a 'compromise' document between the orthodox Melbourne economists (Copland, Dyason and

---

23 'Unemployment and business stability in Australia', AA, A786 z1/1.
24 Walker was one of Mills's students at Sydney. In his recommendation to the Board of Research Studies at Cambridge University in 1930, Mills hailed Walker as the 'most distinguished and brilliant student' he had seen in 10 years of economics instruction at Sydney (R. C. Mills to The Secretary, Board of Research Studies, Cambridge University, 16 October 1930, E. R. Walker Papers, Canberra). Mills and Copland had awarded Walker first-class honours for his thesis on unemployment in Australia. Walker filled the vacancy at the University of Sydney when F. C. Benham left for England (Groenewegen 2009:28).
25 'Memorandum by which greater security of economics be guaranteed to all classes of work', n.d., UMA FECC, Box 9.
26 C. Wickens to L. F. Giblin, 14 May 1928, UMA FECC, Box 213; J. H. Simpson [Bruce's secretary] to L. F. Giblin, 11 May 1928, UMA FECC, Box 213.
27 Hytten autobiography, UT, p. 52.

Wickens) and the more open-minded Brigden and Giblin at Hobart (Coleman and Hagger 2003:16). Their finding, in brief, was to reject the orthodox contention that Australia could have maintained its present population at a higher standard of living under free trade (Dow 1938:114–15). They found instances, however, where the cost of protection exceeded the benefits. They concluded that the level of tariff assistance was now at its optimal level whereas population and the level of real wages had surpassed that criterion (Cain 1973).

The authors were anxious to see how their overseas counterparts would judge the findings (Harper 1989:22). Jacob Viner praised Bruce for having commissioned 'a disinterested and non-political inquiry by competent and unbiased economists into the merits of a policy to which his party and his country are so strongly committed' (cited in Davidson 1977:147). Keynes also applauded the report as 'a brilliant effort of the highest interest' with a 'method of approach most original'.[28] Frank Taussig from Harvard University hailed Copland and his colleagues for their work on the report: 'I wish I could say that work as good came from the immensely larger number of American economists.'[29] The report triggered a long-lasting controversy in existing trade theory (Coleman and Hagger 2003:16–18). For our purposes, however, it marked the start of Australian economists engaging in Australian 'economic problems with gusto'.[30]

This early policy work of Australian economists mirrored, if not anticipated, comparable developments in Britain, where extra-parliamentary economic expertise was pursued with some vigour, especially after the onslaught of the Depression (Howson and Winch 1977). Bruce's 'eyes and ears' in London, Major Casey, the Australian liaison officer with the Foreign Office, wrote of the rising power of economics: 'Economics was beginning to show signs of asserting itself' and was 'being recognised as the sharp and effective tool of those in power' (Hudson and North 1980:502). By 1929, Bruce had a Federal Economics Bureau on the statute books (Scott 1988:16; Roe 1995:119; Castles 1997:26–8).

Copland was the first to raise the idea of such an Economics Bureau (Spierings 1989:132).[31] Giving evidence before the Royal Commission on the Federal Constitution in 1927, Copland said a special authority was required for the development of economic research along the lines of the Commonwealth's Council for Scientific and Industrial Research (CSIR).[32] David Rivett, the

---

28   J. M. Keynes to L. F. Giblin, 28 August 29, UMA FECC, Box 213.

29   F. Taussig to D. B. Copland, 13 December 1929, UMA FECC, Box 48.

30   Melville, TRC 182, NLA, p. 9.

31   D. B. Copland to L. F. Giblin, 6 June 1927, UMA FECC, Box 220.

32   *The Mercury*, 23 March 1928. The Melbourne stockbroker E. C. Dyason was also in favour of a permanent body of economics specialists 'railed off from politics' whose key task would be to issue periodic reports on the economy ('Memorandum on the increase of production in Australia upon a sound economic and social basis', n.d., UMA FECC, Box 8).

Chairman of the CSIR, dissuaded Bruce, however, from attaching an economics research division to his organisation. The British Economic Mission (1927) also advised against it because of the fear that the CSIR would, under the proposal, become politically contaminated (Schedvin 1987:60). The economists were keen on the bureau being self-supporting since it would guarantee the necessary freedom that they would not have if attached to a government department (Rivett 1972:110). Interestingly, the director of the bureau was, as originally outlined, to have freedom from political interference (Scott 1988). Copland hoped that this dimension would allow the director to freely initiate inquiries into wage regulation, unemployment, overseas borrowings, tariffs, development policy and intergovernmental relations before they became politicised. Lastly, Copland saw the bureau as working in cooperation with other policymaking agencies thereby delivering coordination and assessment of the wider effects of public policy.[33] Given his lobbying for the bureau, Copland was shocked when Brigden showed him Bruce's offer to become its first director.[34] Affronted, Copland asked Bruce why he should not be considered for the post. He had earlier written to Simpson to unashamedly offer his services to the bureau, especially if he did not win the Ritchie Chair.[35] Annoyed at the breach of confidentiality, Bruce withdrew the offer to Brigden[36]

The idea of a bureau of economic research was cut short with the defeat of the Bruce government in October 1929. The Labor Party had already voted against the bill. One Labor politician stated that the bureau would have been staffed with economists 'brought up in schools of economic thought and ideas quite foreign to conditions prevalent in Australia'. 'The economist,' Arthur Blakely continued, 'is academic, conservative and anti-working class and lives in a world of his own.'[37] Labor MHR John Curtin saw the bureau's likely agenda as waging an intellectual assault on the wage fixation system with the power of wage determination handed over to quarrelling economists The Labor Party leader, James Scullin, also criticised the ostensibly 'academic' orientation of the people who would staff the office: 'The textbooks teem with the opinions of the so-called leading economists of the world on the subject of free trade and protection...[The people] are not concerned with the opinions of learned persons who talk about a wonderful flow of trade through uninterrupted channels' (cited in Castles 1997:28).

---

33   'New aid to government', The Herald, 25 February 1928.
34   According to Giblin, it was the New Zealand economist J. B. Condliffe who was earmarked for the position of director of the bureau. Hytten corroborated this. After Condliffe began to haggle over the conditions of appointment and before negotiations were complete, the Bruce–Page government was thrown out (R. Wilson to L. F. Giblin, 2 November 1950, RBA, GLG-50-1; Hytten autobiography, UT, p. 57).
35   D. B. Copland to J. H. Simpson, 29 June 1929, FECC UMA, Box 4.
36   Hytten autobiography, 197, pg. 53.
37   'Another weapon against workers', The Worker, 24 May 1929.

With this view of economic expertise, it came as no surprise when Scullin also abolished the Development and Migration Commission. Labor believed that the high volume of imports and heavy immigration were responsible for the escalation in unemployment between 1927 and 1929 (Roe 1994:119). The Scullin government moved therefore to postpone assisted migration and significantly raise tariff protection. Sir Richard Hopkins, a British Treasury official, found this good cause to recommend that London terminate lending to Australian governments (Roe 1995:143). Despite Labor's hidebound attitude to economics expertise there would shortly come a time when it would have no choice but to accept it.

How interwar economists saw the origins of the Depression in Australia

The time is coming when…every battery of science will be required for the defence of our standard of living.

— J. B. Brigden, 1928

This part of the chapter highlights the long-run internal and external factors at play that interwar economists felt made Australia acutely vulnerable to any downturn in the world economy. It is commonly agreed by economists that much of the seeds of the Australian economic malaise that unfolded in 1929–31 were sown in the mid-1920s. In his 'reinterpretation' of the causes of the Depression, Schedvin argued that the interaction between external and internal factors was the clue to understanding the severity of the crash in Australia. Having just undertaken an inquiry into the Australian tariff, the economists were well aware of how the capital-driven rapid expansion in resource development and population could collapse if Australia's export prices crumbled. As we shall discover, economists attributed much of the damage from the fall in the terms of trade to state and federal governments' fixation with overcapitalised 'development' (Shann 1930a; Richmond 1971:248–9; Osmond 1985:148). Frederic Eggleston's studies of Australia's finances in 1928 had already convinced him that 'developmental' policy was 'out of date and inapplicable to our economic circumstances' (cited in Osmond 1985:148). He warned J. G. Latham, the then Federal Attorney-General:

You are in for a difficult time. The finances of the States are so bad and the failure of Government intervention in economics is so conspicuous that I don't think any Government can do what ought to be done without losing office. You people have not seen the drift of things in time [or] prepared the people for a change in policy which is overdue. (Cited in Osmond 1985:148)

Eggleston longed for a prime minister who would have the 'courage' to do little on the development front (Cain 1974:357). Economists would have shared this sentiment. Aware of the incipient economic problems and their perception, at home and abroad, Bruce was reluctant for electoral reasons to act on them (Lloyd 1984).[38] Earlier, Shann had prophesised in his pamphlet *The Boom of 1890— and Now* (1927) that the seeds of the Depression were sown in the 1920s with the first manifestation of crisis sprouting in 1927 when wheat and wool prices fell calamitously on international markets. In the same year, in a lecture aptly titled 'The road to ruin', Giblin expressed concern about Australia's voracious appetite for imports.

Unemployment, which had been chronically high throughout the 1920s, crept upwards as the external blow percolated through the economy. Most Australian economists sheeted the blame for high structural unemployment to high real wages and, by direct linkage, tariff protection (Cain 1974:351; Hancock 1984:72–3). As the Brigden Committee had noted, tariffs had altered production towards labour-intensive ends. By placing a tax on primary production and supporting the workers' livelihoods at the expense of the rural sector, protection allowed Australia's population and economic base to diversify more than they would have under free trade (Brigden et al. 1929). The Brigden Committee warned, moreover, that overseas borrowing could not continue unimpeded 'unless some totally new resources such as a great mineral field, are discovered' (cited in Dow 1938:119). Australia's high real wages, a Tariff Board report noted, were supported not just by protection but by foreign borrowing that underpinned a high level of economic activity (Shann and Copland 1931a:40–52). The Tariff Committee all but admitted that Australian real wage levels were unsustainable and would surely slip in the near future (Cain 1973).

By 1927, two-thirds of Australia's capital borrowings had been undertaken for the purpose of economic development and took the form of public works (Mills 1928:112). The warnings of economists about the dispersal of public-sector borrowings into unproductive ventures were not heeded. In one year alone,

---

38 In post-prime ministerial life, as Assistant Treasurer, then High Commissioner for Australia in London, Bruce made amends for his earlier laxity in monitoring Australian borrowing. So adroitly did he attend to managing Australia's borrowing portfolio or 'loan-mongering' that, together with his command of economic matters, he was touted as successor or alternative leader to Lyons. His decision to withdraw from the Australian political scene as Assistant Treasurer to Lyons in 1933 to take up appointment as Australia's High Commissioner in London was seen by the *Sydney Morning Herald* (6 October 1933) as a great loss to the nation. The inference was that the Lyons cabinet was short of talent and expertise—a view Bruce and Casey shared with each other (see Hankinson to Secretary of State for Dominions, 8 February 1932, Public Records Office, London (hereafter PRO), T160/807/11935/5; Bruce–Casey correspondence, 1933–37, AA, 1421).

Australian governments floated £45 million worth of long-term debt on the London capital market. From January 1929, no long-term loans were issued to placate London's concerns about the escalation in Australian debt.[39] The laxity of the Bruce government found its origin in Walker's view that conservative governments could get away with what a Labor government could not (Cain 1983:10, 16).

Bruce had always expressed confidence that his capital-intensive rural development schemes, operating in tandem with British migrants and underwritten with British capital, would prove remunerative (Cumpston 1989:65; Richmond 1971:248). Bruce had hoped to use the British Economic Mission to alleviate growing concern in the City about Australia's rate of borrowing (Roe 1995:126). The mission, however—in a reprise on London opinion—criticised Australia's new protectionism. The concern about Australian cost levels drew the attention of one member of the mission, who noted: 'The nub of the problem had been identified as the great and growing costs of production, for which growing tariffs and correspondingly growing costs of living and of labour are primarily responsible, and which are further enhanced by all un-remunerative expenditures of borrowed money' (Malcolm 1929:19–20). The mission encouraged the Bruce government to square the circle by attempting to lower production costs while continuing to promote development (Cumpston 1989:86). Their advice encouraged Bruce to embark on industrial relations reform—an action that spelt the electoral demise of his government.

University economists were heartened by the mission because it assailed the intrusive nature of government intervention within the economy, particularly the 'vicious' link between tariffs and wage arbitration—a concern the Tariff Board had alluded to time and time again (Cain 1974:355). Economists made themselves unpopular by railing against the power of the oppressive state and the dangers of overexpansion. Indeed Shann's *oeuvre* had been dedicated solely to tracing the growth and development of, in his eyes, the sacrosanct wage-fixing system that arose in the first quarter of the twentieth century. His work had yet again publicised the effects of protectionism and brought out the key distinction between sheltered and unsheltered industries—a distinction that was to play a critical part in the policy response to the Depression (Hytten 1960:156).

Shann's major work, *An Economic History of Australia* (1930a)—offered up as a blueprint for economic reconstruction—concentrated on the author's lifelong perception of Australian economic enterprise being shackled by a raft of

---

39 The Bruce–Page administration left overdrafts in London of £3.3 million and loan commitments of £71 million maturing within one year of leaving office. There was also a deficiency of £49 million in the London funds (*SMH*, 24 January 1931).

regulations put in place by the 'apostles of restrictions'.[40] The book proclaimed Shann's 'credentials as the leading neo-liberal voice in economic discourse' (Snooks 1993:23). It was a detached view of Australian economic policy written in the splendid isolation of the west (Copland 1935a:599). In an earlier pamphlet, Shann drew parallels with the 1890s and made the poignant remark about overcapitalisation. Three years later, he was adamant that while 'public works are excellent things but only for so long as the balance is preserved between capital and earning power, between equipment and its use in furthering production... overset that balance and they become a burden as voracious as the grasshopper' (Shann 1930b:28). By 1930, Australia had overstepped the mark: 'This is no time for additional public works. One of our main troubles is an interest bill... on public works that do not earn interest' (Shann 1930b:54–5). Shann's words on the capital sunk into public works would haunt the 1930s. He also warned that if the price of Australian staples fell, the interest bill would not fall, *pari passu*. All this came to pass. Shann colourfully extolled the predicament facing the Scullin government:

> We have fixed costs and [living] standards. The markets we serve have fallen away and left on fixtures as high and dry as a steamer on the nor' west coast tied to a jetty when the tide is out, though with the difference that the tide may not return. And all that Labour [sic] can suggest is to build a little dock around the vessel and float it again on the contents of its reserve banks.[41]

Brigden's pamphlet *Escape to Prosperity* (1930) also raged against urban and rural overdevelopment but with an evangelical call for action and community cooperation.[42] Meanwhile, Wood was finishing off his magnum opus, *Borrowing and Business in Australia* (1930), in London under the supervision of Gregory. Casey, allowed to read the draft, feared that its 'depressing' tone would have a bad impact on London opinion (Hudson and North 1980:544). So gloomy was Wood's analysis that Casey got Wood to stress that it was an academic work rather then a forecast of the Commonwealth's future.

In its report, the British Economic Mission commented that Australia 'had been mortgaging the future too deeply and would do well to restrict her expenditure

---

40　By this Shann meant the endless and intrusive government regulation of commodity and labour markets—in particular, the connection between high protection and high wages, which penalised the export sector. Protection all round, Shann maintained, ultimately retarded the rate of economic growth and the rate at which working-class standards could be raised (Snooks 1993:27). In his polemic, Shann staged the argument in terms of a heroic individual struggle against the dark forces of restriction, which wanted to extend wage fixing, tariff protection and protection all round.

41　E. Shann to C. A. S. Hawker, 3 December 1929, Hawker Papers, NLA.

42　Shann so savagely reviewed Brigden's pamphlet—compiled from radio talks: 'it would not be to the credit of Australian economists'—that Copland shelved the idea of having the review placed in the Economic Record (E. Shann to D. B. Copland, 4 July 1930, and D. B. Copland to E. Shann, 3 July 1930, UMA FECC, Box 134).

of borrowed money for development'.[43] The mission praised deflation as 'the cause of wisdom' and urged that a 'cadre' of highly qualified men staff the economic agencies (Roe 1995:128). The general impression formed in London from the report was, as Casey relayed to Bruce, that 'they do not think we have been very clever with our nation planning in the past' (Hudson and North 1980:462).

Copland gave the best contemporaneous account of how Australia's economic difficulties had steadily mounted in the late 1920s. He identified four 'danger-spots' or 'weaknesses' in the economy—namely, the rising ratio of interest payments to export revenue; the increasing levels of tariff assistance; the growing disparity between Australian and foreign price levels; and, not least, state and Commonwealth deficit budgets (Shann and Copland 1931a:95). There was undue profligacy with public expenditure consuming 29 per cent of national income in 1928, which would rise to 45 per cent by 1931 unless otherwise checked (Raws 1931:38). All this, Copland reasoned, would have necessitated some adjustment for the economy notwithstanding the deterioration in the world economy (Shann and Copland 1931a:95). Copland rejected the argument that there had been gross economic mismanagement. A dependent economy, he said, was 'only partially master of its own house'; in that sense Australia had been embarrassed by the calamitous fall in export prices (Copland 1930a:638–40). He did admit, though, that the distorted pattern of development would have required some adjustment, certainly on the wages front, irrespective of adverse external developments (Clark 1981a:21; Cain 1973:20).

Australian economists were not totally against the idea of large-scale development. Melville defended the public works undertaken, underlining the capital-intensive nature of these works as the economy moved from a rural to an industrialised base.[44] Melville held out hope that once export prices recovered, together with more sensible policies pertaining to tariff and wage matters, Australia could resume where it had left off (Cain 1974:354–5; Melville 1929). On loan allocations, economists called for greater disclosure of where the funds were intended to go and the returns of the borrowings. The real priority for Australia was not 'less borrowing but wiser spending' (Mills 1928:116–17). Only Shann, Brigden, Eggleston and, before them, Frederic Benham, were pessimistic about Australia's long-term economic prospects given the amounts of foreign capital recruited into low-return ventures (Cain 1974:355).

---

43 Report of the British Economic Mission, C. P. P. 1929, p. 19.
44 Melville, TRC 182, NLA, p. 13.

Niemeyer and the Australian economists

It seems local economists were probably taken as much by surprise as Labor Party officials when informed that the Bank of England was dispatching Sir Otto Niemeyer to Australia to undertake an evaluation of the economy's finances.[45] It could be said that the local nucleus of economists was grateful for Niemeyer's visit since it added a much-needed degree of gravitas to the unfolding problems. Indeed Giblin, on behalf of his university colleagues, sent Niemeyer a note of welcome.[46] If the 1930s were to be the making of Australian economics in terms of policy influence, it was in no small part due to the public and political reaction against Niemeyer. The concluding part of the chapter shows how this was set in train.

A banker brought home perhaps the true legacy of the Niemeyer visit: 'It is the first occasion in half a century that economic talks may be brought home forcibly to the people of Australia and those who rule over them.'[47] He was inadvertently right, for the controversy surrounding the visit, together with the draconian advice that sprang from Niemeyer's lips, gave local economists an opportunity to exercise what would ultimately prove a more acceptable solution to Australia's woes—for Niemeyer, as Gibson anticipated, brought the house of English orthodox economics down on Australia's head.[48] It would materialise in Niemeyer attacking the 'ark of the covenant'—namely, Australia's living standards, which he considered unsustainable.[49] When the Speaker of Federal Parliament asked Niemeyer if his mission was proceeding satisfactorily, Niemeyer is said to have replied: 'That depends on whether you do as you are told' (cited in Macintyre 1986:258).

The high point of Niemeyer's fact-finding tour was his infamous address to the Melbourne conference of Commonwealth and state leaders, where he told his audience that the 'cold facts must be faced'. He told his audience that came with stern admonitions about how tariffs, in league with arbitration and excessive government borrowing, supported unsustainable living standards (Goodwin 1974). Real wages had to be quickly reduced; the therapy was couched in phrases such as restoring 'equilibrium' and 'equal sacrifice'. His diagnosis of Australia's predicament was blunt:

> In short, Australia is off budget equilibrium, off exchange equilibrium, and faced by considerable unfunded and maturing debts both internally

45   A fuller version of this section appears in Millmow (2004).
46   L. F. Giblin to Sir O. Niemeyer, n.d., Giblin Papers, NLA.
47   A. C. Davidson to Sir O. Niemeyer, n.d., BE, OV9/288.
48   One of the conditions of Niemeyer's visit was that Sir Robert Gibson was to have the first interview with the Bank of England man and be allowed constant access to him (Ricketson diary extract, 25 June 1930).
49   'Sir Otto Niemeyer in Australia', Nation and Athenaeum, 17 January 1931.

and externally, in addition to which she has on her hands a very large program of loan works for which no financial provision has been made. (Cited in Shann and Copland 1931a:21)

Niemeyer visited Australia because Scullin was tempted by the possibility that the Bank of England might accommodate Australia with a loan to cover liabilities to English banks, especially if the federal government followed Niemeyer's advice. Niemeyer's mission was to diagnose the nature of the Commonwealth's economic problems and put forward advice as to its resolution. It afforded London an opportunity to launch another critique of Australia's pattern of economic development (Roe 1995:148).

The British Treasury had been monitoring Australian assisted immigration and development programs through the 1920s and one of its officers, Skevington, visiting the year before Niemeyer, voiced critical remarks about the Australians' self-belief in the great potential of their country. He found 'their ignorance of economics…pathetic' (cited in Roe 1995:136).[50] As an old Treasury man, Niemeyer might have read Skevington's dispatches. For his own part, he would also be articulating only what had already been written on for the Bank of England's edification (Attard 1992:81).

Niemeyer's Melbourne address was composed after he had audited all governmental budgets with assistance from his economic adviser, Professor T. E. Gregory, of the London School of Economics, and an assistant from the Bank of England, Raymond Kershaw. They had also examined each government's portfolio of internal and external debts. Niemeyer made much of Kershaw's data showing the movement in money wages, per capita productivity and unemployment, even finding a spot in his diary (Love 1982). For Niemeyer, it was an open and shut case.

Niemeyer's advice at the Melbourne conference was listened to politely and seemingly consented to. As Tsokhas (1995:20–1) identified, however, the peculiarity of Australia's political and institutional arrangements, especially the federal structure of governance, deprived Niemeyer of having a 'single point' whereupon he could concentrate pressure on the need to reform. Moreover, the states resented having to make greater proportionate expenditure cuts than the Commonwealth (Tsokhas 1995:22–4). It could be said that the Scullin government, while agreeing that budgets had to be pruned, exercised a policy of 'passive resistance' to Niemeyer's advice, in the expectation that something

---

50 He was not alone in this view. Alfred Davidson, the newly appointed General Manager of the 'Wales', bemoaned in a letter to Shann the same problem among his staff. He elected to establish a bank circular that, freely distributed, would attempt to lift the community's level of economic literacy (A. C. Davidson to E. Shann, 14 May 1930, BNSW, GM 302, p. 590). Another bank circular, prepared by the economic department with the same mission, was circulated only to branch managers.

would turn up. It was open to more palatable medicine. Niemeyer found the Australian resistance to buckle under disconcerting, believing they were far too optimistic about their country's future prospects. What irritated Niemeyer most was the boundless optimism of his hosts that there must exist an easier way out of their predicament. In a long missive to Montagu Norman, Governor of the Bank of England, Niemeyer vented his frustration:

> They are occupied half the time saying that the present difficulties are not their fault but somebody else's—either Bruce's or the London Markets or the general perverseness of the world and the other half in trying to find ingenious ways by which somebody else should help them out.[51]

When Niemeyer read in local papers that the British government was still considering a proposal guaranteeing loans for further migration and land settlement, he cabled Harvey:

> Can you tell me whether there is any truth in this, as rumours have bad effect on these optimists? Australia is a poor country probably over-populated with a higher percentage unemployed than UK. Settlement hitherto has been very costly and unsuccessful; future development at present seems to me insane.[52]

Despite Niemeyer warning Scullin that London would not give him a warm reception, Scullin asked whether the bank would provide the money to enable the Commonwealth to pay off some £5 million worth of maturing Treasury Bonds (Tsokhas 1995:25). Harvey, who had visited Australia in 1927 to advise on establishing a central bank, declined because the Australian government had, so far, not moved to implement Niemeyer's advice in any way, shape or form. Earlier, the Bank of England, at Niemeyer's suggestion, was prepared to help finance the maturing of Treasury Bonds in late 1930, but only if the Scullin government implemented the August resolutions that had, in fact, met with the approval of five state premiers.[53] The Treasury mandarin Sir Richard Hopkins annotated a copy of the report of the interview between Scullin and Harvey with the comment: 'It is a bad business.'[54] Scullin also did not impress Beatrice

---

51   Sir O. Niemeyer to Sir M. Norman, 1 September 1930, BE, G1/291.

52   Sir O. Niemeyer to Sir E. Harvey, Cablegram, 14 August 1930, PRO, T161/396/11935/02.

53   Scullin's extraordinary requests might be understood by Theodore having received a letter from a press agent, the *Financial Times*' J. M. Myers, who informed him that the Bank of England might give Australia direct financial assistance as a result of the large gold shipment that had proved extremely useful to the bank in its dealings (J. M. Myers to E. G. Theodore, 6 August 1930, Theodore Papers, NLA). Casey had earlier complained to Bruce that Myers' paper was chiefly responsible for fomenting negative sentiment about Australia's finances.

54   Copy of interview with Scullin and Sir Ernest Harvey, PRO, T161/396/11935/02.

Webb when he told her that Australia would be better off without trade unions. Webb was puzzled about why Scullin remained leader except perhaps as a cover for the 'attractive and gifted Theodore' (Webb 1936:254–5).

Meanwhile, the visiting Niemeyer was unimpressed by the 'personnel all round—political, administrative and banking—is, with rare exceptions, lamentable, a circumstance which is accentuated by the marooning of the Commonwealth Government and administration on a sheep run 200 miles from anywhere'[55] (Tsokhas 1995:24). To E. T. Crutchley, the resident British government adviser on migration matters, Niemeyer confessed 'he had had a lot to do with bankrupt countries but have never seen one more utterly impotent to help itself'.[56] Even Gibson, the only man the Bank of England trusted, 'staggered' Niemeyer by prophesising—correctly as it turned out—that Britain would go off the gold standard within six months.[57] Apart from that indiscretion, Niemeyer told Lady Gibson that her husband was 'the most outstanding figure of all those I met'[58] and in another instance, 'Australia could never repay Sir Robert Gibson in thousands what he had saved the country in millions'.[59] Niemeyer was so impressed by Melville that he probably recommended him to Gibson as the Commonwealth Bank's first economic adviser.[60] Melville, who drew strength from Niemeyer's visit, tried to entice him to give the Joseph Fisher Lecture.[61] Niemeyer declined the honour, as he did many invitations, especially after his August speech, and maintained a studied reticence on economic policy matters—what E. R. Riddle, the Governor of the Commonwealth Bank, called a 'blasphemous silence'.[62]

There were, as will be shown in the next chapter, less austere homespun plans drawn up against Niemeyer's prescriptions, the most outstanding of which was the Melbourne school's. There was no record in Niemeyer's diary or papers of having met or corresponded with its chief architect, Copland. Giblin, in his recollections to Walker, reported, however, frequent clashes with Niemeyer especially over the issue of protection (cited in Cain 1987b:6). For his part, Niemeyer found Giblin 'pretty disappointing' (Love 1983:273). Gregory did, however, see Copland and Giblin a day before Niemeyer's keynote address to the Melbourne conference.[63] Gregory cryptically reported back that the conversation gravitated around two points: the exchange rate and real wage

---

55   Sir O. Niemeyer to Sir M. Norman, 1 September 1930, BE, G1/291.
56   E. T. Crutchley Diary, 14 August 1930, NLA.
57   'Recollections of Sir Robert Gibson', Sir Harold Clapp, Gibson Papers, Latrobe Library.
58   Sir O. Niemeyer to Lady Gibson, 1 January 1934, Gibson Papers, Latrobe Library, Box 3.
59   Manuscript by M. Gibson on her father, Sir Robert Gibson, Gibson Papers, Latrobe Library, p. 50.
60   E. Shann to W. Young, 17 February 1932, BNSW, A 53/409.
61   Professor Gregory (1933:109–11) gave the oration and he took the opportunity to attack, in a digression, the Melbourne school advocates of 'a little amount of local inflation' then extant, whose 'ultimate consequences would be fatal' to not just the banking structure but the economy overall.
62   E. R. Riddle to Sir O. Niemeyer, 17 November 1930, BE, OV9/286.
63   It would not have mattered what the views of these gentlemen were. Niemeyer had already made up his mind what he was going to say and, indeed, had already given an important speech to Commonwealth

cuts. Gregory posed the question to the two academics of what was Australia's optimal path out of its depression—namely, deflation or devaluation? He found Copland more careful in his qualifying analysis than Giblin, but also more likely to be 'inflationist'—by that, meaning a rise in the price level via devaluation. In the record of that interview there is no mention of Copland's expedient, articulated in his 1930 *Economic Journal* article, of a money wage cut that would deliver a real wage cut of 10 per cent. Giblin and Copland spoke, rather, about a 10 per cent devaluation to suppress imports and how, more importantly, it would give a boost to primary and secondary industries. This decision was to be coupled with compensating reductions in the tariff. Gregory insisted that primary producers would not escape rising costs due to the import bill increasing. The Melbourne economists confided that they saw unemployment ballooning to 25 per cent. Significantly, Copland mooted the idea of 'a general scaling down' of interest rates, but Gregory thought it was not 'a considered point of view of what was possible on his part'.[64]

Apart from this interview and his Fisher Lecture, Gregory kept well in the background during his visit. His one contribution to the media, as events unfolded, was to prove an interesting and prophetic one. He categorically refuted the Labor argument that a reduction in interest rates must precede a wage reduction:

> If we look at it strictly as an economic proposition, both rising rates of interest and the growth of unemployment are evidence of maladministration in Australian economic affairs, and, from a strictly economic point of view, you cannot assert that it is unjust that interest rates remain high while wages fall if the high rate of interest is unnecessary to attract capital and a lower rate is necessary to attract a demand for labour.[65]

Niemeyer wrote to the Chancellor of the Exchequer, Sir Philip Snowdon, informing him that Gregory was returning home having had a 'close-up' view of protection, over-expenditure and over-borrowing.[66]

As hopes of implementing the Melbourne agreement faded, an embittered Niemeyer wrote to his old colleagues at the Treasury: 'This is an odd country,

---

and state heads of government the night before along the lines of the Canberra statement of February 1930. Niemeyer had been well briefed on Australian financial affairs while at the Bank of England, and before that at HM Treasury (see Attard 1992:77; Roe 1995).

64   Notes on conversation with Professors Giblin and Copland at Melbourne, 19 July 1930, BE, OV9/242.
65   *Daily Guardian*, 29 August 1930, BE, OV9/288.
66   Sir O. Niemeyer to Sir P. Snowdon, 29 August 1930, BE, OV9/286.

full of odd people and odder theories, but I think it has had a salutary effect…on your friend Gregory who left last week uttering the most orthodox and almost antediluvian sentiments on monetary and other matters.'[67]

Meanwhile, Melville had, at Niemeyer's urging, gone on the attack against the stabilisation views of the 'Melbourne school'. Niemeyer encouraged him to keep up the fight against 'Copland and Co.' and their 'dangerous nonsense', part of which was about letting the exchange rate depreciate.[68] Niemeyer, along with the trading banks, saw little logic in Australia having to pay more to service its debt or imports. It was held that the primary producers, too, would extract little benefit because of the higher costs inflicted by the devaluation.[69]

In a concluding dig at the Melbourne school, Niemeyer remarked how 'curious a commentary it is on human psychology that the same people talk in one breath of the boundless potentialities of Australia and in the next of the necessity of writing down those potentialities by 20 per cent'.[70] A heartened Melville replied that the Melbourne school was technically reduced to monetising the deficits directly since the trading banks would not expedite it by purchasing government securities and, if that were to happen, there would be a flight from currency. He sought Niemeyer's opinion about Giblin's contention, reported in the press, that 'our best efforts at balancing the budget were hopeless at the present time'.[71] Niemeyer felt Giblin's pessimism about balancing the budget was symbolic of a 'quitter' mentality he had found in too many of his hosts. Niemeyer's reply to Melville, a few days before he set sail for England, rounded on Giblin and Copland's 'hopelessly academic' measures as meaning only one thing—inflation:

---

67   Sir O. Niemeyer to P. Hopkins, 1 September 1930, BE, G1/291. While made in jest, Gregory's prompting and pronouncements through the 1930s were certainly, from Australian economists' viewpoint, consistent with Niemeyer's description of him. Copland believed Gregory 'gave economists a bad name' with his emphasis on exchange rate stability (D. B. Copland to R. B. Lemmon, 15 June 1934, UMA FECC, Box 24). Copland added that Gregory 'had learnt nothing since 1925'.

68   Sir O. Niemeyer to L. G. Melville, 1 November 1930, BE, OV9/289.

69   Niemeyer ridiculed too the argument that there had been a bank-led deflation of credit—a view Labor parliamentarians Curtin and Anstey had been pushing. For relaxation on the voyage home, Niemeyer read and scathingly critiqued John Curtin's pamphlet *Australia's Economic Crisis and the £55,000 Interest Bill*. In a letter to W. J. Young, Niemeyer took issue with Curtin's argument that bondholders had gained at the expense of workers, and rather insisted protected workers had gained at the expense of unprotected labour, civil servants and pensioners (Sir O. Niemeyer to W. Young, 16 November 1930, BE, OV9/289). Giblin and apparently Dyason applauded Curtin's views on the desirability of price stability (Giblin Papers, RBA, 366/10/157). Curtin cited Keynes's article 'Commercial reconstruction in Europe' as lending intellectual support to finding a way out of servicing Australia's huge national debt. Curtin expectantly quoted Keynes: 'if the fixed charges of the National Debt bear too high a proportion to the national income, it may offer a problem insoluble by orthodox methods' (Curtin 1930:9).

70   Sir O. Niemeyer to L. G. Melville, 1 November 1930, BE, OV9/289.

71   L. G. Melville to Sir O. Niemeyer, 8 November 1930, BE, OV9/289.

> The fundamental fallacy, of course, is the common Australian assumption that it is the business of the banks in general and the Commonwealth Bank in particular to provide capital in the strict sense of the word. The provision of capital is, of course, no part of the functions of any bank.[72]

Niemeyer pointedly remarked that there had already been some 'considerable inflation' in the financing of deficits; he speculated also where Australia would draw on the resources to balance forthcoming budgets or finance public works. Niemeyer articulated similar forebodings when informed that the Scullin government had, against all odds, managed to raise its December conversion loan of £28 million.[73] Pointedly, Niemeyer—unlike the reaction in London and Australia—pinned the success of the conversion to the public appeals made by Gibson, not Joe Lyons, the Acting Federal Treasurer (see Lloyd 1984:53). It was Lyons' star, however, that shone brightest from the action. Lyons' success, as Hart (1967) shows, was basically assured given the phalanx of conservative and financial interests milling behind him after he had withstood Labor Party plans to defer the conversion.

Niemeyer knew that the provisions of the Melbourne conference were in technical limbo until the outcome of the NSW state elections was known. A victory for the conservative leader, T. R. Bavin, would mean that the process of fiscal consolidation could proceed in the most powerful state in the Commonwealth and that a loan sponsored by the Bank of England might be a prospect. Unfortunately, Bavin used the Niemeyer report as the basis of his campaign, giving the unfortunate impression that he was advocating the economy and retrenchment at the dictate of London.[74] Jack Lang, to Niemeyer's horror, mounted his entire electoral campaign against supporting the August resolutions—arguing instead for some form of repudiation. Victory for Lang would therefore be a severe blow to the Niemeyer plan and, as Norman told Hopkins, '[t]he game would be up'.[75]

Even on the day of departure, Niemeyer still strove to expunge the inveterate optimism of his hosts, remarking to journalists that 'there was not enough pessimism around' (Goodwin 1974:230–1). He remarked that Australians had 'hard times ahead of them but they don't know how to be pessimistic'.[76] While he reportedly left Australia 'to stew in her own juice', one positive outcome was that local sympathisers apprised him and Kershaw of Australia's dwindling finances and the unfolding political crisis. Indeed, communication links were formalised between Australian and British central banks. Niemeyer saw this

---

72   Sir O. Niemeyer to L. G. Melville, 13 November 1930, BE, OV9/289.
73   Sir O. Niemeyer to T. Bavin, 23 December 1930, BE, OV9/289.
74   'Sir Otto Niemeyer in Australia', *Nation and Athenaeum*, 17 January 1931.
75   Sir M. Norman to Sir P. Hopkins, 23 October 1930, BE, G1/291.
76   *Adelaide Advertiser*, 18 August 1931.

as an alleviating factor and cause for some optimism, as long as the perception was not sown that the Bank of England was manipulating Commonwealth Bank Board policy (Tsokhas 1995:28–9). Much later, A. C. Davidson of the Bank of New South Wales, among others, would suspect that the Commonwealth Bank's views on monetary policy were well under the sway of 'a certain influential section of London opinion'.[77] Gibson, and even Melville, would strenuously deny that there was dictation, saying that there was only conferral.

While many, including Montagu Norman, could foresee a looming crisis, some saw it as doing a power of good. Crutchley, for instance, reported that '[t]he Commonwealth Bank felt, as did other competitive authorities, that a "crash" so long as it is internal in immediate effect, was not only unavoidable but should be expected as the only way of forcing the Governments and the public to face facts and accept the hardships of reconstruction'.[78] Theodore, too, reinstated as Federal Treasurer in January 1931 after being cleared of an impropriety, was of the same inclination, wanting a crisis to force the Commonwealth Bank Board to bend to his will.

In hindsight, the Niemeyer mission was to provide Australian economists an excellent opportunity to present a fairer and idiosyncratic solution to Australia's economic problems in the 1930s—a point never made in the extensive literature on the Niemeyer mission. This was no mean achievement since the Labor Party usually shunned the advice of local economists as academic and impractical (Melville 1971:34; Castles 1997). Nothing Niemeyer had diagnosed about Australia's economic difficulties was new. It was Niemeyer's method of application of remedial policies, together with his air of superiority, that proved mindlessly insensitive to political realities and earned him lasting opprobrium. As the British senior trade representative in Australia noted, 'Niemeyer was not the success he might have been; he lost his head a bit, was tactless and did some very stupid things' (cited in Attard 1992:82). Rather predictably, Niemeyer had forsaken Keynes's advice that with Australia's export prices already depressed it was 'not a time to choose for pressing her too hard' (Keynes 1982b:381–2). Even Niemeyer's strongest supporter, Gibson, chided Niemeyer for his pessimism, arguing that he did not give the Australian people enough credit to pull through.[79] Of course, it could have been that Niemeyer was deliberately painting a gloomy picture to force the necessary measures to be taken—a point Copland felt was quite necessary in the circumstances. This did not sway Wood, however, who fumed years later that '[t]he resentment of the Niemeyer mission goes deeper than perhaps you have been led to expect. The personnel was unfortunate, the job was badly handled and the general effect was almost disastrous, despite the

---

77   A. C. Davidson to W. S. Robinson, 12 August 1938, BNSW, GM 302/574.
78   E. T. Crutchley to the Undersecretary of State, Dominions Office, 2 April 1931, PRO, T160/807/11935/1.
79   Newspaper obituary on Sir Robert Gibson, Gibson Papers, Latrobe Library.

necessity for telling the Scullin Government the true facts of the case.'[80] Some years later, Copland took delight at the sharp criticism of Niemeyer's style and therapy among Cambridge economists.[81]

As a mark of things to come, the Melbourne stockbroker Edward Dyason, who had also been in intermittent communication with Keynes over Australia's economic distress, told the Acting Treasurer, Joe Lyons, his concerns about Niemeyer's advice: 'I believe that the present policy is inimical to the national interest and dangerous to the social fabric.'[82] Giblin added his weight, telling Lyons that if deflationary policies were carried out, as intended, Australia would have a 'bad smash with the chance of revolution and chaos' (Clark 1977. The Scullin government had been elected on the promise that they would shelter the living standards of the working man from the economic blizzard. The degree of subtlety required to negotiate through the crisis could come only from economists with an unerring common touch. They had to be able to tell parables to explain abstruse economics in order to generate the consensus for the measures needed. Along with Copland, Giblin would later claim that the Australian economists' solution to their country's predicament was quite removed from the Niemeyer blueprint, which he believed was both harsh and ill founded (Giblin 1951:84). It was only in April 1931 that the Labor leadership, albeit reluctantly, turned for help to the advice of local economists.

Niemeyer, however, would prove a little vindicated when he told Montagu Norman: 'We have given them a concrete plan to pull on and sooner or later even those who now hold back will follow it.'[83] Norman could only agree, cabling 'we have shown [the] Premiers a reasonable way of avoiding bankruptcy'.[84] In a sense, they were right, and a placatory missive from Claude Reading, a member of the Commonwealth Bank Board, assured Niemeyer that the subsequent Premiers' Plan was 'in effect merely going back to everything you said when you were here and adopting the remedies which you concluded would be necessary' (cited in Tsokhas 1995:30). The Australian economists' plan was neither as deflationary nor as iniquitous as Niemeyer's. And even if their plan was a 'makeshift' one, it was to make their fame.[85]

Despite its humble beginnings, the Australian economics profession had come some distance in a very short time. The profession had established a good theoretical founding, taking the peculiarities of the Australian economy into

---

80 G. Wood to W. S. Robinson, 21 April 1932, UMC FECC, Box 14.
81 Occasional notes on his visit to Cambridge, 26 May 1933, in BNSW, GM 302/412.
82 E. C. Dyason to J. Lyons, n.d., Lyons Papers, NLA, Box 1, Folder 2.
83 Sir O. Niemeyer to Sir M. Norman, 8 November 1930, BE, G1/291.
84 Sir M. Norman to Sir O. Niemeyer, 6 November 1930, BE, G1/291.
85 Mauldon's review of D. B. Copland's *The Australian Economy*, in UMA FECC, Box 20.

account. It had, moreover, already established the practice of offering scientific input into community issues. This progress culminated in Australian economists offering a more palatable alternative to Niemeyer's prescriptions.

Part II.
Triumph and Tribulation

5. The Premiers' Plan and the economists

Introduction

Australian economists played a key role in developing the policy alternatives to deal with the nation's economic crisis. Contrary to Schedvin's view that economists played only a superficial role in the Depression, Copland (1934:29) saw it as a defining moment for the economics profession. The purpose of this chapter is to recount how economists responded to the economic crisis of 1930–31. While Neville Cain has undertaken an exacting study of the origins of the Premiers' Plan, this account, using new archival material, will attempt to retrace the subtlety and nuance of the path towards economic reconstruction. When reviewing Schedvin's work, the economic historian N. G. Butlin suggested that 'the Battle of the Plans' was not fought just in academic seminar rooms.[1] That is, it was not just a contest of economic ideas; it was an unfolding political drama. Consequently, there must be some discussion of the political backdrop, especially the two opposing economic plans put forward by the two protagonists: E. G. Theodore and Jack Lang.

This chapter reassesses Theodore's fiduciary issue plan, given its contextual and theoretical importance, and contrasts it with Lang's plan. Both plans fell from grace in quick order. The same could not be said of the economists' composite plan drawn up within the ambit of what the financial community would then allow.

The pugnacious figure of Copland was to prove instrumental in marshalling economists behind a plan that rescued the country from the economic mire.[2] It was a plan that embodied existing economic thought. Reflecting on the period, Copland argued that Australia followed two distinct phases of policy response to the Depression. The first phase was an 'experimental' stage in which the authorities, lacking cohesion and direction, tackled the crisis from a short-term view. The 'battle of the plans' phase, and thereafter, was when the federal government, albeit reluctantly, heeded the advice of economists. Strands of earlier memoranda of economic advice and thought were distilled into the shape

---

1   *The Bulletin*, 5 December 1970.
2   D. B. Copland to McDougall, 19 April 1932, UMA FECC, Box 11.

and elixir of the Premiers' Plan of June 1931. Moreover, as the second half of this chapter will show, the plan also had a touch of Niemeyer about it to allay the concerns of powerful financial and banking interests.

The political economy of the battle of the plans

The Theodore plan

Before the Scullin government succumbed to economic orthodoxy, Theodore had, with the critical support of the left, a last throw of the dice with his 'forward policy for Australia' or Fiduciary Issue Plan.[3] The Scullin government had apparently embarked on such a desperate endeavour because it had become, in Frank Anstey's (Cook 1979:389) words, 'a truculent, valiant, revolutionary' position against the prevailing financial orthodoxy being pushed on them by the banks. The party leadership now embraced theories once regarded as 'disastrous' and 'fantastic' or 'not practicable' by Theodore (cited in Cook 1979:385; Hart 1965:3). Emotive statements such as '[t]he banks denied credit to the government; it was therefore necessary to create it' and 'credit can be expanded at will' disconcerted economists and bankers (Shann and Copland 1931a). Shann told an English correspondent that Theodore was leading a 'debtor's revolt' with his policy of heavy inflation.[4]

The private banks echoed the Commonwealth Bank Board's opposition to Theodore's fiduciary issue scheme. The National Bank denounced the Treasurer's 'quack remedies and stimulants' (cited in Cannon 1996). Another bank and another banker, the enlightened A. C. Davidson, who had written a pamphlet on central reserve banking, wrote '[t]here is a large body in the Labor Caucus at Canberra which holds extraordinary theories in regard to money, credit and banking' (cited in Cannon 1996:33). The imperial view, held by HM Treasury and the Bank of England, was that monetary stimulation to induce a higher level of activity would merely raise domestic costs and price levels above those of other trading nations and thereby exacerbate Australia's trade account difficulties.

The vociferous reaction to Theodore's proto-Keynesian experiment, not least from economists, was to have a subliminal influence on economic policy in the 1930s. Just as economists could prove to be constructive, so equally could they prove destructive in their criticism of the plans and ideas of others. It mirrored in a way Theodore's rather problematic relationship with the economists,

---

3   *SMH*, 28 January 1931.
4   E. Shann to H. Finlayson, 5 May 1931, BNSW, A53, p. 409.

finding at times half-hearted support for his measures, at other times, vehement disapproval. There was also an element of admiration for the Treasurer and, as we shall see, there was to be a sequel to this story in 1939. Economists were not alone in appreciating Theodore's technical abilities. A political opponent, the NSW Opposition Leader, Bertram Stevens, who would come into his own element later, described Theodore as 'possessing the coolest, best, and most experienced financial brain in the southern hemisphere' (cited in Kennedy 1988:278).[5] Bruce reportedly considered Theodore to be Australia's greatest treasurer (Calwell 1972:62). The economists would later find—perhaps to their embarrassment—that some of Theodore's economic vision was ahead of their own (Kennedy 1988).

Initially, Theodore held court with Copland, Giblin and the stockbroker Edward Dyason, but the university men parted company over the fiduciary issue scheme.[6] Dyason remained committed to it.[7] Economically literate, Theodore was allegedly privy to the views of Robert Irvine, the defrocked professor of economics from Sydney University known for his under-consumptionist views (Clark 1974b; Fitzgerald 1994; McFarlane 1966). Irvine had already won notoriety having battled out an honourable draw—intellectually at least—with Copland in the 1930 National Wage Case, arguing, with some support from the business community, that wage cuts would merely suppress purchasing power (Cain 1987b; Clark 1981b). According to David Clark (1975:30), Irvine's evidence on monetary circuits bore a 'remarkable resemblance' to Theodore's proposals that came not long afterwards. Copland, who emphasised the capacity-to-pay argument before the court, won the case but the presiding judge was also swayed by Irvine's submission that reducing wages would, by reducing purchasing power, make matters worse before they got better (Hancock 1984:73; Cain 1987b:11–15). Theodore deplored the court's decision, believing political forces had put the judges up to it.[8] A heartened Shann felt that the court's decision showed that it was partisan free.

---

5 Theodore had already shown his intellectual qualities by bringing the Central Reserve Bank Bill before Parliament. The attempt to redesign Australia's financial architecture was to be abortive. Theodore wanted more effective control over the mobilisation of credit and to split the commercial activities of the Commonwealth Bank from its central banking duties. Theodore had already attacked the trading banks' powers to determine the extent to which credit could be expanded or contracted. In arguing his case for the legislation, Theodore cited A. C. Davidson's work on the subject and claimed 'there is a generally held opinion among economists, bankers and financiers generally, that our existing banking and financial system has proved defective' (CPD Hansard, 1 May 1930). Davidson did not return the compliment, fearing that the Commonwealth's board of directors would become politicised and approve Labor's wild credit schemes (Schedvin 1988:343). While certainly to Melville Theodore's proposal was never taken seriously, some of its attributes, such as concentrating the gold reserves of the private banks into national control, came to pass in the mobilisation agreement of August 1930. This enabled the Commonwealth to obtain information on the trading banks' foreign exchange and thus allow the possibility of exchange control (Cornish 1993b:11).

6 Melville, TRC 182, NLA, p. 43.

7 E. C. Dyason to L. F. Giblin, 27 February 1931, UMA FECC, Box 20.

8 SMH, 9 February 1931.

Having undergone an intellectual metamorphosis in 1930, Theodore saw the Depression as due to a breakdown in the credit creation process. Deflation, he held, was 'the policy of despair'.[9] Monetary stimulation would arrest the economic decline and reignite economic activity. Some parliamentary support for the plan came from the NSW state Labor member, Clarence Martin, who possessed an economics degree from the University of Sydney and was a devotee of Keynes.[10] What became known as the Fiduciary Issue Bill had unclear parentage. It was inspired partly, as Castles (1997) shows, by a memorandum prepared by the Commonwealth Statistician and Actuary, Wickens, for the Acting Prime Minister, Fenton.[11] His memorandum to engage in the process of price stabilisation using a statistical index attracted criticism—not just for his foray into policymaking, but for the very nature of it (Castles 1997).

Castles (1997:29) contends that such was the Scullin government's contempt for 'scientific economists' that Wickens was the only trusted expert to which they could turn.[12] Wickens, however, did not pull his punches: 'Australia had been living in a "fools' paradise" of bountiful harvests, high export prices and borrowed money all of which had now vanished. Australia had to choose between Repudiation, Inflation or Readjustment.'

The last option, in his view, meant the selection of an equitable price level index, an accommodating monetary policy and, with it, a flexible exchange rate. In other words, stabilisation of prices was more important than stabilisation of exchange; it was to become an issue that would dominate the thinking of economists in the 1930s. This attracted the bile and bite of Davidson, who likened Wickens' inflationary scheme to that of alcoholic addiction: 'Another little drink wouldn't do us any harm…but he is in shockingly bad company.' Davidson also ridiculed the very idea of price-level targeting and queried what means were in place to prevent overshooting: 'Who is to bell the cat?' he pondered.[13]

---

9 Ibid.

10 Melville, TRC 182, NLA, p. 43. C. E. Martin presented evidence before the 1930 Basic Wage Case offering alternatives to wage reduction (*SMH*, 13 December 1930). Martin served in the short-lived Lang Labor government (1930–32). In his maiden speech, Martin quoted 'probably the world's greatest economist', Keynes, and his belief that the reason for the slump was due to the high rate of interest inducing a fall in investment. In his speech, Martin put the case for a 'restrictive and carefully managed inflation', which, in turn, would necessitate a reformed central bank along Theodorean lines. Martin was baited for his 'Karl Marxian' theories (see Parliamentary Speeches of C. E. Martin, MLA for Young, 4 December 1930, p. 229, and 9 December 1930, Mitchell Library, Mss 4947, MLK 04389).

11 Arthur Calwell, leader of the Australian Labor Party (ALP) in the 1960s, relates in his memoirs the rather remarkable claim that Theodore attributed Gibson as being the one who suggested the idea of a fiduciary issue (Calwell 1972:68). Simply put, Gibson was quite keen to help the Scullin government but drew back from assisting, in any shape or form, the Lang government. Just possibly Caldwell might have confused Gibson the banker with Giblin the economist.

12 Wickens was a foundation member and president of the Victorian Branch of the Economic Society.

13 'A statistician's advice', A. C. Davidson Papers, BNSW, N2/97.

Theodore's plan was encased within three bills put before the House of Representatives in February 1931

- a rate-of-interest bill
- a Fiduciary Notes Bill
- a bill to amend the *Commonwealth Bank Act* with respect to the note issue.

The less well-known first bill provided for the appointment of a board to make recommendations to the Treasurer concerning bank interest rates. The second authorised the issue of £18 million of public works expenditure facilitated, in part, by the third bill by relaxing the note issue regulations of the Commonwealth Bank. Theodore's plan was a collage of the Melbourne school mixed with the works of Irvine and Wickens' memorandum.

The trading banks were suitably outraged at Theodore's bill.[14] Couching his words within a familiar analogy, Sir Ernest Wreford of the National Bank warned that 'Australia is financially sick and will not get well by drinking the financial champagne of further borrowing or note inflation' (Blainey and Hutton 1983:209). Despite the outrage in Parliament and elsewhere that greeted the initiative, Theodore stressed that he was not an inflationist even though the restoration of price levels to the average of their 1929 levels meant 'heavy inflation'. The economists took action. Shann and Melville lent their imprimatur to the pamphlet *The Menace of Inflation*, condemning outright the Treasurer's policy. Archibald Grenfell-Price, an Adelaide polymath, penned the pamphlet (Kerr 1983:91). The banks financed its mass circulation. Apart from the tacit approval of Wickens and Dyason, the only lasting support for Theodore's plan came from Irvine, who congratulated Theodore on his new financial policy: 'You have gripped the truth that every bank advance means an increase in deposits and every cancellation of advances means a decrease of deposits.'[15]

The highpoint of the Theodore plan was when he gave a virtuoso performance in Parliament in March 1931 defending it by citing the works of Keynes, Hobson and Cassel, all of whom were in favour of reflation rather than expenditure and wage cuts (Kennedy 1988:298).[16] Theodore knew his scheme was bound to provoke furious reaction so he cast it in the verbiage of a reduction of pooling or 'spreading the loss' mentality that economists were keen to convey. Theodore showed an easy familiarity with a crude version of an expenditure multiplier in his advocacy of easier bank credit.[17] He used Giblin's multiplier, showing some

---

14 *SMH*, 23 February 1931.

15 R. F. Irvine to E. G. Theodore, 22 January 1931, Theodore Papers, NLA.

16 *CPD Hansard*, 17 March 1931.

17 It was Theodore who theatrically held aloft a copy of Keynes's *Treatise on Money* in the House of Representatives and declared that, 'as a textbook [it] will stand for fifty years as a guide to the intellectuals of the nation on the subject'. Theodore was the first person in Australia to have a copy, expressly sent to him by the mining magnate W. S. Robinson (Melville, TRC 182, NLA, p. 42). Clark (1975:31), however, records

output elasticity to defend his proposal of injecting credit into the economy (Cain 1987a:21). In the same speech, Theodore noted that achieving budgetary balance was a function of economic recovery itself (Cain 1987a:21). While technically correct, this allowed him to downplay the need to make immediate economies—something that horrified the economists. Theodore proposed that the Australian pound free itself from 'the conservative fetish of parity' and find 'a level commensurate with the disparity in the Australian price levels as compared with those overseas'.[18] The Australian pound had, as we shall see, already been devalued in January 1931, but this scheme spelt further weakness. When Theodore claimed that the Fiduciary Notes Bill had the imprimatur of the Melbourne economists and even Brigden, the Opposition Leader, J. G. Latham, retorted that this was no longer, if ever it had been, the case. In Parliament Theodore responded, 'I did not say that the scheme was supported by them. I quoted their works to show that the same ideas were supported by them.' With Theodore, expediency came before conviction.

Markwell recounts another episode of an intellectual sleight of hand in which Theodore selectively quoted Keynes's remarks disavowing wage cuts as a cure for the Depression yet deleted his preceding remarks that the credit restriction policies carried out by the Bank of England had been relatively mild.[19] As Melville recalls, Theodore was, first and foremost, a politician theatrically engaging in attacking the banks for purportedly restricting credit when the opposite was more true.[20] Theodore's Fiduciary Issue Bill could easily be interpreted as an inspired act to secure the support of the left of the Australian Labor Party (ALP) to advance his leadership aspirations.[21] In that light, Theodore's plan would politically neutralise the Lang camp and sweep him to the party leadership.

The vociferous reaction to Theodore's proposals reflected the widespread fears that linked currency expansion with inflation. His plan consequently ran into fierce institutional and political opposition from the Commonwealth Bank and the Senate. Theodore's plan of financial rehabilitation also did not convince the

---

that the Lang political machine quoted liberally from the *Treatise*. The *Treatise*'s primary policy emphasis was to use cheap money to bring savings and investment into equilibrium at full employment. It was also true that Keynes had described public works as a 'weapon by which a country can partially rescue itself when its international disequilibrium is involving it in severe unemployment' (Keynes 1930:376). But what if in Australia's case the extravagant use of public spending had, to some extent, landed her in that international disequilibrium?

18   *SMH*, 9 February 1931.

19   The *Sydney Morning Herald* detected another misrepresentation of Keynes's views used by Theodore to justify his fiduciary issue plan in its editorial of 11 February 1931. The former NSW Treasurer B. S. B. Stevens noted during the Parkes by-election, in which Theodore unveiled his initiative, that he claimed economists had favoured inflation but he had not disclosed they were equally adamant for cutting government spending and costs (*SMH*, 16 January 1931).

20   Melville, TRC 182, 1971, NLA

21   'Mr Theodore evolving a sound plan', *SMH*, 31 January 1931.

state premiers. Theodore made the mistake of assuming others could understand the mechanism of controlled credit and a purported rise in economic activity (Cain 1987b:18–19).[22]

Copland and Giblin, who months earlier had entertained the notion of price stabilisation, distanced themselves from Theodore's ideas, stating that his strategy diverted attention away from Australia's fundamental problem of a distorted, unfavourable export price–domestic cost relationship.[23] After consulting Melville, Copland also attacked Theodore's plan on the basis that it would destroy confidence and lead to capital flight. The Treasurer's plan also did not make clear the need for substantial expenditure cuts or embody any wage or income cuts.[24] Theodore's sole reliance on using monetary policy to make the economic adjustments necessary to restore employment and national income attracted Copland's ire (Cain 1987a:25–6). No manipulation of the currency, it was held, could restore the real income of the country (Copland and Shann 1931a). Also undergoing a change of heart was Theodore's friend Giblin. He attacked the 'foolishness' of printing notes or releasing credits in one of his John Smith commentaries that appeared in the Melbourne *Herald*.[25] Giblin insisted that the only solution to an 'outside problem which is causing an inside problem' was an interim cut in real wages. He did, like Copland, see merit in having an issue of credits to maintain the price level. Giblin was adamant, however, that monetary stability was necessary for recovery and that it be exercised by an independent but informed authority.[26] Rejection of the Theodore plan would clear the field for a compromise Melbourne plan encompassing balanced budgets, some credit expansion, lower interest rates, money wage cuts and a depreciated exchange (Shann and Copland 1931b:27–8).[27]

The timing was never right for Theodore's scheme; its licentiate expansionism went against the collective guilt-ridden reaction to the profligate borrowing and spending of the 1920s. At a deeper level, schemes of fiduciary currency were held to bring about the collapse of moral standards and the breach of contracts (Nicholls 1992:215).[28] Giblin later told the Sydney University economist Ronald

---

22 Even Niemeyer had Kershaw or Gregory draw up a description of the credit creation process for his own elucidation to help explain what the Federal Treasurer was about (BE, G1/291, Appendix).

23 Theodore's principle to restore price levels to their 1929 level as the means to recovery belatedly met with the approval of financial high authority in London with The Tuesday Club consisting of, *inter alia*, Niemeyer, Keynes, Stakosch, Stamp, Sir Charles Addis and Sir Richard Hopkins (Kennedy 1988:300).

24 D. B. Copland to L. G. Melville, 13 February 1931, BNSW, A53-412; 'Memorandum on the Theodore Plan', 25 January 1931, Brigden Papers, NLA.

25 24 November 1930, Giblin Papers, NLA.

26 Giblin Papers, NLA.

27 'Mr Theodore plan: fundamental weaknesses', *SMH*, 23 February 1931; 'Creating credit; its limitations and dangers', *SMH*, 30 January 1931.

28 Ralph Hawtrey (1928:64) deemed inflationism 'a derogatory term thrown at a school of thought by their opponents, as the term Christian was by the people of Antioch at a new sect…The inflationist dog has been given a bad name'.

Walker that the Theodore plan was intrinsically 'reasonable and sensible' but strikingly at odds with the prevailing psychological mood (cited in Cain 1987a:26). The policy would, like its proponent, have a deleterious effect on business confidence. It threatened the pecuniary interests of the powerful banking and rentier communities.

The Lang plan

Given the colossal political impact Jack Lang wielded in 1930–31, it is remarkable how little economists—apart from Shann, who held the demagogue in utter contempt—spoke out against his debt-repudiation plan. Another view might be found in Brigden's critique of Theodore's plan 'to extend credits to Government as an alternative to equality of sacrifice...[which] would most certainly lead to default abroad with substantial inflation at home. Mr Lang's policy is much preferable, for it would be certain and would not inflate.'[29] Nonetheless it would be drawing a long bow to argue that repudiation, even a moratorium on paying interest on the London debt, had the approval of Australian economists. Perhaps Lang's overt populism and his scathing dismissal of intellectual input, no less economists, did not warrant a considered rebuttal. Giblin was right to believe Lang's plan was circulated to maliciously disperse support for Theodore's blueprint (Young 1963:40). As the previous chapter showed, Lang's rise to the NSW Premiership had already put at risk Commonwealth policy—namely, upholding Australia's good name in the London capital market.

More positively, Lang's crusade brought home to economists the imperative of constructing a recovery plan that would quell community tensions. This could be achieved, as Lang argued, by having all parties contribute to Australia's salvation. Cutting interest rates would help kindle recovery. On an intellectual plane, Lang's under-consumptionist argument, together with his scurrilous attacks on English finance, stemmed from the economic underworld (see Clark 1977). Lang's pamphlets did, however, cite Keynes's *Treatise*, especially on public works and the need for low interest rates (Clark 1981b:180). One of Lang's assistants, A. C. Paddison, who wrote the pamphlet *The Lang Plan*, an *ex post* rationalisation of the makeshift program, sent a copy to Keynes. He received a courteous reply agreeing in part on the need for an altered exchange rate; however, the matter of repudiating Australia's overseas debt or even the idea of a moratorium on paying it struck Keynes as a 'rather crazy' policy.[30] True to his propensity for changing his mind when the circumstances changed, Keynes later told Giblin that default on Australia's sovereign debt might, in some cases, be a defensible option.[31]

---

29 'Memorandum on monetary policy', late 1930, Brigden Papers, NLA.
30 J. M. Keynes to A. C. Paddison, 20 April 1932, KPKC, CO/6/3.
31 J. M. Keynes to L. F. Giblin, 31 August 1932, KPKC, CO/2/213-5.

In the same vein, Cook argued that the ALP at the time was not really interested in radical ideas and theory but, like any political party, was really interested only in retaining office. This might offer some explanation, too, for why Labor ultimately succumbed to the Premiers' Plan, with Theodore admitting that it would restore confidence (Cook 1970). Melville was of the opinion that the government had no other option (Cornish 1993b). What ultimately put to death the Theodore plan, therefore, was not the intermittent attacks of economists but political circumstances such as the 1931 Parkes federal by-election, which was basically fought over the 'controlled inflation' issue. The Niemeyer plan too, one recalls, had been put to the electoral test (Lloyd 1984:Ch. 5).[32] The Parkes by-election result also torpedoed Theodore's Central Bank Bill, since the Scullin government would hardly force a double dissolution over the issue. In a confidential letter to Niemeyer, Claude Reading intimated that Theodore had committed himself to so many positions within the previous 12 months that it was 'only a matter of time' before the Scullin government fell. His letter concluded: 'The drift in Government finances still continues, but as far as the Board is concerned we are determined not to make it easy for the drift to continue.'[33]

Two months later, in April 1931, Gibson effectively put an end to Scullin's vacillation and Theodore's vain hopes of a *deus ex cathedra* by refusing to extend the Commonwealth overdrafts any further. As a last gasp before the inevitable, Theodore had Robinson make further representations to the Bank of England about whether Australia could obtain reasonable credits in London during the next three years if she could balance her budgets with reasonable speed.[34] The request suffered the same fate as Scullin's two meetings with Harvey the year before. Another plan had to be found—one that included economic expertise.

The Premiers' Plan

> The plan, the whole plan and nothing but the plan.[35]

The Premiers' Plan assumes the mantle of folklore in Australian history. As a piece of economic architecture, the plan provided the platform for Australia's economic recovery even though it was, in fact, quite deflationary (Walker 1933a). It did, as one American observer noted, contain some departures from orthodoxy, which, even if they were accidental, as Walker argued, were economically and ethically justifiable (Garnett 1949:100; Cain 1983:4–5). The

---

32 Shann sardonically observed Theodore's economic oratory on the hustings: 'He seems to have swallowed Mr Keynes's *Treatise on Money* but to have found it indigestible' (*The Statist*, 26 February 1931, Shann Papers, NLA).

33 C. Reading to Sir O. Niemeyer, 4 February 1931, BE, OV13/1 453/2.

34 W. S. Robinson to Sir E. Harvey, 28 April 1931, BE, G1/286.

35 E. Shann to D. B. Copland, 5 June 1931.

plan was directed, first and foremost, at establishing budgetary equilibrium. It was to operate for three years and was agreed to by all the premiers and the Commonwealth government, giving it binding force. The measures, moreover, were seen as a comprehensive, indivisible whole, simultaneous in operation. They were also complementary to the Arbitration Court's 10 per cent wage cut of January 1931, together with the devaluation of the Australian pound— measures for which economists had proved remarkably instrumental. The plan was predicated on primary product export prices falling no further than they had in 1931.

In their meetings called to discuss the crisis, economists showed an acute sense of 'practical politics' in coming to some agreement about what precisely to do.[36] As Torliev Hytten, who held the economics chair at Hobart, recalled: 'While the orthodox economic theories were no doubt at the back of our minds…we were really pragmatists.'[37] Copland, who, as one historian later put it, 'sedulously propagated' the role of the economists in the episode, was afterwards more candid about the compelling force of circumstance (Hancock 1972:76). He admitted to an associate: 'Only the logic of events allows pure theory to get any triumph, and what we have been able to do here and elsewhere in this crisis must be attributed not to our own logic but to the inevitability of implementing the policy we propounded.'[38] To another associate, he confessed that '[t]he early severity of the crisis forced drastic methods upon us and we were perhaps fortunate in not being in a position to make a deliberate choice. No doubt we would have failed to have taken the drastic action that we did.'[39] In short, it was the dire circumstances confronting the Australian economy that brought economists to the fore.

These were not inconsiderable.

- A collapse in national income, in nominal terms, from about £645 million in 1928/29 to £430 million in 1931/32—a fall of some 34 per cent.

- Unemployment increased from 9.3 per cent in 1929 to 25.8 per cent by 1931.[40]

- A major diminution in state and federal government finances due to falling customs and railway freight revenue.

- A worsening balance of payments, with the London funds critically low.

---

36   L. F. Giblin to E. R. Walker, 19 April 1934, Giblin Papers, NLA.
37   Hytten autobiography, UT, p. 66.
38   D. B. Copland to R. B. Lemmon, 20 March 1935, UMA FECC, Box 34.
39   D. B. Copland to W. Downie-Stewart, 20 January 1933, UMA FECC, Box 19.
40   These figures were provided by trade union secretaries. Roland Wilson suggested that the trade union secretaries' estimates 'were not worth the paper they were printed on' (Wilson, TRC 1612, NLA). Giblin and Copland, however, set much store by them in 1930.

- A deterioration in confidence such that it was feared Australia could no longer raise loans in its own capital market to bridge government deficits and loan servicing costs.
- A debt deflation problem threatening, with exporters unable to meet their interest payments and their assets, pledged against debts, depreciating rapidly (Copland 1937a:398–9).

Australia was, as Giblin put it, 'in a difficult hole'; her problems were compounded by a trading profile marked by a limited export basket of goods yet acutely dependent on imports of capital and intermediate goods.[41] Australia had to generate very quickly a trade surplus sufficient just to meet the yearly £30 million sterling interest debt. Imports had exceeded exports for almost a decade, while interest payments were drawn from fresh borrowing. On top of this came the problem of maturing debt—external and internal—over the next decade. While Australian authorities had certainly been made aware of the gravity of the problem since Niemeyer's visit, they had dithered in devising a plan of action. The fact that Australia had 'not got its house in order' dealing with these innate problems beforehand made her difficulties all the more burdensome especially when creditor nations such as Britain also became engulfed by depression (Shann and Copland 1931a:x).

The key architect and publicist for the plan, Copland, transposed it into a conceptual framework. It consisted of

- a depreciation of the currency sufficient to restore real income in export industries to 90 per cent of its former level
- a reduction in real wages of 10 per cent
- a general reduction in real government salaries and wages expenditure of 10 per cent
- a super tax of 10 per cent on income from property
- an expansionist monetary policy based on the purchase of government securities by the Commonwealth Bank with a view to maintaining the general level of prices
- a proportionate reduction in rentier income derived from securities (Copland 1934:66–7).

These policy recommendations closely followed the recommendations of the economists and Under-Treasurer's committee—informally named the Copland Committee after its chairman. Three other economists—Melville, Shann and

---

41   Memorandum no. 20, 1932, UMA FECC, Box 32.

Giblin—sat on the subcommittee, together with five state treasurers and Commonwealth Treasury officials. Its brief was to compose a report entitled *The Possibilities of Reaching Equilibrium in Australia.*

What set the Premiers' Plan into formal motion was when a subcommittee of the Loan Council, instigated by the South Australian Labor Premier, Lionel Hill, was charged with investigating the steps needed to balance government budgets by the end of 1934 (Copland 1931:538–90). This action broke the Theodore-imposed deadlock on the Loan Council's ability to act. Gibson had already warned the federal government that the bank's advances of Treasury bills were limited to £25 million. That decision to wrestle control of the public purse away from an overspending government brought forth a riposte from Theodore that would resonate through the decade:

> The attitude of the Board…can only be regarded by the Commonwealth Government as an attempt on the part of the bank to arrogate to itself a supremacy over the Government in the determination of the financial policy of the Commonwealth, a supremacy…never contemplated by the framers of the Australian Constitution. (Shann and Copland 1931b:48)

Compounding difficulties was Lang's precipitate action of defaulting on an overseas interest payment. The federal government hurriedly paid instead, but Australia's credit rating was tarnished (Walker 1933a:142). It was time 'to call in' the economists.[42] It was at that juncture that economists 'rendered their country important service…their advice was taken at a critical moment in the crisis' (Copland 1937a:400). Walker's (1933a:143) contemporaneous account visualised the economists emerging with 'a compromise' to break the deadlock between the federal government, the Commonwealth Bank and the Lang NSW government.

Apart from the influence of Melville, the Premiers' Plan had further South Australian connections with the Adelaide businessman Sir Wallace Bruce, Archibald Grenfell-Price and an accountant, Hardinge Brown, formulating a plan in May 1931 known as the Discount Scheme (Kerr 1983:97). The scheme revolved around the idea of a national sacrifice that included all income recipients. Hardinge Brown wanted all financial institutions and bondholders to take a unilateral cut in their interest income. When Hardinge Brown and Grenfell-Price first showed their plan to Melville, he damned them as 'repudiationists who out-rivalled Lang'.[43] Melville, however, quickly reversed his tune, telling Grenfell-Price that the economists on the Copland Committee placed the discount scheme at the forefront of their recommendations.[44] While

---

42   H. C. Coombs to E. Shann, 4 June 1931, Shann Papers, NLA.
43   A. Grenfell-Price, 'The emergency committee of South Australia and the origin of the Premiers' Plan', p. 24.
44   Ibid., pp. 24–5.

the banks opposed the very idea, Grenfell-Price claimed that his little coterie, backed by the popular might of the mass-based Citizens' League, provided the progenitor for the Premiers' Plan. As he put it: 'The important part for the Adelaide side was that the discount scheme was adopted by the experts in spite of Melville's earlier opposition, and that it did lead to interest rate reductions and a scheme of general self sacrifice.'[45] Grenfell-Price was quite unaware of Copland's earlier work showing how 'heavy deflation' would, using Keynes's *Treatise* schema of savings and investment imbalances, aggravate social tensions within the community (Cain 1980:14).

Copland saw the plan achieve three significant things. First, it took the process of financial rehabilitation out of the political arena. Second, it laid to rest the Theodore policy of inflation. And third, in contrast, the plan solidly committed Australia along the road to deflation 'to an adjustment of her internal prices and costs in conformity with the fall in overseas prices' (Copland 1931). His Sydney counterpart, Mills (1933:221), in a review of the plan, said that it addressed the two key problems of restoring the balance between costs and prices in all industries, not just exports, and arresting the drift in public finances. Importantly, it had to draw on the critical support of the trading banks to be a success. They were to live up to their end of the bargain and promise interest rate cuts. The whole package, nonetheless, made for deflationary economics.

The economists however, as Copland later intimated to Irving Fisher, were about a secret agenda: 'Our economists and monetary advisers knew pretty well what they wanted, but I am quite sure that neither the Treasury authorities nor the Commonwealth Bank Board quite appreciate the nature and importance of the experiment they were conducting.'[46]

Copland (1932a:113) added that banking and financial authorities, too, did not recognise the 'significance' of the policy they were administering under the plan. The 'experiment' was to use Treasury bill finance to cover existing deficits and sustain spending and the price level thereby preventing the burden of indebtedness from increasing. In correspondence to another academic, Copland confirmed that

> Australia did act upon expert advice and it was to some extent because of this she got so reasonable a scheme. Neither the businessmen nor the Labor people completely agreed with the economists…I think, however, it may be said that the policy that was ultimately adopted substantially agreed with the original schemes discussed and put forward by economists.[47]

---

45   Ibid.
46   D. B. Copland to I. Fisher, 23 November 1934, UMA FECC, Box 23.
47   D. B. Copland to S. F. Ferguson, 5 August 1935, UMA FECC, Box 30.

Melville admitted that there was a 'Machiavellian' touch behind the economists' rhetoric: 'We thought that the proper way to get results was to talk about deflation and inflate like hell.'[48] Hytten attributed the plan to economists with 'a solid theoretical background but this was an exercise in applied economics, and the factual situation played the decisive part'.[49] Boris Schedvin has argued that the Premiers' Plan not only avoided a complete economic breakdown, it was dedicated to restoring Australia's external equilibrium—a view Melville (1971) endorsed. In a pointed dig at Copland's prolific rhetoric about the plan's merits, Melville reflected years later that:

> Maybe some of us got a little hysterical about how good it was but it aimed to be only an attempt to get the budgets of the States and the Commonwealth under control and flowing from this we could see an avoidance of default and we would see a more manageable external debt problem, which was no solution to the depression problem, but these were important issues that had to be tackled.[50]

Even Shann, who worked with Copland on the plan and thereafter, was, in private, rather contemptuous of what he considered Copland's 'demagogic egotism'.[51]

Copland always took an extremely positive view of what the package really achieved and the role of economists in carrying it through. No other country had done as much as Australia in its economic readjustment (Copland 1931:549). 'Australia,' he claimed 'came out of the depression earlier than most other countries because of the approach that was made under the Premiers' Plan.'[52] Economists, Copland (1951:9) proclaimed later, 'went over the trenches in the grand manner, to occupy positions that had hitherto been beyond their reach'. Inevitably, there was overstatement in Copland's claims about what the plan had done for Australia and for the economics profession. The plan, it was true, exhibited some element of forceful cooperation between the economic classes, which was Copland's academic *oeuvre*, but, more importantly for our interests, it brought the two contending camps of economic advice—the deflationists and the stabilisationists—under the one roof. In that regard, there was, early on, as Davidson recalled, some antipathy between Copland and Melville with Shann having the task 'poor chap...of trying to bring them together'.[53] There was also no representation from the Sydney coterie of economists with Mills overseas on sabbatical. Apart from uniting the economists, the Premiers' Plan met with

---

48 Melville, TRC 182, NLA, p. 34.
49 Hytten autobiography, UT, p. 67.
50 Melville, TRC 182, NLA, pp. 48–9.
51 W. Somerville, 'A blacksmith looks at a university or the first thirty years of the University of Western Australia', Mitchell Library.
52 Copland, TRC 574, NLA, p. 10.
53 A. C. Davidson to T. Hytten, 27 May 1935, BNSW, A 53/446.

the critical approval of the banks. Five years later, Copland had barely changed his tune. He told an Economic Society gathering in August 1936 that the plan had been 'misunderstood'. He went on: 'Both sides of the controversy had laid emphasis on the orthodox elements of the Plan, although its unorthodox features were the really distinguishing features. The orthodox portions of the plan were only "smokescreens" for the things that were really done under the Plan.'[54]

The Adelaide businessman and political savant W. J. Young conveyed the good news to Niemeyer: 'Copland has discarded any weakness he may formerly have shown and he and Melville are working loyally together.'[55] Young meant by that Copland's earlier advocacy of price stabilisation. Sympathetic to the new breed of academic economist-cum-adviser, Eggleston hailed the plan as 'a magnificent conception' (Osmond 1985:155). As well as the overriding goal of fiscal consolidation, the plan outlined how the burden of economic adjustment would fall equitably. This doctrine of 'equality of sacrifice', which underlay the package, came at the insistence of politicians, but it was Copland and Giblin who had first mooted the idea of all playing their part to restore Australia to an 'equable position'.[56] It struck a pious chord since the overindulgent spending in the 1920s should be followed by collective penance (Nicholls 1992:216).

At the Commonwealth–state conference held in June 1931 to discuss the plan, Copland and Giblin explained the technical provisions especially concerning the loan conversion operation.[57] One premier bemoaned: 'The economists are like our wives; a perpetual plague while they are with us, but we can't do without them' (cited in Hytten 1960:154). When Scullin asked the premiers whether they would consent to a reduction in government expenditure, Lang (1970:102) responded: 'I do not accept it at all; I do not think that the facts are accurate. I do not think that the economists know much about it…We hear a lot of economists telling us what we ought to do. It is like their confounded impudence.'

Lang was also not impressed by the overall package; he insisted that Copland was a 'torchbearer for the Niemeyer plan' (Lang 1962:344). Lang (1970:99) held that neither economists nor Treasury officials should pontificate over policy; that was a duty alone of elected representatives.

---

54 'A professor and his plan', *The Westralian Worker*, 21 August 1936.
55 W. Young to Sir O. Niemeyer, 23 March 1931, BE, OV9/289.
56 'The economic outlook for Australia', *The Age*, 1 May 1929.
57 For an impartial eyewitness account of the proceedings, see E. T. Crutchley, His Majesty's Government representative in Australia, PRO, T160/807/11935/2, and his diary held on microfilm in the National Library of Australia.

The path to the Premiers' Plan

Cain (1987a, 1987b) has covered in exacting detail how the four economists who composed the Premiers' Plan arrived at their great compromise. As is commonly acknowledged, the Premiers' Plan was, despite Copland and Giblin's later protestations, probably closer to the Niemeyer prescription than the Melbourne school of stabilisation. To be fair, however, the two conservative economists, Melville and Shann, yielded ground on the need for some 'inflationary' financing of deficits and scaling down of interest rates just as Giblin and Copland relinquished the idea of price stabilisation. How economists responded to the onset of Australia's economic difficulties demonstrates not only their public spiritedness but their collegiality and mental versatility. The remaining part of this chapter will retell the story using new archival material, but will also emphasise the traverse in economic thought economists underwent as they deliberated over an integrated plan that entailed not just public finance but relative cost adjustment.

The May manifesto and the assault on Australian wages

As economists appreciated the full magnitude of the two external blows delivered to the Australian economy, so too did they tailor their advice to prevailing conditions. At first, the scale of the problem was dismissed lightly; as late as October 1929, for instance, Copland predicted that the recession then affecting Australia might be 'temporary' (cited in Lowenstein 1978:433). As 1930 unfolded, however, a 'violent change' shuddered through the Australian economic landscape (Bland and Mills 1931).

At the end of a social sciences conference in May 1930, the economists, at Melville's behest, moved to issue a statement or manifesto quantifying the loss in national income (Crawford 1960:194–5). Melville recalled Copland leading the cause (Cornish 1993b:5). The manifesto was important because the signatories upheld—as Keynes did in *The Tract*—that internal price stability should take priority over maintaining the exchange rate. The economists bristled, however, at Copland's suggestion to devalue the currency. This informed and considered perspective by economists made little impact simply because of the speed and gravity of unfolding events—not least the arrival of Niemeyer. It was also due to the fact that many Labor politicians, including Theodore, were wary of economists, fanned no doubt by their opposition to further protection, rigid real wages and monetary reform (Harper 1986:45; Hart 1965:4; MacLaurin 1936:256).

Using the analytical framework provided by Giblin's multiplier, the economists argued that the loss in real income to the export sector be distributed across the community. This became a key theme in all their memoranda; indeed it was made the first condition of recovery. To that end, the economists, especially Giblin, Brigden and Copland, renewed their attack on the wage fixation system, especially the tradition of indexation that locked Australia into rigid real wages and high unemployment (Hancock 1984:70–2). In arguing unanimously for real wage reductions consistent with the loss in the terms of trade, the economists were keen to qualify that they were not advocating wage reductions per se as the cure for business depression. It was, however, a point lost on labour minds with the economists perceived to be at the call of bankers (Spearritt 1981). Mills (1929), however, had already publicly exposed this nostrum, in terms of the consequent diminution of purchasing power, at a lecture given at an industrial relations conference. Brigden, too, held that cutting wages should be the last resort as it entailed reducing purchasing power.[58]

An external crisis—a fundamental disequilibrium between domestic costs and international prices—changed all this. The export industries had suffered a fall in their prices and workers there took wage cuts. Consequently, wages in the unsheltered industries were now lower than in sheltered ones. A general reduction in the wage level was therefore appropriate on equity grounds besides giving the export industries some relief (Copland 1931:535). It would also make a greater show at import replacement. This was the nub of the argument that Copland would put before the Arbitration Court (Copland 1946:164). Copland's analytical framework was further strengthened by mastering Keynes's new engine of analysis contained in the *Treatise*. With the savings–investment dichotomy, the goal of enlightened monetary authorities was to use the interest rate to bring savings and investment into equality. Disharmony between the two would cause price movements, which would, in turn, engender output changes.

In his evidence before the 1930 National Wage Case, Irvine, appearing on behalf of the trade unions, accused the economists of committing a fallacy of composition. His argument, however, was set within the wrong context (Shann and Copland 1931a:88; Clark 1974b:52). In his five days of evidence during October 1930, Copland, appearing as an expert witness and with his recently published book, *Credit and Currency Controls*, close at hand, took issue with those who believed that cutting wages made for all-out deflation. Copland rejected the diminution in purchasing power argument on the grounds that it had already occurred with the decline in export prices: 'The present depression was due not only to the lack of spending but to the fact that people did not have the money to spend.'[59] Copland, though, was not prepared to have this adjustment

---

58 'Notes on the economic position of Australia 1929', Brigden Papers, NLA.
59 *SMH*, 21 December 1930.

borne through wage cuts alone. Arguing from a clear analytical framework that Keynes would approve of, Copland said that with devaluation, export prices could rise relative to internal prices, giving the primary sector further relief. He was also in favour of some issue of credits to anchor the domestic price level (Dow 1938:92). In short, Copland upheld balanced budgets, devaluation and lower wages as the correct path to take (Groenewegen and McFarlane 1990:137).

Copland turned Irvine's commonplace argument on its head; any reduction in costs, including wages, that brought about a reduction in the prices of internal goods would lead to an increased output rather than a reduced one. He was emphatic that cutting wages would not reduce spending power in the sense that money saved on the wages bill would be spent by the employer.[60] The transfer of purchasing power would give employers an incentive to produce. Giblin and the other economists shared in this Say's Law perspective of wage cuts. While it seemed counter-intuitive to Labor minds, Copland (1946:166–7) was adamant that there would be no reduction in purchasing power since, to repeat, the reduction in output had already been incurred.

While the court was swayed somewhat by Irvine's testimony and purchasing power arguments, it nonetheless went along with Copland's framework of analysis.[61] Copland informed the English political theorist Harold Laski that the court had sanctioned the wage cut as a 'last resort'.[62] He was well aware how difficult it was to force wage cuts. The wage cut, the court added, 'is not the magic wand which will restore stability. But as part of a reasoned scheme it is unavoidable' (cited in Cain 1987b:15). The court was also insistent that other non-wage income recipients engage in 'sharing the burden' (Dow 1938:92). Looking back over events Copland told Maclaurin that the court's decision to cut 26 federal awards by 10 per cent marked 'the first sign of an adjustment in a community hitherto unwilling or incapable to effect change to straightened economic circumstance'. The first leg of economic adjustment was in place. Copland was effusive in his praise of the court in not just leading the way but of being vigilant and 'much more alive' to general economic conditions than any other official body in the country.[63] The arbitration system, moreover, permitted a more elastic national wage policy than one dictated, say, by decentralised bargaining (Copland 1934).

---

60   *SMH*, 2 December 1930, and 3 December 1930.
61   Apart from trade unions, some employer groups also came out against the wage cuts. A newsletter put out by the Australian Manufacturers' Association in July 1931 entitled *The Folly of Wage Reductions* pointed out that Montagu Norman at the Bank of England opposed the same expedient for Britain because of the effect on internal trade (see Giblin material, UMA FECC, Box 225).
62   D. B. Copland to H. Laski, 12 May 1936, UMA FECC, Box 44.
63   D. B. Copland to R. MacLaurin, 1 October 1937, UMA FECC, Box 55.

The Melbourne manifesto — October 1930

Before the national wage case opened there had been reluctance by the federal government to implement the Niemeyer plan. With Scullin in London and Theodore having stood down the Acting Treasurer, Joe Lyons commissioned Copland, Giblin and Dyason to frame an alternative plan. Copland identified this as the first instance in which economists were called to 'give official advice' against the economic crisis. It came about amid great political drama coming a month after the Niemeyer address in which he had put 'the hard word' on his hosts.[64]

Giblin told Lyons that he was 'our last hope of a peaceful solution—but it is a tremendous perhaps an impossible job' (cited in Hart 1967:67). Giblin's hopes were well placed; Lyons was to prove the man of the hour. In his various guises, Lyons was quite deferential to the views of economists. He had already enjoyed a warm and steady relationship with Giblin and Copland during his tenure as Premier of Tasmania (Hart 1967:39). Copland reminded Lyons how he had saved his native state from insolvency (Denholm 1977:46; Lloyd 1984:47–8).[65] Giblin and Dyason enjoyed early success by persuading Lyons that blindly pursuing the Niemeyer line of parity with sterling would be a 'fatal mistake' and would make the forthcoming loan conversion nearly impossible.[66] Giblin had deprecated earlier attempts at formulating a plan—he told Lyons:

> From the economist side, I don't think we have anything in the way of a plan to offer. But if in any respect they could be useful you know they would be very willing to do anything in their power. For myself, as for the others I don't think I see light on the whole problem.[67]

Copland did not share in his colleague's despondency. He had been assiduously chiselling away on his compromise plan.

Three months earlier, in July 1930, Copland had given a controversial lecture, spread over two meetings, before the Victorian Branch of the Economic Society in which he expounded his 'middle monetary policy'. Copland's model of economic adjustment was inspired by Keynes's *Treatise* dealing with an open economy's adjustment to a disequilibrium situation. It took shape in a chapter from Copland's own work, *Credit and Currency Policy*. The scheme entailed money wage cuts coupled with devaluation and some Treasury bill finance to tide over budget deficits but also to slightly raise the price level. This array of measures would depress real wages (Cain 1987b:2). Apart from the heresy of

---

64   E. T. Crutchley diary, 18 July 1930, NLA.
65   Enid Lyons, TRC 121/30, NLA, p. 49.
66   Giblin to Lyons, n.d., Giblin Papers, NLA.
67   Giblin to Lyons, 9 September 1930, Lyons Papers, NLA.

devaluation there was outrage at its price stabilisation or inflationary aspect. Copland's ambition was open to misinterpretation. He eschewed the argument that printing money would assist employment and could not have been clearer in dismissing the inflation expedient: 'The remedy is much more dangerous than the disease, and no nation should enter upon a course of inflation without complete confidence in the powers and discretion of its banking authorities to check the expansion at the appropriate time' (Copland 1930b:142).

As an indication of their duty to explain the economic predicament Australia was in, economists had, for some years, contributed articles to newspapers.[68] The more famous of these was Giblin's eponymous series of commentaries entitled *Letters to John Smith* (in 1930), which appeared in the *Melbourne Herald*. It was, in essence, the sequel to his well-received inaugural lecture on 'Australia, 1930', which a newspaper lauded as a 'consummately able analysis of Australia's economic position'.[69] The lecture was billed as a tract for bad times and its author dubbed 'Gloomy Giblin'.[70] Apart from the refrain of sharing the burden, the *Letters* were part of a campaign of marrying moderate Labor voters to the idea that the 'experts' were in favour of the largely deflationary policy put forward by Lyons. The commentaries also gave notice that another 'old Labor man' such as Giblin had forsaken the extreme policies put forward by the Labor left.

The Melbourne school of economists circulated their stabilisation plan in September, displaying a middle way between inflation and deflation (Copland 1937a:408–9; Robinson 1986:8–11).[71] Billed as 'A Plan for Economic Readjustment', it was outlined in a lecture before the Victorian Branch of the Economic Society by Copland, Giblin and Wood in October 1930. The Melbourne school feared that with nothing to weigh against the externally imposed deflationary shocks a deflation of the price level would lengthen the process of readjustment and delay recovery. The increase in the level of the real debt would impair enterprise. The Melbourne economists felt a marked devaluation, instead of incremental, market-led moves, was the best means of assisting the export sector (Schedvin 1988:345). This would check the fall in export prices and mitigate the effects of deflation. Using what Copland called the 'principle of equality of sacrifice', the Melbourne economists also wanted

---

68 Sometimes they wrote under pen-names. Copland wrote a series of articles for *The Age* in 1927–28 under the cover of 'Lux'.

69 *The West Australian*, 19 June 1930.

70 'Notes from hither and thither', *The Margin*, vol. 6, no. 2 (June 1930), p. 12.

71 Dyason, while not strictly an academic economist as such, but a stockbroker, was 'a valuable link between academic economists and the business world' (Tucker 1981:391). He was, like Davidson, however, highly involved with the Economic Society of Australia and New Zealand. More importantly, Dyason sought out Keynes's opinion on the feasibility and validity of un-pegging the exchange rate. Keynes replied that he was 'heart and soul' with the line the Melbourne school was pursuing. Interestingly, Keynes added that forcing down wage rates as a means of escape from Australia's problem was likely to be inexpedient (J. M. Keynes to E. C. Dyason, 16 October 1930, KPKC, L/30/57; E. C. Dyason to J. M. Keynes, 3 September 1930, KPKC, L/30/54).

reductions in wages and interest rates.[72] The internal price level would hover near its pre-depression, 1929 price level by monetising budget deficits with Treasury bills. This aspect attracted ferocious criticism from many quarters, including other economists.

Melville was particularly aghast at the Melbourne price stabilisation proposals (Cain 1980:22). Shann, while less opposed, identified the practical difficulties of implementing it with an obstructionist Commonwealth Bank. Shann reassured Davidson that 'Copland and Dyason are certainly not trying to burke the fact of a reduced real income nor the necessity of reduced costs'.[73] Undeterred, Shann wrote a confidential critique of the Melbourne school's plan, pointing out that a credit policy was already in full blast: 'The trio of equilibrists, however graceful and ingenuous their performance avoid finally coming to Earth.' Shann feared that their school of thought was really a 'stalking horse' for Labor interests pushing for a centralised and politically controlled banking system.[74] While critical of Gibson for not enforcing the August resolutions, Shann encouraged him on in 'the good fight against heavy odds in that den of iniquity'—a direct reference to the Melbourne school.[75]

In a newspaper article, Melville, too, criticised the rhetoric and ambition of the Melbourne school: 'To pretend that price levels can be stabilised…is affectation.' He also emphasised its odious political aspects and threw doubt on the institutional competence to carry it out.[76] Melville (1930) believed, in contrast, that the rigours of the deflationist path had been exaggerated. Even the self-made economist Davidson shuddered at the prospect of devaluation coupled with credit expansion.[77]

In a letter to Davidson, Copland vehemently rejected the 'stupid comment' and misrepresentation made of his proposals by Melville.[78] He dismissed his critique as not really an analysis of the economic analysis of the proposals but rather a 'somewhat hysterical outburst' based on the fear that the situation could get out of hand. Copland was emphatic that inflation formed no part of his plan, but it had already been tainted. It left him exasperated that people were 'all too

---

72   D. B. Copland to R. C. Mills, 25 November 1935, UMA FECC, Box 138.
73   E. Shann to A. C. Davidson, 19 September 1930, BNSW, A53, 409.
74   'Memorandum on the paper by Professors Copland, Giblin and Wood on the restoration of economic equilibrium', UMA FECC, Box 30.
75   E. Shann to A. C. Davidson, 16 September 1930, BNSW, A53/409.
76   *Adelaide Advertiser*, 31 October 1930. Melville's stand against the Melbourne school helped no doubt in his appointment to the Commonwealth Bank. Ricketson recalls that the Commonwealth Bank's actuary, B. Latham, did not contradict him when he stated that it was Melville's action of 'trouncing' Copland, Gibson and Dyason over their plan to extricate Australia from its difficulties that had impressed the bank's senior officials (Ricketson diary, 20 March 1931).
77   A. C. Davidson to D. B. Copland, 28 September 1930, and D. B. Copland to A. C. Davidson, 4 November 1930, BNSW, A53/412.
78   D. B. Copland to A. C. Davidson, 10 November 1930, BNSW, A53/412.

susceptible to read inflation into my proposals'.[79] The spirited correspondence between Copland and Davidson secured a bridge between one of Australia's most gifted economists and the nation's leading banker. It was to pay dividends soon after when Davidson locked forces with Melville, Shann and Copland to force the breach with parity (Schedvin 1988:344).

After receiving a copy of Copland's infamous July lecture that had antagonised his Australian colleagues, Keynes replied that he had 'considerable sympathy with the line' taken—namely, price stabilisation via a fluctuating exchange rate as against outright deflation.[80] Recalling the episode, Wood marvelled at how, not much later, Copland was placed in the enviable position of seeing economists who had 'pooh-poohed his stabilisation ideas in 1930 riding to acclaim as the saviour of the country by using his theories two years after they were formulated'.[81] Elsewhere, however, 'Melbourne brains' alarmed the conservatives. Niemeyer, while in Australia, informed Harvey about '[m]uch wild talk in Caucus about expanding credits and tots of brandy inflation has supporters in Theodore and Melbourne economists'.[82]

Meanwhile, the Deputy Secretary of the Treasury, Harry Sheehan, had, in a memorandum to Lyons, corroborated the economists' findings about the loss in national income and the burden falling on the export sector. Sheehan compared the Melbourne school blueprint with the Federal Treasury plan, which comprised four main parts. Apart from the mandatory wage cut, the other measures were: a modest devaluation, the stabilisation of internal prices by monetary control and, lastly, an arrangement with the banks so that credits could be made available for industry.[83] It was a remarkable submission from a Treasury that, like its British counterpart, was prone to orthodoxy. Whether the Federal Treasury took Sheehan's proposals seriously is a moot point but there was evidence that the contemporary outpourings of economists had cast some influence on its making.

Lyons took the Treasury's mildly deflationary plan to Caucus, where it was rejected essentially because of the wage cut clause. Caucus remained in favour of the more expansionary 'heavy inflation' plan put forward by Theodore's backers (Lloyd 1984:49–50). Lyons' dalliance with departures from financial orthodoxy

---

79 Ibid.
80 D. B. Copland to J. M. Keynes, 10 July 1930, and J. M. Keynes to D. B. Copland, 20 August 1930, KPKC. Copland's views were echoed by two authors from the economic underworld: J. A. Gunn and C. A. Alison had penned a pamphlet entitled *Is this Depression Necessary? A short treatise on the stability of prices by control of exchange rate*. Using the *Treatise*, they advocated depreciation, cheap money and government stimulation as a form of domestic price stability (1930). A copy was sent to Keynes, who responded: 'I agree with you that there is a great deal to be said in the case of such a country as Australia, for allowing the exchange to fluctuate in the interest of stability of prices.'
81 G. L. Wood to W. S. Robinson, 21 April 1932, UMA FECC, Box 14.
82 Sir O. Niemeyer to Sir E. Harvey, Cablegram, 3 November 1930, BE, G1/291.
83 Memorandum by H. Sheehan, 30 October 1930, Lyons Papers, NLA.

offered hope for the future, but it went only so far. In his history of the United Australia Party (UAP), Lloyd presents Lyons and his supporters as willing to consider a limited form of economic reflation but totally against schemes of repudiation or inflation.

The November agreement and the second manifesto

By late November, the economists had tired of the Scullin government's drift to the deepening crisis.[84] For two days in late November, a number of economists secretly convened at Dyason's house in Melbourne.[85] The outcome of this gathering was to press for immediate cutbacks to public sector spending, which they now held to be a first condition for the restoration of business confidence. The meeting was also to bring Melville and Shann into some compromise agreement with the others. Brigden's confidential memorandum (cited in Schedvin 1970:224)—the only proof that the meeting was ever held— showed that Copland and Giblin, at the others' urging, had gone cold on price stabilisation by a release of credits, partly because that expedient was already being resorted to with Treasury bill finance.[86] The economists also felt they did not have the degree of confidence in monetary targeting to restore prices to 1929 levels; whether the Commonwealth Bank would prove amenable to the experiment was another matter. Another reason was that restoring budgetary balance was now regarded as the most pressing objective. Henceforth, talk of expansion of credit was removed from the economists' lexicon though Copland, in the verbiage that surrounded the Premiers' Plan, always took semantic licence about the modest inflationary dimension injected by Treasury bill finance of budget deficits. Copland (1930) signalled his *volte-face* in an article in *The Australian Quarterly* Shann interpreted it as a 'counterblast to Wickens and to Copland under the Dyason spell'.[87] Shann encouraged Davidson to get a copy

---

84   The Arbitration Court took matters into its own hands by electing the continuing National Wage Case to focus purely on the need for an emergency reduction in the basic wage given the serious fall in the national income compounded by the sudden cessation of overseas loans. Copland had told a trade union representative, Mr Crofts, that things were so desperate Australia would be lucky to escape with a real wage cut of 10 per cent (*SMH*, 3 December 1930). In the exchange with Crofts, Copland also expressed his displeasure at the failure of governments to curb spending. The Scullin government tried to hold up implementation of the court's judgment, much to Copland's annoyance.

85   Among those invited by Giblin on behalf of Copland, Dyason and Wood for this grand council were Wickens, Walker, Shann, Hytten, Gifford, Brigden and Melville. All attended (Giblin Papers, NLA, 366/15/338-9).

86   A point Niemeyer had made to Melville in his letter of 13 November 1930.

87   E. Shann to A. C. Davidson, 28 November 1930, BNSW, GM 302, p. 509.

of Copland's article to Theodore as '[i]t may help to wean him from Dyason's folly'.[88] Much to Shann's chagrin, Dyason, who had been associating with John Curtin, remained an unreconstructed stabilisationist.

The economists' memorandum ensuing from the conference, which was entitled 'Monetary policy in the crisis', proved a watershed. It honed in on the 25 per cent loss in national income as being perpetrated in part by the lack of economic adjustment and, relatedly, a lack of business confidence. Economists reasserted Copland's submission before the Arbitration Court that real wages had to be uniformly cut by 10 per cent; the mere creation of credits to spend on public works, the economists warned, would not promote recovery. They also reiterated that protection would solve neither the balance–of-payments problem nor unemployment. While they saw the possibilities of synchronising real wage cuts with reductions in the rate of interest, they insisted that the government could not 'safely' force a drop in the latter. Finally, they called for immediate economic adjustment lest Australians suffer even greater losses of income.

Brigden, annoyed at flagrant misrepresentation of his views on price stabilisation and how it could justify 'extravagant inflationary action', put out a memorandum for private circulation.[89] He concluded that price stabilisation was too dangerous because it diverted attention from making vital wage cuts and necessary economies in government spending. Brigden's memorandum also concurred with Shann's view that trying to restore 1929 price levels was too risky a mechanism and that, in any case, Australia 'was least likely' to achieve it. This reflected as much on the Commonwealth Bank's knowledge, personnel and powers of monetary control as it did on Brigden's economic philosophy.[90] As the newly appointed head of Queensland's Bureau of Economics and Industry, Brigden was, like Shann and Melville, sceptical of ready-made solutions or 'plans' and wary about monetary devices such as the scaling down of interest rates (Wilson 1951). According to Colin Clark (1958:223), Brigden was, at one stage, prepared to consider the federal government borrowing and spending heavily once the requisite cuts to incomes had been implemented. That is, he was prepared to alleviate some deflationary pain by expanding credits—to check price deflation, especially if prices fell faster than costs.

Edward Shann's philosophical disposition had always been to back 'the banker against the bureaucrat as the politicians' best economic adviser'.[91] Any economic plan, in any case, had to be congruent with the Realpolitik of economic

---

88 E. Shann to A. C. Davidson, 3 February 1931, BNSW, GM 302, p. 590.

89 'Notes on monetary policy', 5 December 1930, Brigden Papers, NLA.

90 Giblin, in particular, lamented the fact that Australia's public service had few university men. He later told Theodore that Australia did not have the reserve of qualified personnel to staff his and R. F. Irvine's idea of a National Credit Commission (L. F. Giblin to E. G. Theodore, 1933, UMA FECC, Prof. Giblin Papers, 92/141/ Box A-J).

91 E. Shann to G. Gordon, 30 September 1931, Shann Papers, NLA.

policymaking in that the banks, as powerful brokers, together with a vigilant London, had to be appeased (Butlin and Boyce 1988). Shann put it succinctly: 'What we Anglo-Saxons need most is ideas which banks can finance.'[92] Finally, at Copland's and Giblin's behest, the economists sanctioned protection enabling secondary industries to absorb some of those laid off from the cessation of loan works.[93]

The third manifesto—January 1931

With Davidson acting as their lightning rod, the economists publicised their new position with a statement released in January 1931 entitled 'First steps to economic recovery' (Shann and Copland 1931a:72–5; Holder 1970:693). Eight economists signed the memorandum.[94] Noting that the loss was still concentrated on the export sector, the economists called again for a sharing of that loss.[95] This would be enforced by a reduction of real wages, in tandem with cuts to public expenditure and a commensurate reduction in rentier income by scaling down interest rates.

There was some intellectual antecedence for these measures in Keynes's evidence placed before the Macmillan Committee. While it had not recommended devaluation, the committee praised it as 'theoretically the most obvious and comprehensive method of effecting an orderly contraction of money incomes in general'.[96] It was true, however, that Australian economists were, like Keynes, beholden to the idea that regaining equilibrium would be assisted by lower interest rates. The withdrawal of governments from the capital market would, they argued, bring interest rate relief—though Hytten was, to Shann's consternation, impatient for direct action [97] Davidson articulated this very point before the Victorian Branch of the Economics Society in May 1931, arguing that lower rates would materialise only once government borrowing was checked.

Where the economists departed company from the Commonwealth Bank was in their striking advocacy of a flexible exchange rate with no foreseeable return to parity. This was to become their pedigree of distinction throughout the early 1930s; Copland would later hail it as a 'new maxim of advanced monetary authorities'.[98] Copland accepted that Treasury bill financing of government

---

92   E. Shann to J. La Nauze, 11 August 1931, La Nauze Papers, NLA.
93   'Mr Theodore's plans: fundamental weaknesses', *SMH*, 23 December 1930.
94   D. B. Copland to E. Shann, 8 January 1931, UMA FECC, Box 10.
95   Copland, Giblin, Wood, Hytten, Melville, Gifford, Brigden, Shann and Mills signed the manifesto (see *SMH*, 21 January 1931; D. B. Copland to E. Shann, 8 January 1931, UMA FECC, Box 17).
96   Cited in the 'Macmillan report and Australian recovery', *Bank of New South Wales Circular*, vol. II, no. 1, p. 2.
97   Hytten, 1971, pg. 66
98   D. B. Copland to F. S Alford, 2 December 1935, UMA FECC, Box 30.

deficits gave 'sufficient stimulus' to anchor prices. In public writings, and with the economists' and Davidson's encouragement, Copland launched an offensive against the Theodore plan.[99] Indeed Copland wanted to go further and issue another manifesto denouncing the whole fiduciary issue idea. Shann counselled against this, arguing that economists would lose authority if they issued too many statements denouncing the measures of others.[100] Both economists, now working together despite initial policy differences, issued respective denunciations of the Theodore plan in bank circulars; Copland's piece appeared in the National Bank's circular. He was delighted at the opportunity it presented in terms of the edification for bankers.[101] Shann's more strongly worded contribution, 'Political control of banking', appeared in a Wales circular.

The economists' association with the banks led the Labor Party to raise concerns about their true allegiances or what Copland joked to Shann about as 'our year-long worship of mammon'.[102] The enigmatic Giblin, in contrast, with his blunt manner, hobnail boots and homespun clothing and red tie, did not get on with bankers so readily. In January 1931, with the exchange rate crisis extant, he predicted the possibility of dissolution between the banks and the people. At the time, a London banker felt Giblin's sentiments nothing but 'pure bolshevism'.[103] Walker would confirm this dangerous state of affairs in an inquiry into banking and monetary policy in 1936.

Shann found that his involvement in these activities besides his work for the Wales undermined his credibility at his university (Alexander 1963:150–3). His initial appointment at the Wales bemused other bankers who, themselves, had little time for 'theoretical gentlemen'. One local banker was told by his London overseer that 'some banks apparently have money to burn and Professor Shann is fortunate in finding a man like Davidson to provide him with jobs which can be of little practical interest and of no use to the Bank of NSW'.[104] Davidson knew otherwise.

Copland's casual involvement with the banks, particularly the Wales, signified his vaulting ambition not just for his discipline but for himself. His blossoming association with the mercurial Davidson was to be to his future benefit. By June

---

99   'Creating credit: its limitations and dangers', *SMH*, 30 January 1931.

100   To press home the attack, Gibson's letter to Theodore on gold was included in the book as a 'magnificent device' to show how utterly Labor politicians 'had failed to stop the rot' (E. Shann to D. B. Copland, 26 March 1931, UMA FECC, Box 12).

101   D. B. Copland to E. Shann, 31 March 1931, and E. Shann to D. B. Copland, 2 April 1931, UMA FECC, Box 31. While Copland had much earlier joked to Giblin that 'my economic theories will never allow me to make money', he was, however, not interested in leaving academia to become 'bank consultants' like his colleagues Melville and Shann. He was, however, ambitious for his discipline and the more economic analysis the banks invested in, the better for everyone (D. B. Copland to L. F. Giblin, 6 June 1927, UMA, FECC, Box 220).

102   D. B. Copland to E. Shann, 12 June 1931, UMA FECC, Box 31.

103   E. Godward to G. D. Healy, 26 February 1931, Bank of Australasia D/O Letters, ANZ Group Archive.

104   E. Godward to G. D. Healy, 29 June 1933, Bank of Australasia D/O Letters, ANZ Group Archive.

1931, Copland's public status was well established. The South Australian Labor Premier, Lionel Hill, invited Copland to become his full-time economic adviser. Copland demurred, preferring to be associated with the enigmatic Davidson: 'I'd much rather be associated with him than any Government.'[105] The fawning praise reflected, in part, Davidson's ability to re-jig Australia's policy settings by breaking parity with sterling—a step critical in the economic adjustment process.

The role of Davidson and the Bank of New South Wales

The compass has been damaged. The charts are out of date.

— Winston Churchill, Chancellor of the Exchequer, 1930

In his copious writings on the episode, Copland would always perceive the Premiers' Plan as complementary to the measures undertaken on wages and the exchange rate months earlier. Australian economists were emphatic that the 'spreading the loss' clause be implemented across all classes of the economy, including bondholders. This, as we have seen, was the logic that persuaded the Arbitration Court to cut real wages by 10 per cent but to insist on some release of credits. It also resolved the issue of which class would succumb to the first cut in income. In the same month, economists triumphed again by persuading the Wales to forcefully shed the last vestiges of parity. As Australia's strongest bank with many rural clients on its books, the Wales moved the carded rate in line with market pressures. Australia, beset by rough seas, was at last cut free from its sterling anchor. Other banks, including the Commonwealth, lamely followed suit and a new exchange rate regime came into play (Holder 1970:680–6). Gibson was 'apoplectic' at Davidson's actions, regarding parity as sacrosanct even to the point of considering exchange control.[106] Many in the financial circles, including even Davidson at one stage, regarded devaluation as inflationary since it would raise exporters' costs (Schedvin 1988:343). Copland dismissed this, saying that costs were hardly likely to rise during a period of falling prices; in fact, devaluation checked the extent to which cost levels had to be adjusted in order to balance costs and prices (Copland 1932a:116). International prices, moreover, continued to slip.

---

105   D. B. Copland to E. Shann, 19 June 1931, BNSW, A53-412.
106   Hytten, 1971, UT, p. 60. Gibson was perhaps more enraged at the Wales usurping the Commonwealth Bank than by the action itself, for he told Ricketson that he had been in favour of a 10 per cent devaluation but the increase in tariffs obviated this (Ricketson diary, 29 April 1931). Melville told the author that there could be 'two Gibsons': one uttering public views, the other private.

Davidson had been 'egged on' in taking this action by Melville, Copland and especially Shann. The last saw the action as forming part of a broader philosophical crusade: 'It may indeed set in motion forces working in the direction of stability, but in a country so wedded to the manipulation and restriction of economic forces it is an incessant fight to keep these forces unimpeded.'[107] Shann had been advising Davidson for some time on the desirability of a natural change in the exchange rate (Schedvin 1988:346–7). Davidson remained, however, unmoved until late in the piece. Initially, he supported the Niemeyer line against the stabilisationists until self-interest and informed persuasion brought him round.[108]

Contrary to his peers at the time, Davidson was an enlightened soul, free from rigid orthodoxy, who enjoyed the company of economists (Schedvin 1988:338; Holder 1970). He had already, for instance, established his own economic intelligence section within the bank, which would allow his bank to, as he put it, 'be in a position to influence events'.[109] Davidson's appointment as general manager of the Wales in October 1929 was, therefore, to prove auspicious. At the onset of the crisis, he had urged economists to present 'a united front' against Labor's unorthodox policies of inflationism and protectionism.[110] Melville astutely replied that it would be unwise to criticise indefinite policy and ventured that 'interference by university economists in public affairs is a delicate matter, because of the strong financial assistance rendered to universities by Australian Governments'.[111] Instead, Melville suggested that economists issue a statement dealing with the general situation. This, as we have seen, was done six months later, though in a situation worse than Melville could have imagined.

Leading economists attended several weekend retreats at Davidson's Blue Mountains home at Leura to discuss policy proposals (Schedvin 1988:338). These informal arrangements preceded the 'coffee club' culture in Sydney in which intellectuals gathered to exchange ideas about economic policy and Keynes (Coombs 1981:5).[112] Apart from establishing an economics research

---

107   E. Shann to H. C. Findlayson, 25 March 1931, BNSW, A53, p. 409.

108   It was held that a reduction in the rate of exchange would relieve budgeting pressures, while Giblin estimated that though a 130 rate added £10 million to Australia's interest payments to London, there would be benefits to exports, employment and tax revenue. It also gave relief to those paying fixed interest rate charges. Higher monetary values would also keep up taxation proceeds.

109   'Intelligence department', BNSW, GM 302/281.

110   A. C. Davidson to E. Shann, 4 November 1929, BNSW, 302/590/1.

111   L. G. Melville to A. C. Davidson, 25 November 1929, BNSW, GM302/374.

112   Wentworth, TRC 4900, 1994, NLA, p. 5. Davidson built up a huge economics research section totalling 18 economists, which vastly exceeded Treasury's or the Commonwealth Bank's economic advisory capacities (Schedvin 1988:347). Davidson's 'kindergarten', as it became known, was the first 'private sector economic research group in this country' (Schedvin 1988:347). Davidson first appointed Shann as his economic adviser followed by Torleiv Hytten and then Allan Fisher. Hytten and Shann were to remain the most influential economic advisers during Davidson's 17 years as general manager (A. C. Davidson to T. Hytten, 29 October 1949, BNSW, A. C. Davidson Papers, N2/92).

section, Davidson launched bank circulars that presented the steps necessary for Australia's economic reconstruction. Davidson would continue to be a thorn in the side of the federal government, and even more the Commonwealth Bank, throughout the 1930s as he criticised monetary policy settings. It would be wrong, however, to interpret Davidson as entirely the mouthpiece for dissident economic opinion; he was merely supporting a more enlightened approach to exchange rate policy that served his bank's interests (Holder 1970). Nonetheless, Holder (1970:692, 700), who worked in Davidson's economic 'kindergarten', rates Davidson's contribution to formulate a recovery policy so highly that it made him almost a 'godparent' to the Premiers' Plan.

The Treasury Committee plan—February 1931

Against the backdrop of a 30 per cent devaluation and a 10 per cent wage cut, the Loan Council, having abandoned the Melbourne conference resolutions to balance the budgets within one year, opted for a three-year plan. Officialdom was, at last, moving towards a compromise plan but was still some way from achieving it. The Loan Council commissioned a committee of under-Treasury officials to report on Australia's finances. Four economists—Brigden, Melville, Shann and Hytten—were hurriedly and intermittently consulted in the preparation of this report.[113] Brigden recalled that it was Shann and Melville who were most 'influential'. Brigden gave vent to his 'cut and spend' approach but Melville dismissed this.[114] The Treasury Committee plan, reflecting the serious erosion in budgeting finances, proved a marked departure from Sheehan's Federal Treasury memorandum of September 1930.[115] The four state treasurers and Sheehan traced the lack of confidence in the economy to unbalanced budgets and settled for a reduction of government expenditure by £15 million over three years. The committee regarded the level of government expenditure as 'the key to the whole position'.[116] It was, in fact, not enough, with economists reckoning the projected total public sector deficit of £39 million for 1931/32.[117] Perversely, the committee regarded the depreciated exchange rate as a manifestation of that uncertainty and longed for the return of parity.[118] Devaluation, they argued, merely added to the burden of overseas interest payments with the benefit to the export sector deemed purely temporary. It would be too easy, the committee

---

113   In his autobiographical memoirs, Hytten (UT, 1971, p. 58) recalls being astounded by the antics and histrionics of the chairman of the committee—none other than Sir Robert Gibson.

114   J. B. Brigden to L. F. Giblin, 1 April 1947, RBA, GLG-43-1.

115   J. G. Latham, the Federal Opposition Leader, saw the Treasury Committee's views as being one with his own political party's (*The Hobart Mercury*, 13 February 1931).

116   'The plan of reconstruction', *BNSW Circular*, vol. 1, no. 4 (June), p. 2.

117   Ibid.

118   This could not have been the sentiment of the economists. Shann, for instance, called the depreciation of January 1930 'manna in the wilderness' (E. Shann to H. C. Finlayson, 25 March 1931, BNSW, A53, p. 409).

said, to 'gloss over the loss of prosperity by an alteration in the purchasing power of the currency. This was not a road to recovery, but to collapse' (Shann and Copland 1931a:162). The committee argued that extensive government borrowing would only crowd-out private capital expenditure and that genuine interest rate reduction would come only with the return of business confidence (Shann and Copland 1931a:164). The fact that the chairman of the committee, Gibson, confessed in a letter to Scullin that the committee had 'perhaps exceeded' the scope of its instructions in putting forth its recommendations was enough for Scullin to scuttle it.[119]

The political economy of the Premiers' Plan

The economists had all but framed the blueprint of what was to become the Premiers' Plan by late November 1930 but it was only placed before politicians in May 1931. While the economists drew some praise for their efforts, it was their political masters who had to bow to harsh realities. The capitulation of the Scullin government to economic reality was imminent but it underlined the worth of the plan. Australia's first imperative was external solvency and the adjustment of the domestic cost structure to contain and minimise the loss in real income resulting from external shocks.[120] Scullin's reluctance to put into effect the Premiers' Plan until the last moment was encapsulated by C. L. Baillieu: 'If he accepts fully and applies the Experts' report he will be forced to jettison policies which he has never ceased to proclaim…and to see his party ultimately broken by courses which he has sworn he would never take.'[121]

Sir Alexander Hore-Ruthven, the Governor of South Australia, reported that Scullin and Theodore's 'last minute surrender to sound economics' was essentially because the federal government had tested the public's patience.[122] Hore-Ruthven was correct in his assessment that it was the united opinion of five state premiers that kept pressure on the federal government to execute fully the recommendations of the experts.[123] In fact, Theodore pragmatically bowed to orthodoxy and saw the 'equitable reduction' of wages and interest

---

119   *SMH*, 7 February 1931.

120   In his apologia expressed in his *A History of the Central Bank*, Giblin (1951), in reviewing the Depression policy of 1931, defended the middle way, stating that 'it was not far from the best that was possible with a public inexperienced as it was at that time in violent economic vicissitudes and their remedies'.

121   C. L. Baillieu to K. Murdoch, 30 May 1931, UMA FECC, Box 204.

122   Sir A. Hore-Ruthven to the Secretary of State for Dominion Affairs, Sir H. Batterbee, 11 June 1931, PRO, T160/396/11935/02.

123   Hore-Ruthven, at Lyons' behest, became Governor-General Gowrie in 1936 (Wigran to J. A. Lyons, 2 July 1934, Lyons Papers, NLA, Box 2, Folder 18). Hore-Ruthven urged the Governor of New South Wales, Sir Philip Game, to dismiss Premier Lang over the repudiation controversy ostensibly because of the damage it was doing to Australia's credit abroad. Hore-Ruthven had been censored by the Adelaide Trades and Labour Council in 1931 for making blatantly political comments (Blanche 1998:102).

rates 'as the simplest method of economic adjustment' (cited in Clark 1974b:48). He resolutely defended the Premiers' Plan against dissidents in the Caucus and drew Shann's praise for his 'drive and assiduity over detail in piloting it through Parliament'.[124]

Theodore justified his decision, stating that it gave respite for the government (Kennedy 1988:297). He confessed though: 'I never had any belief that the policy would restore employment unless it was accomplished by credit expansionism on a large scale and was accompanied by either an active program of expenditure by government or by a revival of business confidence.'[125]

The irony was that there was, in fact, a revival of business confidence engendered by the Premiers' Plan whereas a policy of huge monetary expansion, with the obvious connotation with inflation, would have undermined business confidence. Then there was Theodore's colourful background. As *The Age*, a paper originally sympathetic to the fiduciary issue idea, editorialised: 'Mr Theodore...is about the worst man who could have proposed it.'[126] The asymmetry was all the more galling since it had been the Scullin Labor government, as economists conceded, that was the only one capable of piloting the Premiers' Plan through—a fact Scullin felt his government was never given enough credit for.

Casey, having returned to Australia in search of a political career, apprised Kershaw at the Bank of England of what had unfolded. He reported it as almost a triumph for Theodore, who had managed the proceedings and

> has developed the situation very cleverly and with admirable political tactics—as he has shown the country that he has tried every possible expedient to avoid direct attack on the small civil service wage earner and on the small pensioner—but owing to absolute lack of government funds, he is obliged at the last moment to give in to the advice of the experts and enforce the cuts—but, mind you, not until he has obliged Capital also to accept cuts of similar magnitude.[127]

Despite Casey's view, historians interpret the Premiers' Plan as a political triumph for Joe Lyons, who had consistently called for balanced budgets and deflationary policy as the best ways to resurrect business confidence (Lloyd 1984; Schedvin 1970; Hart 1967). It was also a triumph for the Australian economics profession.

---

124   Shann Papers, 13 August 1931, NLA, Box 2.
125   E. G. Theodore to J. Curtin, 14 October 1932, Theodore Papers, NLA. Theodore corroborated these views in an interview with Rupert MacLaurin (1936:44), a visiting American scholar writing a thesis on the unique attempt by Australia to extricate itself from the Depression.
126   *The Age*, 26 March 1931.
127   R. G. Casey to R. Kershaw, 7 June 1931, BE, OV 13/1.

Economists *in excelsis*?

It is a great time for economists altogether. Long may they flourish![128]

The critical assumption underpinning the Premiers' Plan was a recovery in Australia's export prices within two years. On that premise, Giblin (1933a:3) figured it was the 'wisest practical policy'. He was unapologetic about how makeshift the plan really was, being the product of a 'number of divergent and sometimes opposing forces of opinion, economical and political'.

It might have been therefore a 'makeshift' solution to Australia's economic predicament but Shann saw an air of purposefulness behind it: 'The economists were under no illusion that their plan was more than a beginning. What they aimed at was a plan to balance budgets and the reverse of all our policies pushing up costs.'[129] June 1931 was, therefore, a defining moment for the Australian economics profession.

Thrust into the spotlight, Australian economists showed considerable political aplomb and a 'native genius' in their deliberations (Cain 1982). Their policy advice underwent a dramatic series of twists and turns within an over-politicised environment—something Melville believed sometimes detracted from ascertaining a real understanding of the economic issues.[130] In the swirl of high political drama, the economists excelled in what the English economist Brian Reddaway later called the 'Australian genius for improvisation'.[131] Also on display was a penchant for social experimentation in dealing with difficult economic problems (MacLaurin 1936:14).[132] In that respect, Australia was singularly blessed with economic institutions and conventions that could bend to the prevailing winds of circumstance (Copland 1934). For instance, the centralised wage-setting apparatus was praised for being 'indispensable to engineer the general fall in costs that was virtually necessary' in 1931 (Reddaway 1938:335). While the Premiers' Plan made for deflationary economics, it did resemble Keynes's notion of a national treaty expedient presented before the Macmillan Committee in 1930, in which all income recipients, including rentiers, shared the burden of economic adjustment (Cain 1973:82–3, 1983:17; Petridis 1994:182).

There were, to recall, consistent themes running through the economists' manifestos and memoranda. These were the restoration of balanced budgets,

---

128   G. L. Wood to B. H. Molesworth, 23 February 1932, UMA FECC, Box 14.
129   E. Shann to Gordon, 30 September 1931, Shann Papers, NLA.
130   Melville, TRC 182, NLA, p. 27.
131   Giblin Papers, 30 November 1940, NLA.
132   MacLaurin visited Australia on a scholarship with the express intention of writing his doctorate on Australia's unique recovery from the depression. MacLaurin turned to Copland as his first contact, who took him under his wing and introduced him to the leading players in the 1931 drama.

a readjustment between export costs and prices, a flexible exchange rate and, under the rubric of spreading the loss doctrine, interest rate reductions. Keynes's *Treatise*, with its savings and investment dynamic, provided the overlapping theoretical framework. The unity between Australia's leading economists was made stronger by the seriousness of the situation.[133] Their advice helped Australia navigate through the Charybdis of repudiation and the Scylla of deflation.[134]

It also allayed the fears of British financial minds. At one stage the situation had become so grave that the British Senior Trade Commissioner, R. W. Dalton, believed that only 'an expert and impartial Financial Commission from the United Kingdom was needed to manage Australia's reconstruction'.[135] An earlier expedient, canvassed by J. H. Thomas, the Secretary for Dominion Affairs, had been to consider sending out the high-ranking Treasury official Frederick Leith-Ross as the next High Commissioner (Leith-Ross 1968:132). While interested, Leith-Ross (1968:132) felt it would be a heavy-handed move, signalling to Canberra Britain's palpable interest in Australia's financial rehabilitation, including the honouring of debt payments to London. After the Premiers' Plan was agreed to, Kershaw dismissed the alarmism of Dalton's missive, telling the British Treasury that 'taking all factors into consideration...putting Australia into commission was neither necessary nor desirable'.[136]

While the plan, as Copland (1935a:600) declared, was a 'composite' one drawn up by Australian economists, it bestowed particular celebrity on him. The Australian newspapers dubbed Copland the 'Keynes of the Commonwealth' (cited in Harper 1986:46). The Harvard economist Frank Taussig saluted him: 'Your own part gives one hope that after all, we economists are not so entirely

---

133   Melville, TRC 182, NLA, p. 41. At the height of this triumph, G. L. Wood somewhat broke the consensus among economists by urging the reconstitution of a body such as the Development and Migration Commission (DMC) to enforce quasi-Keynesian policies of purposeful state action (AA, A786, and D19/2). Two former officers of the DMC, J. Gunn and J. P. Murphy, called on the federal government to boost spending (AA, A786, and T22/8). Much more disturbing for the future, however, was A. C. Davidson's reaction to Herbert Gepp's solicitous advice that the Sydney banker should, as the Melbourne economists had done, gather together a group of young economists for the express purpose of discussing current economic problems (Sir H. Gepp to A. C. Davidson, 6 July 1931, BNSW, GM 302/357). On Gepp's letter, Davidson wrote '[w]hat an atmosphere' and as to Gepp's talk of economic reconstruction, Davidson annotated 'Theodorian or Dyasonian'. Davidson's sarcasm was not sparked by the Melbourne–Sydney rivalry but by the possible fear that the Melbourne school was too 'red' for his liking. In his reply, Davidson minced his words fearing that monthly talks between the same circle of economists could become 'didactic' and 'a little too high in the upper air of economic and monetary theory' (A. C. Davidson to Sir H. Gepp, 13 July 1931, BNSW, GM 302/35).

134   A. C. Davidson drew a comparison between the Copland Committee's advice and the advice contained in a leading article in *The Economist* put forward to deal with Britain's own economic problems (A. C. Davidson to W. S. Robinson, 13 August 1931, BNSW, GM 302/574). For his part, Robinson held 'that the Commonwealth will be setting an example to nearly all other countries' (W. S. Robinson to Davidson, 20 June 1931, BNSW, GM 302/574).

135   E. R. Dalton to Campbell, 20 May 1931, PRO, T160/366/11935/02.

136   R. Kershaw to Sir Frederick Leith-Ross, 27 July 1931, BE, OV 13/1/453/2.

useless as some of the critics allege.'[137] Two years later, Copland told Taussig that the Australian economists' ingenuity in masterminding their country's economic rehabilitation was only one part of the story:

> It has been uncommonly successful, but it has been greatly helped by a run of good seasons. Whether we shall continue...depends more upon the courage we show and the psychology of the people than upon the actual economic efforts themselves. If it succeeds it will at least establish the principle that 'intelligent economic control' is capable of handling a difficult situation with great advantage to all concerned.[138]

The English economist Ralph Hawtrey (1934:120) lauded Australia as the first country to appoint a brains trust of economists to help guide the nation out of depression. At a civic reception given to him in Geelong in 1931, Copland stated that had economists been listened to over the past five years Australia might have avoided the Depression.[139] Apart from being diverted from their academic tasks, the economists involved in the plan's preparation received little remuneration, much less gratitude, for their advice (Alexander 1963:196–7).[140] One instance that exemplified that spirit was Giblin's readiness to 'do his bit' and take up the duties of Acting Commonwealth Statistician in Canberra at great personal inconvenience.[141]

There were, however, some isolated notes of derision about the worth of economists—and from high places. Bruce told Frank McDougall at Australia House in London that Australian economists had seemingly 'reformed' and 'had come down to Earth'. Copland took umbrage, saying that it was not a case of economists deviating from the path of virtue so much as a 'deviation...occurred with other people who now see the light where all was darkness'.[142] Equally, when the Melbourne businessman Sir Harold Luxton reported that it was a sign of 'mental weakness' and 'a drawback in our national life' that economists

---

137 F. Taussig to D. B. Copland, 19 October 1931, UMA FECC, Box 17.

138 D. B. Copland to F. Taussig, 28 February 1933, UMA FECC, Box 19.

139 'The Premiers' Plan and after', *Geelong Advertiser*, 4 September 1931.

140 D. B. Copland to H. Luxton, 23 June 1932, UMA FECC, Box 11. Due recognition perhaps would come in the afterlife. Copland jibed to an associate that 'making the world safe for private profit and preventing the high priests of high finance from ruining themselves would guarantee a very warm quarter in the upper world' (D. B. Copland to Kitto, 29 October 1935, UMA FECC, Box 35). Possibly, but Copland would later find his temporal aspirations spiked by those same interests he ridiculed. The Commonwealth Statistician, Charles Wickens, had suffered an incapacitating illness in February 1931 due to overwork and the controversy his views had embroiled him in (Castles 1997:32). Shann's two-year secondment to the Wales as economic adviser was creating animosity with university administrators and others in Perth (Alexander 1963).

141 Giblin to A. Blakely, Minister for Home Affairs, 27 March 1931, UMA FECC, Giblin Papers, Box 1, 92/141; J. A. Lyons to L. F. Giblin, Cablegram, 24 March 1931, UMA FECC, Giblin Papers, 92/141.

142 F. McDougall to D. B. Copland, 23 December 1931, and D. B. Copland to F. McDougall, 19 April 1932, UMA FECC, Box 11.

were consulted to prise Australia out of her difficulties, Copland replied that businessmen, like everyone else, had been demoralised by the crisis; only economists had conceived a practical, reasonable plan to save Australia.

Bankers, too, were scornful of the intrusion of 'academic gentlemen' into the world of economic advice. Ernest Wreford, Chairman of the National Bank of Australasia, told its directors ,'I am one of many who feel that the world today is getting a little too much advice from professional economists' (Blainey and Hutton 1983:205). Another banker, C. H. Tranter, Chairman of the Melbourne-based Associated Banks, was scathing about the role of economists in urging the break from parity: 'I am not too much influenced by the theoretical opinions of economists who, as a rule, take the academic course and have not had practical experience' (cited in Holder 1970:684). Speaking for the English-owned banks, G. D. Healy pleaded with 'three professors of economics' that devaluation was wrong and 'that even if their contentions were correct' it was not the time to put them into operation and that 'practical men' should be allowed to deal with the situation.[143]

There was resentment, too, from office-holders at the arrival of economists into positions of influence. McDougall agreed with David Rivett of the CSIR that the economists had 'lost their heads' with their newly found sense of importance. Sounding like an aggrieved banker, Rivett went on:

> My interpretation of the position is that the 'homo economicus Australiensis' was a neglected species up to 1929. Then when depression broke upon us the harried politician hurried to him for aid and since that date your Giblins, Coplands, Shanns and Melvilles have been taken very seriously indeed. This sudden promotion of men whose experience in public affairs is limited seems to me to have had an unsettling effect upon their mental equilibrium. (Cited in O'Dea 1997:67)

Others, such as Walter Murdoch from the University of Western Australia, refused to acknowledge the worth of economists:

> The economist has his uses in the world, and one use in particular…The true use of the economic expert is to refute other economic experts…He may have other uses, though I, personally, have not discovered them… My wireless expert did put my set right; what has the economic expert ever put right? (Cited in La Nauze 1977:118)

While the Premiers' Plan was later castigated as deflationary and serving the interests of the banking community, the economists drew praise by their insistence on devaluation, Treasury bill finance and lower interest rates—what

---

143   G. D. Healy to E. Godward, D/O Letters, 20 February 1931, ANZ Group Archive.

Copland called management by 'intelligent economic control'.[144] There was also Copland's imaginative voluntary conversion-of-internal-debt scheme.[145] While Copland (1932b:378) admitted that he did not agree with Australian governments rejecting Niemeyer's therapy *in toto,* he was emphatic that his plan was quite removed from the Niemeyer blueprint. Copland had identified Niemeyer's therapy as akin to an aboriginal circumcision causing 'needless disorganisation and distress' (cited in Clark 1981b:183). For his own part, Copland did not feel that the cure was worse than the disease. Nonetheless, he later regretted that allowing loan expenditures to fall to a nadir in 1931–32 was as much in error as allowing Australian governments to engage in reckless expenditure during the 1920s.[146] In other words, there was no recognition that public works expenditure be increased to the level occurring before the Depression so as to offset the calamitous fall in private investment; nor was Giblin's multiplier analysis ever applied to cutbacks in domestic expenditure until Kahn recast it in 1931 (Karmel 1960; Wilson 1951:195).

In his theoretical outlook, Copland (1934:64) set little store on the value of public works; lasting employment would be found in the export and import-replacement industries. Attempting reflation by public works, it was believed, merely inflated the prices of domestic goods, imposing further hardship on the export sector (Plumptre 1935:133). Public works were held to be effective only when they served as a stimulus to private enterprise and for this to occur business opinion was crucial (Brigden 1934). In Copland's favour were the prevailing psychological circumstances, which called for fiscal consolidation not expansion.

There was contemporary criticism, too, from the Sydney economists F. A. Bland and Mills (1931), who, in their review of the plan, felt that the equity aspect did not wholly extend to pensioners and the low paid. In like spirit, Hugh Dalton, British economist and Labour politician, praised Australia's wielding of the axe on expenditure and incomes but wondered if it was 'truly scientific forestry'. He pointed out the gross inequality within the sharing-of-loss principle in that external bondholders were quarantined from having to partake in the sacrifice (Dalton 1934:441). Although there were engineered interest rate cuts, Copland (1960:21) later admitted that the inflationary aspect of the plan was 'was not pursued by the same vigour and unanimity' as were the expenditure cuts and tax rises. That said, the banks were praised for playing their part and not taking

---

144   D. B. Copland to F. Taussig, 28 February 1933, UMA FECC, Box 19.
145   Even at the hour of triumph, Leslie Melville held grave concerns about whether the loan conversion arrangement would work (L. G. Melville to Sir O. Niemeyer, 6 June 1931, BE, OV9/289).
146   *The Herald,* 30 December 1935.

advantage of the reduction in interest to reduce the rates on their deposits. Looking back, Hytten (1935:132) concluded that the Premiers' Plan, while overly severe, had 'done its work' in terms of reducing deficits and outlays.

In his reappraisal of the Premiers' Plan, the New Zealand economist Allan Fisher (1934) suggested that economists had erred in prescribing devaluation because it induced more unprofitable primary production at a time when the world did not desire it. This critique sprang from his research focus on material progress, showing how it did not lead just to a continuous increase in production but to increasing diversification of goods and services. In 1941, Giblin found time to defend the plan's originality: 'It would have been difficult to find among those concerned with the Premiers' Plan any agreement with the theses of Niemeyer who had, in fact, left Australia long before the plan was thought of.'[147] He was well aware, too, that the plan was bound to be deflationary but Australia, at the time, had little choice. He also defended the 1931 wage cut for being a stimulus—material and psychological—to exporters and import-replacement manufacturers.[148]

In the past 50 years, the Premiers' Plan has assumed a place of infamy in Australia's history. A retelling of its origins and rationale, though, casts it in a much brighter light. The economic and political drama of 1931 represented an opportunity for Australian economists to combine the latest theoretical work of the monetary reformers with some native improvisation. It was, in fact, the making of the Australian economics profession.

---

147 'The myth of the Premiers' Plan', 6 November 1942, Giblin Papers, NLA.
148 L. F. Giblin to E. R. Walker, 19 April 1934, Giblin Papers, NLA.

6. The agonistes of the economists, 1931–1932

Introduction

In his account of Australia's travail through the Depression, Schedvin (1970:225) was dismissive of the efforts of economists in formulating policy dealing with the crisis but also, more importantly for our purposes, in putting forward alternative economic policies.[1] Apart from his main contention that the Premiers' Plan had a comparatively minor effect on the course of recovery, Schedvin suggested that the economic policy decided on in July 1931 retarded, more than promoted, economic recovery. The interwar economists would have concurred; official economic policy in 1932 took a deflationary bias. The purpose of this chapter, however, and those following, is to show how Schedvin's view of the role of economists is not grounded in the facts. In particular, the tracking of the development of Australian economists' thought and policy advice during the 1930s leads to a categorical refutation of Schedvin's (1970:225) claim that instead of economists re-examining traditional economic thought 'they clung to the myth of the efficacy of the Premiers' Plan and implicitly condoned the inept policy of the Lyons Government'.

Australian economists had, in fact, begun to question the traditional patterns of economic thought as well as the appropriateness of the Premiers' Plan's especially as unemployment soared and export prices fell further. Some decided on bold new directions. After 1933, the unity of the economists in promoting anti-depression policies began to fray with a divide re-emerging between the stabilisationists and restrictionists, albeit in muted form. Before then, however, economists were asked to reformulate another bolder plan to retrieve Australia from slump. This advice was not acted on.

To understand why this was, some background on the formation of, and interests behind, the Lyons government is appropriate. There was a revival of economic revisionism with the Commonwealth Bank reasserting its authority over economic policy by ordering a currency appreciation. As the economy

---

1   A useful illuminating exercise is to compare Schedvin's account of economists' activities in the early 1930s with the more uplifting, albeit self-interested account given by Holder in his history of the Bank of New South Wales. Both books were published in 1970.

continued to stagnate, Lyons commissioned a review of economic policy. The subsequent report, which attracted the attention of Keynes, focused on the contemporary dilemma between exchange rate stability and price stability.

The economic policy of the Lyons government

Economists welcomed the election of the Lyons government. It heralded the return, not just of business confidence that would allow the Premiers' Plan to start yielding results, but of a Prime Minister prepared sometimes to act on academic economic expertise. In contrast with the boost in business confidence that marked election of the United Australia Party (UAP) to power, there was only a lukewarm response in the stock market when the Premiers' Plan was first announced.[2] This was partly because Scullin and Theodore had allowed themselves to become, as Casey put it, 'political charlatans'.[3] Pushing through the Premiers' Plan, in any event, merely hastened the self-destruction of the Scullin government and allowed its successor to appropriate the electoral credit for pulling Australia out of the economic mire (Lloyd 1984:164).

Economists were aware of Lyons' backers, particularly a Melbourne-based cabal known as 'The Group', and held some fears that economic policy might revert to outright deflation (Hart 1967). With Britain off the gold standard from September 1931, concern focused on a Commonwealth Bank Board asserting its independence and moving to 'rehabilitate' the exchange. Sterling had begun to appreciate in any case meaning that Australia lost the benefit of the second de facto devaluation when sterling first came off the gold standard. To safeguard the linchpin of intelligent economic policy—that is, an exchange rate that took account of domestic economic conditions—economists engaged in persuading higher authorities to take the correct approach.

Whatever the growing unease among economists over the policy settings put in place by the Premiers' Plan, there were two binding constraints on any other feasible alternative. First, the plan was a three-year program and it was on that platform that Lyons, as the titular head of the conservative forces that crystallised around the UAP, won at the polls; Lyons, whose appeal to the electorate was deeper and wider than any political party, had asked for—and overwhelmingly received—a 'doctor's mandate' from electors.[4] His manifesto was built around three broad themes: a restoration of business confidence,

---

2 A few years after losing office, Scullin was still bitter that his government was not given the credit due to it for putting in place the measures that saved Australia (Molony, 2000, 149).
3 R. G. Casey to M. Hankey, 6 July 1931, Hankey Papers, Churchill College.
4 That term was taken from Ramsay MacDonald's successful re-election campaign in Britain in 1931. It was little wonder Lyons used the slogan 'Tune in with Britain' in the UAP's election campaign.

the balancing of budgets and the reduction of unemployment through the stimulation of private enterprise. The UAP election manifesto was drawn from Lyons' predecessor, Latham, who, even in the dark days of early 1931, saw nothing explicitly wrong with the economic system other than a marked lack of business confidence caused by the dithering of the Scullin government. In that light, Latham, along with The Group, cast a shadow over Lyons' economic views. One consolation was the return of Bruce, as Assistant Treasurer, though Giblin felt he was hamstrung having to 'live down' his reputation for reckless expansion.[5]

The second constraint on alternative economic policy was that Australia's external obligations to British bondholders dictated sound finance and a stable exchange rate. Apart from choking off imports with tariffs, Australia, on the other side of the ledger, had to muster a large enough export push to meet its foreign debt requirements. This was no easy task. For instance, in 1930/31, the surplus of exports over imports amounted to £28.3 million, while the total interest payments on the external debt of Australian government authorities amounted to £36 million. In the succeeding year, 1931/32, Australia recorded a trade surplus that allowed some accumulation in its London funds. The management and servicing of Australia's debt portfolio assumed even greater weight once Bruce was dispatched to London to begin the difficult task of converting maturing Australian government securities to a lower rate (Attard 2000). Apart from Australian tariff levels injuring British exports and the repudiation rhetoric of Lang, London financial opinion was shocked at how voluntary conversion of the national debt had become coercive for dissentients.[6] Melville subsequently told Niemeyer of his concern that the process might give impetus for Lang to push for the compulsory conversion of Australia's external debt since the outstanding Australian loans on the London market exacted a heavy interest burden on government budgets.[7] Even though Britain had a cheap money policy from 1932 onwards, the British Treasury initially opposed the Commonwealth conversion operations on the pretext that the London market could not accommodate the scale of the conversions at hand. London acceded to the Australian request only by July 1933, having by then sorely tried Lyons' patience (Cain 1985). In a cable to Bruce, Lyons vented not only his own frustration at London's 'callousness or thoughtless indifference to our difficulties', but what the riddance of the Scullin government had meant: 'It must not be forgotten,' Lyons intoned, 'that in approaching consideration of this matter that the Australian people voted us…into power in the belief that London would react…and that, with a Government pledged to pay its way, lower rates

---

5   L. F. Giblin to E. Giblin, 9 March 1932, Giblin Papers, NLA.
6   'Toreador column', *New Statesman and Nation*, 12 September 1931, p. 322.
7   L. G. Melville to Sir O. Niemeyer, 6 June 1931, BE, OV9/289.

would inevitably and willingly follow.'[8] The explicit threat to London was that such recalcitrance would result in the return to power of the Labor Party, which would set about reducing the country's external interest rate obligations in a much more 'brutal and direct fashion'.[9]

Some three years later, Bruce informed Giblin of the economic Realpolitik behind the conversion program that had, by then, been successfully executed. It was, he said, not just to give Australia the maximum relief with regard to her interest burden 'but possibly more importantly, to convince Australian public opinion that the policy of respectability is more profitable for Australia's point of view'.[10] Just how far this policy of 'respectability' went would soon present economists with their first challenge.

Lyons' commission, as both Prime Minister and Treasurer, was to carry out the Premiers' Plan to the letter. The electoral call for orthodoxy and respectability had resonance since Latham delighted in exposing the fact that Theodore and Scullin had not totally forsaken the 'policy of inflation…and printing bank notes to make the credits effective'.[11] Scullin and Theodore, annoyed at the banks' reluctance to honour their commitment to cut interest rates, explored new expedients (Holder 1970:705–7). Melville feared that Theodore would use the findings of the British *Macmillan Report* to revive the extension-of-credit idea.[12] In a letter to the South Australian politician Charles Hawker, Melville suggested that Theodore's thunder be stolen by the UAP adopting the Macmillan doctrine urging an international reflation of prices, *inter alia*, and dismissing domestic inflation as an expedient.[13] The three English banks based in Melbourne were delighted, then, at the electoral demise of Theodore because it had removed from circulation notions of inflationary schemes.[14] Or so they hoped.

Elected in December 1931, the new Lyons government, with a majority in both chambers of Parliament, commanded a powerful leverage over economic policy. At first, Giblin sensed that Lyons and Bruce were keen on a new economic plan, but this was only electioneering.[15] It had, of course, been Lyons' overwhelming popularity with the electorate that brought this coalition of conservative interests to power (Lloyd 1984). Lyons' biographer, Philip Hart (1967), got to the nub of

---

8   J. Lyons to S. M. Bruce, 11 March 1933, Cablegram, AA, 1970/559, Bruce Correspondence to Lyons, 1933.
9   Staniforth Ricketson diary extract, 20 June 1932.
10   S. M. Bruce to L. F. Giblin, 11 July 1936, AA, M104/4, Miscellaneous Papers Bruce, 1936.
11   *The Age*, 7 November 1931.
12   The Wales put out a circular on the findings of the Macmillan Committee, which, taken at face value, did not readily accord with Australia's economic readjustment measures. For instance, the Macmillan Committee dismissed 'the resort to competition in wage cutting [as] a counsel for despair, especially for debtor nations'. It did, however, urge financial reflation and international monetary reform to lift price levels back to 1929 levels in a bid to eliminate the discrepancy between manufactured and commodity prices.
13   L. G. Melville to C. A. S. Hawker, 31 September 1931, Shann Papers, NLA.
14   G. D. Healy to E. Godward, D/O Letters, 24 December 1931, Bank of Australasia, ANZ Group Archive.
15   L. F. Giblin to E. Giblin, 17 January 1932, Giblin Papers, NLA.

Lyons' intrinsic appeal to the electorate; it was his essential 'ordinariness' and his folksy 'homely style' that won over the people. 'Ordinary men', perplexed by the monetary schemes of Lang and Theodore, knowing little of economics, turned gladly to Joseph Lyons whose honesty and belief in economy they could easily understand. Lyons expediently played on his unfamiliarity with finance. Such professed innocence and timidity would, as Labor politicians pointed out, cost Australia dear.

Buoyed by the victory of Ramsay MacDonald in the British general election of October 1931, Lyons offered the same sanctuary to the Australian electorate. In similar circumstances to MacDonald, Lyons had also been traduced by conservative interests to be at the head of a motley coalition of conservative groups (Hart 1967; Lloyd 1984). As mentioned, the most outstanding of these interests was the Melbourne group (Lloyd 1984:292; Hart 1967). The Group revolved around the aspiring Victorian politician R. G. Menzies and the Tasmanian-born stockbroker Staniforth Ricketson (Murray and White 1988). It was Ricketson who had marshalled financial opinion behind Lyons' loan-conversion campaign of 1930, which proved the making of his electoral appeal. As his diary entries reveal, Ricketson shared the confidences of Sir Robert Gibson, B. S. B. Stevens, the NSW Opposition Leader, and Casey, a future Federal Treasurer. Other members of The Group were Sir John Higgins, head of the British and Australian Wool Realisation Association, Charles Norris, an insurance magnate, and Ambrose Pratt,[16] a businessman and former journalist with strong links to Keith Murdoch, the Managing Editor of the *Melbourne Herald*. Murdoch's newspapers played a critical part in Lyons' elevation, presenting him as Australia's saviour. Pratt felt The Group would be the channel through which to meet the 'desire to influence public opinion for the public good' (cited in Martin 1999:94). A later recruit, the architect Kingsley Henderson, whom Lyons was especially friendly with, was an intimate of Sir Robert Gibson (Hart 1967; Martin 1993:83). Lloyd (1984) considers that, 'in terms of access to power and influence, the Group's presence could not be surpassed'. Ricketson's diary, however, reveals this applied, perhaps, only to the early days of the Lyons government. Once into his term of office and facing bleak economic times and a divided cabinet, Lyons gently resisted the overtures of The Group, telling its spokesman, Sir Kingsley Henderson, that he was reluctant to call on them for fear that they would think

---

16 Pratt also dabbled in political economy with some reasonably cognate analysis of Australia's economic ills. In 'Disequilibrium—the measure of depression', Pratt identified an overproduction of staples as a besetting global problem necessitating lower production costs for secondary industry to restore the balance. In a weightier offering—'Elements of constructive economics'—Pratt argued that banking policy should be brought under closer partnership with the State. That is, the banking system should be deprived of the power to start cyclic movements, which it could not stop. Pratt was, however, adamant the banks should not engage in financing budget deficits (Ambrose Pratt Papers, State Library of Victoria, Box 327/6, Mss 6547 and Mss 6546).

he was 'imposing on their good nature'.[17] Nonetheless, The Group reassured Lyons that they had a duty to support him at a difficult time of economic adjustment, with Ricketson informing him that '[c]apital has a very definite responsibility at the present time to aid people like yourself who are fighting for the preservation of contracts and the honouring of our obligations'.[18]

Apart from opposing the policies of inflation and repudiation, The Group had earlier struck a discordant note with mainstream Australia by resisting the clause that domestic bondholders partake in the equality of sacrifice. Indeed their trenchant opposition to what Menzies called 'the breaking of contracts' initially hindered acceptance of the Premiers' Plan (Martin 1993:106). Lyons, however, in a rare show of strength, broke from his backers and Deputy Leader Latham and pushed for cuts in interest rates as part of the package (Hart 1971:134). That is, he sided with the economists on the issue of equal sacrifice. Lower interest rates, forthwith, took their rightful place as an integral part of the economic rehabilitation process. Despite this partial reverse, The Group continued to lobby for balanced budgets, the funding (retiring) of Treasury bills and the return to sterling.

Meanwhile, Lyons had to give thought to the formation of his cabinet. Apart from Bruce and Latham, the only other 'brain' in his cabinet was Charles Hawker.[19] While Lyons took the portfolio of Treasurer it was merely to lend an air of psychological assurance; Bruce, as Assistant Treasurer, carried that portfolio's duties. Bruce laid the foundations of the UAP's economic policy until replaced by Massy-Greene in July 1932.

With his genial personality and political acumen, Lyons' leadership was about reconciling conflicting requests from different interests. Rarely, however, did he have the stomach for a fight within cabinet. His biographer, Philip Hart, has described Lyons' modus operandi in policymaking as basically to rely on expert advice that met his philosophical framework and then, in turn, emphasise the non-partisan nature of the path taken. His main role appeared, to many, as merely to occupy office and let the private sector, coupled with the strictures of the Premiers' Plan, bring about recovery. In some ways, this interpretation was correct; as Coombs intimated to Shann, what Australia required after 1931 was not a Bruce or Theodore but a 'steady unimaginative soul'.[20] Lyons was their man; he was, as the leading businessman C. L. Baillieu put it, 'the man Australia had been waiting for'.[21] Lyons disavowed any gift for economics: 'I know little about finance,' he frequently intoned, implying perhaps that

---

17   Ricketson diary, 23 April 1932.
18   S. Ricketson to J. A. Lyons, n.d., Lyons Papers, NLA.
19   Ricketson diary extract, 23 April 1932.
20   Shann Papers, NLA, Box 4.
21   Ricketson diary extract, 17 March 1932.

he would solicit the wisdom of economists and others before making policy decisions.[22] He entertained a fetchingly simple view that equated government debt with personal debt. To be fair, Lyons had been broad-minded enough to accept the Melbourne school's plan of constructive deflation in September 1930. Lyons was also not content to leave economic salvation purely to market forces even if his government was ostensibly a 'private enterprise' one (Hart 1967:243). Indeed with Giblin and Brigden having his ear, and Bruce 'happy to be back in harness', Lyons began his administration by letting slip the comment that 'the credit of the Commonwealth would be utilised' to pursue public works.[23] The Group, along with a 'hard-shelled minority' in cabinet led by George Pearce, the Minister for Defence, feared Lyons coming under the influence of 'the economists' (cited in Hart 1967:264).[24] Sir John Higgins, too, was 'apprehensive' that Lyons would if not be overwhelmed by Bruce and Latham, become entangled by his 'close association [with] economists and Treasury officials [with]…the latter' falling for 'the line of least resistance'.[25] This, perhaps, was a veiled reference to the liberally inclined Sheehan who was years later to become Governor of the Commonwealth Bank.

A consummate chairman of the board, Lyons was, at the last resort, never prepared to breach cabinet solidarity or disappoint his backers by pandering to the advice of experts; nor for that matter was he prepared to leave the comforting confines of the Premiers' Plan or, just as importantly, brook the independence of the Commonwealth Bank on monetary and exchange matters. On assuming office, Lyons' first brief was to hold a premiers' conference—the first of many— to audit the progress of the state governments in winding back their budgetary deficits. They were struggling to rein in their deficits as the full force of the Depression hit. Lyons was, however, intent on placing the Commonwealth in a fiscally strong position from which it could browbeat state governments into submission.[26] In that regard, Shann and Copland might have triggered the new government's attention with a report entitled *The Australian Position*, exposing how some states had still not yet complied with the Arbitration Court's wage cut. Consequently, the Gibson-led revaluation of the currency made the burden of domestic costs on the export sector more onerous. Melville, in a delicate but nonetheless influential position at the Commonwealth Bank, summarised the report for Gibson's edification, agreeing with the authors that a policy to restore

---

22   *Commonwealth Parliamentary Debates*, vol. 128, 13 March 1931, p. 238.

23   Ricketson diary extract, 23 January 1932.

24   Senator Pearce had been instrumental in the destruction of Theodore's proposed *Commonwealth Bank Act* by coming up with the idea of inviting the 'grand old man' of Australian finance, Sir Robert Gibson, to be a witness before the bar of the Senate where in turn a consummate performance dammed the proposed legislation (Pearce 1951:188; Margaret Gibson, draft memoir of her father, Gibson Papers, Mss 10823, State Library of Victoria).

25   Ricketson diary extract, 28 January 1932.

26   L. F. Giblin to E. Giblin, 17 January 1932, Giblin Papers, NLA.

parity, irrespective of the prices of Australian exports, would have disastrous consequences (Booth 1988). To placate Gibson, Melville tactfully added that too much tampering with the exchange rate to adjust costs and prices would not compensate for a direct adjustment in domestic costs.[27]

The battle over the exchange rate

The Bourbons, it would appear, were not unique in learning nothing and forgetting nothing by their days of adversity.[28]

Near the end of 1931, a slight rise in export prices, together with a hefty increase in export production, replenished the London funds. This, in turn, sparked fears among economists that the economic bourbons were in the ascendant. It was another call to arms for the economists as unemployment reached 28 per cent by December. In an attempt to pre-empt efforts to restore parity with sterling, the economists issued a manifesto in November 1931 fortifying the case for further devaluation (Shann and Copland 1933:29–34). The signatories to the statement—basically the whole Australian economics fraternity, bar Melville, who was economic advisor to the Commonwealth Bank—warned that a return to par with sterling 'would, on present and prospective prices, gravely imperil the chances of economic recovery in the near future' (Shann and Copland 1933:86). The economists, together with Davidson, urged the Commonwealth Bank to fulfil its central bank duties by assuming responsibility for the exchange rate. As if on cue, the Commonwealth Bank, in one fell swoop, took responsibility for the exchange rate free from any sectional interest other than what preoccupied the bank board. While economists welcomed the sentiment and principle, they were horrified by the board's decision to revalue the currency.

Gibson's action could have been swayed partly by advice from Niemeyer. He had cabled Gibson in September 1931 'offering some thoughts and observations for reflection only' about Australia's exchange rate. An appreciation of the exchange, Niemeyer held, would 'liberate some of your finances now earmarked to meet budget deficits'.[29] Niemeyer had already advised the New Zealand government against devaluation on the basis that it would widen the budget deficit. This would, in turn, necessitate higher taxation falling on exporters or, even worse, the use of Treasury bills to bridge the shortfall in finances.[30]

---

27 'Notes on the Australian position December 31', 8 February 1932, Gibson Papers, State Library of Victoria.
28 Edward Shann in *The Statist*, 10 December 1931.
29 Sir O. Niemeyer to Sir R. G. Gibson, Coded telegram, 21 September 1931, RBA, GRG-33-3.
30 'The premiers' economy plan; further report by special committee', *National Bank of Australia Circular*, April 1932, pp. 11–12.

In their campaign to prevent any further appreciation, the economists[31] had been vindicated in their arguments by the findings of the Macmillan Committee in Britain that problems caused by fluctuations in the price level were now 'transcending in importance of any others of our time' (cited in Shann and Copland 1933:32). Davidson, with Shann's help, in a *Bank of New South Wales Circular*, analysed the Macmillan Committee's findings. They focused on the key problem facing Australia, which was not the exchange rate per se, but globally depressed price levels. Revaluation would intensify the burden of rural indebtedness and drive debtors to despair. Moreover, the safer option of keeping the exchange rate steady would, if export prices fell, spell further deflation and more adjustment of domestic costs. The logic did not convince Gibson even with Melville's protests within earshot. Tragically, it also did not register with Lyons or Latham until much later.

The economists—correctly as it turned out—held fears that Lyons would fall craven to the weight of Melbourne banking and financial interests. The Prime Minister had already stated that governments 'should not be entitled to dictate to those who are controlling the exchange what the rate should be' (cited in Learning 1934:407). Shann identified a Melbourne–Sydney rivalry over who had primacy in setting the exchange. Melbourne, then the financial and business hub of Australia, waged a tug of war with the Sydney banks and exporting interests over the setting of the exchange rate. Shann, who felt that the 1931 devaluation saved the country from a 'collapse of the whole financial system' (cited in Cain 1985:63), appealed to Hawker to do his utmost in maintaining the 'great improvement' in exchange rate management: 'Don't let the respectabilians and importers in Melbourne stampede you into an impossible attempt at deflation of prices by a further 20 per cent.'[32]

Just after the November 1931 statement was issued,[33] Copland told Latham that the build-up in London funds was the end result of a bumper season and would be further augmented by a renewal of private capital flowing back to Australia with the return of a conservative government. Copland asked Latham to encourage the Commonwealth Bank to exercise its role as a central bank and purchase the surplus funds of the Australian banks held in London. With export

---

31 Signatories to the *Memorandum on the Exchange Position* were Copland, Giblin, Shann and R. C. Mills from the University of Sydney. Melville did not sign because of his position with the Commonwealth Bank, but helped in its drafting.

32 E. Shann to C. Hawker, 3 December 1931, Hawker Papers, NLA.

33 Melville, at this stage, partly broke rank with the other economists—not just because of his position at the Commonwealth Bank, but because he felt there was danger of a lopsided boom in the exportable industries riding on a depreciated exchange rate and recovering prices. This fear rightly struck Shann as 'absurdly thin and pedantic' (E. Shann to C. A. S. Hawker, 18 January 1932, Hawker Papers, NLA). Despite Melville's rather premature prophecy, Shann reminded the Adelaide businessman W. Young that Melville's command of his brief and, in particular, the most appropriate setting for Australia's exchange were vastly superior to anything London opinion had to offer (E. Shann to W. G. Young, 17 February 1932, BNSW, A-53-409).

prices subdued, revaluation would have farmers in despair over the board's decision. Copland asked Latham to make a statement that his party was against 'unnecessary deflation'—that is, it would not allow the exchange to appreciate. If this were done it would enshrine the new exchange rate policy until overseas prices intervened.[34] It was to no avail. This, and subsequent behaviour by Latham, drew Copland's lasting bile that '[h]e has never been prepared to admit that economic policy as such can do very much'.[35] Davidson also did not get much purchase from Latham when he enclosed an article by Keynes that spoke of the precipice of outright deflation the world economy was perched on.[36] Somewhat sinisterly, the article, 'The consequences to the banks of the collapse of money values', published in London newspapers in August 1931, had not been reproduced in the local press because of the political climate (Cain 1985:63; Keynes 1931:150–8). Davidson also made sure that Lyons received Keynes's article with the accompanying plea not to 'press high-handed and thoughtless measures of restoring parity'.[37] His bank released a statement on the dangers of revaluation.[38] Despite the lobbying, the economists' advice went unheeded and the prospects for enlightened economic policy receded. Another opportunity presented itself when Lyons established an expert committee to deal with the worsening economic climate. After the rebuff on the exchange rate only months earlier, economists must have felt heartened that their expertise and input were still in demand. Indeed, with Copland and Wickens incapacitated from overwork, Wood mused, 'I wonder whether Governments will ever realise the necessity of keeping a sufficient staff of scientific advisers against the day when adversity cometh.'[39] It was a salient point.

At the official level, the Commonwealth Bank had Melville on its staff while the Treasury had its first graduate economist even if Wilson was employed as an assistant to Giblin, the Acting Commonwealth Statistician. This internalisation of economic expertise was barely enough for Casey, a new and energetic member of the government, who told his London confidant and mentor, Maurice Hankey, that Australia needed a body similar to Britain's Economic Advisory Council.[40] Such a body was better than having to 'depend upon sporadic and occasional advice by financial and economic experts hurriedly drawn together'.[41] Casey envisaged the body independently advising on the exchange rate. The idea of

---

34 D. B. Copland to J. Latham, 30 November 1931, Latham Papers, NLA.
35 D. B. Copland to H. Gepp, 5 November 1934, UMA FECC, Box 23.
36 A. C. Davidson to J. Latham, 23 December 1931, Latham Papers, NLA.
37 A. C. Davidson to J. Lyons, 23 December 1931, Lyons Papers, NLA.
38 'Statement on the exchange', 11 November 1931, BNSW, A. C. Davidson Papers, N2/71.
39 G. L. Wood to M. H. Baillieu, 10 March 1932, UMA FECC, Box 13. Three young, promising economists—J. K. Gifford, E. R. Walker and H. C. Coombs—had gone abroad to undertake theses with some policy bearing on the Depression's impact on Australia. Two Tasmanian-born economists, Arthur Smithies (Oxford) and Keith Isles (London School of Economics), were already overseas.
40 *CPD Hansard*, 1255, 13 October 1932.
41 *Cairns Post*, 28 October 1932.

an agency of independent economic advice became a hobbyhorse of Casey's though he was joined in it by an assortment of identities ranging from R. F. Irvine to Herbert Gepp. In Niemeyer-like tones, Casey went on and bemoaned to Hankey that '[o]ur Parliament…is a totally inadequate body to discuss economic problems, and our Government Departments are much less able than yours to express themselves on this type of subject'. Casey went on to talk about the magnitude of Australia's problems then extant, including 'our most inadequate civil service', 'our out of balance economy as between town and country' and 'our queer economic ideas about tariffs and bounties'. He closed, inimitably capturing the eternal Australian economic predicament: 'We are swung about, like a tractor after a motor car, at the tail of the world's price levels.'[42]

The *Wallace Bruce Report*

Very quickly an air of economic desperation encircled the new Lyons government. It impelled Giblin to think it time for a 'bold—perhaps desperate—policy to kick things together'. He sounded out Lyons, whose cabinet was already showing signs of division about the direction of economic policy.[43] Possibly swayed by Giblin's advice to do 'something' about mounting unemployment, Lyons commissioned a group of businessmen and economists in March 1932 to hurriedly make a preliminary survey of the economic problem and, in doing so, review the appropriateness of the Premiers' Plan. This part of the chapter discusses the intellectual makings of the subsequent report and its reception.

Melville, Shann and Giblin, in that order and weight, drew up the terms of reference for the inquiry.[44] They were: 'to formulate a long run policy with the aim of maintaining and expanding both the primary and secondary industries; and to explore the possibility of immediate action to tide over the period which must elapse before results can be expected from the long range policy.' The terms of reference were similar to the tasks set before the short-lived Secretariat on Employment and Production set up by Scullin and the premiers in August 1931. The secretariat's mission had been to formulate ways of increasing employment— something the Premiers' Plan was never intended to address.[45] At that forum, Giblin and Dyason, arguing without much theoretical conviction other than pragmatism, pressed the authorities with the need for more public works, or reflation, to stem the alarming rise in unemployment (Wilson 1951:198).

---

42 R. G. Casey to M. Hankey, 30 March 1932, Hankey Papers, Churchill College.
43 L. F. Giblin to E. Giblin, 9 March 1932, Giblin Papers, NLA.
44 E. Shann to J. La Nauze, 11 April 1932, La Nauze Papers, NLA.
45 *Employment and Production: Report to the Premiers' Conference by the Secretariat Committee*, 3 September 1931 (cited in Cain 1983:209).

The other economist appointed to the Wallace Bruce Committee was Mills, who replaced Copland, who had fallen ill in New Zealand. An apprehensive Giblin told his wife that, with Mills's 'conservative instincts', the prospects of a 'positive policy'—that is, public works and credit expansion—were decidedly poor. Copland's absence, however, did not significantly affect the bearing of the committee's findings and he supported their recommendations (Cain 1985:2–3). Cain (1985:4) suggests, in fact, that Copland's report on New Zealand economic adjustment exerted a strong impact on the *Wallace Bruce Report*. Giblin, while more idiosyncratic than the rest of his colleagues, was adamant that its findings be strong and unanimous to help Lyons overcome the 'hard-shelled' cabinet minority demanding orthodox finance.[46]

While the Chairman of the Committee, Sir Wallace Bruce, was, along with G. S. Colmen, a businessman sympathetic to economic discourse, the report was, as Melville recalls, 'very much an economists' show'.[47] Shann, who laboured tirelessly over the committee's drafts, optimistically told a university colleague: 'We economists—an inveterately hopeful band—are doing our best to push the governments into a sound monetary policy' (cited in Alexander 1963:153).

He told his protégé, John La Nauze, that he hoped the report would convince the thinking public, adding that 'the Treasury officials whom we have to use as a medium of transmission to Premiers are as snake-headed deflationists as the bankers'.[48] Despite Shann drafting much of the report, its genus was largely concocted by Melville. Giblin, Melville and Shann gave an in-camera briefing of their findings to leading members of the government at Keith Murdoch's house (Hart 1967). It made for sombre listening.

Analysis

With primary product prices on international markets falling a further 15 per cent since November 1931, Australia's fundamental economic problem—export prices falling below the costs of production—had become acute. Australia was just 'hanging on' even with good seasons and efficiencies in production.[49] Since a general recovery of employment could, given the nature of the economy, come only by way of net exports, the long-term plan had to focus on a reduction of costs since a recovery in export prices was now wishful thinking. To expedite this, the committee settled for a threefold strategy that embraced a further devaluation, compensatory tariff cuts and enforcing the 1931 wage cut. Copland (1937a:409) labelled it 'the middle course' between continued deflation and devaluation of

---

46   L. F. Giblin to E. Giblin, 24 March 1931, Giblin Papers, NLA.
47   Melville, TRC 182, NLA, p. 35.
48   E. Shann to J. La Nauze, 14 April 1932, La Nauze Papers, NLA.
49   G. L. Wood to W. S. Robinson, 21 April 1932, UMA FECC, Box 14.

the currency. Attracted by the idea of exchange rate manipulation, Melville felt devaluation contained its 'own safeguards' since, by penalising governments and importers by forgoing revenue, it prevented the mechanism from being overly abused.[50] Melville also wanted the devaluation executed at a time when the London balances were healthy; to do otherwise would be perceived as a sign of weakness. Their recommendations came also with the reminder that budgetary deficits still be reduced in accordance with the Premiers' Plan. Indeed the committee reiterated that there could be no plan to relieve unemployment until deficits, in the name of business confidence, were progressively reduced. In a key paragraph, the committee assimilated Theodore's line that budgetary improvement was, however, as much a function as a condition of recovery (Cain 1985:11).

The blended formula was, in short, a reprise of the Premiers' Plan strategy with the three measures deemed interdependent and inseparable.[51] The stress was to further improve Australia's relative cost structure so that the nation would be well placed to ride any recovery in export prices (Cain 1985:9). The report also recommended that state parliaments make the necessary amendments to allow arbitration courts and wage boards to fix wages in line with economic circumstances. The economists, however, generally eschewed bridging the gap between export costs and prices by solely resorting to cutting cost levels since this would impair financial stability and, in turn, prevent budgetary equilibrium from being realised. Likewise, electing to let the exchange rate carry the whole burden of adjustment might trigger capital flight. The most revolutionary proposal was not just devaluation but having the Commonwealth Bank Board manage the exchange rate according to economic circumstances and thereby making it an instrument of economic policy. For Melville, this was a calculated risk since he hitherto felt that rational management of the exchange rate required authorities to be not only omniscient, but omnipotent.[52]

Informed by the analytical framework of Keynes's *Treatise*, the committee's thinking on devaluation also had an underlying macroeconomic rationale. It would allow more domestic reflation to be contemplated but only after the relative cost adjustment had been undertaken (Cain 1985:12; Cornish 1993b:12). That is, more public investment or public works would be attempted to counter the drag of excess savings lying idle in bank vaults. This proposal was similar to one of the expedients Keynes presented before the Macmillan Committee in

---

50   L. G. Melville to C. A. S. Hawker, 9 May 1932, RBA, GCM-35-1.
51   An assured Copland, having just recovered from a bout of illness that saw him confined to bed, told the editor of a news magazine that '[t]he Experts' report is curiously enough a restatement of Chapter 6 of my book on *Credit and Currency* control. When this Chapter was first written in 1930 it caused rather a stir among the good folk of Melbourne and the inner councils of the UAP—the middle course is the very one I recommend Australia should take' (D. B. Copland to E. Knox, 16 April 1932, UMA FECC, Box 17).
52   L. G. Melville to E. Shann, 30 November 1931, Shann Papers, NLA.

March 1930 to pull Britain out of the slump. The higher activity and devaluation would prevent the price level from slipping due to lower wage levels. The Australian economy would emerge, then, with steadier prices together with lower real wages and restored profit margins. It was Melville who articulated this strategy. Shann saw some hope of cranking up capital expenditure, which would augment, in turn, the spending power of consumers and thereby stabilise business confidence. It would also allow the orderly retirement of the formidable total of Treasury bills then extant. Giblin wanted an increase in public works irrespective of devaluation. His colleagues felt this might reignite Australia's trade deficit and bring back the spectre of default that had only just been faced down.[53]

Reaction

Within days of the report being released, the economists came under fire from many quarters. As Giblin intimated to Keynes, there had to be something in the report since '[b]anks, Chambers of Commerce, Trades Hall and Mr Lang abuse it in terms of equal intensity'.[54] A month before the report's release, Giblin, working behind the scenes, tried to solicit favourable press treatment for the report by getting on side Keith Murdoch, who, while equivocal, agreed that 'something' was needed and that the *Experts' Report* was the 'only plan in the field'.[55]

Much criticism revolved around the clause to lower money wages to give effect to the 10 per cent real wage initially prescribed by the Arbitration Court. At the premiers' conference held to discuss the report, Premier Lang and the Acting Premier of Victoria, Tom Tunnecliffe, denounced it as an attack on the working man. The West Australian Labor Opposition Leader, Collier, chanced his arm against the economists 'and all their works' even before a copy of the report reached Perth.[56] Even the Acting Vice-Chancellor of the University of Western Australia reproached Shann and the other economists' 'obsession' with wages:

---

53 There were other staunch defenders of the parity besides Gibson and the Commonwealth Bank Board. B. Latham, the actuary of the Commonwealth Bank and a confidant of Ricketson's, told the stockbroker that he was 'distrustful of the professional economist' with his belief that the only cure for Australia 'is to live within her income' (Ricketson diary extract, 28 January 1932). Melville's act of wanting to tread carefully within the bank came unstuck with the release of the *Experts' Report*. Gibson disallowed Melville from going to the Imperial Conference until the Governor of the Bank, Riddle, specifically requested Melville accompany him to Ottawa. Casey informed Sir Henry Battersbee of the Dominion's Office to keep an eye out for Melville, who was 'as near a real winner in the way of an economist as we have produced' (R. G. Casey to Sir H. Battersbee, 10 June 1932, Hankey Papers, Churchill College).
54 L. F. Giblin to J. M. Keynes, 19 April 1932, KPKC, CO/2/188.
55 L. F. Giblin to E. Giblin, 18 April 1932, Giblin Papers, NLA.
56 'Blind critics, and worse', *Adelaide Advertiser*, 22 April 1932. A more highly pitched critique of the report came from Senator Sir Hal Colebatch, who assailed the economists for their penchant to 'fix' wages, the exchange rate and other economic variables as distinct from letting the market rule ('Economists' plan; a criticism: currency, wages and trade', *SMH*, 26 April 1932).

'Why not lift your nose from its persistent sniffing at wages and let us know what you think of the money root of our problems?' (Alexander 1963:153). A mortified Shann, already acutely sensitive about uninformed attacks on the economists, gave a riposte:

> [Y]ou are a little unjust to the economists concerning interest. We did have the 'guts'—your phrase—to press the proposal of a cut in fixed money charges in the teeth of the fiercest opposition from Tories and 'mugwumps'…The Australian economists are not 'concentrating on wages' and have not done so in any conference I have attended. (Cited in Alexander 1963:154)

More effective censure of the committee's report came from a statement issued by Gibson on 20 April 1932, which quelled speculation about the exchange by stating that the board would not be swayed by 'sectional interests' in its decision making; by sectional interests, Gibson meant economists and the self-seeking Davidson. In a sense, the *Wallace Bruce Report* had merely intensified the exchange rate struggle between Davidson, who 'talks too much', and Gibson, 'who understands little and talks less'.[57] Gibson did 'talk' but to bankers more than anyone. The bank board, moreover, rather disingenuously eschewed any notion of directing economic policy even though Gibson had told Lyons in January 1932 that the exchange rate was 'more than a mere banking question and indeed impinges on national policy' (cited in Cain 1985:144).

A week before Gibson's statement, H. T. Armitage, Deputy Governor of the Commonwealth Bank, assured Ricketson that 'their people' would not be rushed into a quick decision about devaluation. Echoing the sentiments of private bankers, Armitage reminded Ricketson that the views of the 'professors' were 'academic' in the sense that their ideas were put forward without any notion of profit on the matter.[58] Nonetheless, Gibson did not take the economists' recommendations lightly. On the day the report was released, he cabled to Montagu Norman the committee's findings, warning that if the economists' views prevailed there would be devaluation irrespective of Australia's foreign reserves.[59] While economists were surprised by Gibson's intransigence, they did not help their cause by invoking the convention that the bank board remain free 'from both the fact and the fear of political control' in its deliberations (Shann and Copland 1933:97–8). Davidson alluded to this likely problem in a cable to Robinson detailing the committee's recommendations but doubting whether the bank board had the 'knowledge and grasp of situation' sufficient to enable them to act wisely.[60] Perhaps the truth was that Davidson and the economists were,

---

57   G. Wood to W. S. Robinson, 21 April 1932, UMA FECC, Box 14.
58   Ricketson diary extract, 13 April 1932.
59   R. Gibson to Sir M. Norman, Cable, 20 April 1932, BE, G1/276.
60   A. C. Davidson to D. Geddie, Cablegram, 16 April 1932, BNSW, GM 302/569.

given the institutional and constitutional constraints facing them, seeking a *deus ex cathedra* to undermine Gibson's campaign for revaluation. The higher authority sought was the opinion of the City.

Lyons and Bruce initially welcomed the report (Shann and Copland 1933:96; Hart 1967:268). Bruce, in particular, facing the prospect of half a million unemployed before him, was, according to Bertram Stevens, 'greatly influenced by the recommendations of the Theorists'.[61] Lyons, the one man who had the power to direct Gibson on the exchange rate, elected to sit on his hands for fear of antagonising his cabinet; the experts' vision proved larger than his own ambition. Bruce, too, cooled in his support for the economists' argument as he looked forward to beginning duties as the High Commissioner in London.

The committee's report was a 'political Godsend' for Lyons. It was critical of Lang for not reducing wages in New South Wales and reaffirmed faith in private enterprise and abrogated the federal government from taking responsibility for economic policy; that should lie with the state wage tribunals, the Loan Council and the Commonwealth Bank (Cain 1985:13–14). The Lyons government had, in any case, an escape clause from the committee's findings by supinely upholding the convention that matters of exchange deliberation remained with the bank board. The board, however, was asked to take into consideration the effect on the economy—internally and externally—of their policy deliberations. On reflection, it appears that Gibson had persuaded Lyons that preserving Australia's financial architecture and international standing was a greater concern than domestic economic activity. Another key consideration was that the economy was beginning to recover, in any case, from the mixture of unintentional expansion from the floating debt coupled with the stimulus of reduced money costs (Walker 1933a:209). Nonetheless, as Schedvin pointed out, the failure to devalue was a major policy error and lengthened Australia's tenure within depression. As it was, the premiers' conference summoned to discuss the committee's report quickly fell into stalemate because Lyons refused to arrange a loan program until the recalcitrant states committed themselves to the report, particularly the need to contain deficits and enforcing the 1931 wage cut. The conference afforded Lang a last opportunity to attack the 'professors' and 'experts' for being inconsistent in having reversed their views about the relationship between the budget and the economy (Cain 1985:35–6). There was a general consensus at the conference that 'economy alone is not the solution'.[62] That is, bearing down on expenditure would merely worsen the prospects of achieving budgetary balance. Lang, together with Acting Premier Tunnecliffe from Victoria, took the economists to task for excluding overseas rentiers from making any sacrifice. Despite the political stalemate, Gibson had, in fact, made

---

61 Ricketson diary extract, 11 April 1932.
62 *CPD Hansard*, 1422, 20 October 1932.

up the government's mind for them. It was a major setback for the economists, but one they were not readily prepared to accept. Their greatest surprise, though, was to find the empire's most eminent economist, J. M. Keynes, playing a key role in undermining their case.

Keynes and Australia

Keynes had always taken an abiding interest in Australia's fortunes, triggered by intellectual curiosity and his private financial portfolio advice. In 1929, he observed how Australia was 'gravely embarrassed' by the fall in the price of their staple exports and was craven to borrow at 'whatever rate lenders demand of them' (cited in Markwell 1985:13; Cornish 1993b:17). At one stage, Keynes even advised against subscribing to Australian loan issues (Gilbert 1973:79).[63]

Having a pecuniary interest in Australian securities, Keynes was in regular contact with two of its leading businessmen, Claude Baillieu and W. S. Robinson, and the two economists, Giblin and Copland, on academic and economic policy matters. There was, in addition, an abiding interest in how a semi-industrialised, rural-based economy could extricate itself from serious economic and financial difficulties. In 1930, Lyons had urged the London-bound Scullin to contact Keynes as he had correctly predicted that the storm centre of the early stages of the Depression would fall on primary good-exporting, debt-laden countries such as Australia. Like other British economists, Keynes was struck that Australian counterparts had been uncommonly influential in the running of their country's economic affairs (Goodwin 1974:235).

Such was Keynes's prestige in Australia that, at one point, Baillieu, Robinson and Keith Murdoch hatched an extraordinary plan to bring him out to Australia for a study tour, writing exclusively for Murdoch's newspapers—for the princely fee of £2500. For six months, Keynes had provided political and economic briefings for Robinson's Collins House group.[64] Oswald Falk, one of Keynes's business associates, relayed the proposal to him.[65] It drew an immediate response. He told his wife, Lydia Lopokova, 'I have an invitation to go to Australia for six months for a fee of £2,500 and all expenses. I shall refuse.'[66]

The counterfactual 'What if?' aspect to this would prove intriguing. One could safely argue that Keynes's advice—the tenor of which we know—would have

---

63 It might be argued that Keynes's views of Australian economic policy were coloured by his advice to friends on the holding of Australian bonds. The equivalent to that line of thought was that since Sir Robert Gibson banked with the National Bank of Australasia he was attendant to the trading banks' views on monetary policy.

64 'JMK and self', W. S. Robinson Papers, UMA FECC, 101/70/file 94, Box 5.

65 O. Falk to J. M. Keynes, 17 March 1932, KPKC.

66 J. M. Keynes to L. Lopokova, 17 March 1932, KPKC.

given him a less frosty reception than that meted out to Niemeyer. Perhaps, too, a greater appreciation of the local facts might have led Keynes to alter his at times rather patronising view of Australia's economic options in 1932. In a sense, Keynes did 'come' to Australia, albeit in the form of an incisive, though lopsided review of the *Wallace Bruce Report*. It came, too, at one-tenth of the cost to the Murdoch chain of newspapers.[67] Apart from also receiving a handwritten summary of the committee's findings from Robinson,[68] Keynes received Davidson's version of the committee's findings,[69] which he found 'very useful'.[70]

The report of the Australian experts

Keynes, as always, wrote his draft quickly but this commission caused him uncharacteristic unease. In enclosing a draft for comment, Keynes admitted to Baillieu that it was 'a responsible task writing it' and it was a struggle 'to strike just the right note'.[71] Keynes's review was dispatched on 25 May 1932 and splashed over the front pages of the *Melbourne Herald* on 27 June when the *Wallace Bruce Report* was released.

The *Report of the Experts' Committee*, as Keynes's précis became known, was an enigmatic account that drew many reviews, the most incisive being Cain's (1985), Markwell's (1985) and Turnell's (1999). While in some ways the memorandum had an 'all things to all men' quality, the general tenor was unmistakably clear— namely, that the Australian (and New Zealand) economists

> are all disposed to be a little too drastic and to attempt to cure troubles that are really incurable so long as the existing international environment persists. The object should be rather to hold the situation than to try and force through impracticable adjustments upon wages and the exchange rate and run the risk in the process of social upheaval.[72]

Keynes (1982b:95) was therefore extremely reluctant to support the committee's recommendation for a further devaluation because he felt that the level of prices countenanced was not 'a practical working hypothesis'—that is, it was too pessimistic and quite unsustainable given the structure of national and international indebtedness. Keynes felt that the proposed action would be the act, therefore, of a bad neighbour and instead of promoting international

---

67 C. L. Baillieu to J. M. Keynes, 7 April 1932, KPKC.
68 W. S. Robinson to J. M. Keynes, 16 April 1932, KPKC.
69 A. C. Davidson to J. M. Keynes, Cablegram, 16 April 1932, KPKC.
70 Summary of *Wallace Bruce Report* in KPKC, A32/1/244. The visiting Latham dined with Keynes and others on the evening of 12 April 1932. Latham might have informed Keynes about Australian political developments including the Lang factor.
71 J. M. Keynes to C. L. Baillieu, KPKC, A/32/1.
72 J. M. Keynes to H. Belshaw, 24 May 1932, KPKC, L/32/113.

cooperation would engender more competitive devaluations. The only devaluation Keynes (1982b:83) was prepared to accept was of sterling, which would lighten Australia's debt and give the global economy a fillip. Keynes also derided the option of further reducing money wages on practical and theoretical grounds. He suggested that further resort to cutting money wages would, in the absence of a new source of fresh purchasing power, be the case when 'prices are related to costs after the same fashion as a tail is to a cat' (Keynes 1982b:99). Devaluation, in any case, would achieve the same outcome. As Colin Clark later recalled, this observation on wage cuts led Keynes to make the only reference to Australia in *The General Theory*, citing that attempts to adjust wages to prices over the business cycle would prove futile. In concluding, Keynes delicately chided his Australian colleagues:

> If, therefore, I were an Australian economist advising Mr Lyons today, I should be decidedly moderate in my view. I should recommend him to ride his difficult and suffering steed with as light a rein as he dare. I should not press for heroic measures. It is a time to chastise gently. Moreover, I should have sufficient confidence to take this line, precisely because Australia has done so much already, and has been relatively so successful in her programme of necessary adjustment—if only, in spite of disappointments, she could, by comparison with the state of others, know it! There is more chance of improving the profitableness of business by fostering enterprise and by such measures as public works than by a further pressure on money-wages or further forcing of exports. The problems of the Budget and of Unemployment are more pressing than that of the Balance of Trade. (Shann and Copland 1933)

While Copland strangely likened Keynes's words to 'a breath of warm, fresh air', the latter was urging his Australian colleagues to lobby for more domestic stimulation regardless of the external account (Markwell 1985:18–20). Copland and Shann (1933:xiii) issued a statement defending the position of the economists on the Wallace Bruce Committee, declaring that 'we are already doing all the things Mr Keynes recommends as much as courage and prudence allows. But they form parts of a policy the central principle of which is and must be the restoration of balanced budgets as the chief test of our success in retaining economic control.'

Giblin begged to publicly differ with Keynes on the devaluation option.[73] He argued that Keynes would be unaware that Australia's trade surplus came by dint of exports having risen due to two exceptionally favourable seasons. In more normal times, however, Australia would need the insurance of a devaluation to generate the trade surplus necessary to meet her external obligations.

---

73 *The Herald*, 27 June 1932.

In private correspondence with Keynes, Giblin advised that his main grievance with the committee was not over the exchange rate but over their reluctance to unequivocally sanction public works.[74] On this, of course, Giblin shared the same view as Keynes though his theoretical case was not as well grounded. Feeling isolated alongside his three colleagues, Giblin intimated to Keynes the inner agenda of the committee had been 'too pre-occupied with the narrowness of the bank and financial people' to the extent that the case for immediate public works to stem the growing rates of unemployment was deemed secondary to that of restoring business confidence. Like Keynes, Giblin felt that the danger of social dislocation from high unemployment should have been given equal billing. Consequently, on signing the report, albeit 'with some hesitation', Giblin issued a private letter to Lyons urging some 'immediate action...be taken to relieve the strain, until the long term policy bears fruit'.[75] His ideas had antecedents in the Scullin-appointed Secretariat of Unemployment, which had been commissioned with identifying feasible, remunerative public works to alleviate unemployment.[76] Giblin's report concluded that 'artificial methods of creating credit' to the tune of £18 million, a la Theodore, be raised to maintain employment on public works.[77] Predictably, the secretariat's report, released in September 1931, was criticised for embracing the 1920s' philosophy of spending for development.

While the Wallace Bruce Committee, for its part, could not identify any 'profitable' short-term public works, Giblin, using a modification of his own multiplier analysis—not Kahn's, of which he was unaware—estimated that a £20m public works program, financed by Treasury bills, would generate employment for 100 000 workers provided the original expenditure continued (Cain 1985:26).[78] The proposed spending, Giblin reminded Lyons, would be not only for 'tiding over a limited period' until export prices recovered, it would be not so large as to endanger business confidence or invoke the wrath of the Commonwealth Bank Board over its method of financing and disbursement (Cain 1985:27). In signing off his missive, Giblin would have known that his proposal was in vain since Lyons' cabinet was increasingly becoming unreceptive to unorthodox advice.[79] Keynes signalled his approval of Giblin's proposal and reminded him that trying to get a commercial return on the projects should be relaxed in the circumstances (Cain 1985:28).

---

74   L. F. Giblin to J. M. Keynes, 19 April 1932, KPKC, Co/2/187-8.
75   L. F. Giblin to J. A. Lyons, 13 April 1932, KPKC, Co/2/189.
76   Hytten 1971, pg. 64
77   Ibid. p. 65.
78   Giblin's stance might have been contemporaneously fortified by a memorandum on unemployment prepared for the cabinet of the Victorian government by former DMC officials, Gunn and Gepp, which posited that the problem would get markedly worse since business enterprise was unprofitable and economic despair widespread ('Memorandum on unemployment', H. Gepp and J. Gunn, 30 March 1932, UMA FECC, Box 15).
79   L. F. Giblin to E. Giblin, 9 March 1932, and 24 March 1932, Giblin Papers, NLA.

Apart from Gibson's intransigence on the exchange rate, and Lyons' refusal to have the Commonwealth government instruct the bank board, Melville recalls that what also helped to sink the committee's report was Keynes's refusal to support a further devaluation (Melville 1992:671). Melville recalls that the Commonwealth government was denied, therefore, the latitude to practise public sector stimulation by Keynes's reluctance to support devaluation.[80] Keynes's qualified support elsewhere for an increase in public expenditure—a second-best solution in the Australian case—proved of little consolation. While Schedvin (1970) and Clark (1974b, 1981b) point out that Australian economists were deflationary in their advice during this period, they rarely point out that Keynes's one and only profound intervention in interwar Australian economic affairs helped Gibson face down the economists. The bank board's trenchant opposition to palliative public works schemes and devaluation meant that the *Wallace Bruce Report* 'fell between two stools' (McTaggart 1992:672).

While Keynes agreed with Giblin that public works be pushed 'to the limits of prudence', neither Giblin's correspondence nor the full, unabridged report he subsequently received enticed Keynes to revise the pitch of his original article. In correspondence with Giblin, Keynes, while acknowledging that there were anomalies between the states in wage levels, took the opportunity to demonstrate, as he had told Horace Belshaw, the New Zealand economist, that they were inclined 'to be too drastic and to attempt what may be socially impossible'.[81] Mulling over this afterwards, Keynes became even more adamant, telling Baillieu that the Wallace Bruce Committee 'is inclined to be too drastic and is aiming at adjustments which are humanly impossible for Australia' (Keynes 1982b:100–1). Keynes now also disputed the commission's figure work over export costs and prices thereby undermining—again—the arguments for devaluation. Keynes felt that artificially restoring prosperity to wool exporters in the then abnormal conditions was 'unnecessary and altogether impracticable'.[82] Before Giblin had a chance to reply, Keynes recycled his doubts about the committee's statistics and recommendations on further relative adjustment, telling Baillieu he found them 'too simpliste'.[83] The letter was reproduced in the Melbourne *Herald*.[84]

If economists were disappointed by Keynes's foray into Australian economic policymaking, they did not readily show it. They had every right, because as Cain (1985:17–20) cogently demonstrates, Keynes had overlooked certain key policy aspects, dismissed further relative cost improvements and been

---

80   Melville, TRC 182, NLA, p. 25.
81   J. M. Keynes to L. F. Giblin, 2 June 1932, KPKC, CO/2/195.
82   Ibid. Meanwhile, Shann and Melville, heading home from the Ottawa conference via London, were to be sorely disappointed when told by Keynes and Hawtrey, inter alia, the same advice—namely, that Australia should focus on achieving internal equilibrium rather than fussing over exchange rates (Holder 1970:744).
83   J. M. Keynes to C. Baillieu, 24 May 1932, and C. Baillieu to J. M. Keynes, 2 June 1932, KPKC, A/32/1/293.
84   'Production costs: Mr Keynes doubts 20 per cent gap', *The Herald*, 5 July 1932.

selective and sometimes self-serving in his arguments. He had, moreover, been disarmingly glib about Australia's economic problems, arguing that, in some respects, Australia was in better shape than other countries and could therefore spend more on public works (Cain 1985:29). In private correspondence, Giblin pursued Keynes on this, pointing out the truly marginal existence of many rural exporters (Cain 1985:31). Nonetheless, the thrust of Keynes's remarks stuck. In this respect, several authors besides Schedvin—namely, David Clark (1976), Colin Clark (1958), and Hancock (1972)—have condemned Australian economists for their position at this time.

These reviewers, however, tend to overlook, as Keynes did, the delicate and problematic circumstances confronting the Australian economy. First and foremost, there was the direct relationship between public spending and the deficit on the external account (Cain 1985:17–18). Second, the guilt and waste of a prodigal past hung in the air. Copland felt that 'Australian governments had... shot their bolts before 1930 and so were in no position for bold initiatives' (Cain 1980:17). That is, Australian governments had exhausted their credit of public borrowing to exercise what Keynes in the *Treatise* called 'nature's remedy' to prevent business losses in a slump (Bland and Mills 1931). Third, greater public spending at this stage would have upset the deficit-reduction strategy enshrined in the Premiers' Plan, which was, in turn, fostering business confidence. Keynes completely overlooked this aspect, whereas the Australian economists—already mindful of the concern the huge amount of Treasury bills was causing the authorities—did not (Cain 1985:20). Latter-day critics of Australian economists also seem unaware of Keynes's earlier praise of their predecessors' involvement in public policy, especially the line Copland and Giblin took.[85] Keynes (1982b), for instance, spoke of being 'intensely sympathetic' to the report's 'general method of approach'. By that he meant the strategy of relative cost adjustment to improve Australia's competitive position. He praised Australian efforts in that regard and acknowledged the use of the 'National Treaty' expedient of an across-the-board cut in costs and debts, which he had raised before the Macmillan Committee.

Nonetheless, Keynes's review of the *Wallace Bruce Report* must have exasperated the Australian economists. They would have agreed with Keynes's (1982b:94) confession at the start of his commentary that '[i]t is a rash thing to write from a great distance on a matter which demands practical judgement more than theory'. While he would not have concurred, Keynes was barging in on an applied and specific economic problem that Australian economists probably knew best how to deal with. It was, however, a different matter on theory. As Cairncross (1996:88) notes, Keynes's infuriating genius was that he would modify his ideas with changing circumstances. Keynes's review of the *Expert's Report*

---

85   J. M. Keynes to C. L. Baillieu, 14 July 1932, KCKP, A/32/1/307.

was a classic case, therefore, of having to discern and identify the changing nature of his ideas as he shifted position on theory and policy. And here the Australian economists were lagging behind. Keynes felt that the reliance on monetary measures such as interest rates and exchange rates to drive a wedge between costs and prices in a bid to revive economic activity was becoming ineffective and outmoded; something bolder, such as public expenditure, was needed to jolt the economy into expansion. In terms of theoretical development, Keynes was at a crossroads, moving in early 1932 from one Marshallian analysis of an economic system in which the *quaesitium* was price changes to one in which it was the change in quantities (Turnell 1999:400).

Aftermath

In subsequent correspondence with Giblin, Keynes returned to the vexed issue of devaluation, arguing that it would 'not be very material' and, in any case, would merely compound the downward pressure on Australia's export prices. This translated into diminishing the sterling or gold equivalent of Australia's exports. In any case, too much rural production for export was hindering the longed-for recovery in export prices. Keynes went on to concede that if Giblin's 'rather pessimistic prognostications' about Australian export prices in the future came to pass, 'it will in effect be impossible for Australia to meet her London charges in a season of only normal productivity. It is no good attempting the hopeless task of reaching adjustment on the basis of meeting your London charges without any rise in the price of your exports.'[86]

In other words, under those trying circumstances, Keynes saw no other option but for Australia to default on her overseas commitments. This startling admission by Keynes was kept from public consumption; Bruce, however, would use the threat of default to force London to embark on a more expansionary monetary policy to the benefit of the dominions (Turnell 1999). Even Giblin was taken aback by Keynes's talk of default. Later, however, after drafting a document, 'The burden of external debt', for official edification, he assimilated Keynes's global view of the problem at hand—namely, that 'the effect of the Australian effort to preserve external solvency must have been to intensify and prolong the depression'. By that Giblin referred to Australia cutting its imports by half and physically increasing its rural exports by one-third.[87] By the end of 1932, Giblin told Melville:

> If every debtor nation strives to meet its foreign obligations and succeeds—whether by exchange or tariffs, or by reducing internal costs and expanding exports—then the result is going to be the further

---

86   J. M. Keynes to L. F. Giblin, 31 August 1932, KCKP, Co/2/214.
87   'Memorandum no 6, the burden of external debt', n.d, Giblin Collection, UMA FECC, Box 213.

drying up of trade, further falls in price and general intensification of the depression. I fancy a condition precedent to recovery is a scaling down of all internal debt...so I should be inclined to use the higher exchange rate as an argument for debt readjustment in the first place— and I'm not sure that I would not default rather than raise the exchange in the last resort.[88]

Melville would tend to agree with this prognosis following the lack of resolve by Britain at the Ottawa talks to activate a concerted monetary expansion that would assist indebted commodity-exporting countries such as Australia. He told Senator Colebatch that Britain's refusal to engage in such action forced Australia to reconsider devaluation or 'a more direct method of cutting debts' (cited in Turnell 1999:65).

Bruce's departure to London removed a player receptive to expansionist thinking, though Davidson had noticed that he was more interested 'with the body of London opinion which takes a deflationary view of the economic problems confronting Australia' (cited in Cain 1985:59). His replacement as Assistant Treasurer, Senator Massy-Greene, was a hard-nosed believer in orthodoxy with a 'great natural gift' for finance (Kemp 1964). Giblin felt the new appointee was a good man with an intelligence to match, 'but with a deflationary bias also a little hampered by the invariable Treasury complex with its preoccupation over Government receipts and expenditure'.[89] For his part, Massy-Greene was distrustful of high officialdom and he did not entertain a high opinion of economists (Kemp 1964:135). He was, for instance, scathing of Giblin's paper on 'Exchange and tariffs' prepared for the July 1932 Premiers' Conference (Cain 1985:54). Giblin had modelled the economic effects of a massive devaluation before settling for one of lower magnitude. The dilemma Giblin faced was how to sustain the level of Australian rural exports without resorting to devaluation. That, he thought, would almost certainly invite retaliation. Massy-Greene felt that 'arbitrary' exchange rate movements did little to elicit any further export gains of either commodities or manufactures but would rather merely reignite a capital flight problem at a most injudicious time.[90] With that rebuttal, and most of the *Wallace Bruce Report*, economic policy took a deflationist turn— something the next part of the chapter will focus on.

---

88   L. F. Giblin to L. G. Melville, 3 December 1932, UMA FECC, Box 15.
89   L. F. Giblin to E. Giblin, 29 June 1932, Giblin Papers, NLA.
90   Sir W. Massy-Greene to L. F. Giblin, 11 July 1932, Giblin Papers, NLA.

Orthodoxy regained

The Premiers' Conference of July 1932 was to prove a setback insofar as enlightened economic policy was concerned. Budgetary, monetary and exchange policy was now, with Lyons' connivance, in Gibson's lap. Perversely, the Australian economists' monetary reform proposals for the Imperial Trade Conference at Ottawa, which met with government approval, helped Lyons fudge the *Wallace Bruce Report* on the premise that the conference would deliver the export bonanza economists were trying to engineer. That is, if successful, Ottawa would deliver an increase in the velocity of trade within the British Empire that, when coupled with cheap money, would allow world prices to rise. While the delegations voted in favour of the monetary resolutions put forward by Shann and Melville, there was little multilateral action to follow up the good intentions. Meanwhile, the approach of the Chancellor of the Exchequer, Neville Chamberlain, to raising prices—restricting production rather than by monetary expansion in the locomotive economies—was anathema to the Australian economists (Turnell 1999).

Giblin attributed Lyons' *volte-face* over the *Wallace Bruce Report*, besides the promise of greater inter-imperial trade represented by Ottawa, to tiredness and the loss of Bruce.[91] Lyons spoke of feeling 'isolated' in cabinet.[92] His isolation was accentuated in September with the departures in quick succession of Fenton, over tariff levels, and Hawker, who resigned over politicians' salaries (Sawer 1963:43). It was difficult, however, to ascertain whether there were more sinister forces at play behind Lyons' backdown, other than to tailor a policy that curried favour with a conservative cabinet. In this critical instance, Lyons' decision to defer to Gibson's wishes was ultimately borne of the conventional belief that the Commonwealth Bank should exercise full, untrammelled authority over money and banking matters—a position he spelt out in detail while responding to Country Party calls for more expert management of the exchange rate (Cain 1985:56–7; Giblin 1951:142).[93] Lyons would later declare that no-one had been closer to Gibson than himself and no-one knew the problems confronting the bank board better than its chairman.[94] The *Wallace Bruce Report* had not helped matters by agreeing that the exchange rate be managed by the Commonwealth Bank 'free from both the fact and the fear of political control' (cited in Cain 1985:9). The caveat here was that the committee wanted the bank board to take into account economic considerations in their brief.

---

91   L. F. Giblin to E. Giblin, 6 July 1932, Giblin Papers, NLA.
92   Ricketson diary, 23 April 1932.
93   'Overseas exchange: government's policy defended by Mr Lyons', *SMH*, 16 July 1932.
94   *SMH*, 27 August 1934.

The necessity of having an independent monetary authority was reinforced by the repudiation antics of Lang. Lang held up the rehabilitation process simply because no constructive economic policy was possible while the strongest state, New South Wales, was out of kilter with the rest of Australia. The removal of Lang from office in May 1932 steeled Gibson and Lyons to apply the plan to the letter on the pretext that an economic spring would now be in the offing.

Neither, however, had reckoned on the feisty, independent mind of the newly elected Premier of New South Wales. Bertram Stevens would prove just as big a thorn in the side of the federal government as Lang (Cain 1985:61). Stevens used his accounting background to circumvent the federal government's *Financial Agreement Act*, which limited loan expenditure. State authorities bypassed that legislation to spend money on public works (McFarlane and Healey 1990:8). The NSW electorate had elected Stevens because they wanted a 'strong man' who 'would get things done' (McCarthy 1979:155). Lyons complained to Bruce that with Stevens 'one is continually sabotaged from behind'.[95] The first signs of this appeared when Stevens, briefed and egged on by Copland and Davidson, put the *Wallace Bruce Report* back on the agenda at the July 1932 Premiers' Conference.[96] The NSW Assistant Treasurer, E. Spooner, was equally adamant that Australia 'must blaze a new trail' and that 'deflation had gone too far' in terms of economic reconstruction. Before the NSW Branch of the Economic Society, Spooner sang the praises of the Wallace Bruce Committee as 'the first really comprehensive proposal for reconstruction that had been placed before the Premiers'.[97] There was good cause for this position since rural export prices had tumbled 30 per cent since July 1931, spelling further blowouts to budget deficits. Furthermore, with a huge state deficit to wind back, Stevens told Gibson that cutting back public expenditure was 'counterproductive', besides being undertaken within a completely unrealistic time frame.[98] Earlier, Davidson had briefed Stevens that 'while the balancing of budgets is essential to economic recovery it cannot itself promote such a recovery. The budget situation is indeed as much an effect as a cause of existing economic difficulties.'[99] Duly enlightened, Stevens held that the *Wallace Bruce Report* 'pointed the way' with its hydra-headed emphasis on wages, exchange and tariff revision. It was 'a sound economic policy of reconstruction' (cited in Cain 1985:43).

Lyons relented, issuing a resolution that, while adhering to the Premiers' Plan, the federal government would thereupon 'conduct public policy with a view to reviving industry so as to restore normal employment'.[100] This was an admission

---

95   J. Lyons to S. M. Bruce, 2 November 1932, Lyons Papers, NLA.
96   D. B. Copland to B. Stevens, 13 July 1932, UMA FECC, Box 32.
97   'Reconstruction: Mr Spooner's views', *SMH*, 6 August 1932.
98   B. Stevens to Sir R .Gibson, 11 October 1932, UT, 21/4-6.
99   A. C. Davidson to B. S. B. Stevens, 2 July 1932, Lyons Papers, NLA.
100   W. C. Hankinson to Sir H. Batterbee, 12 July 1932, PRO, T160/808/11935/7.

that there would be more public works. Brigden (1932a:1) feared the effect on business confidence of the confusion of opinion over the exchange rate, public spending and funding. The issue of the extent of Treasury bills in circulation was hard to reconcile since there were no standards for judgment with the emergency being faced. The Commonwealth Bank Board wanted to 'play for safety' and reduce their circulation.[101] Backstage, the economists were waging a campaign, via the press, to again bring the spotlight back on the exchange rate. Copland reminded Davidson and Premier Stevens that '[t]he exchange problem is a matter of public policy on which the bank must have a direction from parliament'.[102]

Getting to the nub of the issue, Davidson lamented to Lyons that there had been clear signs of a marked 'reorientation towards a policy of deflation' commensurate with 'dangerous tendencies of financial thought' circulating (Holder 1970:737). In his 1932 Crawford oration, Davidson argued that the Commonwealth Bank did everything in its powers to keep prices up as it was 'the most hopeful expedient of relief from the torment of depression in the midst of abundance' (Shann and Copland 1933:206).

Deaf to such sentiment, Lyons spoke optimistically about how the upcoming international conference on imperial trade and monetary reform would bide Australia well if only she maintained an even keel in domestic economic policy.[103] The new Labor Premier of Queensland, W. Forgan Smith, argued that the Premiers' Plan was insufficient to generate recovery—nor did waiting for international cooperation console him.[104] Citing Brigden and Keynes, Forgan Smith, a Theodore protégé, rejected fears of crowding-out if the Commonwealth should open its purse strings and begin spending (Cain 1985:45). Unlike Stevens, Forgan Smith agreed with Keynes's conclusions about the *Wallace Bruce Report* and looked instead for the government to take the lead. Stevens, impatient with Lyons' preference for leaving the exchange rate issue to lie until after Ottawa, accused him of 'fiddling while Rome burns'.[105]

As a consequence, Lyons asked Giblin, as Acting Statistician, to model the necessary exchange rate alteration in lieu of a wage cut, which would give Australia a competitive advantage (Cain 1985:47). Giblin and Copland had already accepted Keynes's point that relative cost adjustment was in the

---

101 L. G. Melville to R. Kershaw, 21 December 1932, BE, OV13/2.
102 D. B. Copland to A. C. Davidson, 18 July 1932, UMA FECC, Box 32; D. B. Copland to B. S. B. Stevens, 13 July 1932, UMA FECC, Box 32.
103 Keynes also did not entertain high hopes of the Ottawa conference since proceedings would be in the hands of the 'ultra-conservative' Neville Chamberlain and Montagu Norman and, as he told Clive Baillieu, 'they can be relied on to nip anything constructive in the bud, and no one else will have sufficient knowledge and energy to force them along the right lines' (J. M. Keynes to C. Baillieu, KPKC, A/32/1/302).
104 W. C. Hankinson to Sir H. Batterrbee, 12 July 1932, PRO, T160/808/11935/7.
105 *SMH*, 2 July 1932.

circumstances best expedited by devaluation rather than wage cuts (Copland 1932a:118). Meanwhile, the Commonwealth Bank became nervous about the growth in the floating debt and was increasingly critical about using Treasury bills to finance public works. Even Shann warned that 'the swelling tallies' of Treasury bills could result in a distorted, public sector-led economy; it was a curious admission given his position as economic adviser to Davidson's bank, which had been instrumental in taking the bills up.[106] The trading banks had been at first reluctant to hold the bills as part of their cash reserves until Davidson, realising their generous returns, led the way and absorbed them as bank reserves (Holder 1970).[107] The purchase of the bills by banks involved no reduction of their reserves but rather they grew as the credit provided to governments gave rise, in turn, to new deposits.

The issue of funding—that is, retiring short-term government debt by raising public loans—was to prove the next testing ground over which the economists waged battle with the bank board. The issue revolved around the tendency to inflation as against deflation. In the debate, Casey (1933:62) commented on how some of the 'most orthodox economists in Australia' were now in favour of the former expedient. Not denying the palpable benefit Treasury bills had on his bank's balance sheet, Davidson argued that reducing their volume in circulation would not just tighten credit generally, it would prevent a much-needed reduction in interest rates.[108]

Since trading banks regarded Treasury bills as part of their reserves, the fear of the bank board, articulated by Melville's input, was that as the economy improved these reserves could form the basis of a massive and inflationary expansion of bank lending. Alarmed at this prospect, Gibson 'put a pistol' to the heads of the premiers by insisting on a speedier reduction in budget deficits before he would allow credits for public works.[109] One English observer at the July 1932 Premiers' Conference, W. Hankinson, likened the spendthrift states to recalcitrant children, who, having refused their breakfast, would face the same bowl of 'cold porridge' later before something more palatable was served up.[110]

Meanwhile, Stevens' advocacy for devaluation saw him perceived as being under the sway of Davidson. It was Copland, however, who supplied the arguments to Stevens, demonstrating how a revaluation would be disastrous

---

106   E. Shann to C. A. S. Hawker, 18 January 1932, Shann Papers, NLA.
107   R. N. Kershaw to L. F. Giblin, 29 May 1947, BE, G1/288.
108   A. C. Davidson to J. Lyons, Telegram, 21 October 1931, Lyons Papers, NLA.
109   R. G. Casey to Sir H. Batterbee, 13 July 1932, Hankey Papers, Churchill College.
110   W. Hankinson to Sir H. Batterbee, 12 July 1932, PRO, T160/808/11935/7.

for the country.[111] Stevens had brought Copland up to Sydney to brief him on finance and economic matters, overlooking therefore the economics expertise at the University of Sydney.[112]

Stevens and Forgan Smith's refusal to toe the line exasperated Gibson. The sniping attacks by economists, and Davidson, on the exchange rate, and now funding, together with the states stonewalling on their deficits, brought Gibson to the end of his tether.[113] Feeling his authority slipping away, Gibson wanted a public loan of some £20 million floated with more than half of the proceeds intended for funding. Stevens accused Gibson at the October 1932 Loan Council meeting of behaving like a banker towards borrowers caught short and imposing humiliating conditions on them. Intending to put Stevens in his place, Gibson, in a bravura performance, thundered that he was 'the horse and cart and the dog under the cart' as far as the Australian financial system was concerned.[114] The truth was that he was not and it was the economists, including Melville, who were undermining him.

'Deflationists in the bag' — orthodoxy challenged

Apart from the states' resistance to funding, Gibson's outburst was probably sparked by frustration at having been unable to press on with returning the Australian pound to parity with sterling. When Gibson announced his intention to regain parity in late 1932, economists, in league with exporters and the Country Party, engaged in a campaign to prevent it. Copland and Giblin met with Sheehan over the matter but both were wary that Gibson might see this as undue interference.[115] After another meeting with Sheehan, Copland told his Sydney-based colleague Claude Janes that it had been 'a great comfort' to talk to the Treasury official, who, fearing too many deflationary impulses were being unleashed on the economy, wanted the board to take a 'reasonable view' of things with respect to the exchange rate and funding.[116]

In the gathering light of the mixed outcomes from the Imperial Trade Conference, economists felt that conventional opinion had to be made more exchange-rate conscious than hitherto. Economists, therefore, eagerly lent their support to Senator Hardy of the Country Party, who called for a royal commission into

---

111   D. B. Copland to B. S. B. Stevens, 25 August 1932, UMA FECC, Box 32.
112   F. A. Bland to E. R. Walker, 20 November 1932, Bland Papers, University of Sydney Archives.
113   Sir Robert Gibson's daughter movingly records in her unfinished memoir of him the strain the contretemps was having on him (Gibson Papers, State Library of Victoria).
114   Ricketson diary, 26 October 1932.
115   D. B. Copland to L. G. Giblin, 2 September 1932, UMA FECC, Box 15.
116   D. B. Copland to C. Janes, 12 October 1932, UMA FECC, Box 15.

the exchange rate matter. To further that end, Janes, head of the economics section at the Wales, liaised with the leader of the Country Party, Earle Page, over the likely personnel for the commission as well as drafting tentative terms of reference. Janes told Copland that it was his impression Lyons might welcome the opportunity of shifting the responsibility of exchange rate policy to a body of experts.[117] Copland, happy to lend his support, informed Janes of the Realpolitik behind the issue:

> My feeling is that you must persuade the people in London and the Government to do this by a little well-organised propaganda there as to the meaning of the exchange rate to Australia. Moreover it should not hesitate to deal with the attitude of shareholders of the London banks operating in Australia. They are the real devils in the piece.[118]

To that end, Copland, spurred on by Davidson, engaged in an attempt to educate high opinion in the City and, no doubt, financial interests in Australia by penning a piece for the *Economic Journal* attacking Niemeyer's and Gregory's recommendations that New Zealand neither devalue its exchange nor engage in Treasury bill finance as Australia had done (Copland 1932b:378–9). While the article was ostensibly about New Zealand's likely economic course, it had resonance with the policies Australia was pursuing. Although Copland had completed the article as early as April 1932, it appeared only in the September issue of the journal. Davidson in fact expressed his annoyance to Keynes that the article had not appeared earlier, stressing '[t]ime is the essence of the contract and September may be too late. Criticism of such deflationary policy is urgently needed on this side and you should lend support to opponents of deflation on your side.'[119]

Towards the end of the year, Copland (1932c) penned another piece for the same journal, further extolling the anti-deflationary virtues of Treasury bill finance, the rapid issue of which concerned not just the bank board but the City. In a reprise of his earlier article, Copland warned that the zealous pursuit of funding and rehabilitating the exchange rate would be detrimental to Australia's financial system by intensifying the real debt burden. He closed by noting how the bank board seemed oblivious of the dangers of falling back into deflation, nor did it 'realise the enormous powers it now possesses for guiding Australia along the present course of credit creation to avoid unnecessary deflation' (Copland 1932c:587).

At the academic level, Copland told the University of Yale economist Irving Fisher that he believed he had basically anticipated his debt-deflation theory,

---

117   C. Janes to D. B. Copland, 5 September 1932, UMA FECC, Box 15.
118   D. B. Copland to C. Janes, 9 September 1932, BNSW, A53-413.
119   A. C. Davidson to J. M. Keynes, 3 June 1932, Keynes File, BNSW.

which predicted that orthodox economic policy efforts to work off debt in fact intensified it. Australian banks, he told Fisher, quickly found that they had fixed money claims to meet but with assets that would shrink as deflation proceeded. While he did not pursue the matter, Copland drew Fisher's attention to a series of press articles he had written in 1930, later consolidated in his *Credit and Currency Control*, on the dangers of following deflationary policies.[120]

While Copland and Janes doubted the ability of Page to get the exchange rate on the agenda, it all became academic when Reading, informed by Melville and Shann, reported about London opinion concerning the future for the global economy, alerting the board to the likely precariousness of export prices in the near future (Turnell 1999:49; Cornish 1993c:443). This persuaded the bank board to override Gibson's wishes and keep the exchange rate steady. The Bank of England decreed, moreover, that it had no objection to the Australian exchange rate moving in accordance with internal conditions (Schedvin 1970:363). Giblin sought out his *bête noire*, Sir Otto Niemeyer, to confirm the change of heart. He received a letter from Niemeyer, full of English understatement, precisely to that effect.[121] This was enough for Copland to tell his colleague at the Wales: 'I think at the moment we have the deflationists in the bag, but how long we can hold them there is another matter.'[122]

Apart from Gibson wanting to 'rehabilitate' the exchange rate, Lyons knew that devaluation would have a detrimental impact on Bruce's brief in London of converting Australia's loan portfolio. Australia continued to import more than what her export income could warrant and this, in Copland's view, could be checked only by devaluation. Theodore felt more tariff protection was the answer. Giblin disparaged this line of thought, believing it would only make Gibson 'an even greater menace to Australia than he is' (cited in Cain 1985:56–7). Copland told Stevens that the bank board was 'acting imprudently' over the matter and that the bank should be brought to account over it just as any other recalcitrant was for not playing their part in the economic rehabilitation of Australia.[123] At last, official and academic opinion had penetrated through to the bank board that Australia could ill afford the revaluation Gibson dearly wanted to impose.

Copland's (1932a:113–17) temperate optimism about the deflationists 'being in the bag' was also based on how Gibson had been checked about raising a huge public loan intended purely for retiring short-term public debt. Lyons complained to Bruce that Stevens should be treated warily since he 'is

---

120   I. Fisher to D. B. Copland, November 1933, and D. B. Copland to I. Fisher, 23 November 1933, UMA FECC, Box 23.
121   Sir O. Niemeyer to L. F. Giblin, 19 October 1932, BE, OV13/2.
122   D. B. Copland to C. Janes, 16 September 1932, UMA FECC, Box 15.
123   D. B. Copland to B. S. B. Stevens, 7 December 1932, UMA FECC, Box 32.

persistently advocating a policy on monetary matters directly opposed to our own'.[124] Gibson's public loan proposal, however, also met with the disapproval of the Assistant Treasurer, Massy-Greene, who told his predecessor, Bruce: 'He [Gibson] is very strong for carrying through a big funding operation only. Personally I regard this as a mistake. I think that it would be considered in many quarters as a further deflationary move.' Massy-Greene was further of the mind that the bank board should have much less say in determining the extent of the states' loan programs. He felt a more liberal view of financing state deficits with Treasury bills was in order since these deficits were bound to continue for some time.[125]

Even the arch-conservative Latham could now see how the subtle use of Treasury bills to finance deficits was keeping prices buoyant. In a public speech, Latham noted that '[t]he greatest menace to our economy is not to be found in any incipient boom or expansion of the note issue but rather, if I may speak frankly, in a certain indifference on the part of the Commonwealth Bank to the effects on public opinion of a "stand–pat" policy and of a falling price level'.[126]

With Gibson under fire from several quarters, Copland reported that '[t]he general feeling…is that the Old Man of the Bank…cuts a sorry figure'.[127] Yet Copland (1936:16) later paid tribute to Gibson for his financial stewardship. It was Gibson's reassuring presence with the capital market that also allowed Australia to resort to the use of Treasury bills from July 1931 onwards (Copland 1937a:418). Almost incapacitated—and succumbing to his infirmities not long after—Gibson's influence would continue to exert a conservative bearing on the making of Commonwealth economic policy.

---

124 J. Lyons to S. M. Bruce, 2 November 1932, Lyons Papers, NLA.
125 W. Massy-Greene to S. M. Bruce, 4 October 1932, AA, M104, Item 1, 1932.
126 Speech given at the Constitutional Club, 6 March 1933, Latham Papers, NLA.
127 D. B. Copland to C. Janes, 2 November 1932, UMA FECC, Box 15.

7. The Australian recovery, 1933–1936

Introduction

In September 1932, a year in which unemployment peaked at 28 per cent of the available workforce, Lyons told Parliament of a growing return in business confidence now that the Premiers' Plan was being implemented. Lyons relentlessly played on the psychological comfort of having a conservative government in power (Lloyd 1984). It was, as the economists knew, barely enough. At one point, Lyons was reduced to enumerating the number of new telephone connections as proof of the green shoots of recovery.[1] In another instance, he made an appeal reminiscent of Keynes's public broadcasts:

> What we need now is not to button up our waistcoats tight but to be in a mood of expansion, of activity…to do things, to buy things, to make things. Activity of one kind or another is the only means of making the wheels of economic progress and all the production of wealth go round again. (Cited in Lloyd 1984:240–1)

While MacLaurin (1936) dated the economic recovery from the last months of 1932, it was to take another three years before unemployment rates fell below 10 per cent—the rate it had been during the 1920s (Copland and Janes 1936).

This chapter discusses the nature of the Australian economic recovery and how economists reacted and adjusted to it in thought and advice. In terms of theoretical development, some economists were groping along proto-Keynesian lines and stressing the case for public spending and exchange rate flexibility. Others, however, were more beholden to Hayekian themes and insights. By 1935–36, Australia's economic recovery had become so robust that the foreign exchange reserves were judged inadequate to meet overseas obligations. Copland (1936) marvelled at the nature of recovery and the unique novelty of having to check spending in the mid-1930s. Economists, whose advice had been neglected for some time, were consulted before remedial action was taken. That advice sprang from the latest views on the art of monetary management. Initially, the

---

1   Budget speech, 1934/35, *CPD*.

academic economists were in favour of keeping the expansion going but it was the 'inside' economists—those within the policymaking agencies—who won the day.

Some background on the conventional economic policy at the time and the policymaking process in which the various players were involved is necessary before proceeding. Issues of public works, funding and the exchange rate predominated. The thinking of academic economists was to advocate strengthening the recovery with public spending. Economists still had to contend with the view of the Commonwealth Bank Board, which wanted short-term debt quickly retired. Sometimes economists found their perspectives shared by a new Federal Treasurer. This step forward, though, was tempered by the schism within the economic fraternity that came to the fore over curbing public sector spending and funding.

Conventional economic policy

In 1934, Lyons proclaimed that the Australian economic recovery was 'one of the most spectacular...the world has known'.[2] He asserted that unemployment due to the Depression had been cut in half. By 1935–36, Australia regained the peak of pre-depression output achieved in 1927–28. Certainly, the business and financial constituencies, having had their fill of economic experimentation, were, like high opinion in London, comforted by the fiscal consolidation and the marked lack of adventure in economic policy. To help ensure this, the Lyons government gained notoriety for its lack of parliamentary sessions and the frequent use of the guillotine to suspend debate on economic policy.[3] In 1934, for instance, the Federal Parliament sat for just four weeks. This was done in the name of fostering business confidence. Scullin, now Opposition Leader, saw it, however, as representative of an intellectual torpor gripping the government's thinking. Newspaper proprietors assisted the government by not publishing the attacks of its critics or by censuring them such that their impact was dissipated. Lyons returned the favour by giving editors advance notification of cabinet decisions to forestall any criticism (Hart 1967). The Lyons government won electoral support by not taking risks with the currency or exchange rate. In close cahoots with its financial backers, the government's faith in supply-side policies to deliver economic salvation did attract criticism from some backbenchers. One former minister, Charles Hawker, complained of the

---

2   'Mr Lyons' Sydney speech', *SMH*, 14 August 1934.
3   'Federal session: the guillotine', *SMH*, 30 November 1934.

'flabbiness' and 'flapdoodle' within cabinet, its outlook 'bounded by Collins Street' (Pike 1968:21). Labor politicians echoed this, attacking the government for its 'shilly-shallying' over policy.[4]

While the patchy economic recovery was seen as vindicating the Premiers' Plan, the truth was that recovery, as Walker (1933a) recounted, was probably as much to do with rising commodity prices and propitious climactic conditions as it was with policy. Nonetheless, the recovery was protracted, punctuated by dissension emanating from within and outside the government. One source of that dissent, of course, was academic economists and this chapter charts how they attempted, admittedly with little success, to influence economic policy in the mid-1930s. Their frustration, as seen in the previous chapter, became all the more evident as monetary policy became markedly deflationary from 1932 onwards. In the mid-1930s, their frustration turned to the pace of the recovery. The key policy question revolved around the funding debate and the ambit given to public works. Given that a private sector recovery was vital to reduce the country's external debt, it meant that the diversion of credit resources into public consumption expenditure—represented by Treasury bills—could be ill afforded unless, of course, there was an excess of savings. Apart from upholding the Premiers' Plan, official policy enshrined external balance and exchange stability as priorities—certainly for first half of the decade (Reddaway 1960:192).

Academic economists noted, too, with some dismay, that the more the economy recovered, the less their advice was heeded. A document drawn up by Copland and Wood in early 1933 suggested that the improvement in the business climate was quite precarious, in part because the causes of the improvement were not clearly recognised in financial circles and partly because some of it was, as Walker noted, due to good fortune.[5] Another fly in the ointment, identified in the report, was the low level of private investment. Yet other perennial concerns were the disparity between farm prices and industrial prices, high long-term interest rates and the bank board's desire to revalue the exchange rate as soon as export prices recovered. Moreover, as recovery began to take hold, the Commonwealth Bank became insistent on funding irrespective of interest rates. As prosperity gradually returned, the bank board, in league with the Federal Treasury, suppressed notions that there was more opportunity to finance public works (Cain 1988a). Recovery was made conditional on the government not doing anything rash in policy. As Lyons told Parliament after presenting the 1932/33 budget, '[c]onfidence has in a large measure been restored. All that is necessary now to enable us to reach the haven of complete recovery is an increase in world commodity prices.'[6] The Ottawa Trade Agreement, despite its

---

4   Holloway in *CPD Hansard*, 1333, 18 October 1933.
5   'Report on the Australian economic position 1929 to 1932', Wood Collection, UMA FECC, Box 206.
6   'Federal budget', *SMH*, 2 September 1932.

early promise, prevented Australia from increasing its export revenue to match the rise in imports that came with the improvement in business confidence.[7] The London balances were already under strain, meaning those calling for more internal economic stimulation would remain voices in the wilderness. This would never appear more evident than in 1933.

At the political level, Lyons was lumbered with a hostile and unimaginative cabinet. With Lang removed, the mind-set was to merely await the return of business confidence. This squared with the view of Latham, who considered wise governance was not just the good one did but the evil one prevented others from committing. Casey was not happy to settle for such lassitude. He told his London friend Hankey that he was agitating for 'the dirty work' to begin. He went on: 'If it becomes apparent in the next couple of years that our side is not prepared to risk its hide to save the show then my present feeling is that I will chuck it in and try some other form of entertainment.[8]' Casey would have his chance with his elevation to Assistant Treasurer in late 1933. For the moment, however, he could only agree with Keynes that high interest rates were the 'villain in the piece' and that 'a great reduction in long term interest rates…may even be a necessary condition for the survival of the existing financial structure of society' (Shann and Copland 1933). Casey pinned the blame for stubborn rates on the local banks being run by 'such hidebound old conservatives and rather ignorant money grubbers' (cited in Hudson 1986:102). For their part, the Melbourne banks looked on Casey with suspicion, with Healy telling his London overseer, Edmund Godward, that Casey was inexperienced and inclined to be 'too academic'.[9]

A floating debt of £50 million maintained spending and liquidity, while the devalued Australian pound anchored the price level ensuring that the real burden of the internal debt did not worsen. As detailed in the last chapter, however, the bank board feared that the Treasury bills portended a massive and highly inflationary expansion of bank lending if the trading banks chose to 'unload' them on to the central bank (Brigden 1932b:4). If, on the other hand, full-scale funding of short-term debt was vigorously pursued it would, by being intrinsically deflationary, intensify the internal debt and thereby endanger the whole banking and financial structure. Casey showed his colours by writing against the practice of using Treasury bills to finance deficits and public works though he did not believe their retirement was as yet practically possible. In the

---

7   L. G. Melville to R. Kershaw, 21 December 1932, BE, OV13/2.
8   R.G. Casey to Hankey, 1932, Hankey Papers, Churchill College.
9   G. Healy to E. Godward, 8 December 1933, D/O Correspondence, ANZ Archive. It was an accurate assessment. Casey, an engineer by training, had written to Hawtrey inquiring whether the attached summary of his work, *The Trade Depression and the Way Out*, was accurate. He mentioned to Hawtrey that it was his intention to keep abreast of all the contemporary works on economic affairs (R. G. Casey to R. Hawtrey, 19 June 1933, Hawtrey Papers, Churchill College).

same article, he dismissed devaluation as an option, preferring instead cheap money as the way out of depression (Cain 1988a:5). In a parliamentary exchange in 1932, he opposed wresting control of the exchange rate away from the central bank because it would then merely become 'a shuttlecock of party politics'.[10]

The first federal budgets brought down by the Lyons government added to the deflationary pressures placed on the economy. When Lyons discovered, for instance, that the projected budgetary outcome for 1932/33 was likely to be a deficit of some £3 million, he quickly moved to cut industry bounties, aged pensions and politicians' salaries—measures supplementary to those already taken under the Premiers' Plan. In seeking these economies, he rejected the idea of levying more taxes, preferring to cut outlays instead.[11] Correspondingly, budgetary surpluses in subsequent years were dissipated in the form of tax remissions to rural producers and the propertied. Academic economists were, by this stage, pushing for something different.

First stirrings of expansionist economics

As Chapter 6 discussed, most economists had begun to express doubts that the measures taken within the Premiers' Plan were entirely appropriate. Keynes's critical comments on the *Wallace Bruce Report* swayed minds towards new expedients. Meanwhile, the *Treatise* won over more converts. Some Australian economists, it was true, had their concerns about the Premiers' Plan before Keynes did. It was Giblin who was the first to recognise just 'how deep and abiding…the stagnation in investment' really was.[12] That revelation came as early as August 1931. In his 1933 Marshall Lectures, Copland (1934:145) conceded that not allowing more monetary stimulation at that time was a 'serious lapse' on the part of the economists. Loan expenditure on public works in 1931 was £9 million down from £40 million the year before. More public spending and liquidity would have checked the deflation caused by falling wages and costs. While deflation was a wonderful tonic for the export and import-competing industries, its general effect was income depressing. This did not mean, however, that Copland accepted public works as the means to a higher level of economic activity. That realisation only came some time in 1934, even though Copland had been in Cambridge during 1933 when the firmament of the *General Theory* was being discussed by Keynes and his circus (Cain 1988a).

It was Giblin and Dyason who developed the line that businessmen were too demoralised by deflation to be revived by cheap money and fiscal balance. In

---

10 'Budget debate: control of the exchange rate; Mr Casey's views', *SMH*, 14 October 1932.
11 'Rigid economy', *SMH*, 28 July 1932.
12 L. F. Giblin to E. R. Walker, 20 April 1934, Giblin Papers, NLA.

terms of the framework of the *Treatise*, savings was vastly in disproportion to investment. Both argued in a supplementary report to the premiers and Scullin in September 1931 that public spending be undertaken to mop up the liquidity in the banking system (Cain 1983:206; Wilson 1951). Public works, however, were regarded as only a palliative, with the central strategy being a long-term one of restoring relative competitiveness. By March 1932, Shann (1932:100–1), after reviewing the British *Macmillan Report*, was saying the same thing—that is, accumulating savings in bank vaults was hardly to the common good. In addition, it did not, as monetary policy should, ensure stability in purchasing power. Ten months later, Shann (1933:11) wrote a more forthright piece lamenting 'the cancer of hoarding', particularly in the United States, with savers reluctant to deposit their funds in the banking system. Perceiving 'consumers' outlay as the crux of the problem of recovery', Shann (1933:12) embraced Keynes's expedient of public works, together with a rudimentary notion of the multiplier, as the way out of the muddle. It was, as Turnell (1999:64) identifies, 'an extraordinary journey' for Shann given his polemical outbursts against public works in 1930.

Brigden, head of Queensland's Bureau of Industry, was also becoming more receptive to the idea of more public spending and relaxing the campaign to cut costs. Deflation and cost cutting, taken too far, could extirpate business confidence. While concerned about unwise borrowing by the government, he saw how 'the motive power of industry—the aggregate of individual willingness' did not respond quickly enough to lower costs. It was a case, Brigden concluded, not of 'what ought to be done' but of 'what can be done'; if the private sector would not spend then governments must (Brigden 1932b:1). Four months later, Brigden, seeing no end to depression in sight, was now having doubts about Australia's economic strategy of fiscal consolidation. Brigden wondered whether Australia should continue to pursue the policy of balanced budgets. He was concerned that the taxation required to fulfil that objective might impair the possibilities of recovery (Brigden 1933:1). The 'awkward dilemma' was that the means to ensure balanced budgets and, in turn, business confidence, could dampen the spirit of enterprise. That is, employment and production were speculative, driven by net profit, yet the burden of taxation meant that the surplus was diminished. Should taxes be lowered there would have to be recourse to more Treasury bills and their portent for inflation. It was a choice, Brigden concluded, 'between evils'.

The next shot in the expansionist campaign came from Davidson's bank in the form of circulars. Copland was commissioned to write a commentary showing how Treasury bills kept the domestic price level up. This was followed by another circular that focused on price levels and economic activity. Davidson wanted what Australian economists had been advocating at Ottawa applied domestically. That is, the price level should be raised by devaluation and Treasury bill finance, which would give a stimulus to local enterprise. Devaluation gave exporters, of course, a higher local price for their produce. Another circular entitled 'Towards recovery', issued in May 1933, put the case for a major sea change in economic policy (Cain 1985:65–8). Instead of trying to equalise savings and investment with deflation and cheap money, the article suggested that falling prices destroyed business optimism. The alternative, as Keynes had recently spelt out in his 1931 Harris Foundation Lectures, was to increase demand by greater public spending. This, in turn, would lift the domestic price level and close the gap between producers' costs and receipts. Public works, financed by Treasury bills, would not crowd-out private expenditure simply because the banks had plenty of idle balances on their books.[13] By the same token, insisting that public works projects yield a positive or commercial rate of return was silly when the opportunity cost of using what were idle resources was set at zero.

Melville was wary about the wisdom of further public spending, feeling that devaluation alone rather than 'playing about' with Treasury bills and the note issue was the answer. He told a federal senator:

> My only position is that of 'wait and see'. But then I cannot see how the tail can wag the dog. I do think that by management of the exchange and a suitable credit policy, we should keep the tail well up. No more than that is possible. If the dog is ill the tail cannot but feel the effect.[14]

There was no suggestion, though, of restoring the bold developmental policy of the 1920s since Australia had learnt its lesson about unremunerative public works and reckless borrowing.

Proposals to increase public works were, of course, what Keynes was then advocating for the British economy. In Australia's case, further government borrowing, executed by Treasury bills, would make it easier for banks to lower their rates to the private sector by giving them an increased return on their investments through the placement of surplus funds.[15] Strictures, therefore, about always balancing the budget should not come at the expense of unbalancing the economy. Scullin was an active proponent for public works, though only in the sense of alleviating unemployment rather than a means to recovery. He did, however, echo economists' views that cheap money by itself would not trigger recovery (Robinson 1986:121).

Copland, meanwhile, was heading overseas for a sabbatical, part of which would be spent at the University of Cambridge giving some lectures on Australia's

---

13 'Towards recovery', *BNSW Circular*, vol. III, no. 2 (May 1933).
14 L. G. Melville to H. Colebatch, 16 January 1933, RBA, GGM-33-1.
15 *BNSW Circular*, May 1933, p. 11.

economic experience at the express invitation of Keynes.[16] Ultimately, that proposed set of lectures, which Keynes had suggested as early as late 1931, would materialise as the 1933 Marshall Lectures. While Copland would speak on Australia's economic rehabilitation, he was not to know that Walker, who was undertaking doctoral work at Cambridge, had already given a lecture on that subject before the Marshall Society in 1931.[17] Casey felt the sojourn would do Copland a 'lot of good', explaining that he 'had been going to the left a great deal lately and is much too sure of himself. London and the rest will affect a little bloodletting.'[18] By that, Casey meant Copland's involvement with the expansionist cause, especially his dealings with Davidson and Stevens. The Melbourne man had been intermittently advising Stevens since mid-1932 and helped articulate the case against funding and strict budgetary economy. Casey's prophecy of Copland being brought to earth by sharper minds abroad did not eventuate. Indeed, it was to prove the contrary and Herbert Gepp's appreciation of Copland and his policy work that appeared in *The Herald* on the day of his departure portended even greater recognition abroad.[19]

Keynes's invitation to Copland was, in some way, representative of the standing of Australian economists in the world. Australia's attempt at economic rehabilitation and the role of economists in bringing it about had not escaped the notice of London. Nigel Davenport, who penned the weekly Toreador column in the *New Statesman and Nation*, felt that the Commonwealth government was unique in heeding the advice of their economists.[20] It augured well for the country's further adjustment, he held, should the external account deteriorate.[21] Such an exigency would certainly arise if the run of good export seasons came to an end. For the moment, Australia was managing to meet the annual interest on its external debt—some £36 million—with comfort. In that regard, *The Spectator* warned that, whatever the plaudits of Australia's economic readjustment, she had been doubly fortunate, not just with the generous trade concessions extracted from Britain at Ottawa but by the fact that global interest rates were subdued.

While the Lyons government had more latitude concerning the repayment of imperial debts than was commonly realised, a visit by a Bank of England officer apparently to appraise the Australian economy guarded against any laxity

---

16   J. M. Keynes to D. B. Copland, 19 May 1932, KPKC.
17   E. R. Walker to F. A. Bland, late 1931, Bland Papers, University of Sydney. Copland later reported that while at Cambridge he had heard 'excellent accounts' of Walker (Occasional Notes, 26 May 1933, BNSW, GM302/412).
18   R. G. Casey to S. M. Bruce, 20 February 1933, AA, A1421.
19   'Professor and Premiers' Plan: an appreciation of D. B. Copland', *The Herald*, 13 April 1933.
20   In his autobiography, Davenport (1974:18) recalls being given a brief by Montagu Norman to secretly write a pamphlet critical of the inflationary nature of Australian government financial policies in the Theodore period.
21   *New Statesman and Nation*, 12 December 1932, p. 866, and 16 September 1933.

(Hart 1967).[22] The officer apparently asked Melville for briefings on the budget, banking, employment and the exchange rate.[23] On this score, Theodore would later raise the spectre that perhaps the Lyons government's monetary policies were somewhat under the dictate of Threadneedle Street.[24] While this claim of interference could never be proved, London was certainly appeased by Gibson's insistence on containing the growth in floating debt and operating monetary policy to reduce further the risk of devaluation.[25] Davidson took up the baton, telling the London-based Robinson: 'There are repeated rumours that "friend Gibson", as you call him, and the Commonwealth Bank are more influenced by a certain influential section of London opinion than their duties to and responsibilities for the welfare of Australia.'[26]

Davidson's remark was also prompted by his and others' annoyance at the tardiness of London in passing interest rate relief on Australia's debts to the City, but, more importantly, that Gibson's fixation to restore parity with sterling might be at the behest of English financial interests in Australia.[27] In an earlier letter, Davidson bemoaned to Robinson that Gibson 'was unable to grasp the big disparity between prices and costs'. If the pressure from London continued, Davidson warned that Australia would not just default, it would see extremists back in power.[28]

Shann concurred with Davidson, noting that he had observed from Gibson's 'own lips' that he seemed more impressed with London opinion regarding Australian monetary problems than that of local commentators. In Shann's mind, here were the views of the Commonwealth Bank's own economist, Melville, whom the bank board greatly 'underestimated' primarily due to his youth. Shann felt that relying on London financial opinion was risky since '[s]uch people, no matter who they may be, cannot be as well informed as Melville is, both in a general and statistical way, upon Australia and its very complicated politics and finance'. That said, Shann advised his London-bound friend and businessman, Sir Walter Young, to tell those in the City that before expressing

---

22   Sir M. Norman to Sir R. G. Gibson, 7 July 1933, RBA, GRG-33-5.

23   M. McGrath to Skinner, 8 February 1934, BE, OV13/3.

24   'Commonwealth Bank: alleged control by the Bank of England', *SMH*, 3 October 1932.

25   In his book of speeches on current events, *The World We Live In*, Casey disputed the contention that Gibson was influenced by the views of Montagu Norman. He went on: 'As a matter of fact, it is fairly well known to many that Mr Norman has been of the opinion for many years that he has not been taken sufficiently into the confidence of the Commonwealth Government' (1933:66). Casey also took the opportunity in the book to renew his call for a permanent economics body along the lines of Britain's Economic Advisory Council (1933:68). That body, he hoped, would help the Commonwealth Bank in its deliberations on exchange rate policy.

26   A. C. Davidson to W. S. Robinson, 12 August 1933, BNSW, GM 302/574.

27   Writing about the controversy, Copland told a Canadian economist that he had asked 'some of his friends in the Commonwealth Bank about the influence exercised upon them by the Bank of England. Melville says that the influence is precisely nil' (D. B. Copland to A. F. W. Plumptre, 6 May 1934, UMA FECC, Box 36).

28   A. C. Davidson to W. S. Robinson, 26 September 1932, BNSW, GM 302/574.

any opinion about Australia's financial position they might seek out Melville first.[29] Perhaps, by that conduit, the bank board might just realise what a 'find' they had in Melville. The Commonwealth Bank's resident economist would soon come into his own (Cain 1988a:4).

Theodore took up the expansionist cause in 1933 with an address to the NSW Branch of the Economic Society on the matter of monetary management with a proposal for a more scientific, less doctrinaire basis from which to conduct monetary policy. Giblin told Theodore that the country would be hard put finding enough suitable men to sit on the proposed National Credit Commission that would deliberate on monetary policy.[30] By this time, the Labor Party was fancifully consumed with the notion of bank nationalisation and the socialisation of credit (Robinson 1986; Kuhn 1988). It had little interest for what economists, such as Giblin, were saying. His enthusiastic review of Keynes's (1933) 'The means to prosperity' in the *Economic Record*, for example, went unnoticed because the Labor Party shunned university-educated men and 'experts' just as much as bankers did (Giblin 1933).

According to Giblin (1951:120), Keynes's pamphlet popularised the notion of using 'credit expansion in a depression' though Australian economists had already advocated it in a minor way. The pamphlet used Kahn's employment multiplier, showing how a public stimulus was almost self-financing in the tax revenue generated. Giblin (1933:141–2) drew strength from the pamphlet, stating that Australia had already been practising what Keynes was urging but only, alas, in a 'piecemeal' fashion and 'without any general acceptance of principle'. Giblin corresponded with Keynes over the figurework behind Kahn's multiplier (Coleman and Hagger 2003; Markwell 1985:29–30).

Having returned to Melbourne, Giblin gave a lecture at the Shillings Club, a political economy club he had founded for university staff and students. Giblin spoke, again, of the need for expansionist policy (Downing 1960:46). Inspired by Keynes's pamphlet, Giblin used Kahn's multiplier analysis to show how a net increase in public spending could trigger a bountiful jump in employment. Giblin made his proposals in the light of an expected substantial federal budgetary surplus. Judging from the notes of the minute-taker, the reception from staff and graduate students was hardly welcoming, perhaps because Hayek's *Prices and Production* was then more in favour than Keynes's *Treatise*. Roland Wilson, down from Canberra, believed that the added expenditure would put pressure on the exchange rate. Jack Horsfall, a graduate student, said that the expenditure would not compensate for the cessation of overseas loans together with the adverse terms of trade. Another critic maintained that

---

29   E. Shann to Sir W. Young, 17 February 1932, BNSW, A-53-409.
30   L. F. Giblin to E. G. Theodore, 6 October 1933, Giblin Collection, UMA FECC, Box 1.

the expansion would pander to the greed and avarice of trade unionists—a problem Giblin, like Keynes, felt would be allayed by a sense of community mindedness. Another questioned the elasticity of supply assumptions behind Giblin's figure work. Lastly, Frank Mauldon, a departmental colleague, felt the plan was 'too easy...as economists we could not be satisfied with any simple means of recovery'.[31] Apart from the stigma of public sector borrowing going to wasteful ends, Mauldon's reservation reflected the concern of his colleagues that Giblin's expedient was all too similar to proposals bubbling up from the economic underworld. One economist who was not there and who would have appreciated Giblin's line of thinking was Walker. He had compared the anti-depression policy prescriptions of Keynes with Hayek and found the latter's approach 'not relevant to the problem of recovery from a slump' (Walker 1933b:201).

Politically, 1933 was to prove an *annus horribilis* for Lyons, with questions raised in the press about his leadership. Bruce's departure to take up loan-conversion duties in London left the front bench, as Casey put it, 'tragically weak' (Hudson 1986:83). Casey kept Bruce informed about the condition of the government and pandered to the notion of him staging a return to Australia to assume the prime ministership. After some thought, Bruce thought a return to the leadership would reignite 'the old prejudices and passions' held against him and that he was better off serving his country in London.[32] Meanwhile, Latham's 'grandstanding' in driving policy together with Gibson's refusal to budge on financing more public works tested Lyons' patience.[33] The Prime Minister's hands were tied since he had promised in the 1931 election campaign that the UAP would not interfere with the decisions of the Commonwealth Bank (MacLaurin 1936:103).

In addition to moving towards budgetary equilibrium, Gibson wanted a considerable fraction of the public loans raised put towards retiring debt (Tsokhas 1993:109; Cain 1988a). Initially, Gibson, in what Davidson called a 'diabolical scheme', wanted all the proceeds from the public loan to be used to fund short-term debt rather than to finance public works. Gibson was forced to back down by the united opposition of Lyons and the Loan Council.[34] Davidson told Shann that Gibson's gambit was the exact opposite of what 'the rest of us' had been about for some years (Holder 1970:795). Premature funding of Treasury bills would have starved industry of funds. It came at a time when there were repeated calls from Labor and the Country Party for an inquiry into the banking system. Lyons decided to wrest the political initiative and meet

---

31 'Minutes of Shillings meeting', July 1933, author unknown, UMA FECC, Box 219.
32 S. M. Bruce to R. G. Casey, 13 September 1933, Casey–Bruce Correspondence, AA, A1421/1.
33 S. M. Bruce to R. G. Casey, 19 January 1933, Casey–Bruce Correspondence, AA, A1421/1.
34 A. C. Davidson to E. Shann, 24 October 1933, BNSW, GM 302/590.

the call for economic expansionism by putting pressure on the banks to further cut their rates. With the rural sector unhappy with bank overdraft rates, Lyons reasoned that cutting interest rates might nip the problem of an inquiry in the bud.[35] Lyons browbeat the trading banks by predicting that if they did not cut advance rates the 1934 federal election would be fought on the issue of bank nationalisation.

Davidson told Lyons that the rate on advances was 'now lower than it has ever been'. He took the opportunity to point out the 'logical results' of the bank board's decision to reduce the amount of Treasury bills in circulation. It would, he claimed, spell higher rates in the future since the bills were a key part of a trading bank's cash reserves. Interest rate relief would also not come from the Commonwealth Bank taking the lead and cutting the rate on fixed deposits. Davidson reminded Lyons that when it came to the issue of bank nationalisation 'a show of excessive nervousness' by the central bank merely played into the hands of 'the forces working towards this end'.[36] Stevens also felt lower rates would be 'insurance' against moves towards controls over interest rates.[37]

The prevailing mind-set in government and banking circles was that economic prosperity would tamely follow as world commodity prices recovered.[38] In 1933, Lyons presented his 'prosperity' or 'restoration' budget. The budgetary surplus was dissipated in the form of tax relief rather than dispensing it to the states. This, Lyons figured, was the best way to cut producers' costs. The stock market boomed the day after the budget with press reaction, local and abroad, giving it a chorus of approval.[39] The London *Times* hailed the budget as 'the nearest approximation to a prosperity budget anywhere since the beginning of the depression'. It went on to record how it was 'fitting' that the first country to go into depression would 'also be the first to be able, in a national budget, to take account of the definite signs of improvement'.[40]

Notwithstanding the exchange rate issue, the cautious budget strategy facilitated the task of converting Australia's huge stock of debt on the London capital market. In that respect, the collateral for Australian securities in London lay solely with Lyons. Another plaudit for Australia's economic achievement came from the English financial expert Sir Henry Strakosch. He attributed it not to favourable wool prices—as some now did, including Toreador—but to the Premiers' Plan. It struck him as 'a daring [plan], yet logical, comprehensive and wholly consistent with accepted economic theory'.[41] Strakosch's utterance

---

35   E. R. Riddle to Sir M. Norman, 24 August 1933, BE, OV13/3/454/1.
36   A. C. Davidson to J. Lyons, 4 December 1933, BNSW, GM/5/46.
37   B. S. B. Stevens to Sir R. Gibson, 25 March 1933, RBA, GRG-33-33.
38   'Recovering: Australia's achievements: Premiers' Plan result', *SMH*, 24 June 1933.
39   *SMH*, 6 October 1933.
40   'Opinion in London: unstinted praise', *SMH*, 6 October 1933.
41   'Australia's recovery: financial expert's praise', *SMH*, 11 December 1933.

might have been prompted after reading press reports of Copland's Marshall Lectures at Cambridge University. Copland had warned that Australia could ill afford to return to a policy of 'forced economic development' with heavy overseas borrowing, public works and immigration, but he praised devaluation and cheap money and suggested that the large internal debt might well remain a 'permanent' feature of the money market. Should the expansion of credit prove troublesome in the future by overstimulating activity, it could be checked by devaluation and open market operations. With economic nationalism resurgent, Copland felt Australia would have to rely on its internal market and that, in turn, could be harnessed by cheap money and tariff protection as long as it did not penalise the export sector.[42]

When Copland's lectures were published in 1934, they drew the attention of Montagu Norman. In a confidential, never disclosed review, Norman believed Copland was about '90 per cent right' in claiming that the remedies applied were suitable to the Australian economic situation and national character. The 'ambitious, dogmatic' Copland, however, had a 'marked tendency "to rationalise" Australian experience' in order to make it fit 'a monetary pre-conception of a Keynesian—or more probably Hawtreyan—cast'. Like most commentators, Norman praised Australian economists for their ingenuity in saving their country from economic disaster though full recovery was ultimately dependent on the revival in the creditor and industrial countries.[43] There was no reaction from Niemeyer.

As wool prices recovered and the psychological stakes improved in 1933, Gibson took the opportunity to put the exchange issue back on the agenda.[44] It was to be Gibson's last piece of executive action.[45] A Commonwealth Bank briefing backed it up, with Melville positing the thesis that the economy was more in danger of boom than deflation. This surprised Shann.[46] Melville had, in fact, raised the same concern a year earlier fearing the 'risk' of an inflationary boom in the exporting industries due to the combination of devaluation and rising commodity prices.[47]

The Secretary of the Federal Treasury, Harry Sheehan, who was also a director on the Commonwealth Bank Board, told Bank of England officials that there were not enough grounds to warrant the revaluation Gibson wanted. Kershaw felt that Australia could practically appreciate its exchange only if there was a recovery in the industrialised countries in tandem with her diversifying her

---

42 'Recovery: Australian policy: Professor Copland urges continuance', *SMH*, 29 November 1933.

43 Copland's Marshall Lectures ('Australia in the world crisis 1929/1933', 29 September 1934, P. J. Grigg Papers, Churchill College, Cambridge).

44 Memorandum on exchange—from Chairman to the Board of Directors, 9 October 1933, RBA, GRG-33-5.

45 W. S. Robinson to J. M. Keynes, 30 January 1934, KPKC.

46 A. C. Davidson to E. Shann, 23 November 1933, BNSW, GM 302/590.

47 E. Shann to Sir W. Young, 17 February 1932, BNSW, A-53-409.

export markets. Melville, on the way home after the Ottawa trade conference, sounded out London high opinion on the Australian pound's preferred value. He was told, unequivocally, that the Australian currency should not be realigned with sterling at parity (Markwell 1985:22–3).

Economists and the funding debate

While Gibson's death put an end to thoughts of revaluation, it did not dispel the bank board's concern about the floating debt, which was approaching £50 million by the end of 1933. It was a matter that was to unite academic economists against the Commonwealth Bank. Indeed, with Melville articulating the reasoning, the bank came out stronger than ever for retiring them. Melville found support from the Treasury, where Wilson was becoming a key source of advice. Brigden (1932a), too, expressed public alarm at the build-up in Treasury bills, believing their number undermined business confidence. Brigden (1932b:4) reiterated his warnings about the 'latent' inflationary potential of this borrowing, especially when business confidence revived. Yet Brigden (1932b:1) could also see the other side of the ledger—that is, the 'motive power of industry' needed more than reduced costs to become stimulated.

The bank board informed the Loan Council that public works projects, henceforth, must be financed by public loans in a bid to rein in government spending, particularly the spendthrift habits of Queensland and New South Wales (Tsokhas 1993:108–9). The other fiscally weaker states became what Colin Clark later called 'mendicant' states and joined the federal government in opposing the expansionist policies of New South Wales and Queensland at Loan Council meetings (Higgins 1989:301). The bank board and the Loan Council agreed to reduce the amount of Treasury bills in circulation and also to reduce the rate of discount, or return, on them. This, Davidson feared, would put upward pressure on interest rates at a time when there was a clamour, from the Prime Minister down, for lower rates. Davidson also felt this deflationary policy would become an obstacle to achieving balanced budgets. The more enlightened approach, he argued, would be to continue with more central bank credit, which, with lower rates, would help revive business activity and, in turn, restore government budgets.[48] As recovery proceeded, it might have been thought the controversy over short-term debt would diminish since public works could be financed by public loans hand-in-hand with piecemeal funding. The bank board, however, remained vigilant. Besides its philosophical reservations about public works, the board was wary that borrowing for public works was a greater drain on Australia's credit resources than before the Depression. Melville

---

48   A. C. Davidson to W. S. Robinson, 20 February 1933, BNSW, GM Files, 302/574.

felt that the level of internal debt was too large for the economy to cope with. Public deficits had to be wound back, as the Prime Minister put it, to 'free money for investment purposes'.[49]

This debate over government finances and funding highlighted the differences between Melville representing the bank board's view of things and that of academic economists (Cain 1988a:10–11). By 1934, Melville had shifted position, not just on funding and public spending, but on the related issue of the flexibility of the exchange rate, which he felt was an invitation to overexpansion. He insisted that devaluation not be triggered by overstimulation of the economy. There had been enough of the latter in any case with the amount of Treasury bills extant already making monetary management difficult (Cain 1988a:9). Instead of exchange flexibility, Melville suggested a managed exchange rate as the best means of ensuring economic progress. As he later told John La Nauze, 'My conclusions…are so fundamentally different from that of my economic brethren in Australia that I am anxious to get as much criticism as possible.'[50] Reflecting on it a decade later, Roland Wilson felt it was Melville's 'rigidity rather than the essential substance of his views which made us regard him at the time as a pain-in-the-neck'.[51]

When someone, therefore, under the pseudonym of 'Bystander' penned a piece in the *Australian Quarterly* outlining economic arguments for funding Treasury bills, suspicion fell on Melville as the author. Baillieu sent a copy to Keynes suggesting that he could easily 'divine' the authorship of the article.[52] Keynes was puzzled why the author was so intent on funding. Keynes added that while Treasury bills did make it easier for governments to spend, he felt the author's claim that a large volume of bills impeded credit control was somewhat 'exaggerated'. The main thing, according to Keynes, was whether Treasury bills afforded a cheap form of government borrowing. He did, however, agree with the author's contention that there were dangers in over-borrowing but Keynes did not feel that the article demonstrated that the 'limits of prudence' had been yet reached. Moreover, Keynes felt that while the author had set out to show why funding would not do much harm, he had not established whether it would do much good either.[53]

Fresh from his sabbatical abroad, where he had taken note of how other countries were promoting recovery, Copland marked his re-entry into domestic public affairs by calling for lower interest rates. In a speech before the NSW Branch of the Economic Society in April 1935, Copland stressed that '[w]e must revise

---

49 *CPD*, vol. 145, 1 November 1934, p. 99.
50 L. G. Melville to J. La Nauze, 26 July 1935, La Nauze Papers, NLA.
51 R. Wilson to L. F. Giblin, 7 December 1949, RBA, GLG-51-5.
52 C. L. Baillieu to J. M. Keynes, 28 March 1934, KPKC.
53 J. M. Keynes to C. L. Baillieu, 6 April 1934, KPKC.

our ideas about rates of interest'. Investment, which had been stagnant for four years, could be restored only by cheap money and if that meant more public debt it had to be faced: 'The world cannot get richer unless its debts are greater. The modern capitalist world must feed on its own fat or it will be destroyed.'[54]

Copland might at this stage have been reading the doctrines of the early Australian economist William Hearn. An invitation to deliver the Macrossan Lectures at the University of Queensland in May 1935 presented an opportunity to deliver a timely lesson and also shed light on a neglected Australian economist. Hearn had emphasised that with depression the economy was not the key to economic recovery. To wit: 'The world which refuses to increase its debt must increase the impoverishment; it will grow richer by increasing its debts and not by reducing them.' Hearn's premise, identified by Copland, was that '[w]e have much that we may expend more. The World that refuses to expend more because it has much will very soon have less, until it reaches the stage where it will have nothing at all' (Copland:1935b).. Copland's lectures, later published, caught the ire of Hayek. He lamented that the expedient attempt by Copland to use Hearn 'as a peg on which to hang an exposition of the views of a particular group of modern Australian economists will do little to enhance Hearn's reputation' (Hayek 1936:101).

Copland dismissed the policy, put forward by some, including a federal parliamentary secretary, Frederick Stewart, of following Franklin Roosevelt's strategy in the United States of increasing wages as a means of generating recovery. Wages, Copland felt, would rise as recovery proceeded, which could be sustained only by a prior increase in investment spending.[55] Brigden and Shann publicly backed Copland's call for lower interest rates.[56] Shann reasoned that lower interest rates would encourage internal spending without impairing the export surplus.[57] Lower interest rates would also alleviate rural indebtedness,[58] especially since a scheme drawn up by Copland and others to write down farmers' debt had been received by banks as if it were 'marking the beginnings of the end of Australian capitalism' (Hart 1971:131).[59] An angry Copland pinned the government's U-turn on rural debt relief on the reaction from Melbourne financial interests (Hart 1971:131).[60]

---

54 'Lower interest: to revive investment', *The Argus*, 28 April 1934.
55 D. B. Copland to E. Harding, 16 October 1934, UMA FECC, Box 24.
56 'Interest rates', *Brisbane Telegraph*, 1 May 1934; 'Interest rates: further reduction needed', *The West Australian*, 20 July 1934.
57 'Liberal credit: Prof. Shann's views', *The West Australian*, 22 August 1934.
58 Senator Massy-Greene, the Assistant Treasurer, had floated a scheme to alleviate—indeed liquidate—rural indebtedness using ideas from the Douglas credit movement. It was designed also to counter the Labor Party's election proposal to nationalise credit while getting the Country Party onside. It disappeared without trace (Sir W. Massy-Greene to J. Lyons, 15 February 1934, AA, AA1068/391, Item 66).
59 D. B. Copland to D. Heaton, 18 June 1934, UMA FECC, Box 24.
60 D. B. Copland to W. S. Robinson, 27 June 1934, UMA FECC, Box 26.

Copland now detected a lack of leadership within the Commonwealth government, especially on matters of economic policy. According to Copland, Lyons' only really hope was Stevens, who, as he later put it, 'can understand the economic position better than most economists'.[61] In a memorandum written for a business associate, Copland noted an inconsistency in economic policy with the government lamely pushing for lower rates yet happy to indulge the bank board with thoughts of more funding. Copland, too, detected that Casey, for all his energy and promise, was captive to the bank board's view of things (Tsokhas 1993:109).[62]

As the economic recovery gathered momentum, the board, along with Melville, was still nervous of the possibilities of inflation if the trading banks presented the bills for rediscount and the note issue expansion that would subsequently ensue. The board took the view that the bills were issued only as an emergency measure to finance governments when loan markets were closed and it was never contemplated that they would reach such a high level. Expansionist economists, such as Giblin and Walker, however, dismissed such concerns, adopting the Keynes–Kahn view that with so much supply potential available there was little chance of inflation as expenditure rose (Cain 1988a:10). Any move, therefore, to curtail the issue of Treasury bills met with the opposition of Stevens, the Wales and, as Casey noted, 'the majority of economists of consequence in Australia' (Copland and Janes 1936:318). The odd economist out was Melville, who, as Wilson noted, had 'views on these matters…not shared in government or Treasury circles'.[63] In fact, Wilson was being a little disingenuous since the Federal Treasury also took a hard line against public spending (Cain 1988a:11–12).

The Assistant and Acting Treasurer, Casey, would moderate his views on funding, arguing later that the issuance of Treasury bills was defensible 'so long as it roughly does no more than is necessary to offset the reluctance of the community to use its savings'.[64] The new Chairman of the Commonwealth Bank Board, Claude Reading, however, relentlessly hammered home the message over the next few years that there was too much short-term debt for the Australian financial system to carry and that public loans be raised to reduce the number of Treasury bills in circulation. Casey was convinced by Reading's argument that it left the central bank with no margin for emergencies such as adverse seasonal conditions or the 'recrudescence of depression'.[65] Reading informed Norman at the Bank of England of the 'carefully considered and energetic propaganda in favour of expansion' being peddled by certain political and financial interests.

61 D. B. Copland to C. Baillieu, 24 March 1936, UMA FECC, Box 41.
62 'Confidential memorandum for Mr Clive Baillieu', 5 April 1934, UMA FECC, Box 21.
63 R. Wilson to L. F. Giblin, 7 December 1949, RBA, GLG-51-5.
64 'Memorandum on the present monetary position in Australia', 1935, AA, RGC 5.
65 Meeting with C. Reading, 10 May 1935, AA, CP503/1, R. G. Casey Records of Conversations.

Reading noted that the campaign was aimed directly at changing public opinion away from the allegedly 'short-sighted' policy of the Commonwealth Bank, which was being painted as the scapegoat. Reading said this alternative view was 'warped', with the correct policy being some moderation in the rate of recovery.[66]

In a switch in policy consistent with Melville's new outlook, the bank board adopted a more cautious attitude to public works, emphasising the psychological and open economy repercussions of too much loan expenditure (Cain 1988a:11). Funding would deliver an appropriate check to economic activity, which was being fuelled by public spending, deficit budgets and good export prices (Cain 1988a:12). The bank held that a paucity of savings, not investment, was the problem. It criticised the expansionists on their 'primrose path' for having no sense of proportion or limitation about the carrying capacity of the Australian economy (Cain 1988a:12).

Armitage, now a London-based officer of the Commonwealth Bank, relayed news of the contest of ideas between the economic expansionists and restrictionists to Montagu Norman:

> The desire of the States to spend money on public works continues, whether or not, the money can be raised from the public. Indeed a preference exists in some influential quarters for continuing to finance deficits and public works by Treasury Bills. This view is not held by this Bank.[67]

Emboldened by news of a turnaround in the global economy, the bank board informed state governments that central bank credit would be no longer available for either deficits or loan expenditure except as a temporary measure. Treasury bills, it held, were only a form of emergency finance.[68] Stressing the integrity of the Premiers' Plan, the bank board served notice that it would not finance deficits from 1934/35 onwards (Copland and Janes 1936). The bank board had become impatient with the states' tardiness in balancing their budgets. Budgets had to be balanced first before further expenditure would be considered. This view was in stark contrast with what expansionist economists and Davidson believed—namely, that the sporadic signs of recovery should not be mistaken for the return of general prosperity and that stimulatory measures must continue (Holder 1970:795).

---

66 C. Reading to Sir M. Norman, 15 October 1935, BE, G1/287.
67 H. T. Armitage to Sir M. Norman, 24 January 1933, BE, OV 13/2, 453/3.
68 'Financing of deficits', *SMH*, 21 June 1934.

When the mercurial Davidson visited London, Niemeyer thought it would be good if Montagu Norman saw him soon before he got up to mischief.[69] Kershaw's brief on the governor's visitor noted that Davidson was 'strong and brutal, a good banker...not instinctively theoretical...impressionable with all'.[70] Norman, alas, was not impressed by the Australian, finding that he put 'self and profit' before country.[71] Davidson wanted to raise a number of matters with Norman, including Treasury bills, Australia's exchange rate and rebuilding her sterling reserves. Apart from quizzing Davidson on his opinion on state budgets, Kershaw suggested Norman might 'shift your ground' by asking the visitor whether it might not be wise for 'Australia to go slow for a little while'.[72] That rather puzzling concern, at a time when Australia still had 20 per cent unemployment, invites a closer look at the peculiarities behind Australia's continuing economic recovery and the role economists—inside and outside—played in sustaining it.

'On the side of the angels': economists and recovery

> This bleeding country seems to impose severe exertions upon the nervous energy of economists. We are about to have an election and the banks are showing a little disenchantment to proceed with further reductions in interest rates and to encourage the Government to spend a reasonable amount on public works...when one sees the light so clearly it is difficult to keep one's patience with nit-wits.[73]

Lyons had won the federal election of spring 1934 promising nothing other than continuing economic recovery.[74] In the election campaign, he reminded the electorate of the ALP's policy on bank nationalisation before declaring that the trading banks had been the country's 'sheet anchor' and had 'saved the country from complete failure'.[75] This was a direct riposte to the Labor Party's campaign, which focused almost entirely on the reform of the banking and monetary system, including giving Parliament the authority to direct the central bank (Sutherlin 1980:12–13).[76] The private banks gave Lyons election material to wage

---

69   Davidson also met Keynes in London (A. C. Davidson to J. M. Keynes, 18 June 1934, L 34/62, and J. M. Keynes to A. C. Davidson, 28 June 1934, OC/2/171, KPKC).

70   E. Skinner, Secretary to the Governor, Memorandum, 13 April 1934, BE, OV 13/3 454/1. 'McKennaish' was a reference to the chairman of the Midlands Bank and former Chancellor of the Exchequer, Sir Reginald McKenna, who was of the expansionist bent. McKenna had incidentally praised Copland's efforts at economic reconstruction contained in his Marshall Lectures.

71   A. T. Lewis to L. G. Melville, 27 March 1937, Melville Papers, NLA.

72   Memorandum to Sir O. Niemeyer from R. Kershaw, 18 April 1934, BE, OV13/3.

73   D. B. Copland to H. Innis, 1 June 1934, UMA FECC, Box 24.

74   'Australia's recovery: rising tide of prosperity', SMH, 27 January 1934.

75   'Mr Lyons defends banks', SMH, 6 April 1934.

76   'Labor's policy explained by Scullin', SMH, 16 August 1934.

an 'essentially negative' campaign focusing on the disunity within the Labor camp, together with its unorthodox economic policies (Sawer 1963:72). Despite their grumbles about the professionalism of the government, both Davidson and Copland drafted a series of briefs for the Lyons election campaign highlighting the positive role the banking system played.[77] Shann penned articles for the press depicting the Australian banking system in a favourable light compared with those operating abroad. During the campaign, Lyons pledged to spend more on welfare and reproductive development work such as the unification of railway gauges. That came with assurances to state governments that the Commonwealth would work closely with them on major developmental and welfare projects. These plans for greater public spending were later shelved, being too much for the financial backers of the federal government to stomach (Lloyd 1984:241).

By this time Australia was, in any case, no longer 'feeling her way' but was treading the path towards full recovery (Copland and Janes 1936:xvii). Copland and other economists, however, felt that, with the mood of national emergency no longer present, a sense of complacency was creeping into the minds of policymakers. Copland told a Sydney University economics graduate, Ian Potter, that economists had to be prepared to see their advice thwarted by political pressures.[78] Copland showed some hubris, however, when he told his Sydney colleague Mills that '[i]t is always necessary to exert constant pressure on the politicians to keep them moving at a satisfactory pace in the right direction'.[79]

One national issue was the continuing high level of interest rates, which Copland attributed to a 'rentier psychology' and 'hard money' view within the Commonwealth Bank.[80] Copland assured a friend that he was 'on the side of the angels and…working behind the scenes' trying to change it. Economists attributed the nascent recovery to improving export prices, favourable business sentiment and rising levels of public and private investment (Copland 1936). Copland told Per Jacobsson of the Bank of International Settlements that the key force behind the 'extraordinary improvement' in Australian economic activity during 1932 and 1933 had been the combined effect of reductions in money costs and credit expansion.[81]

---

77 The hand of Copland can be palpably detected in a broadcast Lyons gave on the financial system in which he defended the role of the banks in the crisis and recovery and rejected the notion that the Bank of England influenced the Commonwealth Bank Board ('Banks' administration', *SMH*, 1 August 1934). This is scarcely surprising because Copland had written to Irvine Douglas, the Prime Minister's publicity officer, listing the positive role the banking system played in the economic crisis (D. B. Copland to I. Douglas, 29 May 1934, UMA FECC, Box 27).

78 D. B. Copland to I. Potter, 26 March 1934, UMA FECC, Box 25.

79 D. B. Copland to R. C. Mills, 24 May 1934, UMA FECC, Box 24.

80 D. B. Copland to E. H. Stinner, 8 June 1934, UMA FECC, Box 27.

81 D. B. Copland to P. Jacobsson, 27 August 1934, UMA FECC, Box 24.

In June 1934, the NSW Branch of the Economic Society conducted a forum on 'The economics of recovery' with Walker, Melville, Mills and a newcomer, Allan Fisher, all contributing. Fisher spoke of how the individual capitalist had been prevented from doing his duty due to fear and a lack of confidence. Melville complemented this by suggesting that it had to do with expectations that interest rates might fall further. Mills made noises about how properly banded action by the government might trigger private investment.[82]

With the re-election of the Lyons government one might have expected a steady-as-you-go approach to economic policy but this was not to be. The UAP was forced into a coalition with the Country Party, meaning that some inquiry of the monetary and banking system was now imminent (Sutherlin 1980:18–19).[83] The return of the Lyons government quickly brought attention to the state of the recovery—in particular, the reluctance of interest rates to fall. By the start of 1935, export prices had begun to slip again.

Besides commissioning an inquiry into the monetary system, Lyons also had to contend with younger blood unhappy with the government. The new member for Kooyong, R. G. Menzies, found the workings of the Lyons' cabinet amateurish compared with the Victorian state government he had just left. Casey, too, after a year of being Assistant Treasurer, felt that '[o]ur methods of giving consideration to matters of importance would disgrace a girls' school. The absence of study and research into important matters and the off hand decisions "on the voices" is a constant menace to the best interests of the country.'[84]

His friend Hankey, a former British Cabinet Secretary, found on his visit to Canberra that procedure within the Lyons cabinet was quite 'loose and rambling' (Martin 2000:124).

Long enamoured with economics expertise, Casey brought in Roland Wilson to advise 'on Treasury questions proper'.[85] Not long after, Wilson became Casey's key economic adviser.[86] The Treasurer had, however, to fight to secure his services by matching an enticing offer from his alma mater, the University of Tasmania. Wilson elected to stay put because it was 'the bigger job' (Cornish 2002b:20). Casey told Bruce that the young man 'had turned out very well' and 'besides knowing all the economic nonsense…has a good head, good judgement

---

82 'Economics of recovery', *SMH*, 13 June 1934.
83 The Country Party Leader, Earle Page, also wanted the inquiry to examine the relationship between export prices and domestic costs ('Country Party policy; Dr Page's reconstruction plans', *SMH*, 15 August 1934).
84 R. G. Casey to S. M. Bruce, 3 November 1934, AA, A1421/1; D. B. Copland to R. C. Mills, 24 May 1934, UMA FECC, Box 24.
85 R. G. Casey to S. M. Bruce, 3 November 1934, AA, A1421/1.
86 Copland congratulated Wilson, one of his former students, telling him, somewhat presciently, that 'I hope it will be a further step towards freeing you for consideration of the larger issues of policy' (D. B. Copland to R. Wilson, 1 March 1935, UMA FECC, Box 40).

and general balance'.[87] Casey arranged, probably with Giblin's help, to get a young economist to assist Wilson. It came in the form of another Tasmanian, Arthur Smithies, who returned from the United States with commendations from Joseph Schumpeter[88] and Copland.[89] There was also Ian Potter, who was for a brief time Casey's personal secretary.[90] Casey also toyed with the idea of adding Giblin to the Commonwealth Bank Board in a bid to put monetary policy on a more scientific footing. He assured Latham that the idiosyncratic Giblin would not be a risky appointment since '[t]here are sufficient "practical men of affairs" on the Board to dilute and, if necessary, to offset any radical tendencies that he may have'.[91] That counsel did not assuage the London manager of the Bank of Australasia, who felt Casey's appointment was, in itself, unwise since having 'had practically no business experience to the post he [Casey] now holds lays itself open to a danger of the introduction of revolutionary ideas and methods which a more experienced man would hesitate to employ'.[92] Their fears were misplaced for Casey rarely strayed from the bank board's economic perspective.

Apart from the homecoming of Smithies and Copland, three other economists returned to Australia after engaging in study overseas. Each would try to enlighten public opinion using the latest in overseas economic thought. Walker returned with one of the first doctorates in economics earned from Cambridge University (Cairncross 1998:43–4). Like Syd Butlin, Walker was supervised by D. H. Robertson, meaning that he was distant from Keynes's inner circle.[93] Walker, nonetheless, had invested much of the *Treatise*'s analytical framework into his doctorate on wage cuts and unemployment in Australia and would quickly become the most erudite Keynesian of interwar Australian economists. Butlin, who was undertaking another degree, fell under the influence of Robertson and was, like his mentor, wary of Keynes's doctrines (Butlin 1978). J. K. Gifford from the University of Queensland returned home also having completed a thesis, at Kiel in Germany.[94] H. C. 'Nugget' Coombs, too, returned home having completed a doctorate from the London School of Economics on 'Dominion exchanges and central bank problems' (Rowse 2002:65). Against the flow came a young visiting

---

87 R. G. Casey to S. M. Bruce, 20 February 1935, AA, A1421/2.
88 Schumpeter felt Smithies was an economist of 'unusual force and ability and of a very wide range of possibilities' (J. A. Schumpeter to L. F. Giblin, 18 August 1934, UMA FECC, Giblin Collection, 92/141, Box 2 k-t).
89 Smithies told Copland on 22 April 1935, 'I know that it is likely due to your efforts that I got the job in Canberra' (UMA FECC, Box 38).
90 Ian Potter was one of the first graduate economists to become fully engaged in stockbroking.
91 R. G. Casey to J. Latham, 16 January 1934, Latham Papers, NLA. Casey had a hand in the appointment of Coombs to the Commonwealth Bank in 1935 having interviewed him beforehand in Perth (Rowse 2002:73).
92 E. Godward to G. Healy, 11 January 1934, D/O Letters, Bank of Australasia, ANZ Archive.
93 Apart from a few statistical quibbles, Giblin favourably reviewed Walker's book in the *Economic Record*. He later confessed that the review did not do Walker full justice.
94 Gifford's thesis was also published. Entitled *Devaluation and the Pound*, it dealt with the general problem of correcting the balance of payments and the deflationary effects of the British pound devaluation and the advisability of returning to the gold standard.

scholar from Harvard to expressly compare Australia's recovery experience with that of the United States. Copland took Rupert MacLaurin under his wing and introduced him to the key players in the drama. The American duly reciprocated by trotting out the economists' line that the Australian recovery had not been fully effective because of mistakes with exchange rate policy and the lack of a coherent public works program. In a lecture, however, he told his audience that the Australian recovery had been a more effective one than the US effort.[95] The scaling down of interest rates on internal debt, engineered through a special clause of the Premiers' Plan, MacLaurin felt worthy of imitation elsewhere. When MacLaurin's book was published in 1936, it was warmly received by local economists.

The nature of the Australian recovery had attracted considerable international attention, which Copland, and less so Walker, appropriated with their accounts. Walker's treatment of the issue was, of course, more theoretically weighted than Copland's account. It was also closer in spirit to Keynes's world view of the conundrum than Copland's account, which had not theoretically developed from his position of 1931. Copland, for instance, still eschewed public works as the way out of the Depression. Walker found that the Australian wage cut of 1931—in terms of purchasing power analysis—had in fact done little to engineer economic recovery other than to give the export trades some breathing space. For a year after the wage cut, employment had not risen. Facing another burst of deflation, entrepreneurs would use the lower costs to reduce their overdrafts rather than to hire more workers. In short, wage cuts would do little to stimulate investment and bring it into line with savings. This, of course, was the advice Keynes conveyed to Australian economists in 1932. Public works was the answer; it would absorb savings and trigger a multiplier effect in consumption spending. If this was attempted, entrepreneurs' expectations would focus more on expansion than on retiring debts. Walker was insistent that public works be financed by borrowing from the public rather than resorting to bank credit. This was crucial in the name of business confidence (Cornish 1990:61). Once recovery was under way, some wage cuts, Walker mooted, might be of advantage though it opened the door to international retaliation. On that score, Walker held that the Australian devaluation of 1931 had been effective, not by giving a stimulus by way of more net exports, but rather by allowing more space for domestic stimulation to take place (Cornish 1990:61).

Copland's book, too, gave hope for some degree of economic enlightenment. The Canadian economist A. F. W. Plumptre (1935:131–3) said Copland's account demonstrated that Australia was indeed a land where 'the plans of Economic Men have been put into practice'. In his own mind, Copland was intrigued by Roosevelt's 'unorthodox' attempts at recovery but complained that he could

---

95 'Recovery plans: American and Australian', *SMH*, 9 October 1934.

not 'get any line on the point of view of American economists' in tackling the slump. This drew a compliment from the polymath Archibald Grenfell-Price that the lack of progress in the United States made one realise 'how good has been the job that you and the other Australian economists have done'.[96]

Copland's account of the crisis, however, sparked a feud in the expansionist camp. Davidson was incensed with Copland's account because it omitted mention of the Commonwealth Bank Board's doctrinaire position on funding and the exchange rate. The book also did not mention the role of the Bank of New South Wales in forcing the 1931 devaluation (Plumptre 1935:132). Copland had praised the coordinated, albeit improvised, strategy effected by Australia's economic institutions, including the central bank, in leading the country out of the slump. In fact, the local banking system had, by creating an amount of credit greater than any other country, pulled Australia out of the slump. Moreover, Copland (1937a:411) also held that the Commonwealth Bank's appreciation of the currency in December 1931, while at first glance 'an act of deflation turned out to have strong expansionist tendencies'. That is, the action lent confidence to local and overseas capital markets that the Commonwealth Bank was taking control of matters. Capital inflow piled in.

Davidson was annoyed at Copland's faint praise of the Commonwealth Bank, fearing that 'it played into the hands' of those opposed to the expansionist school. Copland tried to mollify Davidson by replying that the Commonwealth Bank did not really understand the good it had done by adopting 'unorthodox' financial measures.[97] Unmoved, Davidson still felt Copland had made a blunder in making benign reference to an institution that was still following a 'dreadful deflationary policy'.[98] Copland told his contact at the Bank of New South Wales, Claude Janes, that while Davidson's charge was 'absurd' he did not want to jeopardise the unity within the camp. Knowing his chief's vanity and, indeed, that of his mentor, Janes suggested letting the matter rest. Besides placing Janes in an invidious position, the disagreement opened a divide between two of the most powerful players within the expansionist camp.[99] The feud festered into the new year with Copland feeling that the headstrong Davidson—'His Royal Highness'—was, for all his good work in promoting the discipline, prone to dismissing the worth of economists especially when their views did not match

---

96   D. B. Copland to A. Grenfell-Price, 6 March 1932, and A. Grenfell-Price to D. B. Copland, 6 April 1932, UMA FECC, Box 204 A.
97   A. C. Davidson to D. B. Copland, 7 December 1934, and D. B. Copland to A. C. Davidson, 19 July 1934, UMA FECC, Box 22; D. B. Copland to C. Janes, 12 December 1934, and C. Janes to D. B. Copland, 14 December 1934, UMA FECC, Box 24.
98   A. C. Davidson to D. B. Copland, 21 December 1934, UMA FECC, Box 22.
99   Another economist with an Australian connection not entirely swept along by Copland's work was F. Benham. Copland told Austin Robinson, the Associate Editor for the *Economic Journal*, that Benham did not fully understand the point of view of the Australian economists circa the early 1930s (D. B. Copland to E. A. G. Robinson, 24 October 1934, UMA FECC, Box 25).

his own.[100] One instance of this was when Melville took the line from late 1933 onwards of pursuing exchange stability. Davidson warned Kershaw not to take the advice too seriously as Melville 'is really an actuary and statistician, and owing to that training, finds it extremely difficult to take into consideration the general economic, financial and business aspects of the problem'.[101] It was also inaccurate. Melville wanted the exchange rate to move 'in accordance with internal conditions' (Schedvin 1970:364–5).

The Sydney plan

When a businessman suggested to Copland that it was time for the Wallace Bruce Committee to reconvene to consider the state of the economy, Copland assured him that economists already had another plan in the offing.[102] Copland had already been invited by Stevens to contribute towards devising a 'new Premiers' Plan', or better still, one that would complement it, by dealing with problems of public finance, unemployment, trade and marketing.[103] With unemployment still at 20 per cent and national income at £500 million compared with the pre-depression level of £650 million, and world export prices sliding again, Stevens had a point. Impatient with the pace of recovery, Stevens commissioned a group of Sydney University economists in May 1934 to devise major changes to economic policy. The resulting submission was presented to a Loan Council meeting.

Led by Mills, the committee comprised Walker, Copland and Hermann Black with William Wentworth from the premier's office assisting (Cain 1988a:7). In the press, Walker had called for more public works with the economy still in depression. The committee's report was full of expansionist precepts and policies, meaning that Sydney and Melbourne academic economists were now of the same ilk. In fact, there had been some undercurrent of antipathy between the two schools with Mills and Butlin having 'limited sympathy' for the public activities of the Melbourne school (Butlin 1978:104). Walker's arrival on the stage helped to bridge the divide.

The Sydney plan or 'forward policy' was one of controlled inflation achieved through a concerted plan through increased public works expenditure. The plan was 'forward' in the sense that the slow rate of world recovery made pre-emptive, constructive policy imperative. Some fundamental changes in the economy were necessary even if export prices continued to hold up. Interestingly,

---

100   D. B. Copland to C. Janes, 13 March 1935, UMA FECC, Box 34.
101   A. C. Davidson to R. Kershaw, 20 August 1934, BE, OV 13/3.
102   H. V. Howe [NSW Chamber of Manufactures] to D. B. Copland, 6 July 1934, UMA FECC, Box 24.
103   B. S. Stevens to D. B. Copland, 21 May 1934, UMA FECC, Box 27.

the preamble on public works expenditure was regarded primarily as a means of generating consumption demand. Copland claimed the rise in income from the public spending would generate the savings to fund the operation (Cain 1988a:8–9). The plan, as presented to Stevens, bore the imprint of Walker's latest research in establishing that the two principal economic problems were unemployment and the transference of workers from uncompetitive industries. The final polished version sounded almost like Keynes in his public writings. It began with the words: 'In times of depression the resources of a country are not fully employed but men and equipment are idle. This idleness arises from a failure of consumers' demand and can only be overcome by an expansion of that demand.'[104]

Its premise was that the slower and more uncertain the world recovery, the more necessary it was to revive consumption spending. The Sydney plan also envisaged reducing interest rates while suspending funding operations, if not increasing the amount of Treasury bills in circulation. There were also clauses on debt reduction, the exchange rate, wages policy and trade preferences. Copland was so heartened by it that he told Stevens that he must make a serious play to enter federal politics. Only he truly understood and had the technical ability to push the expansionist cause. If Stevens chose to remain where he was he would be driving policy 'from the back seat'. It was better and indeed far easier, Copland assured him, to be driving from the box seat, and that meant the position of Federal Treasurer.[105] If Stevens entered the federal arena it would buttress Lyons' position, which, while partial to the philosophy of the plan, was neutralised by a cautious cabinet.

Despite the memorandum raising the hopes of the economists this remarkable proto-Keynesian document registered little impact at the intergovernmental level. Stevens did, however, extract from Lyons the promise to authorise more public works after the election.[106] While Copland bemoaned to W. S. Robinson that things would be much easier 'if the forces of conservative finance were a little less strong', London was told a different story.[107] Dalton, the British trade representative, told his superiors in London that there was 'a strong tendency to indulge in expansionist policies', entailing borrowing 'for public works and the like'. There was also the suspicion that the Commonwealth Bank was not exercising the same degree of restraint since state government deficits persisted with the total public sector borrowing nearly £25 million per annum. Dalton pondered whether the resort to public works might lead to 'conditions of

---

104   'The case for expansion', n.d., UMA FECC, Box 27.
105   D. B. Copland to B. S. B. Stevens, 11 June 1934, UMA FECC, Box 27.
106   W. Wentworth to D. B. Copland, 13 June 1934, UMA FECC, Box 27.
107   D. B. Copland to W. S. Robinson, 18 June 1934, UMA FECC, Box 24.

artificial prosperity', which had triggered Australia's financial crisis in the first place. While he thought this recurrence unlikely, he was still anxious about whether Australia could meet her liabilities without assistance.[108]

In his missives to powerful business associates such as Robinson and Baillieu, Copland fathomed the layers of the psychological mind-set financial circles held against expansionary policies. Most business and finance houses were, quite simply, unaware and unappreciative of the fact that Australia had extricated itself from the slump by a policy that was no less unorthodox than it was inflationary. Sir Robert Gibson, for instance, had always interpreted the rehabilitation of Australia's finances as 'something in the nature of a fairy tale'.[109] Despite Australia's heavy resort to credit most bankers were still unable to see how Treasury bill finance had helped them and were now resisting cutting rates, which would 'only require a small effort on their part'.[110] When the unorthodox policies of economists failed to generate a full-bodied recovery it merely confirmed bankers' doubts about the efficacy and worth of experts' plans. This, as Copland told Jacobsson at the Bank of International Settlement, led to 'a greater agitation than ever for deflationary policies'. Moreover, even when the economic situation did improve conservatives were just as likely to attack not just the heretical measures that were found necessary during the crisis but to prevent other progressive changes from occurring lest they disturb the equilibrium.[111]

Copland closed his letter to Jacobsson with the hope that 'a counsel of moderation' would prevail and allow Australia to tread further along the path of mild inflation.[112] They would face, however, the unremitting and quite uninformed opposition of the rentier class. The opposition from Collins Street mounted against Copland was particularly galling since the Trades Hall frequently charged him with being in the pay of the banks. For their part, bankers, as one had half-jokingly told Copland, would like to see him and his doctrines 'floating down the Yarra'.[113] Nonetheless, Copland was happy to foresee the day when the Commonwealth would assume greater responsibility for the relief of unemployment by more loan expenditure. He was joined in this wish by Sydney economists. Walker gave an address before the NSW Branch of the Economic Society in March 1935 contesting the view that once public works

---

108   R. W. Dalton to Sir E. Crowe, Department of Trade, 6 November 1934, PRO, T160/808/11935/7, File No. 8.

109   *The Argus*, 19 December 1934.

110   D. B. Copland to P. Jacobsson, 27 April 1934, UMA FECC, Box 24.

111   D. B. Copland to W. S. Robinson, 26 September 1934, UMA FECC, Box 26.

112   D. B. Copland to P. Jacobsson, 18 June 1934, UMA FECC, Box 24.

113   D. B. Copland to Laing, 7 December 1934, UMA FECC, Box 24.

slowed the economy would slip back into depression. Rather, if undertaken correctly it would trigger private investment spending that would use up idle savings thus allowing public expenditure to gradually taper off.[114]

Copland astutely read the prevailing psychological mood as having reached a position of security such that business and finance were impatient with further experimentation. The consequence was that, as in 1932, Australia faced a reoccurrence of 'a somewhat reactionary phase' with the danger of undoing the good already done.[115] This manifested, as we have seen, in the advocates of funding raising the cry of over-borrowing and the Commonwealth Bank insisting that all deficits be financed by public loans. Copland felt the federal government might cave in to the board's demand since 'it is not a government with great convictions about anything and it has very few strong Ministers'. Despite this, Copland was optimistic that 'the pressure of public influence in favour of spending is so great' that the Commonwealth would abide with its program of public works even if it meant a hardening of interest rates in the future.[116]

Giblin also attacked the government's lassitude and deference to the Commonwealth Bank by sending a memorandum to Casey in late 1934 warning that falling export prices again compelled the need for a more proactive policy stance. Calling for a new Premiers' Plan 'to meet known tendencies and prepare for the unknown', Giblin felt the only way of preventing an economic relapse was more public expenditure financed by Treasury bills (Cain 1988a:7–8). He took the opportunity to wage on Casey the augmentative power of the multiplier. Should the Commonwealth Bank prove recalcitrant Giblin encouraged the re-elected Lyons government to take charge and not 'shelter behind a Bank Board of their own creating'. In closing, Giblin warned Casey that if the federal government failed to act an alternative government would, with consequences as disastrous as the present administration's complacency.[117]

The calls made, therefore, by both Melbourne and Sydney economists for more boldness and adventure in policy settings during 1933/34 gives the lie to Schedvin's (1970:375) claim that they were still bound to the Premiers' Plan framework. In the light, too, of Schedvin's thesis about the leading, if accidental role of manufacturing in generating recovery, the Melbourne and Sydney economists had also focused their minds on generating internal recovery rather than relying on exports to deliver salvation. The former Assistant Treasurer

---

114   'Public works', *SMH*, 13 March 1935.
115   D. B. Copland to F. Taussig, 23 November 1934, UMA FECC, Box 27.
116   'Memo on the financial policy of Commonwealth government', 16 November 1934, UMA FECC, Box 27.
117   Untitled manuscript, November 1934, UMA FECC, Box 23.

Massy-Greene drew attention to this after receiving a copy of the Sydney plan.[118] Primary production for export was, in any case, not as employment intensive as manufacturing. Massy-Greene told Copland that the development of secondary industry was the only means to absorb the unemployed. Moreover, with the drying up of foreign loans, Massy-Greene felt Australia would be stretched accumulating foreign balances sufficient to pay her way in the world.[119] On this point, Copland admitted his concern that any upturn in economic activity would, with rising imports, jeopardise the external account.[120] Those fears were soon to materialise.

Before then Massy-Greene informed Copland that he had asked Casey to reconvene the committee of experts who had drafted the Premiers' Plan to make some reappraisal of economic strategy. This was something the economists welcomed. Like Giblin, Copland felt that with the election over, it was time for the government 'to take a risk', even if both sides of politics would object to 'the Government calling in wicked economists again' for advice.[121] Copland believed that a strong report from a competent committee would allow the government to disengage itself from the fetters of Melbourne high finance—a sentiment Massy-Greene agreed with.[122] That hope depended on the advocacy powers of Casey.

Casey at the helm

We are all 'expansionists'—it is only a matter of degree.

— R. G. Casey, 1936

While he would not fully assume the mantle of Federal Treasurer until October 1935, Casey had effectively been in command of the portfolio since 1934. He was a ball of energy, matched by an equal intensity 'to be in the limelight'; but whether his usually homespun economic proposals would win over cabinet was another matter entirely (Hudson 1986:93).[123] There was no doubting Casey's industry and mental versatility, but his biographer, W. J. Hudson, argues his subject did not have the forbearance to overcome the cut and thrust of cabinet.

---

118 Working alongside Copland within the Austral Development Company in an advisory capacity, Massy-Greene changed his tune on the worth of economists. He had even begun to appreciate the outpourings of Keynes, particularly on public sector stimulus. At the same time, he grew wary of 'The Hard Money School', who trenchantly opposed a more liberal central bank policy (W. Massy-Greene to D. B. Copland, 2 September 1935, UMA FECC, Box 45).

119 W. Massy-Greene to D. B. Copland, 27 June 1934, UMA FECC, Box 34.

120 D. B. Copland to W. Massy-Greene, 28 June 1934, UMA FECC, Box 34.

121 D. B. Copland to W. Massy-Greene, 19 November 1934, and W. Massy-Greene to D. B. Copland, 17 November 1934, UMA FECC, Box 34.

122 Ibid.

123 E. Godward to G. Healy, 13 December 1934, D/O Correspondence, ANZ Archive.

Casey's own view on pushing matters through Parliament showed a lack of combativeness (Hudson 1986:92–3); he told Bruce: 'I never look for a fight in the house as I can find I can get business through much easier and quicker by a reasonable degree of courtesy and without bombast. This may or may not be the way to get on in the show.'[124]

Casey was quite happy to placate Lyons' wish to invite Bruce back and was even prepared, just days after becoming Federal Treasurer, to step aside and allow him to take his place (White 1987:175). Equally disarming was that while Casey always made a good early impression on his cabinet colleagues, the second impression of his knowledge and depth was never as flattering (Hasluck 1996:85; Spender 1972:32–3). Colleagues and opponents quickly sensed Casey's irresolution behind the confident facade.

Economists, too, starting with Copland, would quickly appreciate W. S. Robinson's observation that Casey 'lacked understanding' and was 'timid' when it came to confronting the bank board.[125] Copland, for instance, had to remind Casey that there was no relationship between Australia's level of imports and her level of exports. Rather, the level of spending determined imports.[126] Casey had energetically marked his first year in the job by personally drafting a stream of memoranda on a whole series of economic policy issues.[127] It met with a lukewarm response from a cabinet convinced that their orientation was too radical (Hudson 1986:93). Casey had already been unhappy with the nature of cabinet decision making, intimating to Bruce that

> we amble along as a collection of individuals doing the obvious things that come to mind—but doing no forward thinking—and generally managing to avoid or sidestep the difficult problems until they are on our doorstep—then we make a snap, line-of-least-resistance decision which is usually costly, in which we merely always sacrifice principle. Heaven knows how we have kept out of real trouble.[128]

By drawing up a series of informative briefs—partly for his own edification—Casey idealistically hoped it would improve policy deliberation.

One of Casey's first memoranda addressed Giblin's call for a more active attack on unemployment (Cain 1988a:13). While agreeing that it was the main social and political problem facing the country, Casey did not believe the problem could be resolved by government action. Rather the problem was attributable

---

124   R. G. Casey to S. M. Bruce, 9 December 1934, AA, A 1421/2.
125   D. B. Copland to W. S. Robinson, 27 June 1934, UMA FECC, Box 26.
126   D. B. Copland to R. G. Casey, 19 August 1935, UMA FECC, Box 32.
127   By 1934, Casey was, in effect, Federal Treasurer with Lyons having not set foot inside the Treasury building in the past 18 months except once while dodging pressmen.
128   R. G. Casey to S. M. Bruce, 9 December 1934, AA, A 1421/1.

to the general economic 'tone' of the community and it would diminish only when 'things improve'. After discussing the two main ways of increasing employment—that is, stimulating private enterprise and maintaining, if not increasing, loan-financed public works—Casey came to the conclusion that 'no major line of attack upon unemployment had come to light' (Cain 1988a:13–14). Even the last-ditch methods of 'the most radical experimentalist' approach of injecting a 'shot' of more public works expenditure into the economy, a la Giblin, would be inflationary and jeopardise the jobs of the majority. Casey also contended that more funds could not be found over the amount expended on public works. He concluded that the present ensemble of policies continue with cheap money enshrined by making the Commonwealth Bank go easy on funding. This position was, in retrospect, not much of an advance on the UAP's earlier position on unemployment, as enunciated by Latham, who felt that the problem was best tackled by tax relief rather than commissioning more public works.[129]

In subsequent memoranda, Casey turned his attention to the matter of Australian governments' finance. The deficits of the state governments and the bank board's refusal to accommodate them were, together with the aggregate public works program, putting pressure on the local capital market. After considering the alternative of an open market for bills, which Casey initially favoured, he swung around to a position whereby if the states cut their deficits the bank board would relax its strictures about financing deficits.[130] That way the bank board would get its way without seeming to dictate to the states about their spending levels. Rather, the limits of deficits and the public works programs would be ultimately determined by how willing the public was to lend. Casey feared that these loan requirements had a tendency to outstrip the means to supply them. In this he was proved right, since the Commonwealth Bank, after representations from the Loan Council, relented and allowed some Treasury bill financing of state deficits for 1934/35.[131] Casey told cabinet that the government should place pressure on the states to trim their public work programs, which had soared from £6 million in 1931/32 to £22 million by 1934/35. Otherwise the total public sector borrowing would amount to £30 million for each of the next two years and this would be quite beyond the local market's capacity to control. If it was unchecked, it would mean petitioning the Commonwealth Bank to allow further deficit finance with bills for 1936/37 and only a modicum of funding. Bruce praised Casey's stance as ideally balanced between the ultra-expansionists and those who felt that all deficits and public works should be sourced from loan

129   J. Latham to E. A. Kemp, 18 February 1933, Latham Papers, NLA.
130   R. G. Casey Papers dealing with public finance, 15 November 1934, AA, CP503/1, Item 3.
131   'Loan Council problems: memorandum for the subcommittee', 5 December 1934, AA, A1421/1, Item 1.

finance.[132] Casey was also not initially prepared to advocate the creation of an open market for bills, essentially because it would put the government offside with the trading banks.[133]

In his November memorandum referred to earlier, Casey took the opportunity to reflect on the two schools of economic expansionism then in vogue. The Labor or Scullin line, which no economist supported, was critical of public works but in favour of the nationalisation of credit. The other school of expansionists followed the government line with its ensemble of policies including public works, cheap money and Treasury bills. This school believed it was 'the proper function of governments' to authorise public works until prices and private enterprise recovered. Casey, however, was not prepared to take up the cudgels in persuading the bank board to adopt an accommodating monetary policy, or even issuing more bills if the recovery faltered. He was grateful for what had already been achieved. When, in contrast, it came to considering restrictive monetary policy, Casey proved more amenable. Such was the prospect facing the country by the end of 1935.

A 'sharp cleavage of economic opinion': containing the economic expansion

After years of dealing with the economics of slump, by late 1935 Australian economists found themselves dealing with an economy in apparent semi-boom (Copland 1936:10). The delineation or 'sharp cleavage of opinion' between inside and outside economists over how to rectify the problem was informed by each camp's theoretical premises (Copland and Janes 1936:xvi).

In March 1936, Casey wrote to Sir Maurice Hankey informing him of how he had been struggling for the past eight months with the Australian balance of payments and 'at long last have come to some sort of conclusion in my own mind about it all'.[134] The nub of the problem was that, in the absence of overseas borrowing, Australia had to generate an export surplus to pay for her imports and maintain debt payments to London. With her appetite for imports resurging, and export prices still 30 per cent below their pre-depression peak, Casey was hard pressed coming up with a solution other than the traditional respite of depreciation or tariffs, both of which he loathed. Buttressed by advice from Treasury, Casey told Hankey that '[y]ou can depreciate your currency as easily

---

132   S. M. Bruce to R. G. Casey, 9 March 1935, AA, A1421/2.
133   'Loan council problems', 5 December 1934, AA, A1421/1, Item 1, p. 24.
134   R. G. Casey to Sir M. Hankey, 30 March 1936, Hankey Papers, Churchill College.

as kiss your hand, but it is almost beyond mortal power to appreciate it again. If your exchange rate slips, it apparently slips for good.'[135] Bruce added to Casey's fears about devaluation, warning him how dimly London would see it.[136]

The other alternative was to stage manage an economic slowdown. Put another way, the crux of Australia's difficulty was that expansionary policy only applied internally; nothing could be done to lift the prices and volume of exports. Eventually Casey stumbled on a long-term structural solution to the perennial problem of the external account. It was an idea that Giblin and other economists had come to six years earlier—namely, that the country attract British industrial interests to manufacture locally behind a tariff wall. Casey said the benefit to Britain was that Australia, at last, would neither have to depreciate nor default on her debts (Ross 1995:190).[137] In the meantime, however, some adjustment of macroeconomic policy was imperative. The economic circumstances that brought Casey to this revelation are worth examining since it was, in a sense, redolent of the crisis of 1931.

A cabinet submission, written by Casey in March 1936, detailed not just the economic policy dilemma facing Australia but the circumstances leading up to it. Since mid-1935, the economy had been recovering too fast and the key issue was whether economic activity should be checked to protect the external account (Copland and Janes 1936:i–vii). Merchandise imports had soared from £44 million in 1931 to almost £83 million by 1935/36. The level of London funds was comparatively low compared with previous years. Domestically, the rate of interest was tending to rise at a time when state governments were still intent on securing more central bank credit. The increase in public spending, especially by the states, provoked fears of a rerun of the 1920s. It left Casey horrified at the prospect of devaluation as the London funds dwindled due to imports and a speculative outflow of capital. Puzzled by the dilemma, Casey noted '[i]t is a queer thing that you cannot embrace a liberal domestic policy without having to accept the probability of unpleasant counter-reactions arising directly from that policy'.[138] Countries with debts and a trade-dependent profile could also not expand the domestic level of activity without due regard for the exchange rate (Cain 1983).

The advice from the official economic advisers—Melville, Smithies and Wilson— was to curb domestic expenditure before disaster befell Australia. Systemically, investment was racing ahead of savings caused by monetary overextension;

---

135   Ibid. The advice came from a briefing from Smithies. He in fact added that there was also a tendency for the exchange rate to have recurring depreciations a la Niemeyer and Gregory (in 1930) (Cain 1988a:26).
136   S. M. Bruce to R. G. Casey, 14 September 1935, AA, A11857, The Treasury Secretary Papers 1934–37, Correspondence with S. M. Bruce.
137   R. G. Casey to M. Hankey, 30 March 1936, Hankey Papers, Churchill College.
138   R. G. Casey to S. M. Bruce, 2 September 1935, AA, CP503/1, Item Bundle 3.

if unchecked, this would result not just in devaluation but in a boom–bust. Against this lay the members of the expansionist camp, who felt that it would be premature to deflate the economy just because of pressures on the external account (Cain 1988a:20–1). They contended that the point had not yet been reached when public loan expenditure should be wound back. Besides Giblin and Copland and their Sydney counterparts, Mills and Walker, the expansionist school had political, even financial muscle, with the respective support of Stevens and Davidson. Against them ranged the trading banks, the Commonwealth Bank, the Federal Treasury and, of course, the federal government.

Lyons, who had been abroad for the past eight months, was aghast at the prospect of higher rates as it would signify not just the end of the recovery but a resort to deflation. One response was to place his old economic adviser, Giblin, on the Commonwealth Bank Board in a bid to defuse the problem. It would also raise the technical level of policy deliberation within the board with Giblin, a monetary specialist, peppering his colleagues with statistical data and a review of economic conditions—something Gibson would never have allowed in his heyday (Millmow 2000:61). Giblin was probably as surprised as anyone with his appointment since months earlier he had given another address at the Shillings Club warning of dire consequences if public spending contracted (Millmow 2000). He followed this up with a memorandum full of grim foreboding if the Commonwealth Bank fell craven 'to the primitive deflationary instincts of the less intelligent sections of the business world'.[139] With unemployment still at 18 per cent, Australia could fall into recession if deflationary policies were pursued. To forestall this, and having to undergo what he now considered the futility of cost cutting, Giblin proposed public works with some monetary accommodation to prevent interest rates rising.

Copland detected that Giblin's appointment had to do with Lyons' fear that the banks would—with Casey apparently seduced by the virtues of deflation—take the opportunity to increase their rates.[140] Adverse publicity of that spectre came when the Melbourne *Herald* ran an editorial querying the wisdom of raising interest rates with unemployment still widespread. The same newspaper had warmly welcomed Giblin's appointment to the bank board.[141] Copland believed his contacts with Sir Keith Murdoch, and his editorial staff, had pre-empted—so far—the rise in interest rates. In this instance, he reminded Brigden: 'There is no doubt that occasional statements from one or other of us...

---

139 'The progress of recovery', 1935, UMA FECC, Box 214.
140 D. B. Copland to J. Burton, 21 October 1935, UMA FECC, Box 30. The trading bank community, still unrepentantly dismissive of the worth of economists, was delighted that Copland was not the appointee to the board since he was perceived as 'thick' with Davidson and a 'credit expansion man' (G. Healy to E. Godward, 27 November 1935, D/O Correspondence, Bank of Australasia, ANZ Archive).
141 *The Herald*, 26 September 1935, and 'The best man for the job', *The Herald*, 21 October 1935.

has a considerable influence at critical times.'[142] Since coming to Melbourne, Copland had assiduously built up relations with newspaper editors, especially Murdoch (Younger 2003:140–2). An overlooked factor in the influence and ideas of economists in this whole period was having powerful players interested in what enlightened economic policy could achieve.[143]

Perplexed by the issue of whether it was possible to keep the recovery going without jeopardising the current account, Casey turned to his personal economic adviser. Wilson penned a long, philosophical letter, poignantly written from Chicago, outlining the two contending schools of economic thought about the Depression. While relaxed about the short-term debt, Wilson echoed Melville's advice that extensive resort to public works would indeed result in a boom–bust scenario together with incipient devaluation. In Hayekian tones, Wilson spoke of the economy's 'natural and recuperative tendency' being hamstrung by an 'unfortunate combination of circumstances' coupled with the endemic feature of cyclical instability. Given this, Wilson settled for policies that would keep industry profitable including tariff reform, low interest rates and keeping public works to 'a reasonable level'.[144] Cain (1988a:26) finds Wilson's letter bereft of any awareness of what Keynes and Kahn were saying about the economy's ability to deliver supply and was focused purely on monetary, not expenditure, flows.

At the same time, Copland, in a conversation with Smithies, argued for continuing the expansion on the premise that the exchange rate be flexible (Cain 1988a:19). Deploying Giblin's multiplier, Copland was prepared to go as far as having employment return to normal levels and budgets brought into balance. Smithies took issue with this view (Cain 1988a:25). If anything, public works, taken too far, would leave the economy distorted with rising costs, inappropriate real wage levels and a bloated public sector. The purgative would be depreciation and, ultimately, deflation—the result expansionist economists had all along wished to avoid. Moreover, real wages would have to be adjusted downwards. Smithies (1936 would also cross swords with Walker on the matter of wage cuts.

As the London funds fell, Melville hurriedly organised an informal committee involving Mills, Copland, Giblin and Smithies to discuss what to do.[145] Melville dismissed the idea that the central bank stand ready to inject liquidity into the

---

142   D. B. Copland to J. B. Brigden, 28 November 1935, UMA FECC, Box 31.

143   Copland gave letters of introduction to Murdoch to several influential economists including Keynes for his visit to England in 1936. He described Murdoch as someone who 'has given quite valuable assistance to the economists in Australia in their public work during the last six years…and has taken a very active interest in the economic policy of Australia over the past six or seven years' (D. B. Copland to Prof. Daniel, 14 April 1936, UMA FECC, Box 44).

144   R. Wilson to R. G. Casey, 11 September 1935, AA, CP503/1, Item Bundle 3.

145   D. B. Copland to W. S. Robinson, 14 September 1935, UMA FECC, Box 37.

economy to allow unemployment to return to normal levels; instead, the role of monetary policy was to allow 'voluntary' savings and investment to find balance (Cain 1988a:22). Initially, Copland was sceptical of the Melville line that private investment would take up the slack created by cutting back on public loan expenditure. Robinson kept Keynes informed of the debate and would have also recycled the latter's views to Copland.[146] While the three academic economists were ardent expansionists and came to the September meeting armed with memoranda, a compromise was reached whereby it was agreed that only a moderate expansion of public spending was now deemed desirable in order to safeguard the external account (Cain 1988a:15–20).[147] Devaluation was apparently ruled out. Keynes was happy to hear of it.[148] A week earlier, Keynes had told Robinson that after reading memoranda on the matter he remained unconvinced that devaluation was desirable. Keynes volunteered the view that the 'relief' from devaluation was exaggerated, but more importantly, frequent resort to this expedient, even discussion of it, would establish a precedent that capital movements could exploit, resulting, therefore, in 'an indefinite progression of devaluation'.[149]

Besides this insight from afar, Cain (1988a:18–21) has adroitly covered the reasons why the expansionists did a remarkable *volte-face* in their position. Melville exploited a 'hesitance' within his opponents and persuaded, perhaps reminded, them of the immediate past. Probably apprised of Keynes's disposition, Copland lost interest in devaluation. This was besides the fact that the Commonwealth Bank would do all in its powers to preserve the rate. In explaining Walker's conversion to the official line, Cain (1988a:21) speculates that he was perhaps satisfied that public expenditure be tapered as unemployment drew closer to its pre-depression rate. Walker had not timidly fallen prey to the monetary overinvestment thesis that an unchecked boom will lead to bust. Rather he was confident that the tapering-off process could be proportionate to the recovery in employment in the private sector provided there was also no sharp contraction in public spending.[150] Nonetheless, it had not dawned on Walker, or his opponents, that a rising level of investment would generate more savings via a higher income level (Cain 1988a:23). Lastly, Walker was well aware of the negative business sentiment being sown by an inappropriately high level of public works.

Giblin's view of things was only really revealed six months later when he issued a press statement or memorandum justifying the Commonwealth Bank Board's decision to further dampen economic activity by raising interest rates in March

---

146   W. S. Robinson to J. M. Keynes, 8 October 1935, KPKC.
147   'Memorandum on conference of economists', October 1935, AA, A 1968/391, Item 48.
148   J. M. Keynes to W. S. Robinson, 22 October 1935, KPKC.
149   J. M. Keynes to W. S. Robinson, 16 October 1935, KPKC.
150   'Loan expenditure facilitates general recovery', *SMH*, 12 February 1936.

1936.[151] Australia, he said, was close to 'normal' unemployment and had to 'mark time' by slowing down the rate of expansion. This was the consequence, of course, of expanding faster than Australia's trading partners and the need to protect her external account. Giblin's statement, as we shall see, was a double-edged sword.

At the policy level, Casey invoked the authority of these 'outside' experts in warranting the cutback in public works that occurred in November. He went on to articulate his ideal of a 'forward' monetary policy holding that credit should not continue to the point where all the unemployed were absorbed but rather only until private investment picked up. Only when that process began was recovery assured. Pure expansionism, on the other hand, would merely end in an inflationary boom. This was a rebuttal of the Davidson–Stevens line. They had, with Copland's help, been debating—later feuding—with Casey, alleging that the Commonwealth Bank had deliberately, and quite unnecessarily, engaged in monetary tightening to protect the London funds. This portended higher interest rates and renewed agitation to write down debts.[152] Claude Janes told Smithies that the trading banks were restricting credit 'to the point of curtailment' and that they would soon be unable to accommodate overdraft requests unless relieving action was taken by the central bank.[153] Davidson wrote to Casey warning him of an imminent rise in rates unless monetary stringency was eased.[154] In an internal note to Sheehan, Casey, echoing the Reading interpretation of events, vented his anger at Davidson's impertinence at blaming the Commonwealth Bank and 'inferentially' the government for the Wales' liquidity problems. Casey blustered: 'The business of the General Manager of a Bank is presumably to manage his Bank—not to direct the monetary policy of the country, nor to run the Commonwealth Bank.'[155] Melville investigated the Wales' liquidity problems and concluded that its embarrassment was due mostly to aggressive lending rather than monetary policy per se.[156]

At first, Stevens contested Casey's view that any check on imports, other than currency depreciation, would retard recovery. Should the need to curb imports be necessary it was best expedited by devaluation, not, as Casey favoured, by credit restriction.[157] Consequently, when Casey's memorandum was circulated, William Wentworth wrote an incisive critique of it. Apart from attacking Casey's 'childish view of the processes of savings and investment', Wentworth argued that credit restriction inevitably raised the prospect of Australia defaulting on

151   Giblin sent Keynes a copy of the untitled memorandum dated 6 March 1936 (KPKC, L36-46).
152   A. C. Davidson to R. G. Casey, 14 August 1935, BNSW, GM 302.
153   C. Janes to A. Smithies, 16 September 1935, Janes Correspondence, BNSW, A53/451.
154   A. C. Davidson to R. G. Casey, 26 September 1935, AA, A11857.
155   R. G. Casey to H. Sheehan, 26 September 1935, AA, AA 1968/39, Item 1.
156   C. Reading to R. G. Casey, 17 September 1935, AA, A 11857.
157   B. S. B. Stevens to R. G. Casey, 1 October 1935, UMA FECC, Box 37.

its foreign debts.[158] The key criticism of the Casey memorandum was its failure to recognise the link between the London funds and the liquid resources of the trading banks.

Copland informed Stevens of the economists' findings, advising that the premier be sympathetic to a general plan of 'tapering off' in expenditure, provided recovery and cheap money continued. The agreement also promised no funding operations together with the acceptance of an open market for bills.[159] In a letter to Casey, Stevens flagged his qualified acceptance of the economists' findings.[160] The letter was accompanied by a lengthy dissection of the memorandum that he, in concert with Wentworth, had written. Its main concern was that 'because recovery is rapid, it therefore has elements of instability in it'. Stevens traced this sentiment to the economists' supposition that '[i]t was boom times which precipitated the depression, and that, if we are to avoid a future depression, we must avoid boom times'.[161] Instead of extrapolating from past experience, Stevens suggested that perhaps a rapid recovery might just be as 'sounder' as a slow one. Nonetheless, despite the tensions between the camps, Stevens was happy to fall into line with Lyons, Reading and Casey that recovery continue, albeit at a slower tempo.[162]

Copland felt confident that the Commonwealth Bank would be committed to a more sane policy than hitherto. He told the Cambridge economist Austin Robinson that getting state governments to take a more moderate view of their position would be 'the chief difficulty' in tapering off expenditure.[163] The odd man out was Davidson. On hearing of Copland's U-turn on monetary policy, Davidson felt that Copland had again compromised his integrity.[164] In truth, Copland was, as he put it, carrying out a 'Dr Jekyll and Mr Hyde trick of establishing a *via media* between the Commonwealth Bank and Stevens'.[165] Davidson's idea of a 'forward' policy was one that allowed more monetary liquidity even if that spelt depreciation (Cain 1988a:31). A sense of animus between the Treasurer and Davidson had already set in since the former had, in his memorandum and elsewhere, basically accused the Wales of being the *force majeure* behind the upward pressure on rates. The Wales' bond selling had also frustrated the Commonwealth Bank's ability to curb liquidity. The fact that Casey saw Stevens as a mooted challenger to his position only added to the animosity since Davidson had been in cahoots with the premier. As Casey intimated to Bruce, with Stevens 'breaking his neck' to get into federal politics,

158 'First criticisms of memorandum', n.d., UMA FECC, Box 32.
159 D. B. Copland to B. S. B. Stevens, 10 October 1935, UMA FECC, Box 37.
160 B. S. B. Stevens to R. G. Casey, 12 October 1935, AA, CP503/1, Item Bundle 3.
161 Comments by B. S. B. Stevens on memorandum, 12 October 1935, AA, CP 503/1, Item Bundle 3, 29A.
162 D. B. Copland to W. S. Robinson, 21 October 1935, UMA FECC, Box 37.
163 D. B. Copland to E. A. G. Robinson, 8 October 1935, UMA FECC, Box 37.
164 A. C. Davidson to D. B. Copland, 8 October 1935, UMA FECC, Box 33.
165 D. B. Copland to W. S. Robinson, 7 October 1935, UMA FECC, Box 37.

it would be a 'national calamity' if he succeeded since his mind 'does not work as yours and mine does'.[166] As for Davidson, Casey felt that he palpably suffered from an 'aggressive form of personal megalomania'.[167]

A reluctant Bank of England was brought into the problem of Australia's overexpansion because Casey and Reading wanted to shore up Australia's foreign reserves to pre-empt a capital flight problem. In couching his argument, Reading told Norman that 'active deflation' as distinct from funding was 'politically impossible'.[168] A brief, written by Melville, put the view that a loan, in tandem with comprehensive credit restriction at home, would be the best means of addressing the problem rather than resorting to devaluation or trade restrictions. Only that resort would stamp out the 'strong inflationary sentiment' in Australia.[169] A memorandum written by Bank of England officers concluded that, ultimately, the remedy lay with Australia. If she adhered to restraint at home she would probably not need the assistance being sought.[170] Liquidity was mopped up by selling Treasury bills at a higher interest rate. Casey warned Bruce that if the representations to London failed trade restrictions were in the offing.[171] A loan would, moreover, facilitate a more sophisticated method of credit restraint to be put in place with trading banks' cooperation.

Norman lectured Bruce that a debtor nation must always ensure a trade surplus to meet its external obligations before assuring him that '[y]ou can rely upon me that I will not let the Commonwealth Bank down'.[172] Meanwhile Giblin, in the memorandum explaining the Commonwealth Bank's decision to raise rates, refloated the devaluation option, not just to shore up the London funds, but to allow more domestic expansion.[173] He pursued the matter with Keynes and Bruce.[174] Until now, Giblin reflected, Australian economic policy had rejected the 'suicide club of competitive devaluation or sadistic deflation', settling for something more moderate. Devaluation should be undertaken only when the business sector was resigned to some check on the rate of domestic expansion. This was necessary because of the absence of an effective apparatus to control trading banks' lending, together with the Commonwealth Bank's ineffective control over the London funds. Like other economists, Giblin wanted a more effective mechanism that would insulate the lending activity of the banks when

---

166   R. G. Casey to S. M. Bruce, 17 February 1936, AA, A 1421/3.
167   R. G. Casey to S. M. Bruce, 30 September 1935, AA, A1421/2.
168   C. Reading to Sir M. Norman, 2 December 1935, Cablegram, BE, OV181/7.
169   R. G. Casey to S. M. Bruce, 15 February 1936, and attachment, 'A loan in London', AA, A 1421/3.
170   'Memorandum to Sir O. E. Niemeyer', 3 December 1935, and 'Note upon Australian economy', written by J. Farmer and G. E. Jackson, 10 December 1935, BE, OV13/3.
171   R. G. Casey to S. M. Bruce, 22 February 1936, Cablegram, AA, A 1421/3.
172   S. M. Bruce to R. G. Casey, 12 March 1936, AA, A1421/3.
173   RBA, GLG-43-1.
174   L. F. Giblin to S. M. Bruce, 30 March 1936, AA, M104/4; L. F. Giblin to J. M. Keynes, 10 March 1936, KPKC.

the London funds fell. Keynes replied that with Australia's London balances falling away she did indeed face pressures for devaluation though he was 'sceptical' there were adequate grounds. He suggested Australia consider capital controls to protect the pegged rate.[175]

Given a copy of Giblin's memorandum, Melville rejected this advice arguing that funding, or passive deflation, was still the best means to check the boom. Devaluation, moreover, would not work because of international retaliation and the likelihood of rising wages and prices at home.[176] In his reply to Giblin, Bruce, reflecting London opinion, warned that were Australia to 'break the truce' on exchange rate pegs it would result in a loss of international goodwill. It would, moreover, make difficult his task of loan conversions.[177] Bruce also reminded Giblin that devaluation would impede the flow of British investment capital into Australia. In any case, all such deliberations were unnecessary since, first, the Bank of England agreed to make a loan to Australia to buttress its London funds. And second, revised figures for the balance of payments showed that the feared deterioration in Australia's trading performance did not materialise.[178] Meanwhile, concern about the level of London funds abated a little with export prices improving amid new forecasts that the external account would now balance for 1935/36 (Copland 1936:18). Giblin was thereupon content to settle for a stable rate unless there was a change in economic fundamentals.[179]

The delicate negotiations with London had little impact on Stevens, who gave Lyons a copy of his economic plan for 'militant expansionism'. He asked the Prime Minister, who had been warmly received in London as Australia's saviour, to petition Norman to double the level of loan assistance so that domestic economic activity would not have to be checked. Further adding to Casey's consternation was the rise in interest rates in March 1936 that signified not just the end of cheap money, but a political controversy. There was a witch-hunt to find the party responsible. Davidson's bank, hitherto the champion of low interest rates, had pushed up deposit interest rates by 0.5 per cent in response to, and in conformity with, the Commonwealth Bank's experimental selling of Treasury bills in the open market. While Stevens publicly labelled the Commonwealth Bank's action 'extraordinary', Davidson sheeted the blame for the rise in rates squarely to the Commonwealth Bank Board.[180] The matter embroiled Lyons and Casey in a controversy about who ran monetary policy, with the government uninformed about the bank board's initiative.[181] Lyons lamely issued a statement

---

175   J. M. Keynes to L. F. Giblin, 22 April 1936, KPKC, L/36/46-7.
176   L. G. Melville to L. F. Giblin, 3 April 1936, AA, M104/3.
177   S. M. Bruce to R. G. Casey, 14 September 1935, AA, AA1968/391, Item 50.
178   R. G. Casey to S. M. Bruce, 8 April 1936, AA, A1421/1.
179   L. F. Giblin to S. M. Bruce, 4 August 1936, RBA, GLG 43-1.
180   'Interest rates and Treasury bills: Mr Stevens' comment', SMH, 19 March 1936.
181   'Monetary policy: bank board's action', SMH, 7 March 1936.

saying that his government was not responsible for the rise in interest rates.[182] Apart from patently demonstrating the independence of the bank board, it also showed a manifest lack of coordination between it, the Loan Council and Treasury.

Casey, invoking Copland, admitted that the rise in rates was not due to selling Treasury bills per se, but rather the increasing tempo of economic activity.[183] Behind the scenes, a flustered Casey confessed to Bruce that '[i]f there was more than one A. C. Davidson in the banking system' he would come close to being an advocate for bank nationalisation.[184] Casey had, in fact, already come to that conclusion, following the Wales' precipitate actions in 1935 of selling its bills on the market to achieve more liquidity, which put pressure on interest rates. Davidson's encore actions in March 1936, with the Royal Commission on Banking and Monetary Systems in session, could not, therefore, have been more ill timed. As the General Manager of the National Bank, L. J. McConnan, put it: 'The action of the Wales has done more in a month to bring about some form of control of the trading banks than the yelping of the Socialistic Douglas Creditites and the like over the past years.'[185]

McConnan's gumption was correct: Casey intimated to a banker that Davidson's precipitate actions meant that the banks would have to be 'fettered' in the near future.[186] Moreover, the government's visibly limp response to the Commonwealth Bank's actions meant that the issue of ultimate control over monetary policy would have to be reconsidered.

The political debate over monetary policy, especially interest rates, would flare again and involve the same combatants. Casey was apprehensive about what mischief Stevens would get up to once he reached London on official business.[187] One appointment was with Keynes, which Copland had helped to arrange (Clark 1983:38).[188] Copland, in fact, felt that Stevens was capable enough to give a paper before the Political Economy Club. He told Keynes that no other Australian politician had practised expansionist economics so consistently or 'taken economists so much to his heart' as Stevens had.[189] Keynes did not accede

---

182 'Treasury bills: Mr Lyons' statement', *SMH*, 5 May 1936.

R. G. Casey to S. M. Bruce, 30 March 1936, AA, A1421/3.

L. J. McConnan to Lord Inverforth, 1 April 1936, McConnan Papers, National Bank Archive.

183 *Courier Mail*, 26 March 1936.

184 R. G. Casey to S. M. Bruce, 30 March 1936, AA, A1421/3.

185 L. J. McConnan to Lord Inverforth, 1 April 1936, from 'A Selection of Letters of Leslie McConnan, 1935–52', National Bank Archive.

186 R. G. Casey to G. Healy, 9 April 1936, D/O Letters, Bank of Australasia, ANZ Archive.

187 P. Liesching to Sir H. Batterbee, 14 April 1936, BE, OV13/4.

188 D. B. Copland to B. S. B. Stevens, 29 February 1936, UMA FECC, Box 47.

189 D. B. Copland to J. M. Keynes, 24 February 1936, UMA FECC, Box 44.

to this request but he did meet Stevens in Cambridge and found him 'a very sound man'.[190] Colin Clark, who attended the meeting, recalled that Keynes was 'interested in this very earthy politician' (McFarlane and Healey 1990:7).

In a confidential memorandum drawn up for Stevens, Copland, using themes from an important address, outlined a program of progressive social legislation that the premier could use for his possible entry into federal politics.[191] Copland kept Stevens informed about political developments and the agenda facing Lyons and his cabinet:

> Nothing ambitious is being done or contemplated in making policy, and the Government is sure to lose ground because it is not tackling problems with any imagination. More and more it becomes clear that the real problems that will confront us during the next five years are national insurance, the 40-hour week, increased provision for social services, the adjustment of Commonwealth and State financial relations, and the improvement of money wages.[192]

Contrary to the prevailing views, Australian economists were engaged in considerable rethinking of their theoretical positions about macroeconomic matters during the mid-1930s. They recorded some success in the funding debate but bold and radical policy initiatives such as the proto-Keynesian 'Sydney plan' were stillborn, partly because economic recovery made the federal government complacent. Events were turning, however, in the economists' favour especially the forthcoming inquiry into banking and monetary policy.

---

190   J. M. Keynes to L. Lopokova, 18 May 1936, KPKC, PP/45/190/7/126.
191   'Immediate political policy: programme for the Commonwealth', 4 June 1937, UMA FECC, Box 55.
192   D. B. Copland to B. S. B. Stevens, 11 June 1936, UMA FECC, Box 47.

Part III.
The March of Keynesian Ideas

8. The Royal Commission on Monetary and Banking Systems

Introduction

One of the ironies of the 1936–37 Royal Commission on Banking and Monetary Systems was that while the input of professional economists dominated the commission's findings they were barely influential in pushing for the inquiry in the first place. Not perhaps since the 1930 Macmillan Committee on Finance and Industry in Britain had a gallery of economists been afforded a public forum to express their views on economic policy. The evidence given by economists advanced the key issues on which the commission would deliberate. That evidence, among a sea of words, was impressive, representing the state of the art of central banking and also economic theory.[1] Furthermore, it exhibited the latest in contemporary economic wisdom that sprang from Keynes's *General Theory*, which was published just as the commission began sitting. The arrival of that book in Australia is discussed along with an outline of its main theoretical and policy themes.

While the inquiry had been brought to fruition by political pressures on the Lyons government, there was also, as Casey put it, 'the cry of the monetary reformer' shooting through the air (cited in Robinson 1986:79). The prospect of an inquiry into Australia's financial system filled Commonwealth Bank officials with dread. Their apprehension was at odds with what one of the commissioners, Professor R. C. Mills, told a Sydney bank manager—namely, that 'the Commission was superfluous except for giving some people a chance to blow off steam and giving him the opportunity to improve his own education'.[2] Casey was more equivocal, telling a church congregation that the inquiry would be useful even if it only showed how the present system could be improved.[3] Privately, he told Bruce that, while he was initially 'horrified' by the prospect, some good might nevertheless come out of the exercise (Sutherlin 1980:41).

As this chapter will show, Mills's pessimism about the worth of the commission was to be completely dispelled, not just by the evidence given by economists, but by the findings that heralded new milestones in effective monetary

---

1   '2,400,000 words: banking commission evidence', *SMH*, 5 September 1936.
2   G. Healy to E. Godward, 5 December 1935, Bank of Australasia D/O Correspondence, ANZ Archive.
3   'Banking inquiry; Treasurer's explanation', *SMH*, 21 October 1935.

management. The proceedings, dutifully reported on in the press, were useful in clearing minds on the art of central banking (Giblin 1951). Under examination, therefore, will be the evidence put before the commission by economists. Apart from drawing on hitherto unused archival and newspaper material pertaining to the commission, this chapter will also draw on three relatively neglected studies of the royal commission by Cain (1988b), Booth (1988) and Sutherlin (1980).

For the first time, macroeconomic goals were enunciated in a public forum. The contribution from economists revolved around the priority that should be given to the competing goals of exchange rate stability and economic activity. That debate, apart from causing a minor schism in the economics fraternity, still crystallised the advance made in economic understanding by policymaking authorities. Before examining that debate in some detail, some background on aspects of the commission's raison d'être and membership is in order. There is no doubt that the establishment of the inquiry, taken in the scheme of things, formed part of the push towards greater control and regulation of the economy. The economists had, of course, been predisposed in that direction for some time and this chapter underscores that shift in their economic outlook.

The embrace of planning and control

Among Australian economists there had been a growing reaction against the market as a form of coordination. Two depressions in 40 years meant Australia was 'swept up' in the global tide against capitalism (Schedvin 1995:54). Mauldon (1933) had first raised the issue of 'planning' and an advisory council consisting of experts to help the federal government. As a precursor to the future, the Australian Institute of Political Science in early 1934 conducted a summer school on 'economic planning'. A number of economists, including Walker, Wilson, Giblin, Melville and Shann, contributed papers on the 'blessed' issue of planning (Melville 1934:96). In his address, Walker linked planning with self-sufficiency, arguing that, in Australia's case, self-sufficiency had been pressed on her by the trading policies of other nations (Melville 1934).[4] Wilson gave a more forthright address, arguing 'that the competitive system, neither in its operation nor in its results was justifying the faith of its votaries'. He went on to lament that there were uncoordinated schemes of planning extant but 'with no integrating purpose', so that there was no 'body of principles that could be used as a criterion in perfecting a system of economic planning'. He was pessimistic about whether, in fact, the capitalist order could be preserved (Whitwell 1986:2–5).

---

4 'Political science summer school', *SMH*, 27 January 1934.

Giblin defined economic planning as 'applying foresight and reason to economic activities', but he agreed with Wilson that, at that time, there was 'no such agreed aim for Australian development'.[5] It was all at this stage still 'an attitude of the mind' (cited in Whitwell 1986:5). In a radio talk aired in 1935, Giblin asked his countrymen to 'experiment boldly' with new models of economic coordination.[6] Like their counterparts in Britain, Australian economists had swung to a marked acceptance of supplementing the market with more 'planning'. As Whitwell (1986:14) amply shows, the Depression brought about an unequivocal shift to the left among local economists insofar as it entailed more regulation and control over economic activity. Brigden conveyed these sentiments in an Australian and New Zealand Association for the Advancement of Science (ANZAAS) Presidential Conference speech given in 1935. He was prepared to recognise that the profit motive was not enough of a guide and rationale for economic life. Instead, he spoke of an economists' utopia where social responsibility and public accountability would prevail among business leaders and bankers (Whitwell 1986:150). Brigden's utopia also encompassed a better technical knowledge of economic management. Like Wilson, he envisaged a central thinking agency that would exhibit technical proficiency and thereby inspire public confidence that events such as the Depression would not reoccur. Finally, he made the very apposite point that catastrophes such as the Depression 'bring about a very radical reform' in, say, central banking or economic management (Whitwell 1986:15). Much later, Kershaw told Giblin the same thing in discussing the speedy evolution of central banking in Australia during the interwar years.[7]

Even before Brigden's landmark speech in 1935, he had enthusiastically given a series of six radio talks on the subject of economic planning in October 1933.[8] To Brigden, planning meant economic stability. As director of the Queensland government's Bureau of Industry, his duties, apart from matters of economic investigation, were to recommend how loan moneys were allocated. It formed part of Premier Forgan Smith's idea of 'orderly planning' (Molesworth 1933:107). The only drawback in Brigden's mind was that he could not always 'speak his mind...on matters of economic policy', lest he become 'an enemy of the people'.[9]

In Western Australia, Shann invited one of his former students, H. C. 'Nugget' Coombs, on to a radio program and asked him to say 'what impresses you most... about our situation'. Coombs bemoaned the penchant for 'palliatives' and the 'evasion of positive action towards recovery'. He felt that Australia had done

---

5 Ibid.
6 'Shaping the future of Australia', September 1935, Giblin Papers, NLA.
7 R. N. Kershaw to L. F. Giblin, 3 April 1947, RBA, GLG 43-1.
8 Brigden Papers, NLA, Folio 34.
9 J. B. Brigden to F. Mauldon, 26 March 1935, and F. Mauldon to J. B. Brigden, 5 April 1935, UMA FECC, Box 138.

well since 1931 but complacency was now creeping back (Rowse 2002:2). On a higher methodological plane, Melville could see how ignorance, uncertainty and irrationality reduced the neoclassical concept of a self-regulating economist to fiction (Whitwell 1986:8).

The economist who perhaps personalised the shift to planning and intervention was Copland. Radicalised by the events of the 1930s, Copland confessed to a friend that he was impressed with the need for a change in the control of investment and production to endow the economic system with some stability. Even the Lyons government had, against conservative financial opinion, embarked on expanding investment under government control. Copland predicted that there would be a steady movement to the left and he was more than happy to encourage that movement.[10] This allegiance had, of course, already been well noted by colleagues and detractors alike. Many would have felt that surrendering the economic levers to politicians would result in the return of 1920s-style waste. At times, Copland despaired of convincing some of his associates that the political ground had shifted. He told the Canadian economist Harold Innis: 'It's no use arguing with people who have built up dream pictures about the workings of the economic system. They are like young people in love, and it is only the hard fact of the depression that would shake them out of their state of infatuation.'[11]

In September 1936, Copland along with Denis Robertson and Wesley Mitchell was invited to give an address at Harvard University as part of its tercentenary celebrations. Copland's address, which he proudly distributed afterwards, was entitled 'The state and the entrepreneur'. Thematically, it was about injecting greater social control into the economic mechanism and touched on the 'old problem' of the relationship of state control to private enterprise.[12] He told Premier Stevens that his address would find him 'moving still further to the left'.[13]

Copland reported back to his colleagues that all three contributions had independently arrived at the same theme—namely, that 'unfettered enterprise would not produce an economic and social order that would satisfy the aspirations of the common man'.[14] Robertson (1940:118) introduced Copland to the podium saluting him as 'that skilful designer of cunningly mixed cordials for depressed economic systems'. This was high praise from someone whom Copland regarded as one of the 'ablest economists in Britain'.[15]

---

10 D. B. Copland to Laing, 7 December 1934, UMA FECC, Box 24.
11 D. B. Copland to H. Innis, 4 November 1936, UMA FECC, Box 43.
12 D. B. Copland to F. Alford, 30 March 1936, UMA FECC, Box 41.
13 D. B. Copland to B. S. B. Stevens, 23 July 1936, UMA FECC, Box 47.
14 Harvard Notes 1936, UMA FECC, Box 47.
15 D. B. Copland to B. S. B. Stevens, 16 March 1936, UMA FECC, Box 47.

Copland was delighted with Robertson's comment that there was now general agreement among economists as to the cause of the crisis and even the remedy, though there was still debate as to how far the remedy should be applied (Robertson 1940:126–7). In passing, Copland noted, among his hosts, 'quite a cult' over Swedish economic policy with its 'middle way' between individualist capitalism and extensive state control. That philosophy was, of course, nothing new to Australian economists, though Copland raised no complaint at the neglect of Australia. He did, however, express bemusement at how resistant US economists were to the idea of state control: 'To a visitor from a country which had long ago gone far in this direction the controversies about state control in the US appear a little unreal.'[16]

All Australian economists did not welcome the orientation towards planning and an extensive public sector. The ideologically conservative pair, Shann and Melville, for instance, was loath to be swept along by the collectivist tide. For Shann, the encroachment of government into economic affairs went against his elliptical embrace of neo-liberal political philosophy. It also made for tragedy. Shann's aforementioned discourses into Australian economic history raged against tariff protection and industrial regulation, both of which were perceived as conspiracies against the public (Schedvin and Carr 1995). Yet in 1933, as aforementioned, he had turned to Keynes's popular writings to lament the waste of excess fixed deposits in bank vaults as the economy stagnated. While he was wary of economic interventionism, Shann had some faith in a 'wider planning, a monetary policy that would permit the recovery of equilibrium and an expansion of consumers' demand' (Duncan 1934:167).

Later, with economic recovery in prospect, Shann shifted ground and re-embraced his earlier philosophy. His antipathy to public works and, presumably, the extent of debt to finance them, resurfaced. Melville agreed, consoling Shann with the thought:

> Can we really expect a democracy in a hurry to spend its way out of depression, to exercise any discrimination in the works on which it spends its money? To encourage Governments to spend money on public works is, I think, to encourage them to spend it more or less indiscriminately.[17]

Shann conveyed his complaint of wasteful public expenditure to Davidson, explaining how loan expenditure was futile in 'priming the pump' of private enterprise. It was akin to having money 'poured down a rat-hole'. He believed such borrowing kept up interest rates and gave the economy a distorted or 'false'

---

16   'Harvard Material', UMA FECC, Box 45.
17   L. G. Melville to E. Shann, 27 November 1934, RBA, GGM-35-2.

structure.[18] In an unsent reply, Davidson defended public works programs, stating that they were remunerative and, in the last resolve, were an 'investment in human welfare'.[19]

As the world retreated into protectionism and regulation, Shann became increasingly pessimistic about the prospects of a return to a market-driven order of liberal internationalism. The truth, too, was that Shann had also become unsettled since he returned to university life. University colleagues in Perth noted his newly found intolerance of criticism (Alexander 1963:156). In the interim, he secured the chair at the University of Adelaide vacated by Melville and left unfilled due to the effect of the Depression on university finances. It was a position that involved a tradition of teaching theoretical economics when he was, first and foremost, an economic historian (Alexander 1963:178). He also did not have a good grasp of economic theory, particularly its mathematical aspect (La Nauze 1939:227). Nonetheless, the prospect of a 'fresh start' at Adelaide excited him.[20] Shann's last letter to Davidson, together with his commentaries for *The Statist* magazine, for which he was the Australian contributor, struck Davidson as an astonishing return to old patterns of thought. He blustered to Hytten that

> [p]oor old Shann has gone over to the sentimental Economists for the present...I am afraid that he is suffering from...an idea that almost every thing in [the] Australian past and present policy is weakened or endangered by wrongful spending, uneconomic propositions etc. I am afraid he, too, has gone up a side street for the present.[21]

Davidson was cruelly accurate. Like others, however, he was shocked when Shann died in rather mysterious circumstances.

Schedvin and Carr (1995:69) speculate that his death, which the coroner found to be suicide, could be attributable to the sea change in political philosophy as the 'pendulum swung to the economics of J. M. Keynes'. The introspective Shann probably felt he was a spent force. Another authority on Shann, Graeme Snooks, also links his death to personal depression brought on by the move to intervention. In short, Shann could not fathom how more regulation could help when too much intervention in markets had caused the problem in the first case (Snooks 1993:28). In contrast, Melville felt there was nothing sinister in Shann's death other than the stress of overwork.[22]

---

18 E. Shann to A. C. Davidson, 23 April 1935, BNSW, 302/590/1.
19 Draft of A. C. Davidson letter to E. Shann, n.d., BNSW, 303/590/1.
20 E. Shann to J. La Nauze, 12 October 1934, La Nauze Papers, NLA.
21 A. C. Davidson to T. Hytten, 27 May 1935, BNSW, GM/302/386.
22 L. G. Melville to J. La Nauze, 26 July 1935, La Nauze Papers, NLA.

At the memorial service for Shann, G. V. Portus, a professor of Political Science at Adelaide, alluded to the mental torment Shann had been undergoing by remarking how he had begun in the last three months 'to relearn his economics' (Snooks 1993:28). On the day of his death, Shann wrote to Copland regarding commissioning another in the series of anthologies on Australian economic documents. He agreed with Copland's earlier missive that it will 'do me a deal of good to sort out my ideas with you again'.[23] While he was later to pedantically note that Shann was not really an economist, Copland ensured that he was honoured by a memoir of him penned by Melville. Copland was happy with the tribute because it emphasised the 'mutual dependence of each of us on the others who cooperated in influencing economic policy during the depression'.[24]

Shann's demise meant, of course, that his leavening influence would be absent from the forthcoming Royal Commission on Banking. More surprising, however, was the omission of any form of evidence from the loquacious Copland, who had been the first economist to call for an inquiry into the monetary system (Sutherlin 1980:9). Before turning to the giving of evidence by economists, some remarks on the constitution of the commission are in order.

An inquiry into monetary policy

The political origins of why the commission came to be have been exhaustively covered by Sutherlin (1980) and need not unduly concern us here. In her discussion of the genesis of the inquiry, however, Sutherlin made no mention of early Country Party efforts to push for a royal commission into the setting of the exchange rate. That said, the terms of reference and, more especially, the selection of the officials who would sit on the commission are of palpable interest because, ultimately, they would have a bearing on the inquiry's findings. It is, for instance, sometimes assumed that Copland did not appear before the inquiry or submit written evidence because he was disappointed not to be one of the presiding commissioners. This is quite false. Copland did not present any evidence because, as he told Jock Phillips, the secretary to the commission, he was preoccupied being Acting Vice-Chancellor at Melbourne University and, after that, would be abroad visiting Harvard and Cambridge while the commission sat.[25] In any case, Copland had some indirect input into the commission. Melville, for instance, sent him the *Statement* he was to place before the inquiry. Copland would also write articles on the key findings of the commission. Copland told Melville, nonetheless, that it was 'a thousand pities' that university administration prevented him from taking part in the inquiry.

23   E. Shann to D. B. Copland, 21 March 1935, UMA FECC, Box 38.
24   D. B. Copland to L. G. Melville, 5 June 1935, UMA FECC, Box 36.
25   D. B. Copland to J. G. Phillips, 6 April 1936, UMA FECC, Box 48.

He went on to say that 'the enforced absence from controversy would help in a small way to repair my damaged reputation'.[26] By that, Copland presumably meant his poor standing with the authorities over his philosophical views and, perhaps, his association with Stevens. On the key issue of the political interference in banking, Copland considered that it was nonsense to suggest that banking could be quarantined from politics. He told a friend that '[b]anking has far too powerful a social influence to be ignored in politics'.[27] On this issue, Copland would have been heartened by his colleague Gordon Wood's submission, which was dedicated to arguing the case for greater supervision of the financial sector.

After a year or more of backsliding, Lyons announced in October 1935 the terms of reference for the royal commission and the personnel to preside on it.[28] The terms of reference, drawn up by Casey and Treasury Secretary, Harry Sheehan, were suitably broad (Sutherlin 1980:37). They were: 'To inquire into the monetary and banking systems at present in operation in Australia, and to report whether any, and if so what, alterations are desirable in the interests of the people of Australia [as] a whole, and the manner in which any such alterations should be effected.'

Apart from inveterate opposition to the inquiry from elements such as 'The Group', the private banks and even the top echelons within the Commonwealth Bank, delay was also caused by finding suitably qualified commissioners (Sutherlin 1980:20–31). Initially, the federal government was in favour of appointing a foreign-born chairman. Names such as Lord Macmillan, Denis Robertson, Bertil Ohlin and Per Jacobssen were put forward (Sutherlin 1980:32–3). Political and logistical factors swung the choice towards an Australian chairman. Casey was, at one stage, initially inclined to offer the chairmanship to Giblin (Sutherlin 1980:38). Like Copland, however, Giblin had once too often aired his views on monetary reform in public and was, as discussed above, placed on the Commonwealth Bank Board. Eventually, Justice Napier from South Australia was given the job of chairman of the commission. While some of the six commissioners were specialists in some of the fields pertaining to the inquiry it came as some surprise that only one economist was selected. After screening all the likely candidates, Casey chose Mills because he was the only one 'who has not nailed his opinions to the mast in the press, as practically all the others have done' (cited in Sutherlin 1980:41). Apart from being, therefore, a 'safe' choice, Mills was selected because he had some expertise in the field of inquiry, having written textbooks, with Walker, on the monetary system (Groenewegen

---

26   D. B. Copland to L. G. Melville, 9 March 1936, UMA FECC, Box 46.
27   D. B. Copland to F. S. Alford, 30 March 1936, UMA FECC, Box 41.
28   'Banking royal commission', *SMH*, 4 October 1935.

2003:7). In the academic sphere, Mills had neglected his research to build, as he put it, a 'factory' of overseas-trained economics ability (Randerson 1953:43; Butlin 1953:181).[29]

Mills's position as the sole economist on the commission drew Janes to comment that 'Mills should have our deepest sympathy. It looks as though he will have to do a lot of carrying for the others.'[30] Janes, however, overlooked the fact that one of the commissioners chosen was H. A. Pitt, a Victorian Treasury official who had served on the Copland Committee in 1931. He was also President of the Victorian Branch of the Economic Society. The other commissioners were J. P. Abbott, a pastoralist and federal politician, E. V. Nixon, a Melbourne accountant, and J. B. Chifley, a junior minister in the Scullin government who professed an interest in economics and banking. While Janes' comment was, therefore, unfair, it was prescient in another sense. Mills was to have a considerable influence on the commission, including drafting the final report (Butlin 1953:182; Markwell 1985:39). Later, his fellow commissioners would praise Mills's diplomatic skills in getting six opinionated men to agree on the path to take. It was Mills's intention, however, to bring down a unanimous report even if it needed his active stewardship. Having missed the excitement and ferment of the Premiers' Plan, Mills now had an opportunity to make his mark. When the report was published, Copland congratulated him for his work, stating that 'it will take its place' with other reports in other countries on central banking.[31] S. J. Butlin (1937:40), an economist from Mills's department, said the inquiry was 'worth the money'.

At the start of the inquiry, Mills was charged with drawing up, with Chifley, a detailed questionnaire that all witnesses would have to complete (Sutherlin 1980:49). Framing the questions being addressed to bankers and economists allowed Mills and Chifley to have some bearing on the agenda. Belying the tag that they were both politically 'safe', Chifley and Mills were, along with their assistant, Phillips, an economics graduate from Sydney, quite predisposed, in fact, to strengthening central bank powers in the name of sane economic management (Sutherlin 1980:49). It was a view not initially shared by Napier, Nixon and Abbott. After questioning one witness, Napier commented that, after six months of taking evidence, it was not clear to him what more the government could have done to meet the situation created by the Depression

---

29 Among the key personnel in the economics department during the mid-1930s and their place of higher study were E. R. Walker (Cambridge), S. J. Butlin (Cambridge), Hermann Black (Harvard) and R. Madgwick (Oxford).

30 C. Janes to D. B. Copland, 9 October 1935, UMA FECC, Box 34.

31 D. B. Copland to R. C. Mills, 24 July 1937, UMA FECC, Box 54.

other than to expand the supply of treasury bills, which was undertaken. That said, Napier was open to hearing whether there were other 'measures that might have been adopted that would have had a more beneficial result'.[32]

Before examining the contributions of economists to the inquiry and how they shaped the final report it will be necessary to gauge the early reception that Keynes's *General Theory* received in Australia. This is necessary since several economists, without any attempt at grandstanding, referred to it or, indeed, based a considerable part of their evidence on this new revolutionary book.

The arrival of the *General Theory* in Australia

Looking back over the post-World War II period, 'Nugget' Coombs (1981) recalled it as a time of being guided by 'the star' of Keynes. It was, however, a more daunting experience in the prewar years. Australian economists, while not totally opposed to Keynes, were hardly swept along by a tide of new economic thinking. The diffusion and assimilation of the new paradigm in economic thought would preoccupy Australian economists up to the outbreak of World War II. Unlike Keynes's *Treatise*, which was introduced into Australia's Federal Parliament with a dramatic flourish by Theodore in 1930, the *General Theory* had a more prosaic entry into Australia.

Keynes's envoy to Australia

A former King's College student now working with the Bank of England, W. B. Reddaway came to Australia in March 1936 with the 'oven-hot' galley proof in his suitcase (Arndt 1976:282).[33] Reddaway had read it on the voyage and, as this chapter will show, played a leading part in disseminating its contents to his hosts, even using the royal commission as a forum. Reddaway had come out to Australia expressly as the first research fellow at the University of Melbourne, a position funded entirely—and somewhat controversially—from Giblin's directorship fees from the Commonwealth Bank Board (Priestley 2002:135). Given the shortage of economists in Australia, the fellowship was designed to invite

---

32 'Judge's comment: at the inquiry', *SMH*, 18 July 1936, p. 13.
33 Interestingly, Reddaway was not the only Bank of England officer to arrive in Australia at that time. A month before, two officers—Kershaw and Jackson—arrived. It was a prospect that so concerned Reading that he cabled Montagu about the visit with his worry that it might somehow be linked with the royal commission. Montagu cabled back that Kershaw was in Australia primarily to visit his family while Jackson was here to take an appraisal of the Australian economy and also to consider Australia's case for a loan from the Bank of England to strengthen its London funds. Kershaw further mollified Reading by assuring him that if news of the visit caused the Commonwealth Bank any embarrassment Jackson would immediately return to England (C. Reading to Sir M. Norman, 28/2/1936, BE, GI/287). Both officers did meet important personages, including Casey, while here. News of the visit did not leak.

a scholar to come to Melbourne and perhaps shed new light on contemporary economic problems.[34] It would also keep Melbourne abreast of the latest economic debates in Britain and the United States. Keynes had recommended Reddaway as 'the best King's College trained economist in recent years'.[35] While Copland had wanted Austin Robinson as the first research fellow—much to Keynes's consternation—Reddaway would live up to his commendation.[36] H. V. Hodson, editor of the *Roundtable* magazine, briefed La Nauze about the visitor: 'He was Keynes's star pupil…and is strikingly intelligent to talk to. He hasn't, I think, got the rarefied intellectual atmosphere of the set-apart genius of any science but he has common sense and intelligent perception raised to a very high power.'[37]

Copland greeted the young economist with the remark: 'You will not find Australia as interesting as Russia, but I think it has many things to interest anyone who has the blood of the pioneer in them.'[38]

It was to prove a prophetic challenge and one that Reddaway accepted with alacrity.

Indeed, even on landing on Australian shores, Reddaway found himself in the unexpected position of having to recommend a gentle braking of economic activity since Australia's London balances were threatened.[39] In reply, Keynes admitted to being somewhat 'perplexed' by the Australian problem, attributing it to capital flight on the premise that the royal commission might recommend another devaluation.[40]

Reddaway presented his findings and summary of Keynes's work to a Shillings meeting held on 28 April 1936. So momentous was the arrival of Keynes's book that it was agreed that the book be the focus of attention at further meetings. Reddaway's attempt to convey the meaning of the *General Theory* to the gathering, which included Copland and Giblin, was obliquely entitled, 'Is the idea of a fair rate of interest a mere convention?' (Brown 2001:54–5).[41] The review, which reduced Keynes's system down to a system of simultaneous equations, was the progenitor of John Hicks's IS/LM framework of analysis. The savings–investment dichotomy of the *Treatise* was retained but now the difference between the two aggregates determined output, not the price level. The policy import was much

---

34   'Conditions of the research job', Giblin Papers, NLA.
35   D. B. Copland to Vice-Chancellor R. E. Priestley, 2 December 1935, UMA FECC, Box 37.
36   L. F. Giblin to J. M. Keynes, 17 September 1935, UMA FECC, Box 34; D. B. Copland to J. M. Keynes, 13 September 1935, KPKC, L/35.
37   H. Hodson to J. La Nauze, 16 January 1936, La Nauze Papers, NLA.
38   D. B. Copland to W. B. Reddaway, 1935, UMA FECC, Box 37.
39   W. B. Reddaway to J. M. Keynes, n.d., KPKC, L/36/48.
40   J. M. Keynes to W. B. Reddaway, 11 April 1936, KPKC, L/36/50.
41   'Minutes of the Shillings meeting', 28 April 1936, Giblin Collection, UMA FECC, Box 219.

clearer; with resources unemployed, it was investment that determined savings, not the converse, and more importantly, they equalised not through variations in the price level but by changes in output. Unemployment could be reduced by increasing aggregate demand up to a point when supply constraints came into play.

Cain felt that Reddaway's interpretation of Keynes was excellent and gave a 'flying start' to the technical discussion that followed (Cain 1984:367). The paper was rushed into print and became the first published academic review of the *General Theory* (Reddaway 1995:6). It also met with Keynes's approval even though Reddaway was critical that his mentor oversimplified discussion of several matters. Interestingly for our purposes, Reddaway (1936:35–6) felt that Keynes tended to underplay 'the dangers of expansionism'.

The economists in Sydney were not to be outdone by Melbourne having an 'envoy' from Keynes within their midst (Millmow 2003b). Walker and S. J. Butlin had both undertaken higher studies at Cambridge while Keynes was cogitating on the *General Theory*. Both were supervised by Denis Robertson and were, therefore, more observers than participants in the 'Keynesian ferment of the early 1930s' (Schedvin 1978:243). Butlin (1946:9) in fact attended Keynes's lectures at Mill Lane during 1933 and 1934 when the central themes of the *General Theory* were being laid out. Walker adapted a proto-Keynesian view that deficit budgets and public outlays were quite defensible when private spending was lagging (Whitwell 1986:11; Cain 1984:83).[42] Before Reddaway had delivered his lecture, Walker wrote a lucid precis of Keynes's new book in the *Sydney Morning Herald* on 14 March 1936.[43] Walker used the opportunity to damn the deflationary policies of the Commonwealth Bank selling Treasury bills to the public in a bid to further slacken the pace of economic activity. Walker stated that the central bank's actions were wrong-headed and that the 'right remedy' was, in fact, to lower interest rates to keep the economy at the highest level of activity possible. He followed it up by giving a lecture on the *General Theory* on 9 June to the NSW Branch of the Economic Society.[44] That address would be good preparation for his evidence before the commission, where he outlined the new wisdom.

While the first green shoots of the Keynesian 'revolution' in Australia were appearing, not everyone was swept up by it. It certainly did not conquer Australia with 'a speed and a thoroughness' akin to the 'Spanish Inquisition',

---

42 'Financial; a sound policy; public works and recovery', *SMH*, 2 February 1935.
43 'Employment; interest and money; Mr Keynes; again', *SMH*, 14 March 1936. Walker's review is surprisingly not listed in a recent anthology of newspaper reviews of Keynes's great work, probably because the Australian press was never surveyed (see Backhouse 1999).
44 There is no material evidence of what Walker said in that address since the archival records of the NSW Branch of the Economic Society appear to have been lost.

as King (1997:298) claims. Copland, for instance, informed Keynes that being Acting Vice-Chancellor left him little time to absorb his new book.[45] Two months later, R. B. Lemmon, a member of the Economic Society, asked Copland when he would outline Keynes's new book. Copland could only reply that he had 'not read more than 150 pages'.[46] It was a marked difference from the past when Copland had been Australia's leading monetary theorist and the first to digest Keynes's latest work.

A 'worried' Copland told Sir Keith Murdoch that university administration was consuming his time, meaning that he had to neglect 'a good deal of economic literature that I ought to be reading. Any reputation I have will quickly dissipate if this goes on for much longer.'[47] As Australia's most prolific economist of the interwar era, Copland must have felt his professional standing among his peers, or at least keeping abreast of new developments in theory, was beginning to suffer. He told an American academic:

> If we could only make a resolution that we would completely abandon the world and its…affairs periodically for a year or two, I believe we would greatly enrich our science. The ideal is to spend some time in dealing with economic policy and handling practical affairs and then to live the life of a recluse so that there is ample time to think it all over. Once the job of thinking has been done, we should then sally forth again and become embroiled to some extent in practical affairs.[48]

This was, of course, precisely what Keynes had done in order to conceptualise and compose his magnum opus.

Hytten recalled that Giblin had 'been bitten' by Keynes's prophecy of the euthanasia of the rentier.[49] Yet for all his proto-Keynesian leanings, Giblin struggled with swallowing whole Keynes's new theoretical schema. One such incidence was on his voyage to England in December 1937, when Giblin still confessed to lingering doubts about the sweep of Keynes's theoretical schema (Downing 1960:45). A sabbatical spent at King's College, Cambridge, researching the latest developments in monetary theory would clear away conceptual doubts. Copland, knowing how Giblin wrote only under pressure, suggested

---

45   D. B. Copland to J. M. Keynes, 9 March 1936, UMA FECC, Box 44; D. B. Copland to W. S. Robinson, 14 April 1936, UMA FECC, Box 48.
46   D. B. Copland to R. B. Lemmon, 16 May 1936, UMA Economic Society of Australia, Victoria Branch Files, Box 140.
47   D. B. Copland to K. Murdoch, 14 April 1936, UMA FECC, Box 44.
48   D. B. Copland to Prof. Williams, 1 July 1936, UMA FECC, Box 50.
49   Hytten autobiography, UT, p. 87.

to D. H. Robertson that he should encourage Giblin to compose, especially if he saw 'virtue in his ideas' and especially when they might 'stir up the monetary theorists'.[50]

While Copland had to diffidently translate the meaning of Keynes's new theoretical framework to his honours students, in Sydney, Mills 'kept away from Keynes'. According to one of his old students, Noel Butlin, Mills did so because he felt 'it was beyond him' (cited in Snooks 1991:8). All this flies in the face of Mills and Chifley being exposed to the meaning of Keynes's revolution to the extent that the latter, allegedly, became a 'Keynesian-of-the-first-hour' (Crisp 1961:169; Battin 1997:34).

Like other studies looking at the transmission of Keynesian ideas in the interwar era, Markwell (1985:26) observed that in Australia the process generally 'declined with age and increased with the extent and recentness of direct contact with… Cambridge economics'. This rule of thumb could help explain Walker, Copland, Melville and Giblin undergoing a rapid conversion to the economics of Keynes. Yet Melville felt that his two Melbourne colleagues were, even in 1939, 'not altogether convinced' of Keynes's new schema though strongly beholden to his policy prescriptions (Cornish 1993b:18–19). Similar-sounding sentiments about public works and contra-cyclical monetary policy had been 'floating around' for some time before Keynes 'generalised them in his general theory' (Melville 1971:21). For his own part, while he 'accepted Keynes's general conclusions', Melville remained 'very unconvinced by a lot of the theory in his *General Theory* and it didn't seem to me to be very rigorously thought out but I didn't think his conclusions were not generally correct'.[51] Unlike his colleagues Giblin and Copland, Melville later developed some of Keynes's concepts such as expectations, equilibrium shifts and uncertainty.

Closer to the action were two young Australian economists studying in England at the time and each focused on absorbing what Keynes was all about. One was D. H. Merry, a Melbourne economics graduate, working with the Wales, which financed his studies in London. Merry found the *General Theory* a difficult book and recalled one occasion when Keynes came to give a lecture at the London School of Economics: 'I marvelled at how a man that could talk so simply, clearly and correctly would write something like that. I put it down to the fact that he was something of a mathematician.'[52]

The other economist was Jean Polglaze, who was undertaking research at Cambridge on investment spending and business cycles, which was funded by a Rockefeller Scholarship. She told her mentor, Copland, how she attended one of

---

50 D. B. Copland to D. H. Robertson, 24 December 1937, UMA FECC, Box 55.
51 Melville, TRC 182, NLA, p. 158.
52 Author's interview with Don Merry, 2001.

Keynes's lectures in 1937 entitled 'Footnotes to the General Theory'. She wrote: 'Mr Keynes himself, like the Pyramids, is so exactly what's "expected as to be" almost disappointing, but his lecture was full of interesting stuff and far more intelligible than the General Theory itself.' She noted how Keynes's disciples 'will not allow one sentence of the General Theory to be misapplied'.[53]

'Nugget' Coombs was an even greater puzzle (Rowse 2000). While often regarded as the greatest local convert to Keynesian economics—deeming it the 'most seminal intellectual event of his life'—Coombs' (1981:30) early days of exposure to the General Theory were days of frustration. At first, he was not 'impressed' by the new book though he felt Keynes's 'practical implications' were important.[54] Now working under Melville as an assistant economist at the Commonwealth Bank,[55] Coombs had the advantage of a study group with Black, Mills, Madgwick, Walker and Butlin meeting in a Sydney coffee house once a week to discuss Keynes (Cornish 1990:62). This was, of course, the nucleus that had supported the expansionary efforts of Premier Stevens. Despite this arrangement, Coombs could still empathise with La Nauze, who found assimilating Keynes on his own 'a pain-in-the-neck. I am struggling with him, too.'[56]

By September, Coombs was getting to the nub of Keynes: 'I have been trying to make sense out of the theory of the rate of interest. Keynes's work I found unsatisfactory and yet it seems to me to have one aspect of truth and that interest is predominantly a monetary phenomenon.'[57]

The New Zealand-based economist Allan Fisher, who now held Shann's old job at Perth, also confessed to having problems 'digesting' the import of Keynes. Fisher held out hope that Keynes would soon 'provide a text for some general reference upon the conditions for a moving equilibrium'.[58] Fisher later admitted that, like Giblin, he had reservations about accepting the precepts and assumptions underpinning Keynes's theoretical framework.[59]

The import of the *General Theory*

The message implicit within the *General Theory* was that aggregate demand— that is, consumption and investment spending—governed the level of output

---

53   J. Polglaze to D. B. Copland, 17 February 1937, UMA FECC, Box 130.

54   H. C. Coombs to J. La Nauze, 22 June 1936, La Nauze Papers, NLA.

55   Coombs' thesis had been on a study of public works as a stabilisation policy. On returning to Perth, he rejoined the Education Department. He sought a position with the Wales Bank in 1935 but Shann, acting as his referee, was 'quite abusive' about his former student and thus dissuaded Davidson from recruiting him (Hytten, UT, pp. 127, 172).

56   J. La Nauze to H. C. Coombs, n.d., La Nauze Papers, NLA.

57   H. C. Coombs to J. La Nauze, 9 September 1936, La Nauze Papers, NLA.

58   A. G. B. Fisher to J. La Nauze, 19 November 1936, La Nauze Papers, NLA.

59   A. G. B. Fisher to J. La Nauze, 26 March 1937, La Nauze Papers, NLA.

and economic activity. The level of that expenditure, supplemented by public works, could be either too much or too deficient a level in terms of employing resources. The powerhouse variable of investment spending—determined by the interplay of marginal efficiency of capital and interest rates—was also subject to rank uncertainty. Interest rates were determined by the interaction of liquidity preference and the supply of money. The economy's self-corrective properties were not as effective as classical economists believed: full employment was rarely the natural state for market capitalism. Therefore, aggregate demand had to be manipulated to ensure full employment and price stability. This could be achieved, not by planning or arbitrary controls but by the discrete but subtle use of fiscal and monetary policy by the authorities. These instruments could be used not just to rectify economic disturbances but to maintain equilibrium and economic stability. That said, Keynes had a fairly modest definition of what really constituted full employment. He was equally conservative too about budget deficits, believing budgetary balance should prevail at the end of the business cycle. From his earlier work, Keynes knew all about the perils of inflation just as much as he abhorred the hellfire of dear money. Many of these insights, alas, did not immediately spring out from his book.

The difficulty for policy-focused economists in absorbing the *General Theory* was that, while it was a transcendental work on a new theoretical vision, it was hardly a handbook on counter-cyclical macroeconomic policymaking. Keynes (1937:121–2) reminded his fellow travellers that his suggestions for economies in semi-slump 'are not worked out completely; they are subject to all sorts of special assumptions and are necessarily related to the particular conditions of the time'. Moreover, the *General Theory* was sparing in how to apply this new wisdom to policy. Keynes openly acknowledged this; his book was intended for economists, not mandarins. He admitted '[i]t would need a volume of a different character from this one to indicate even outline the practical measures in which they might gradually be clothed' (Keynes 1936:383). In a letter to Joan Robinson in late 1936, Keynes indicated that he did not want his mind to crystallise on the 'precise lines' of the *General Theory* just yet. He went on:

> There is a considerable difference between more or less formal theory, which my existing book purports to be, and something which is meant to be applied to current events without too much qualification by people who do not fully comprehend the theory. So I am against hurry and in favour of gestation. (Keynes 1982b:185–6)

In another place, Keynes insisted on debate, trusting that 'time, experience and the collaboration of many minds will discover the best way of expressing the ideas' (Keynes 1973:111)—ideas that Keynes held to be 'extremely simple and…obvious' (1936:xxxii). These qualifications did not console Copland, who voiced, with others, his impatience at what Keynes was really saying: 'It is not an easy book…later on, when his ideas are clearer, Keynes may be able to set out the problem in simpler language. This however cannot be done until the theory is more clearly defined.'[60] Keynes himself felt the need for a simpler statement but only after he had absorbed the criticisms of others and had become clearer in his own mind about the sweep of his theoretical system (Keynes 1973:47).[61] His heart attack in 1937 and convalescence prevented this, resulting, as Hyman Minsky (1976:14) noted, in Keynes having 'never fully participated in the hammering out of a polished version of Keynesian doctrine'. There was, then, to be considerable delay in working out the policy implications of Keynes's great book. According to the historian Peter Clarke (1998:50), Keynes was well aware of the process by which his ideas would become more politically telling and 'would undergo a selective process of simplification and distortion'. To have, for instance, his radical ideas on war finance accepted, Keynes wanted them to be 'dressed up' in familiar terms so as not to alienate officialdom (Skidelsky 2000:476). Keynes delivered the modus operandi of the *General Theory* in the pamphlet *How to Pay for the War* (1940),[62] in which the problem, of course, was not an economy in slump but one supply constrained.

Most Australian economists, bar Fisher, would eventually accept Keynes's theoretical framework, but some, such as Melville (1939) and Smithies (1936), put their qualifications and reservations into the public domain. Their respective concerns revolved around the theory of interest rates and expectations, the marginal efficiency of capital construct and, in Smithies' case, the marginal propensity to consume and the alleged futility of money wage cutting. To that end, Smithies, who fancied himself more an economic theorist than Treasury economist, told Copland that after reading Keynes he felt 'there were some pretty serious weaknesses in his argument'.[63] Copland tended to agree, responding that the Australian experience of 1931 showed that, apart from reducing real wages, it was indeed possible to get some benefit from the expedient.[64]

---

60   D. B. Copland to Sir W. Leitch, 22 July 1936, UMA FECC, Box 44.
61   A political economist of the highest order, Keynes was always well aware of the practicality of economic ideas, of what was possible and advisable within the prevailing political and administrative system.
62   Earlier, of course, Keynes had, along with many other economists, spoken in favour of counter-cyclical public works to counter the slump. His most famous efforts in that regard were 'Can Lloyd George do it?' (1928) and 'The means to prosperity' (1933). Unlike the classical economists, Keynes's call for these programs had some theoretical underpinnings, sourced from the *Treatise on Money*, prompting him to say in 1929 that 'I know of no British economist of reputation who supports the proposition that schemes of National Development are incapable of curing unemployment' (Keynes 1973:813).
63   A. Smithies to D. B. Copland, 17 April 1936, UMA FECC, Box 48.
64   D. B. Copland to A. Smithies, 23 April 1936, UMA FECC, Box 48.

One step in that journey would be to convince authorities of the need for a sound monetary policy that took macroeconomic balance into account before exchange stability. It is to that we now turn.

The intellectual contribution of economists to the inquiry

The tabling of evidence

A central bank sets out upon an uncharted sea when it adventures forth to control credit.

— J. B. Brigden, 1936

Acting in their private capacities, 11 economists—Mauldon, Melville, Brigden, Gifford, Fisher, Hytten, Walker, Reddaway, Giblin, Wood and Wilson— presented evidence before the commission. It also included each giving a written statement addressing the issues posed in the questionnaire. Some of these submissions and the discourse through them ran to exorbitant length. Hytten's submission, for instance, meant he was in the witness box for five days.[65] Melville, too, took one day of proceedings just to read his statement.

The remarkable thing about the evidence presented by the economists was that it was, barring idiosyncrasies and nuances, fairly uniform. It was, moreover, more coherent and better informed and thought out than the evidence put forward by the other witnesses, including in particular Commonwealth Bank officials. Giblin (1951:215) found the evidence by Riddle, Bell and Reading to be technically poor, with their answers safe rather than instructive.[66] It was also discordant. Riddle, the first witness to be called before the commission, placed the 'utmost importance' on exchange rate stability.[67] He also stated that, unlike in the immediate past, now the bank had little anxiety over the Treasury bills issue. Sutherlin (1980:96) indicates, however, that the governor was insistent that the bank's primary aim was to prevent fluctuations in the price level. Reading, the chairman of the bank board, was emphatic about exchange rate

---

65 Hytten appeared in his own right, not representing the Wales Bank. His superior, A. C. Davidson, presented his own submission and testimony. His submission was prepared by the bank's research and intelligence section. Claude Janes had the task of putting the submission together and to the satisfaction of Davidson. He suffered a nervous breakdown from the stress of doing so and was sent off on a tour of Europe to recuperate.

66 The exception here was the submission by A. F. Bell, a member of the bank board who felt the existing powers were inadequate. Bell wanted more banking powers including the liquidity controls mooted by Giblin and Melville ('Central bank: views of the Acting Chairman', SMH, 31 July 1936).

67 'Bank Royal Commission Sir Claude Reading gives evidence', SMH, 16 January 1936

stability (Sutherlin 1985:118). For Commonwealth Bank officials, preserving the exchange rate was a shibboleth but for others it was a means to a greater end. In this respect, Melville felt the commission's task was to 'select one factor in the economy and attempt to fix it, at the same time endeavouring, as far as possible, to make every other factor in the economy adapt itself to the fixed factor' (cited in Cornish 1999).

Melville saw the exchange rate and the level of foreign reserves underpinning it as fulfilling that role. It was an appropriate marker for a small, open economy dependent on foreign capital. It would serve as a 'compass' by which authorities could steer the economy. This meant pegging the exchange rate and then guiding the economy along that course with appropriate domestic policies (Booth 1988:26). As we shall see, it was the import of Melville's independently crafted and cleverly systematic submission that provoked the most comment from his colleagues (Cornish 1999:122–34; Scott 1992). The economists plumped for achieving economic stability and, to varying degrees, pursuing full employment. Most economists advocated preventing economic fluctuations through counter-cyclical monetary and, in some cases, fiscal policy. To that extent most would have welcomed the report's key finding that '[t]he Commonwealth Bank should make its chief consideration the reduction of fluctuations in general economic activity in Australia, thereby maintaining such stability of internal conditions as is consistent with the change which is necessary if economic progress is to take place'.[68]

That is, the commission decided that exchange rate stability should play second fiddle to overall economic stability. This was the general view of the economists in their evidence to the commission. What, however, was of revolutionary change stemming from the proceedings was that domestic economic activity no longer had to dance to the tune set by the exchange rate. Rather, the exchange rate would be kept stable only as long as domestic economic activity was being maintained. The commission's preference was for the prevention of domestic economic instability and the maintenance of as near as possible full employment (Sutherlin 1980:97). While the commission conceded therefore that 'reducing fluctuations in general economic activity' was not as precise as exchange rate stability, it felt it was a stance of 'fundamentally greater importance'. The same paragraph went on to say that this entailed expanding credit when the economy was in need of stimulus and the reverse when the economy was overheating, with the exchange rate generally kept stable.

---

68 *Royal Commission to Inquire into the Monetary and Banking System at Present in Operation in Australia, 1937, Report and Minutes of Evidence* (hereafter RCMB), p. 204.

In his evidence, Melville had expressed doubt about whether one could truly use this criterion, rather than the exchange rate, as the compass by which to steer economic policy (Cornish 1999). In fact, Melville was never impressed by the commission's final report, commenting that

> [i]f you went with domestic policies and just let the market decide the exchange rate, you would not get good value. The movements in the rate would be very volatile with no management, and the market would just be motivated by waves of optimism and pessimism...That is not a practicable way of running an economy. (Cited in Booth 1988:38)

Following the approach of Sutherlin (1980), we will delineate the evidence of economists between the objectives of internal economic stability and exchange rate stability.

What the economists were saying

Internal stability

The issue of internal balance came to the fore not just in the evidence of the witnesses but in the commission's final report, which recommended institutional changes to the banking system, either by direct means or by establishing an open market for Treasury bills to manipulate liquidity levels within the economy. In the report, brought down in July 1937, the commission emphasised:

> The general objective of an economic system for Australia should be to achieve the best use of our productive resources...This means the fullest possible employment of people and resources under conditions that will provide the highest standard of living. It means, too, the reduction of fluctuations in the general level of economic activity.[69]

These desiderata required that an intelligently managed central bank, under government direction, had to regulate the volume of credit and currency in the light of the 'general objective of the monetary and banking system'. The exchange rate, together with foreign reserves, had to be brought under the ambit of the central bank (Sutherlin 1980:156–8). By placing the central bank under government supervision—or to be more exact, under the Federal Treasurer's ambit—monetary policy would become better integrated with other arms of economic policy (Butlin 1937:47). Monetary policy was to be made subordinate to the general objectives of the economy. The commission also conceded recourse to public works as an effective remedy for economic depression.

---

69   Final report of RCMB, 1937

Melville, Giblin, Reddaway and Hytten all reminded the commission that monetary policy had limited effectiveness when taken in isolation from other measures (Sutherlin 1980:160). Among one of the commission's bolder recommendations was that the Commonwealth Bank should have the power to confiscate a percentage of each of the trading banks' deposits that could be varied according to economic conditions. This was advanced because the commission felt that the central bank's power to restrict credit was circumscribed. Both Melville and Giblin proposed this idea to the commission—an idea that was, to be fair, also supported by a member of the bank board, A. F. Bell, in his evidence.[70]

Looking over the conduct of economic policy, the commission was critical of the shibboleth of exchange stability that the Commonwealth Bank Board had upheld since 1931 (Butlin 1937:44). It felt that the internal level of economic activity should take priority. This meant manipulating money supply, or credit, in inverse proportion to the level of economic activity. The Commonwealth Bank, in contrast, by engaging in funding, had inappropriately contracted credit during 1931–34 and failed to take the lead in setting interest rates (Butlin 1937:44).

It was a finding, perhaps, that mirrored what Keynes was saying in the *General Theory*. Apart from the commission's reference to full employment, however, the principal of regulating the level of credit to prevent fluctuations in economic activity was probably of mixed vintage involving elements of old and new economic thought and a fair degree of pragmatism. A royal commission investigating Canada's monetary system in 1933, for instance, had already concluded that management of credit, including the use of liquidity controls imposed on banks, would ensure a more effective economic policy. Most economists agreed that it was the interest rate that was the most important regulator of borrowing. The commission's enlightened approach to economic policy was not just derivative of new economic wisdom but, more importantly, of the hard lessons of policy mismanagement stemming from the early 1930s, including the embarrassment over interest rates between the Commonwealth Bank and the federal government in March 1936. These errors, catalogued by several witnesses, included not devaluing quickly enough, the failure of the Commonwealth Bank to take the lead on interest rates and its relentless pursuit of funding. Apart from allowing the Depression to develop more rapidly than was really necessary, the Commonwealth Bank compounded errors by retarding the recovery process.[71] The consensus from the economists was that the Commonwealth Bank had been too preoccupied with taking precautions to avoid a boom, thereby making the economy more vulnerable to recession.

---

70 'Central bank: views of acting chairman: powers inadequate', *SMH*, 31 July 1936, p. 12.
71 'Banking: errors of policy: retarded recovery: Dr Walker's views', *SMH*, 25 July 1936, p. 18.

In other words, the bank saw little virtue in expansion, always figuring that it meant increased imports, not increased exports or import substitution (Giblin 1951:217). The Commonwealth Bank's fixation with funding was indicted, with one witness drawing attention to the tangible lack of inflation even with so many Treasury bills extant.

In his damning evidence, Walker exorcised some commonly held falsehoods by demonstrating that the trading banks' credit squeeze of 1931 was the outcome of pressure on the London funds. He was critical, moreover, of the Commonwealth Bank for its failure to act to alleviate the situation by increasing credit at the time.[72] Certainly, some of the economists presented evidence articulating the newly minted wisdom of Keynes. Older economists, such as Giblin and Brigden, did not make direct reference to full employment but rather stressed maintaining a steady level of economic activity.

It was a testing time for some. A few days before he was due to give evidence before the commission, Hytten disarmingly told Giblin:

> The more I think of monetary theories and evidence for our ills the less I see in them. I suppose most parties will regard my conclusions as hopelessly muddled but I can't see any really clear-cut issue. To my mind 'a stable price level' [and] 'a stable exchange rate' are just as much catchcries as 'the single tax' and 'social credit'.[73]

Hytten, however—backed up with technical support from the Wales' economic research department—mounted an articulate, if overlong case for credit management but opposed the idea of liquidity controls.[74] Along with Davidson's submission, Hytten felt the contributions from the Wales were the 'most comprehensive evidence' presented.[75] Hytten enunciated the Keynesian resort of deploying fiscal policy in a slump.[76] His exposition, however, on how that expenditure would fall between output, income, prices and employment displayed some confusion.[77] It was tinged with Hayekian overtones since Hytten believed, like many of his contemporaries, that 'every expansion…carries with it the seeds of another crisis and depression'.[78] Like other economists, Hytten agreed that the main purpose of economic policy, all things considered, should

---

72   Evidence, RCMB, 1318.
73   T. Hytten to L. F. Giblin, 15 July 1936, Giblin Collection, UMA FECC, 92/141, Box 2 K-T.
74   Evidence, RCMB, 1228.
75   Hytten autobiography, UT, p. 136.
76   'Central bank: currency guardian', *SMH*, 21 July 1936, p. 12.
77   Evidence, RCMB, 1223.
78   Evidence, RCMB.

be to achieve the 'maximum employment of men and natural resources consistent with long term stability'.[79] The exchange rate should be kept stable—not for stability's sake, but to be subservient to domestic economic activity.

Allan Fisher, Hytten's predecessor at the Wales, stressed the more microeconomic role of the central bank—namely, to ensure an efficient distribution of the nation's savings. This, together with avoidance of inflation, would lead to the optimum use of economic resources. Elsewhere Fisher, in passages reminiscent of Shann, argued that the Depression in Australia was the consequence of overexpansion of credit in the wrong areas, especially primary industry.[80] Fisher was sceptical of the use of credit to achieve full employment.[81] With that outlook, it could well be understood why Fisher had differences with Davidson and returned to academe.[82]

Giblin's submission was, like his character, idiosyncratic, ranging over issues such as income distribution, population policy and the need for the Commonwealth Bank to formulate economic policy that would have a bipartisan grounding. Giblin emphasised that discussion of monetary policy was, in a sense, too technical a matter for the commission to handle. It also had to be understood that monetary policy could only ease the pain of any external shocks on the economy and prevent the secondary effects of that first loss in real income.[83] Unlike Copland, Giblin was in favour of an independent central bank. His colleague Wood argued that the chief function of the financial system 'was to keep capital accumulation and purchasing power in balance…and there is justified impatience with a system which fails to assume the power to correlate production, consumption, and saving'.[84]

The submissions by the younger economists, particularly Walker, Reddaway and Gifford, confidently displayed an appreciation of Keynes's new vision. Walker, of all the young Keynesians, was probably the most astute in urging the prevention of the recurrence of deflation, but also inflation, though mitigation of the first should take priority. He also showed the greatest technical command of Keynes's theoretical system by invoking a number of key constructs (Cornish 1990:62). Interestingly, neither he nor Gifford favoured the idea of liquidity controls, believing that the Commonwealth Bank had enough power to manipulate credit efficaciously. Walker favoured the use of monetary and fiscal policy working in tandem, though he felt only the latter would be effective in tackling a slump. Monetary policy would play an accommodating role in easing the financial

---

79   Evidence, RCMB, 1222.
80   Evidence, RCMB, 1215.
81   'Banking inquiry: evidence in Perth: Prof. Fisher's views', *SMH*, 25 June 1936.
82   C. Janes to D. B. Copland, 15 March 1935, UMA FECC, Box 34.
83   Evidence, RCMB, 1345.
84   Evidence, RCMB, 1235.

constraint. More importantly, it would assist in the mitigation of depressions and 'the stabilization of the purchasing power of money' (cited in Cornish 1990:61). Walker was the consummate Keynesian, emphasising the extreme importance of business confidence when resorting to fiscal policy action. Like Keynes, he felt that only the persuasion of elected officials would lead to better policy and better outcomes. Cooperation between the Commonwealth Bank, the Federal Treasury and the Arbitration Court was ultimately required for economic stability (Cornish 1990:62). Price stability could be addressed partly by enshrining money wage stability with due allowances for skill differentials.[85]

The University of Queensland economist J. K. Gifford burst into the public limelight with an accessible presentation on the meaning of Keynes. Despite his Kiel school background, Gifford confessed to being a devotee of Keynes and 'was very pleased to see the recent development of his theory in his last book'.[86] In his statement, Gifford swept aside the boom–bust trade-cycle views of Hayek and Von Mises and articulated a hydraulic version of Keynes's new schema and policy implications. Consequently, Gifford was bolder than both Walker and Reddaway in taking the line that the central bank should keep the economy in semi-boom without fomenting inflation. He was, in short, an ardent expansionist. He attracted Chifley's attention by advocating massive credit creation to counter a slump (Robinson 1986:133).[87] The year before, Gifford (1935a) had written an article in the *Economic Record* calling for a 'moderate credit expansion to stimulate industry and cause the absorption of the unemployed' even if it meant devaluation.

Reddaway presented an equally synthetic account of the 'new' economics. He rejected price stability as a policy objective because it was the symptom of domestic and international turbulence.[88] Rather, monetary policy should be targeted at maintaining a high level of employment and income. Public works was an effective antidote to a depression while a budgetary surplus was apposite in boom conditions. Reddaway felt that Treasury bills were an unmitigated blessing and did not impede management of the credit base as long as there was an open market for them. Melville had also exaggerated fears of an excessive amount of bills in circulation.[89] An improvement in the London funds would, however, warrant some funding to counter the threat of a boom.[90] Melville's view, in contrast, was that it was hard to build up London funds without some degree of funding beforehand. Reddaway likened it to being fearful that low

---

85   'Banking control: Dr Walker's views', *SMH*, 23 July 1936.
86   Evidence, RCMB, 1199.
87   Evidence, RCMB, 1197.
88   Evidence, RCMB, 1333.
89   Evidence, RCMB, 1334.
90   Evidence, RCMB, 1335.

interest rates while in the midst of depression might ultimately induce a boom. The two young protagonists came closer on the matter of exchange stability, to which we now turn.

External stability

Melville was insistent that the stability of the exchange rate was not the objective of monetary policy but rather the means to make that policy and its objectives more effective (Cornish 1999). Hytten, to name one, became confused about what really were the ends and means in Melville's scheme. Melville felt that the objective of monetary policy was, like the other economists, to achieve economic stability, price stability and as near full employment as practicable.[91] Melville despaired, however, of conducting an intelligent monetary policy by using a raft of monetary indicators. The conduct of monetary policy would become 'so complex as to be capable of solution only by supermen with absolute power' (cited in Johnston 1993:213).

After reviewing the possibilities, Melville opted for pegging the exchange rate as the datum point for monetary policy. There would be one target and one instrument. Moreover, the target chosen would focus continual attention on the nation's economic bugbear: the external account. This was, of course, the channel through which Australia endured losses and gains in real income from her dealings with other nations. It would be necessary to monitor economic activity to keep the exchange rate steady. The central bank would smooth out any undershooting or overshooting of credit creation by having liquidity controls and an open market for bills. This would ensure 'a sensible sort of discipline' in operating monetary policy. There would still be, however, conflict about achieving the three objectives of full employment, stability in general business activity and a maximum output of production. Indeed Melville suggested that full employment would, more or less, follow as a consequence of achieving the other two objectives. The implication, then, was that pursuing full employment in its own right was likely to jeopardise attaining the other two objectives (Cornish 1999:135).

In his schema, Melville wanted the exchange rate to have an element of 'elasticity' and it was this aspect that separated him from the views of senior bank officials and kept him more within the orbit of the economists (Sutherlin 1980:104–5). Melville's view was that the exchange rate could be changed in exceptional circumstances or cases of fundamental disequilibrium. In that sense his stance was not so removed from the other economists. Reddaway, for instance, sounded almost like Melville in stating that Australia needed an agreed fixed point of

---

91   Evidence, RCMB, 1116.

reference or a stable exchange rate since it was 'a dependent economy'. That fact alone set limits on furthering Australia's prosperity no matter how adroit monetary policy was.

As an experienced exponent of exchange rate policy, Melville reminded the commission that there was 'no glow of prosperity when the currency is overvalued'.[92] He did not, however, think the rate should vary with seasonal movements in the London funds otherwise the currency would tend to oscillate. Implicit within Melville's analysis, as Cain (1988b:9) points out, was the notion that money wages and domestic prices might have to adjust in times of economic duress to preserve the exchange rate. Melville, however, would not brook deflationary policies just to preserve the exchange rate. He also conceded here that money wage rigidity—one of 'the consequences of Mr Keynes'—might throw a spanner in the works. He also did not envisage in his schema that domestic expansion could ever pose a threat to the stability of the exchange rate; only deep-seated external factors could portend that.

Giblin was struck by the degree of uniformity there was among economists on the exchange rate question. It was really all a matter of degree.[93] That is, there was general agreement among economists that the rate could not be sustained if it was impairing domestic economic stability. For the short run, all of them suggested exchange rate stability and, in the longer run, any conflict between upholding the pegged rate and achieving near full employment should resolve in favour of the latter. Cain (1988b) suggests, however, that for Melville these circumstances would have to be quite special given his general philosophy that ultimately governments could do little about alleviating the economic cycle. It was better, therefore, to make the management of the money supply knave-proof by regulating it through pegged exchange rates than surrender it to government authority. To have his system operate effectively, Melville plumped for liquidity controls on the banks. They were a necessary evil. Melville felt the liquidity controls were 'a cause for worry' as the accounts could interfere and jeopardise private banking operations.[94]

Giblin was one of the few witnesses to bring out the political and partisan aspect of exchange rate setting.[95] His view—shared by other economists—was that exchange rate stability should be welcomed since it would encourage more inflow of private investment (Sutherlin 1980:107). Like the other economists, Giblin eschewed Australia resorting to competitive devaluation because it 'would be fatal to world prospects and in the long run to her own interests'.[96] That said, all

---

92   RCMB, Evidence, 1143.
93   RCMB, Evidence, 1344.
94   L. G. Melville to A. H. Lewis, 10 August 1937, Melville Papers, NLA.
95   RCMB, Evidence, 1344.
96   RCMB, Evidence, 1344.

the economists praised the 1931 devaluation as a proper, if belated, response to countering Australia's economic difficulties. Reddaway felt that with normalcy returning, devaluation should be used only as an emergency measure.[97] Walker was not so dogmatic, insisting that the trauma of further devaluation was less onerous than the alternative of credit contraction.[98] He was, like Gifford, prepared to swap exchange rate flexibility to gain more employment (Sutherlin 1980:112).

What the other witnesses were saying

Apart from Davidson's lengthy submission, the evidence tendered by the trading banks was predictably antediluvian. Their evidence was focused more on matters of banking and the allocation of capital than on national economic policy (Sutherlin 1980:89). Like all the bankers, Davidson wanted exchange stability but he aligned himself solely with the economists when it came to the debate between internal stability and the exchange rate.[99] His colleagues hardly stirred themselves on that policy dilemma (Sutherlin 1980:114). Reflective of the contretemps of March 1936, Davidson eschewed the notion that the Commonwealth Bank did not have the power to set interest rates. Like other trading bank representatives, Davidson dismissed the notion that banks had deliberately restricted their advances during the Depression except, of course, to speculators or those purchasing luxuries.[100] In fact, Davidson said his bank had directed loans to import-competing and export industries. Darvell, General Manager of the Commercial Bank of Sydney, correctly attributed any decline in loans and advances during the Depression to economic factors.[101] This view was backed up by G. D. Healy of the Bank of Australasia, who denied there was a consensus among the banks to restrict credit during the Depression.[102]

The proposal to establish a compulsory deposit scheme for the trading banks drew the bile of private bankers. Edmund Godward of the Bank of Australasia felt the measure would fit a 'communistic government'. As for its key proponent, Melville, '[h]e is like all the other economists—evolves an ideal and will not see the dangers of his proposals'.[103] Earlier, Healy had noted that allowing the Commonwealth Bank to have more control over banks' credit creation raised the question, '*Quis custodiet custodes?*'[104] Healy told Mills at the hearings that

---

97 RCMB, Evidence, 1325.
98 RCMB, Evidence, 1298.
99 'Exchange rate: stability needed', *SMH*, 2 June 1936, p. 12.
100 'Banking commission; Mr Davidson's evidence', *SMH*, 9 April 1936, p. 16.
101 'Banking commission; Treasury bills; banker's evidence', *SMH*, 25 March 1936, p. 14.
102 'Trading banks: competition for business', *SMH*, 12 January 1936, p. 10.
103 E. Godward to G. Healy, 25 June 1936, and G. Healy to E. Godward, 21 May 1936, Bank of Australasia, D/O Correspondence, ANZ Archive.
104 Ibid.

the scheme would impinge directly on the private banks' business.[105] The enlightened Davidson agreed, but in his technically sophisticated submission, which ranged over 12 days of testimony, he argued that the art of central banking was better practised by influence rather than by decree (Holder 1970:818).

In his submission, McConnan stated that the private banks had also taken their fair share of sacrifice in the Depression and that they had deferred to the last moment any credit restriction.[106] W. A. Leitch, General Manager of the Union Bank, related the then contemporaneous decline in the trading banks' deposits to excessive government borrowing in the market together with rising import consumption.[107]

Aftermath

Most commentators, including all the economists, held that the commission's hearings and findings contributed to the dissemination and improvement of modern central bank practices. Reviewing the legacy of the royal commission, Melville believed, many years later, that though nothing much was achieved it did get people accustomed to the idea of some regulation of the banking system (Cornish 1993b:16). These powers, alas, due to political and institutional resistance, became operational only with the outbreak of war (Sutherlin 1980). Before that economists remained hopeful that the era of a more effective and coordinated monetary policy was not far off. Certainly, all the reviews of the commission's findings suggested that the age of enlightened central banking had arrived (Sutherlin 1980:178).

In a letter to Mills, Copland was blithely hopeful that, with prosperous economic conditions extant and the trading banks liquid, the Lyons government would quickly implement the commission's findings so as to remove the problem of banking and monetary policy from political controversy.[108] It was, in truth, a vain hope, with another general election about to be fought and the banks already up in arms over the commission's findings.

As Sutherlin's study shows, the Lyons government prevaricated even after the 1937 general election was over—and by that time, the banks' liquidity levels suffered as export prices faltered. This made the prospect of monetary control more untenable. Once again, then, the aspirations of economists in promoting the idea of an enlightened economic policy were nipped in the bud. Massy-Greene informed Copland that Lyons was 'a tired man' and, while eager to adopt

---

105 'Bank inquiry: lodging of cash minimum', *SMH*, 3 June 1936, p. 12.
106 'Australian banks: full sacrifices in depression', *SMH*, 13 February 1936, p. 12.
107 'Government borrowing bank manager's warning', *SMH*, 20 February 1936, p. 10.
108 D. B. Copland to R. C. Mills, 24 July 1937, UMA FECC, Box 54.

a 'more progressive policy', Page, Menzies and Casey were not of the same ilk.[109] It was Casey, alas, who had the odious task of implementing the commission's findings and winning over the Melbourne trading banks' support. He later told Bruce how he had 'sweated blood' to devise measures that 'will do most good and least harm'. He anticipated, however, that the reforms would be greeted by alarm from bankers who were 'really a most unintelligent crowd'.[110] The technical and political negotiations over, the drafting of the proposed legislation would prove a complicated and protracted exercise (Sutherlin 1980).

The trading banks arrogantly held the view that the Commonwealth Bank Board did not have the professional competence or vision to have greater monetary powers invested within it. In that regard, Davidson issued a Wales Bank circular highly critical of the commission's findings. Interestingly, it was written by a visiting English economist, Noel Hall, along lines suggested by Hytten.[111] It was imbued with Davidson's fears about surrendering monetary policy to the whims of the Treasurer—a figure who showed a penchant for deflationary policy (Holder 1970:826–7). He was joined in this by McConnan, who resented the proposed changes as undue coercion.[112] Both exchanged correspondence on this aspect of control and how they would be at the mercy of the Federal Treasurer. McConnan doubted whether the commissioners could appreciate the 'serious danger' of their recommendation that the Auditor-General be authorised to investigate the affairs of any bank at the whim of the Treasurer.[113] Davidson's and McConnan's dissent also applied to the commission's other key recommendation: that the Commonwealth Bank have greater leverage over the London funds to ensure that Australia's reserves were at the appropriate level.

Copland was annoyed with the mischievous nature of the Wales' *Circular*, believing that its views on banking practice were sound neither in theory nor practice. The *Circular* caused him to 'revise my ideas a good deal about the place of economists in business life'.[114] This was a direct reference to the activities of Hytten and Hall, who provided intellectual support to Davidson in opposing the banking sector reforms. Copland was also incensed at how Hytten was appropriating the title of 'Professor' in his public utterances when he now worked exclusively for the Wales and was, moreover, speaking on matters on which he had apparently little expertise.[115] Behind this pedantry, perhaps, lay Copland's annoyance that the Wales was reducing its support for the Economic Society. That aside, Copland decided to counter the Wales' *Circular* by penning

109   Sir W. Massy-Greene to D. B. Copland, 15 June 1937, UMA FECC, Box 54.
110   R. G. Casey to S. M. Bruce, 3 May 1938, Casey–Bruce Correspondence, AA, A1421 (4).
111   A. C. Davidson to T. Hytten, 14 August 1937, Cablegram, BNSW, GM302/386.
112   'Greater powers for the Commonwealth Bank', *SMH*, 1 September 1936, p. 8.
113   L. J. McConnan to A. C. Davidson, 7 August 1937, National Bank Archive.
114   D. B. Copland to C. Janes, 14 October 1937, UMA FECC, Box 53.
115   D. B. Copland to C. Janes, 2 November 1937, UMA FECC, Box 51.

two favourable articles for the press on the commission's report. He also promised Keynes a brief review of the commission's report for the *Economic Journal*. The resulting article was to the taste of Keynes, who had, incidentally, read the Wales material.[116]

The thrust of these commentaries by Copland, as he told one banker, was to regard the report as forming the basis for building better relations between the banks and the central bank and, more generally, the relations between the banking system and the federal government. It represented an opportunity to institute the safeguards the commission recommended in order to underline the public responsibility of the banking system but to do so in a way inoffensive to the banks.[117] Copland, however, did not think that the commission recommendations on liquidity controls went far enough. As currently proposed, the controls could be sidestepped by the trading banks resorting to keeping part of their mandatory liquid reserves in the form of Treasury bills and London funds (Sutherlin 1980:190).

In his review of the commission's report, Butlin (1937) welcomed the finding about placing the central bank under political control of the incumbent government, as was now the case in New Zealand. This would allow economic policy to be integrated with other arms of policy, not least public expenditure— something that had been sometimes lacking in the past. Butlin (1937:73) mused about how little the idea of bank nationalisation had been considered except for Chifley's three-page addendum to the final report. Chifley wrote the addendum only to give mandatory voice to Labor Party policy, especially its new platform on monetary policy that had been incidentally released as the commission sat (Weller 1975:140–1; Kuhn 1988:62). The objectives set out in the ALP's new monetary policy sounded similar to the commission's goals but there was ominous mention of having a 'national control of [the Commonwealth's] credit resources'. Chifley wrote the addendum without reference to any of the evidence presented before the commission. By the same token, Chifley admitted that none of the evidence he had heard led him to accept the continuation of private banking (Crisp 1961:169).

Butlin also praised the idea of variable minimum liquidity controls believing it would be effective in reining in lending during a boom. Walker and Reddaway, who in their evidence had not supported the idea of liquidity controls, changed their tune on the report's release. Both agreed with Butlin regarding the minimum-deposits option as arming the central bank with the power to check a boom (Sutherlin 1980:181). Only Fisher voiced some apprehension

---

116   D. B. Copland to J. M. Keynes, 17 December 1937; J. M. Keynes to D. B. Copland, 28 October 1937, UMA FECC, Box 53.
117   D. B. Copland to L. J. McConnan, 14 August 1937, UMA FECC, Box 54.

about the 'radical' and somewhat vague powers the central bank now had to compel trading banks to hold minimum deposits (Sutherlin 1980:182–3). More perhaps was made of it than it really deserved. Mills later pointed out that the power to call up deposits from the banks—the percentage of which had never been stipulated—would be likely to be used only in periods of acute crisis or when trading banks were proving recalcitrant. Even then, the action had to meet with the consent of the Treasurer. Mills reminded his detractors that the whole spirit of the report was to allow the Commonwealth Bank to continue to regulate the monetary system through the exercise of its existing powers and with the cooperation of the trading banks.[118]

The clause that Federal Parliament, and through it the government, be ultimately responsible for monetary policy would arise only if there were irreconcilable differences between the government and the bank. In that event, the government would give an assurance to the bank that it took responsibility for the policy and its implementation. In short, there would be no repeats of March 1936.

The operative question was whether the delay in arming the Commonwealth Bank with the powers recommended to it by the commission would make the passage through future economic seas more difficult.

---

118   'Finances in emergency', *The Argus*, 17 October 1938.

9. Australia, 1936–1938: the nascent Keynesian state?

Introduction

The two grand themes of this monograph are, to repeat, the influence of economists' ideas on Australian public policy in the 1930s and whether their assimilation of Keynesian economics made any imprint on official policy. In this, and the following chapter, these two themes coalesce as we inquire into whether there is any indication of what might be called a 'Keynesian revolution' in Australian economic policy before and just after the outbreak of World War II. It is not an unrealistic prospect since Australian economists had already assumed a position of considerable influence by the late 1930s. On the other hand, the growth of knowledge in economics, and its infiltration into the corridors of power, is rarely linear and orderly (Coats 1992:426).

In the history of economic ideas it was the case that most capitalist countries adopted—more by accident than design—Keynesianism in order to effectively wage war. Keynes had despaired of seeing the central policy contribution of the *General Theory* implemented except under dire emergency. Total war would allow the scale of public sector expenditure to give life to his 'grand experiment' in economic coordination (Winch 1969:266). The British historian Patrick Renshaw (1999:359), however, has suggested that war was hardly 'a true test bed for Keynesian economics'. That is, mobilisation, conscription, rationing and planning might be the stuff of war but they do not intrinsically amount to a conversion to Keynesian economics per se. Cornish (1992) has argued along similar lines in examining the Australian experience. Other tests of a conversion to Keynesianism might include assimilating Keynes's theoretical constructs, language and, of course, his policy precepts.

This and the following chapter will argue that the lack of a Keynesian consciousness at the higher levels of the Lyons government meant that, even with a prosperous economy, it still had to confront a daunting policy dilemma between financing civilian compared with war needs (Ross 1995). Resolving that dilemma not only jeopardised the government's supply-side economic strategy of low interest rates and low taxes, it thrust it into political turbulence. The federal government discovered to its dismay that the 'recovery of prosperity' seemed to be the signal for more, not less, controversy over monetary policy especially central bank credit.[1]

While Gilbert (1973) has claimed that the Commonwealth Bank Board, in the late 1930s, exuded a Keynesian vision in its monetary policy settings, the conventional view was that official economic policy was still decidedly pre-Keynesian until the outbreak of war. In contrast with official policy, Melville has claimed that most of the Australian economists had, more or less, adopted a Keynesian outlook by 1939—a view shared by Downing (1972). This division in outlook between economists and policymakers will be examined against the backdrop of a number of episodes. While some, like Brigden and Melville, held positions of some influence, they could not penetrate through the philosophical mind-set gripping policymakers and office-holders in Canberra. To be fair, the constitutional constraints meant that the Commonwealth government was ill suited to undertake the scale of spending expansionists urged on it. By the same token, however, state governments could embark, with Loan Council approval, on some modest attempts at pump priming. In that regard, three state premiers continued to criticise the prevailing policy of restrictive expansion. Keynesian voices, therefore, were not confined to the cloisters. Moreover, the Arbitration Court, guided by academic expertise, issued a national wages decision seemingly imbued with Keynesian logic.

This period was not one therefore of repose but one punctuated by a difficult policy choice. Yet, remarkably, it is a period of Australia's economic and political history often overlooked in the literature, with more attention given to the threatening international environment and the country's response to it. While the threat of war, together with a leadership crisis, overshadowed domestic politics, there were still discernible controversies over the direction and bearing of Commonwealth economic policy. Of particular concern was the recurrent matter of managing the economic boom that gave Australia near full employment in 1937/38. Issues, too, such as the National Insurance Scheme, preparing legislation from the findings of the Royal Commission on Money and Banking and defence preparedness preoccupied policymakers. The period would end with the economists, as in 1931, being 'called in' to help with the war effort and imparting Keynes's precepts into budgetary policy in late 1939. This was some time before Britain did likewise with Kingsley Wood's wartime budget of 1941.

While the march of events swung in the economists' favour, it was a struggle to have their services recognised by the federal government. There was also the

---

1   This observation was made in a speech prepared for Casey by Treasury officials in November 1938 (Treasury Secretary Papers, AA, A11857/1).

problem of the public perception of economics. An *Age* editorial, for instance, had the temerity to lambast the profession for its opaqueness, stating that it had delivered a 'singularly meagre service' to the public good.[2] It was ironic that three of Australia's most powerful voices railing against the timid economic policies of the Lyons government would find their reputations and authority diminished by 1939. Davidson was undermined by a new manager who had the Wales' board 'clip his wings' with his beloved kindergarten of economists 'scattered to the winds' (Randerson 1953:51).[3] Premier Stevens, openly regarded as a Keynesian by at least one economist, was still pitching to become the next Federal Treasurer. He was soon, alas, to be toppled from power, ironically, on the grounds of being unable to balance New South Wales' budget (McCarthy 1979:155). Copland, too, would suffer a humiliating rebuff in his aspirations to become Vice-Chancellor of Melbourne University. Yet it was these three figures who gave the Lyons government a hard time in 1936–37 over its monetary policy settings.

Managing the boom

The remarkable thing about 1937 was how the internally generated upswing in economic activity showed little sign of abatement. Private capital expenditure, rather than government spending, led the recovery (Brigden 1938:1). It placed pressure on interest rates, with the local money market 'being milked dry'.[4] Since 1931, construction had increased sixfold and iron and steel production fourfold, while imports, mostly of capital goods, trebled. The last was matched by a corresponding rise in export revenue along with an infusion of foreign investment meaning that the London funds were augmented considerably. Unemployment fell below the pre-depression level of 10 per cent. Giblin wondered just how long the rate of expansion could continue.[5] He noted how it was due more to internal factors than exports, though any economic expansion was ultimately circumscribed by the amount of London funds. Nonetheless, the recovery was almost in defiance of the policy maxim of ensuring that the primary producer was given the utmost assistance. While prices were now healthy, export production had not risen markedly in volume terms since 1932–33.

---

2   'The importance of being intelligible', *The Age*, 15 August 1936. The attack was redolent of a mock trial held at the London School of Economics in 1933, when the British politician Robert Boothby, representing 'the state of the popular mind', accused economists of 'conspiring to spread the mental fog' and declared that they 'were unintelligible', that they had been proved wrong and, lastly, that they were always disagreeing with each other (Davis 1975).

3   L. Bury, TRC 121, 121/70, NLA, p. 8.

4   R. G. Casey to S. M. Bruce, 2 February 1937, Casey–Bruce Correspondence, AA, A1421.

5   'Australia in 1937', UMA FECC, Box 220.

In a pre-election speech before the Australian Chamber of Manufactures in August 1937, Lyons deemed the rise in the manufacturing sector and manifested by the establishment of new factories 'unprecedented in the industrial history of the Commonwealth'.[6] Unlike Britain, moreover, all of Australia's manufacturing output was for consumption, not armaments.

In a commentary in 1937, Copland reminded his readership of how economists had been instrumental in laying the plans for the manufacturing sector to develop and prosper. He stressed how changed international economic circumstances had given those plans further ambit. Manufacturing helped, too, in absorbing the unemployed and gave Australia a defensive capacity in terms of self-sufficiency.[7] Manufacturing, Copland informed Fisher, allowed Australia to achieve full employment without lower public investment than hitherto.[8] Indeed by the end of 1937, public works had returned to its traditional role of promoting economic development rather than as a tool for stabilisation (Brigden 1938:1). Copland felt Australia had little choice but to expand manufacturing following the widespread restrictions on international trade. Besides employing 500 000 workers, manufacturing added to the expansion of national income just as effectively as exports.[9]

The height of the boom was 1937/38, with Australia reaching, and then surpassing, the pre-depression level of output—the remaining unemployment being attributable solely to structural factors. There was a very strong rise in loan advances from June 1937 to June 1938, with the Bank of New South Wales leading the charge. Moreover, the federal government recorded another budgetary surplus, while the accounts of all the state governments, bar drought- ridden Queensland and Western Australia, also showed a net surplus for the first time.[10] This economic largesse induced Casey in the 1937/38 Federal Budget to fully restore the pension and to embark on an ambitious scheme of national insurance. These developments were meant to answer criticism of the government's lack of constructive legislation. The government also did not oppose the trade unions' submission before the Arbitration Court for a wage rise premised on the gathering prosperity. Casey also had to increase the outlays on defence spending, some of which were financed by a loan from the Bank of England. The debate over Australian economic policy was reduced to the Labor Party trying to establish that it was it, not the UAP government, which had put the Premiers' Plan in place. Not to be outdone, the UAP, in its 1937 federal election campaign, focused on what had been achieved in economic terms. Bruce

6 'Bright times had come again', SMH, 20 August 1937.
7 'Expansion of manufactures in Australia: how it helped recovery', Smith's Weekly, 1937, UMA FECC, Box 56.
8 D. B. Copland to A. G. B. Fisher, 27 January 1939, UMA FECC, Box 77.
9 'Commodity prices and Australian exports', Smith's Weekly, December 1937, UMA FECC, Box 56.
10 'Budgets for 1938/39', Economic Notes, no. 4 (July 1938).

told Lyons to stress how Australia had become 'the social laboratory for the rest of the world'.[11] Copland, however, felt that Australia had, in recent years, been overtaken in progressive social legislation by other countries—a view shared by the politically ambitious Stevens, whom Copland advised.[12] This was one reason why Casey set out, almost single-handedly, to introduce national insurance after the election (Richards 1975:1)

The Stevens controversy

As Casey had predicted, when Stevens returned from Britain there was renewed agitation over the direction of economic policy. Armed with more justification for hastening economic expansion, Stevens wanted, and indeed conspired, to have semi-governmental authorities sidestep Loan Council restraints by borrowing directly from abroad. Both the federal government and the Commonwealth Bank already had some difficulty in restraining New South Wales, Tasmania and Queensland from wanting to borrow locally or offshore. Casey had become 'fed up with the shouting match' over the matter between the bank board and the premiers serving on the Loan Council.[13] According to Melville, dissidents were targeting the Commonwealth Bank for allegedly falling under the influence of London and exceeding its powers with respect to other authorities.[14]

The controversy started when Stevens penned three widely publicised articles focusing on Britain's supposedly innovative policy of cheap money and insinuated that Australia, in contrast, had abandoned its expansionist policies.[15] When Copland had visited Cambridge—'his second home'—in late 1936, he would have noted Britain's cheap money policy and could have played some part here in encouraging Stevens.[16] Davidson was the other antagonist—certainly in Casey's eyes. Stevens and Casey clashed over the issue in the Sydney press. The former was annoyed that Australian interest rates were likely to rise against world trends and that action by the Commonwealth Bank could pre-empt this if it were not so timid. Casey responded by stating that this was the 'argument of an inflationist' and that '[y]ou cannot get a quart out of a pint pot'. Stevens correctly replied that it was central bank action on liquidity and credit that ultimately 'decides the capacity of the pot'.[17] It was an interesting metaphor that captured the debate between the Keynesians and the Hayekians.

---

11 S. M. Bruce to J. Lyons, 9 July 1937, Miscellaneous Correspondence, AA, M104/5/1.
12 'Immediate political policy-program for the Commonwealth', 4 June 1937, UMA FECC, Box 55.
13 R. G. Casey to S. M. Bruce, 6 February 1937, Casey–Bruce Correspondence, AA, A 1421.
14 L. G. Melville to G. E. Jackson, 8 February 1937, BE, OV13/4.
15 *SMH*, 18 November 1936, 19 November 1936, 20 November 1936.
16 'Notes of discussions in England', 12 November 1936, UMA FECC, Box 43.
17 *SMH*, 12 November 1936.

The Commonwealth Bank and Casey, were, as always, extremely sensitive to charges that the bank was following a deflationary policy. Casey went to the length of asking the former Treasury official, S. G. MacFarlane, now Official Secretary and Financial Adviser to Bruce at Australia House, to prepare a brief repudiating Stevens' argument that Britain was practising a cheap money policy. He, in turn, approached the Bank of England to help repudiate Stevens' claims.[18] So seriously did Casey consider the matter that he prepared a cabinet memorandum on monetary policy repudiating the legitimacy of Stevens' claims. Apart from stating that the cabinet was satisfied with the current arrangements with the Commonwealth Bank, there was a further decree opposing new borrowing in London for public works. Further, the federal government was to attempt to vacate the local loan market as soon as possible. It was, however, to continue to encourage the migration of capital to Australia. Stevens' idea of pumping more credit into the economy would, in Casey's eyes, see it 'spill out in London'.[19]

Reddaway also came to the Commonwealth Bank's defence by a forceful rebuttal of Stevens' argument for more credit-based finance.[20] Stressing that he, too, was a 'whole-hearted believer' in economic expansion, Reddaway stated that the Australian economy did not need a stimulus, which, if it occurred, would certainly spell devaluation and, therefore, damage the continuance of capital flows. Much of the rise in manufacturing industry was underpinned by this investment. In his own three-article riposte to Stevens, Reddaway pointed out that comparing Australia's monetary outcomes with Britain's was wrong-headed since the latter was a creditor nation and could expand the money supply without fear of devaluation. Reddaway expressed bemusement that Stevens was upholding the timid economic policies of the Chamberlain government in stark contrast with the relatively enlightened economic policies instigated by Australia.[21] Having, as we shall see, just played a part in altering Australian wage levels, one could see Reddaway's point. The Englishman did concede that low interest rates had their place in maintaining economic momentum but the main lesson Australia could draw from Britain was its establishment of efficient labour exchanges.[22]

Stevens also seemed quite unaware of just how dimly the Bank of England would regard his proposals. One of Stevens' articles, for instance, pushed the case for more public expenditure with another article visualising overseas borrowing as the means to facilitate it. This idea would have horrified the Bank

---

18 Memorandum by Kershaw, 30 November 1936, BE, G1/287.
19 'Monetary policy: cabinet memorandum', by the Treasurer, 6 December 1936, AA, A6006, microfilm, p. 21.
20 *SMH*, 28 November 1936.
21 'A contrast: Australia's monetary policy', *SMH*, 27 November 1937.
22 'Australia's monetary policy', *SMH*, 30 November 1936.

of England, including R. N. Kershaw and G. E. Jackson, who, in their secret visit to Australia in 1936, briefed cabinet ministers over the matter of renewed borrowing from London.[23] That resort, the two argued, would lead to a flurry of imports. They also cautioned their hosts that renewed borrowing by Australia might undermine her credibility unless the loan was put to remunerative ends. Kershaw took the opportunity to pour cold water over Casey's idea of establishing more manufacturing industries in Australia. He warned Casey that it was not a medium-term solution and that it was still 'possible to become inflated even in a closed economy'.[24] With the prospect of active deflation 'politically impossible' with a federal election due, Kershaw felt a better way to solve Australia's recurrent external account problem was to develop better means of monetary control. That idea would not become part of the economic policy machinery for some time. As for Stevens, his crusade for more expansionism was far from over.

Copland and 'the coming boom'

For the economists, a booming economy spelt just as much of a challenge as did depression. The preconception held by most economists at the time, even Keynes, was that a bust usually followed a boom. Giblin had already gathered notes in January 1937 ominously entitled 'The next depression', precisely because he and his colleagues were concerned by that prospect. Much of his note taking sprang from a lecture given by Keynes at the London School of Economics.[25] Giblin deduced that, hitherto, there had been no 'obvious, cut and dried' technique of checking a boom without precipitating a slump. Keynes wanted to devise the means by which it might be possible to do so. For Britain, this would involve a 'rightly distributed' aggregate demand, increasing taxes and restricting credit. Britain's unemployment rate at the time was 12 per cent. Keynes felt that using high interest rates to temper a boom was unnecessary (Keynes 1936:323). It also would not stamp out speculative behaviour. Credit rationing was preferable. Keynes, in fact, suggested that the remedy for a boom was to persist with low rates. Another lesson from Keynes was that the longer the life of the boom, the greater the time to prepare the economy for the bust. The trick of economic policy was to avoid this by keeping the economy in semi-boom.

In the Australian context, the problem was compounded, in Copland's estimation, by the forecast that export prices would reach the heights they had attained in 1928.[26] Fixated by the problem, Copland drew up a memorandum

---

23   15 April 1936, BE, OV13/4.
24   Memorandum by Kershaw, 11 May 1936, BE, OV13/4.
25   RBA, GLG-43-1.
26   Telegram from D. B. Copland to B. S. B. Stevens, 11 November 1936, UMA FECC, Box 55.

discussing policy responses to it.[27] He and fellow colleagues met in Melbourne over a few days in March 1937 to discuss expedients that might be adopted by the authorities. Interestingly, the unofficial meeting was held immediately after the Commonwealth Bank Board meeting. The timing was not accidental; Reading had specifically requested it. Melville believed the arrangement 'would be a useful precedent'.[28]

The gathering of 'concentrated wisdom', as Copland put it, included Melville, Giblin, Coombs, Reddaway, Mills and Hytten.[29] Melville, whose views on policy had usually been discordant with those of his colleagues, reported that '[t]here was a remarkable unanimity of opinion about practical measures although there were some differences of opinion on matters of theory'.[30] The discussion was expressed not in terms of monetary aggregates but in wording almost akin to aggregate demand.[31]

One section of the memorandum, entitled 'Mr Keynes and Australian policy', envisaged what Keynes might recommend for Australia, which was at about the same stage of the economic cycle as Britain. The operative strategy agreed on was that the general aim of policy should be to conserve public works projects to help cushion the economy against the inevitable downturn. It entailed postponing public works with a firm promise to restart them when private investment spending turned down; in short, the tap of public works was now an essential part of stabilisation policy. The economists also favoured some funding of Treasury bills. Lastly, they aimed for a £70–80 million levelling of London funds to forestall any fears of devaluation. In contrast with Keynes, the Australian economists suggested that another way to moderate the boom was to increase award wages (Cain 1988a:14). This was to prove, as we shall see, very prescient.

For the first time, even private bankers found the cautionary deliberations of the economists tolerable though Godward could not resist a jibe: 'What an opportunity for a wholesale destruction of the pest! But…I agree with the conclusions arrived at.'[32] Bank of England officials, too, were 'staggered' at the unanimous nature of the economists' meeting, as they 'seemed rather impressed by the strength of the expansionist folk in Australia'.[33]

The economic situation was complicated by the fact that the government had shortly to go before the polls. Copland speculated that if the Lyons government

---

27 D. B. Copland to C. Janes, 24 February 1937, UMA FECC, Box 53.
28 L. G. Melville to L. F. Giblin, 4 February 1937, Giblin Collection, UMA FECC, 92/141, Box 2 K-T.
29 D. B. Copland to C. Janes, 24 February 1937, UMA FECC, Box 53.
30 L. G. Melville to A. H. Lewis, 9 March 1937, Melville Papers, NLA.
31 'Confidential: a review of Australian economic conditions', March 1937, Brigden Papers, NLA.
32 E. Godward to G. Healy, 9 April 1937, Bank of Australasia, D/O Correspondence, ANZ Archive.
33 A. H. Lewis to L. G. Melville, 2 April 1937, Melville Papers, NLA.

was returned 'we may anticipate a rather interesting experiment on methods of controlling an expansionist movement'.[34] On that prospect, Copland gave a lecture entitled 'The coming boom' before the annual meeting of the Victorian Branch of the Economic Society. Copland knew that what he would now have to say would be unfamiliar and invite hostility. He told Smithies that 'after the lecture no one will be able to call me an inflationist'.[35] In short, he was parting company with the militant expansionism of Stevens and Davidson and aligning himself with the official policy line. The switch in direction would have done him no harm in attracting University Council support in a bid to become the next Vice-Chancellor at Melbourne. It would also restore his reputation as one of Australia's leading economists.

He sought solace in Keynes's famous propensity to change his mind when things had changed; Copland asked Smithies, 'Is it not said that a snake changes its skin seasonally? I think a good economist, not to be likened to a snake, should change his skin cyclically.'[36] Copland outlined the objectives of economic policy during boom conditions. They included maintaining cheap money and securing full employment at rising standards of living. To achieve this, the government had to reduce loan expenditure with the Commonwealth Bank mopping up excess liquidity by funding. Also there had to be some qualitative control over bank lending to control the rate of expansion in investment. In that context, Copland would welcome the Arbitration Court's decision, a few months later, to increase the basic wage as consistent with the economists' advice of moderating but not extinguishing expansion. The wage rise would distribute the prosperity and trigger more consumption. More importantly, it would dampen employers' expectations of further profits. Copland felt that Australia now had only 'residual unemployment' and that the economy could have a boom with a higher rate of unemployment than it had in the 1920s.[37]

In his lecture, Copland expressly wanted to expose 'the folly of the argument that we prophesy a depression because we talk of a possible boom'.[38] In this, he expressly failed. While he agreed with Janes that a boom need not necessarily be followed by a depression, Copland was pessimistic enough to think that 'the avoidance of depression under modern conditions is about as far off as the settlement of international disputes'. He gamely predicted, therefore, a boom and depression within the next five years. His despair here sprang from economists being unable to convince bankers, businessmen and politicians about resolving the problem.[39] Indeed by the end of 1937, with some slackening in

---

34 D. B. Copland to J. Sanderson, 1 June 1937, UMA FECC, Box 61.
35 D. B. Copland to A. Smithies, 22 April 1937, Economic Society of Australia Files, UMA FECC, Box 141.
36 Ibid.
37 'Another boom', *SMH*, 25 June 1937.
38 D. B. Copland to C. Janes, 3 July 1937, UMA FECC, Box 53.
39 Ibid.

economic activity and export prices evident, Casey began speaking of a coming depression. To Melville, this was premature; his view was that 'we should be ready for a depression without believing in its inevitability'.[40]

Copland's pessimism provoked a public reproach from Reddaway, who argued that a boom need not be followed by a depression. In the community, there was unwarranted pessimism because parallels were drawn with the situation in 1928–29 and what came after. Janes, too, informed Copland that his 'John the Baptist' sermonising was making people fearful of prosperity.[41] This was hardly Copland's intention; rather it was to control expansion so as to avoid the economy falling into a crisis. Davidson tried to counter the prosperous but unsettled business climate by asserting that Australia need not pass into another depression because of the 'fear of prosperity'.[42]

Things were not helped when the Cambridge statistician and economist Colin Clark, who had arrived to take up Copland's offer of a visiting lectureship at Melbourne, predicted in a public lecture that Australia had reached her economic peak and a slowdown was now inevitable.[43] Melville was annoyed at this prediction, telling a colleague that Clark 'was talking us into depression'.[44] Clark did qualify his remarks by stating that the decline would be mild and that, in any case, the authorities were aware enough to increase expenditure when things turned sour.[45] In a bank circular at the time, Clark said that public sector spending in times of boom was likely to be more damaging than an excess of private spending.[46] The sentiment was echoed by the editorial in the same circular warning that Australia needed to wind back public expenditure. Casey rebuked Clark's prophecy, declaring that it was not time to 'batten down the hatches' because the economic storm was not yet upon Australia and 'might not be on us as soon as Mr Clark assumed'.[47]

Clark's public lecture, with its emphasis on the purposefulness of fiscal policy, would have been music to the ears of Queensland Premier, Forgan Smith (Higgins 1989). It did not, however, impress the ardent expansionist Gifford, who, in a remarkable outburst, accused some of his colleagues of being economic jeremiahs. Gifford was annoyed that a 'boom control' policy, elements of which were apparent in Australia and the United States, drove down share prices

---

40   L. G. Melville to A. H. Lewis, 15 December 1937, Melville Papers, NLA.
41   C. Janes to D. B. Copland, 23 June 1937, UMA FECC, Box 53.
42   'Fear of prosperity', *SMH*, 4 June 1937.
43   *Melbourne Sun*, 29 July 1937.
44   L. G. Melville to A. H. Lewis, 1 December 1937, NLA. When Clark went to see Melville to inquire about the likely rise in unemployment, the latter replied, 'Well, Colin, this is your recession' (Interview with the author).
45   'Signs of decline', *SMH*, 26 November 1937.
46   'Government loan expenditure', *National Bank of Australia Circular*, October 1937, pp. 12–13.
47   'Forestalling the slump', *The Age*, 24 September 1937.

and made business confidence precarious. The motivation behind this form of economic 'wowserism', Gifford held, was the fear that some sectors of the economy would overdevelop if the boom persisted.[48] Consequently, the boom had to be checked because of the inherent imbalances in the economy. Doing this, however, would throw the economy back into depression. Forestalling that bleak scenario was the fact that Australian workers had received an officially sanctioned real wage rise—a matter to which we briefly turn.

The 'Reddawage'

There has been much folklore created about the wage decision reached by the Arbitration Court in June 1937. This section briefly recounts the circumstances behind that finding, highlighting the role of the 'Melbourne school' in telling how this historic wage decision came about. With Downing's help, Reddaway was appointed as the assessor of the wage case, launched by the trade unions, because on the surface, at least, he appeared to be independent and less celebrated than either Copland or Giblin (Reddaway 1995:7; Arndt 1976:282). Copland, of course, had achieved infamy with the trade unions by giving expert evidence in late 1930 that helped the Arbitration Court justify its decision to implement the emergency clause and cut wages in January 1931. Copland was unrepentant about it six years later.[49] Copland also held that the Arbitration Court's refusal to restore the level of the basic wage until 1933/34 aided the process of recovery (Groenewegen and McFarlane 1990:128). Now Copland told Stevens that 'the next step' in economic policy was to increase wages and improve the provision of social services as a means of making the economic system more tolerable.[50] Reddaway's submission reflected the wishes of most economists, bar Walker, who, in his evidence before the Royal Commission on Money and Banking, subscribed to Keynes's view that the level of money wages should not be tampered with.[51] In an earlier incarnation, Walker had opposed rescinding the 1931 emergency adjustment to wages before the Arbitration Court in 1934 because business expectations and business psychology were still too fragile (Louis and Turner 1968:89).

By 1937, economic conditions were, by all accounts, much better. Copland and Giblin discussed the submission Reddaway would put before the Full Bench of the Arbitration Court. Copland advised Reddaway, in his draft submission, that there was no need to refer to the views of other economists. It was a strange remark given what Melville had elsewhere said about the purgative benefit

---

48 'Trade booms: control may bring depression', *SMH*, 7 December 1937.
49 D. B. Copland to A. Smithies, 19 May 1937, Economic Society Files, UMA FECC, Box 141.
50 'State of the economy', Memorandum from D. B. Copland to B. S. B. Stevens, 14 January 1937, UMA FECC, Box 60.
51 'Basic wage: stabilisation encouraged', *SMH*, 24 July 1936.

of high wages.[52] Copland suggested that the economic argument, advanced in 1930—that costs be shifted away from the export sector—could be reversed.[53] Copland agreed with Reddaway's submission that real wages be restored to the 1929 level though he went on to suggest a form of words: 'In view, however, of the desirability of checking investment and encouraging consumption so that the present level of prosperity may be long lived, the case for raising wages a little above the 1929 level is very strong.'[54] The idea, then, of attaching an increment to the award to restrain investment optimism to temper the boom was not strictly Reddaway's, even if the subsequent award was christened 'the Reddawage'.

In brief, three arguments were put forward to justify a higher real wage. First, there was greater productivity per capita. Second, there had been an increase in efficiency since firms were working close to capacity, meaning that overheads were now spread over a larger output. Lastly, there had been an increase in export prices. In short, there had been an increase in real national income greater than in proportion to the numbers employed. Following Copland's lead, Reddaway argued that the real wage increase was justified not just on social justice grounds but on economic ones. Increasing real wages meant that capitalists' profits would not remain inflated and thereby stem the capacity of 'entrepreneurs to start superfluous enterprises' (cited in Brown 1997:248). Instead, consumption would rise and underpin the profitability of recent investment spending. The Australian economy would have, therefore, a self-sustaining growth path. While Reddaway subsequently went on national radio to explain his submission, certain employer groups seethed about his 'prosperity loading'.[55] Reddaway was in the witness box for a whole day facing cross-examination by employers' advocates. Reddaway recalled not just being protected by Justice Dethridge from some of the employers' more inane questions but how he found his submission useful in coming to a determination.[56] It resulted in the Arbitration Court restoring its 'living wage' maxim and also giving a prosperity loading to award wages.

Contrary to Colin Clark's statement that Reddaway was the only economist prepared to give evidence on the subject of wages, it seems clear that Giblin worked behind the scenes to ensure that the Englishman was called to provide

---

52 In writing a damning critique of the New Zealand Labour Government's economic platform, Melville defended the role of high wages: 'High wages may prevent profit from getting too large in the imminent boom and help to check the orgies of speculation and unwise investment that usually occur at this time.'
53 'Memo from Copland to Mr W. B. Reddaway', 19 April 1937, UMA FECC, Box 55.
54 Ibid.
55 'Higher wages and higher prices', ABC Radio Broadcast, 22 July 1937, Typescript courtesy of W. B. Reddaway.
56 Author's interview with Reddaway, 21 January 1997. The other justice in the case, Justice Beeby, asked Reddaway to come to see him in his rooms. Beeby had in mind a dual wage structure in which the eastern states would get a bigger wage rise than Western Australia, which was ravaged by drought at the time (Reddaway interview, 21 January 1997).

expert opinion.[57] Reddaway appeared as an expert witness who 'identified with neither side' (Hancock 1984:77). Copland would, however, have been annoyed when Vice-Chancellor Priestley informed him that some Melbourne business houses were revising their donations to the university because they had been 'incensed' and were 'hurt and sore' at Reddaway's evidence before the Arbitration Court (Priestley 2002:332, 353). Relations between Copland and Reddaway became more strained after the Englishman ridiculed Copland's predictions of a boom–bust. Copland felt that the younger man needed some criticism from the likes of Davidson because '[j]ust at this stage of his career, he requires deflation more than anything else. Whether I shall have to do the sticky business again or not I cannot say, but it is a pity to see an able man have his head turned so early in his life.'[58] Copland did not follow up on the threat. Reddaway was, in any case, soon to be heading back to Cambridge.

The wages decision proved a safety valve not just in terms of redistributing aggregate demand; it also pre-empted Labor orchestrating a campaign to lift wages beyond the rise in the cost of living. Copland sang the Arbitration Court's praises to W. A. Robson, a LSE academic, and also to Rupert MacLaurin for bringing down a judgment that not only reflected the economic situation, it gave a valuable lead in economic policy.[59] Just as in 1931, when the Arbitration Court took the lead in making the adjustments that Australia had to take, so, too, in 1937 was the court vigilant in noting underlying economic conditions—and the evidence of economists—before bringing down a judgment.[60] Moreover, the decision by the court was congruent with the decision of the Loan Council to moderate the amount of public borrowing, meaning that economic policy was now pulling in the same direction.

While the economic recovery had another year to run, the wage rise was the crowning glory in Australia's economic rehabilitation. In a land said to despise scientific economists all these good tidings might have led to some acclaim for the profession (Hancock 1930). Certainly those in the Labor movement undertook some revision in their views about the worth of economists (Kuhn 1988). In the wider community, too, there might have been little affirmation, but within policymaking circles economists continued to make some inroads. The public-minded businessman Sir Herbert Gepp again called for the creation of a

---

57 Ibid.
58 D. B. Copland to C. Janes, 23 June 1937, UMA FECC, Box 51. Much later, when reflecting on his two-year stint in Australia, Reddaway recalled that the level of economics teaching at Copland's beloved faculty was fairly 'low level'. As for Copland, Reddaway felt that 'he was not a great economist' (Tribe 1997).
59 D. B. Copland to W. A. Robson, 3 December 1937, UMA FECC, Box 55.
60 D. B. Copland to R. MacLaurin, 1 October 1937, UMA FECC, Box 55.

specialist economic research staff to advise the federal government on economic problems—an idea, of course, first mooted by Bruce and Casey.[61] It was an idea slowly, but surely becoming accepted by both tiers of government.

The yellow-brick road to utopia

> There is now an army of economists confident that, given sufficient bricks of the right type and quality, a way can be cleared to heaven. It is the Statistician's job to provide the bricks.

— E. T. McPhee, Commonwealth Statistician, 1937[62]

True to Commonwealth Statistician McPhee's boast, economists had by their advice helped get Australia's unemployment rate down to 9 per cent by the end of 1937; it was even lower in New South Wales and Queensland. Having just spent an instructive six-month sabbatical with Keynes and other economists at Cambridge researching monetary policy, Giblin would later deem that, by 1937/38, Australia was at 'normal full employment'. That is, any additional spending would raise prices and incomes leaving real income unchanged. Giblin told a leading businessman that full employment could range between 4 per cent and 10 per cent and was, therefore, a 'matter of practical judgement on a mass of relevant data'.[63] Quoting Colin Clark, Giblin went on to say that, symmetrically, when not at normal full employment, there was justification for 'unprofitable' public works that would prevent the secondary effects of unemployment from unfolding.

As discussed, Australian economists were already held in some renown in government circles for their anti-depression policies but the later 1930s brought a burst of renewed praise from several quarters. It also brought, as this section will show, an increase in the demand for their services. The Indian economist B. P. Adarkar unwittingly validated Brigden's earlier wish by nominating Australia as 'the practical utopia of economists' (cited in Goodwin 1974:236). When the British Labour politician Hugh Dalton visited Australia in 1938, he expressed a desire to meet some of the economists whom he had once criticised for being behind the Premiers' Plan.[64] More reserved in his praise, Montagu Norman felt his peers at the Commonwealth Bank Board were coming too much

---

61 'Economic research: Sir Herbert Gepp address', *SMH*, 10 October 1936; 'Gepp's proposals: an advisory council', *SMH*, 28 August 1935.

62 Transcript of speech given at the Conference of Economists 1996 by Dennis Trewin, Deputy Australian Statistician.

63 L. F. Giblin to Haynes, President, Victorian Chamber of Commerce, 9 February 1939, Giblin Collection, UMA FECC, 92/141, Box 1 A-J.

64 F. L. McDougall to D. B. Copland, 3 December 1937, UMA FECC, Box 54.

under the 'economistical' influence of Melville and Giblin.[65] Walker, meanwhile, was tutoring a coterie of NSW government UAP politicians on the nuances of economics.[66] Copland could rightfully claim to a colleague that '[t]he economist is going to be more important rather than less important in public affairs during the next 10 to 15 years'.[67] Concurrent with his work for Stevens, Copland was appointed Chairman of the Victorian State Economic Committee. It prompted him to comment that 'at long last the Victorian Government has noted and recognised the official work of economists'.[68] Copland's job was to advise the Victorian government on long-term patterns of public finance with a view to avoiding economic fluctuations.

'The white light of publicity', as Mills called it, continued to fall on the economist and no more so than on Copland (cited in Brown 2001:80). In 1938, he used his public profile, somewhat controversially, in a bid to become the next Vice-Chancellor at Melbourne. He failed in this quest though in quite remarkable circumstances. Unbeknown to him, perhaps, was the fact that Mills and Brigden were among those on the list of early contenders sounded out by the University Council. Both names came with flattering references. In Mills' case, the referee was Justice Napier, who had, of course, worked alongside him with the Royal Commission on Money and Banking.[69] A university colleague reported that Copland's unpopularity with the Melbourne business establishment—some of whom served on the University Council—was 'cruelly damaging' his candidature (Selleck 2003:694).[70] Copland was too 'commercially minded' and 'lacked the cultural background' to become Vice-Chancellor (cited in Selleck 2003:694). Herbert Brookes suggested that it was this, together with the 'rough angles' of Copland's personality, that led him to being overlooked for the position.[71] Bailey told Giblin that the University Council did not favour Copland because he did not have the 'culture' and might be liable to 'phobias'.[72] The popularity of Copland's faculty with students and the fact that he was an internationally renowned economist were more hindrances than help given the conservative nature of the University Council, which shared views with the Melbourne Club (Selleck 2003:693–7).

While it was to Australian economics' gain that he failed to win the post, it was not to Melbourne's. An aggrieved Copland solicited for jobs elsewhere. He

---

65   A. H. Lewis to L. G. Melville, 27 March 1937, Melville Papers, NLA.

66   'MPs at university: improving knowledge of economics', *SMH*, 17 August 1936.

67   D. B. Copland to K. Isles, 6 June 1937, UMA FECC, Box 53.

68   D. B. Copland to H. Brookes, 3 October 1938, Brookes Papers, NLA.

69   Justice J. M. Napier to Sir J. Barrett, Chancellor of Melbourne University, Referee letter on Mills, 2 January 1938, and J. L. Gibson to Sir J. Barrett, 31 December 1937, Referee letter on J. B. Brigden, 31 December 1937, Mss 1924/27/362, Brookes Papers, NLA.

70   K. H. Bailey to L. F. Giblin, 4 June 1938, UMA FECC, Box 220.

71   H. Brookes, Notes on vice-chancellorship, Mss 1924/27/1341, NLA.

72   K. H. Bailey to L. F. Giblin, 4 June 1938, UMA FECC, Box 220.

asked Giblin, in residence at King's College, whether Cambridge might offer him an academic post in 'statistical economics' with a college fellowship.[73] This request apparently came after Copland had declined an offer, for family reasons, to become a full-time economic adviser to the Stevens' government. Copland also wrote to Menzies asking if he could be made chairman of the Interstate Commission, an economic agency yet to become established in Canberra.[74] Only a position like that, Giblin believed, would keep Copland's talents within Australia.[75] After regaining his composure, Copland told his friend Brookes 'that I am finding my real interest in the work of the School. It is astonishing how much has to be done in advanced economic theory.'[76] Copland wanted to establish a study of business fluctuations and the control of economic activity.[77] Giblin and Jean Polglaze, along with Melville, were the personnel Copland had in mind for the project. The political bickering at Melbourne University still unsettled Copland, leading him to apply for his old job back in Hobart.[78] Walker beat him to the post but there was no acrimony from Copland.[79] Indeed Copland felt the move would do Walker good as it also involved giving detailed economic advice to the Tasmanian government. 'Economists, like doctors should be GPs for a while,' he told a young colleague.[80]

There was still a paucity of economists within Australia. Despite healthy numbers at undergraduate level, there were still few research scholars coming forward in economics. Copland would have agreed with Keynes's lament: 'If only we could produce competent economists in greater number!'[81] Interestingly, too, membership in all 11 branches of the Economic Society within Australia and New Zealand had, with the passing of the crisis, fallen from 846 in 1932 to 737 in 1938. The Melbourne Branch remained, by far, the largest.[82]

Given the fact that professorships and public service positions in Australia frequently fell vacant, any economist likely to settle in this country from overseas would have had an assured future. To that end, universities such as Melbourne, and even the Bank of New South Wales, tried to entice English economists to come to Australia and redress the shortage. Gerald Firth, for

---

73 D. B. Copland to L. F. Giblin, 7 April 1938, UMA FECC, Box 220.
74 D. B. Copland to R. G. Menzies, 17 May 1938, UMA FECC, Box 60.
75 D. B. Copland to J. Lyons, 5 June 1938, The Interstate Commission, AA, 1972/341.
76 D. B. Copland to H. Brookes, 23 June 1938, Brookes Papers, NLA.
77 D. B. Copland to H. Brookes, 20 April 1938, Brookes Papers, NLA.
78 D. B. Copland to E. M. Miller, Vice-Chancellor, University of Tasmania, 16 January 1939, UMA FECC, Box 66.
79 Walker's referees were probably D. H. Robertson and A. C. Pigou, who wrote flattering references for him in 1935. Robertson had a high opinion of his 'power of analysis...[and] mature judgement' and predicted that Walker would 'occupy a position of authority with wisdom and success' (D. H. Robertson, Statement, 3 July 1935, E. R. Walker Papers, Canberra).
80 D. B. Copland to J. Crawford, 12 April 1939, Economic Society Files, UMA FECC, Box 143.
81 J. M. Keynes to D. B. Copland, 24 July 1937, UMA FECC, Box 53.
82 Economic Society of Australia and New Zealand Files, UMA FECC, Box 141.

example, who came out to replace Reddaway as a Ritchie Research Fellow in 1938, did not return home. Another English economist, W. A. Prest, was appointed to fill the senior lectureship at Melbourne after Mauldon took the chair at Tasmania. Prest's appointment came about only after Copland wrote to several English universities telling them of the desirability of getting 'a new overseas man' to fill the post.[83] Copland soon discovered that he had chosen 'the right man for Melbourne' (Polglaze and Soper 1977:xiv). Hytten recruited Leslie Bury, a Cambridge graduate, for the Wales' economic section while attending a conference in Europe. Hytten's brief while abroad was to recruit young economists of 'open, liberal thought'.[84] Janes went to England in 1938 and visited Cambridge in August 1938 to attend an economics conference. He came away a little 'disappointed' because the economists and the papers presented were of no higher quality than he had been exposed to in Australia.[85] Janes apparently criticised 'with some nervousness' a paper written, but not presented, by Keynes on buffer stocks.

Meanwhile, Colin Clark was offered the chair at Adelaide but declined it.[86] Like Keynes, Copland quickly appreciated the worth of Clark: 'He is a rare find in that he has an unerring instinct for the right figure. Apart from his knowledge of economic theory, he is one of the most ingenious persons with statistics I have ever come across.'[87] Giblin equated Clark's statistical genius with turning 'straws into bricks' (cited in Groenewegen 1994:9). In collaboration with another Australian economist, J. G. Crawford, Clark had made early attempts to estimate the size of Australia's national income, and also to quantify the size of the expenditure multiplier.

Keynes feared that the Australians would wrest Clark away from Cambridge: 'I hope very much you will fail in taking away Colin Clark from us. He is much too needed here.'[88] It is worth recalling that, as late as 1939, Britain did not have official national income statistics (Moggridge 1992:631). Keynes's hope that Clark would return to help establish 'a proper department of statistical realistic economics at Cambridge', implying that Clark would head it, was to be dashed (Castles 1997 cited in Markwell 1985:36). When Casey recruited Brigden in 1938 to spearhead the National Insurance Commission, a suitable replacement had to be found for his post at Queensland's Bureau of Industry. While Hugh Dalton suggested Clark as its next director, Premier Forgan Smith,

---

83   D. B. Copland to E. A. G. Robinson, 29 April 1937, UMA FECC, Box 53.
84   A. C. Davidson to T. Hytten, 27 May 1935, BNSW, A53/446.
85   C. Janes to A. C. Davidson, 26 August 1938, BNSW, GM 302/412.
86   D. B. Copland to J. M. Keynes, 14 September 1937, UMA FECC, Box 53. Walker and Smithies, probably the two most gifted theoreticians in Australia at the time, applied for the position but it fell to Keith Isles, another Tasmanian-born economist (H. C. Coombs to J. La Nauze, 14 December 1937, La Nauze Papers, NLA).
87   D. B. Copland to T. Waites, Government Statistician for New South Wales, 13 October 1937, UMA FECC, Box 56.
88   J. M. Keynes to D. B. Copland, 28 October 1937, UMA FECC, Box 53.

already had him in mind (Higgins 1989:300–1). While Dalton wanted Clark to start 'making things happen', Clark found that Dalton and the premier had discussed Keynesian economic approaches 'even if they did not call it that by that time'.[89] The Queensland Premier wanted Clark's services to prepare the state's case for increased public borrowing allocations from the Loan Council. Clark used his statistical prowess to support the Keynesian case for more funds (Kenwood 1988:108). The post came with positions of Government Statistician and advisor to the Treasury. Later Clark dedicated his book *The Conditions of Economic Progress* (1940) to Forgan Smith, citing him as '[a] far seeing patron of economic science'. Clark told Keynes why he found life in Australia increasingly attractive:

> Economics ranks after cricket as a topic of public interest…People have minds which are not closed to new truths, as the minds of so many Englishmen are and with all the mistakes Australia has made in the past, I still think she may show the world, in economics…in the next twenty years. (Cited in Castles 1998:146)

While those telling words dismayed Keynes, he was not altogether surprised by them; Australia was the place for economists to put their science into practice. Australian economists would find the demand for their services increasing as the re-elected Lyons government introduced unemployment insurance and other social reforms. There was, however, an even greater challenge about to confront Australian economists: the spectre of another depression.

The coming recession

> We, out here, read of these great doings with anxious eyes. We can't affect these major movements—and we get swung along at the tail of the world cart. Depressions don't start in Australia (except temporary ones arising from bad seasons)—they come to us from overseas—and we are quite unable to make financial provision from the effects of important depressions or recessions.[90]

While Casey's concerns to Montagu Norman reflected those of economists, the intriguing thing about the international recession of 1937/38 was that, for the most part, the Australian economy had, 'in some miraculous fashion', withstood any adverse affects from it until 1939.[91] In the United States, the recession had rekindled fears of another depression. The impact from the recession in

---

89   C. Clark to B. Pimlott, 18 February 1980, UQRF, 87.
90   R. G. Casey to S. M. Bruce, 3 May 1938, Casey Correspondence, AA, A1421.
91   R. G. Casey to Sir M. Norman, 7 March 1938, Casey Correspondence, AA, A1421.

Australia took some time to register on domestic economic activity. Amazed that the severe recession in the United States had not affected Australia in any way, Casey believed that it would once the slowdown reached Britain.[92] For the moment, then, Australia was riding her luck. Casey repeated his mantra that depressions did not start in Australia and 'we get swung along at the tail of the world cart'.[93] Australia was relying on what Melville called the 'natural optimism of Australians', which outweighed the pessimism abroad.[94] Copland conveyed to a Victorian Treasury official that what kept the local business climate buoyant was that few opinion-makers dared speak of depression lest it induce the very conditions everyone wished to avoid.[95] In that vein, Melville, too, recorded that the '[p]essimism of our Colin Clarks seems to have singularly little effect upon business activity'.[96] Melville felt that as long as Australian export prices did not continue to fall there was no reason why the recession abroad would check domestic economic activity, particularly when businessmen chose to ignore it. In that regard, Melville speculated that what would bring the boom to an end was the construction of factories on the assumption that the rate of economic expansion would continue.

Until August 1938, the international or Roosevelt recession registered little impact on domestic activity. The economists, however, were clearly worried by the portents. Four months earlier, Copland undertook an audit of the economy for a corporate client. Australia, Copland found, was in a condition of full employment with real income per capita having risen by 10 per cent since 1936/37. He attributed this resounding process to six factors: an increase in primary production, gold production, a favourable terms-of-trade, the greater level of defence spending, the continuing revival of business investment and, lastly, a greater amount of import replacement in manufacturing capacity. With the last aspect, Copland cited work by Melville showing that, between 1927/28 and 1935/36, there had been an expansion of import-replacing manufacturing of some £30 million per annum. This meant considerable relief for the external account, which benefited further from lower servicing costs on Australia's foreign debt. Despite the rise in manufacturing industry, Australia was still, however, at the mercy of the global economy. Copland felt that any further fall in export prices would have Australia 'skating on thin ice'.[97]

Besides that prospect directly reducing national income, it would cause stringency in the money market. Montagu Norman laid down the challenge squarely facing Casey:

---

92   Ibid.
93   Ibid.
94   L. G. Melville to A. H. Lewis, 19 November 1937, Melville Papers, NLA.
95   D. B. Copland to A. T. Smithers, 17 August 1938, UMA FECC, Box 61.
96   L. G. Melville to A. H. Lewis, 29 December 1937, Melville Papers, Mss 8671, NLA.
97   'The economic situation in Australia', April 1938, UMA FECC, Box 63, p. 4.

If you can make it possible to build up a volume of London Funds, adequate to the needs of Australia, without at the same time permitting an over expansion of domestic credit (and hence at the same time a dangerous increase of imports) you will have solved one of the most thorny problems and rendered a great service to the Commonwealth.[98]

With that in mind, Casey and Reading ensured that central banking techniques were improved such that the Commonwealth Bank would, even in the face of falling export prices, start purchasing securities and bills to sustain the reserves of the trading banks.[99] Copland called this new policy one of 'insulation'.[100] He reminded his business associates that the policy did not, however, offer much relief for the export sector, which also had to contend with rising domestic costs. The bank board, briefed on the 1937 Roosevelt recession in the United States, now appreciated the ephemeral aspect of the decline in export prices. With the adverse external account, the central bank engaged in monetary operations to prevent a credit squeeze unfolding (Copland 1946:116–17). There was, furthermore, a defence program and a conversion loan to be financed. The board, still smarting after the criticism aired in the Royal Commission on Monetary Systems, was prepared, therefore, to take remedial monetary action at the first sign of international-borne recession. Indeed, Reading put out a public statement to that effect. This was an assurance to the trading banks that the Commonwealth Bank would no longer allow a fall in the London funds to axiomatically trigger a credit crisis. There was also a political motive behind this preparation. Curtin, the new Leader of the Opposition, predicted that depression would soon engulf Australia. Casey challenged Curtin to nominate his sources before admonishing him about how economic depression could in fact ensue from 'a state of mind'.[101]

Gilbert perceived the readiness to take proactive policy action as a sign that the bank had adopted a Keynesian perspective. It went hand-in-hand with the appointment of the Secretary of the Treasury, Harry Sheehan, as the new Governor of the bank and, in turn, the board's apparent willingness to integrate monetary policy with that of the Treasury (Gilbert,1973:208–9).[102] This is congruent with Gilbert's more encompassing thesis showing how the steady rise of the Loan Council gave the Commonwealth a greater voice in economic policy formation. It came at the expense of the Commonwealth Bank's independence. Politically, this development was matched by a greater show of resolution from the federal government in its dealings with the trading banks.

---

98   Sir M. Norman to R. G. Casey, 29 March 1938, BE, G1/288.
99   'The economic situation in Australia', April 1938, UMA FECC, Box 63, p. 8.
100   'Australian economic conditions: report no. 2', 27 March 1939, UMA FECC, Box 64.
101   'Mr Curtin rebuked', *The Argus*, 15 August 1938.
102   There was criticism of Sheehan's appointment since it meant the Commonwealth Bank Board had no members with banking experience on it ('Bank appointment criticised', *The Sydney Sun*, 18 May 1938).

Lyons, for instance, informed Davidson that if the trading banks did not curtail their campaign against 'government control of banking' his government would consider legislative action to bring that prospect to bear (Gilbert 1973:208). Casey, too, in October 1938 reportedly dismissed the notion that the Commonwealth Bank would oppose the financing of greater defence spending. It would, he is alleged to have said, be 'swept out of the way' if it did.[103] He later disowned such remarks. In the next year, the central bank subscribed to a loan issue from the federal government, ensuring that the cash reserves of the trading banks were maintained and rates did not have to rise (Copland 1946:119).

Despite these developments, Gilbert draws a long bow in arguing that the bank's proactive monetary stance in 1938 was a Keynesian one. It was more a case of improvisation and pragmatism than any act of revelatory Keynesianism. Reddaway (1960:192) is probably more correct in stating that, after 1936, the Commonwealth Bank Board was more prepared to address economic stabilisation issues rather than just uphold external balance and debt repayment. Apart from smoothing the loan-conversion process, the defence program required an expansion in public investment. Given Australia's good record in not defaulting on her debts, London was favourably disposed towards giving the Commonwealth short-term finance to bolster the level of London funds. The trading banks, meanwhile, were mischievously circulating literature against the proposed system of minimum deposits, which when operational would result in a credit squeeze (Sutherlin 1980:227–9). This fear had particular resonance in 1938 with trading banks' liquidity suffering due to the combined effects of drought and falling export prices (Sutherlin 1980:209). Even if the Federal Treasury had more input in determining economic policy, its new Secretary, S. G. MacFarlane, did not comprehend the new doctrines of Keynes (Cornish 2000:211). Indeed MacFarlane's almost arithmetical approach in preparing the Federal Budget astounded one Federal Treasurer for the lack of any doctrine other than merely balancing the 'sums' (Whitwell 1986:54). This was also apparently Casey's approach towards preparing budgets (Spender 1972).

Moreover, Copland still expressed concern that a recession could arise if investor sentiment turned negative, if there was timidity on the part of the central bank or a drastic scaling down in public works.[104] Countering that last contingency was the fact that economists were now agreed on the principle of contra-cyclical spending. In that vein, Colin Clark, in a lecture before the Economic Society in Melbourne in August 1938, warned that internal loan expenditure should be expanded at the same rate as the decline in export income. Clark told his

---

103   Fred Coleman column, *TheSydney Sun*, 30 October 1938.
104   'The economic situation in Australia', April 1938, UMA FECC, Box 63, p. 11.

audience that while the prospect of deficit budgets might be 'repugnant' to those with 'preconceived ideas', there was no other expedient to prevent unemployment and falling wages.[105]

Davidson was also fearful that the forces behind the slowdown could, if left unchecked, leave the economy in a weakened position, from which it would take years to recover. In a memorandum shown to Hytten and apparently requested by a NSW Treasury official, Davidson advised that governments should not increase taxation but instead have the Loan Council authorise more public works financed by Treasury bills. While acknowledging that budgets must be balanced, he said this could be achieved over a number of years. He confidently referred to how the economic and financial knowledge now available would allow 'an intelligent handling of the variations of the trade cycle…to iron out many problems of the past'.[106] The trick was to act now to avert a worsening situation.

Copland's forecast for the 1938/39 balance of payments warned of a net loss in London funds if export prices remained subdued and the volume of imports did not abate. Giblin, in a speech to the Carlton Club in London, which Claude Janes attended, expressed an extremely pessimistic long-term prognosis for Australia's future export prices.[107] Clark could have had a hand in the projections. Janes was sceptical about whether one could, in fact, make such long-term forecasts. As Chairman of the State Economic Committee, Copland advised a Victorian Treasury official, as Davidson had, of the importance of bringing these grim tidings to the attention of the Loan Council.[108] With recession and now war imminent, the economists reconvened to discuss matters.

The economists reconvene

An unofficial two-day meeting of economists was held in Sydney in December 1938 to discuss the state of the Australian economy and propose measures to prepare for the onset of an internationally transmitted recession. They would have noted the success of the Roosevelt administration's large-scale spending program in dragging the US economy out of recession. Certainly, Butlin noticed it.[109] Janes informed Davidson of a similar tale in Britain, where the government was assuming a larger responsibility within the economy.[110] In Australia it was common knowledge that economic activity was slackening and it would

---

105   'Setback threat in Australia', *The Argus*, 12 August 1938.
106   A. C. Davidson to T. Hytten, 12 September 1938, BNSW, GM 302/412.
107   C. Janes to A. C. Davidson, 14 April 1938, BNSW, GM 302/412.
108   D. B. Copland to A. T. Smithers, Director of Treasury, 17 August 1938, UMA FECC, Box 61.
109   'The overseas recession: signs of recovery appear', [by S. J. Butlin], *SMH*, 15 July 1938.
110   C. Janes to A. C. Davidson, 25 August 1938, BNSW, GM 302/412.

be only a matter of time before unemployment rose. There was, in truth, still a hard core of structurally unemployed, which could be overcome only by training programs.[111] There was, moreover, a rise in the price level, which Butlin attributed to the interaction between resource bottlenecks and monopolistic competition.[112]

Mills, Hytten, Copland, Walker, Clark, Melville and Wilson attended the meeting, all in a private capacity. The participants were each given an aspect of the economy to report on so that an accurate audit could be formed. Each came armed with memoranda on their assigned brief. Colin Clark's submission, which Giblin had suggested Clark contribute, warned of a sustained fall in Australian export prices with the world recession and the possibility of British trade controls.[113] Countering this were domestic sources of expenditure—namely, investment, public spending and consumption. Clark displayed a familiarity with the Keynesian multiplier. Economic activity could be kept buoyant by resorting to devaluation, import restrictions, easy credit, budget deficits and public works. Clark preferred easy money as the more palatable expedient. It was a stance shared by his colleagues. Not only would an expansionist monetary policy keep trading banks liquid, it would forestall a rise in interest rates. This view found its way into a summary of policy conclusions prepared by Copland.[114] When it came to public expenditure, the economists, while admitting that unemployment would probably rise, considered fiscal prudence the safest course. This stance was explicable in the sense that existing public works were already putting a strain on the money market. As it was, the increased expenditure on defence, together with borrowing by state and local authorities, would offset some of the decline in export income. On that matter, Copland felt the mooted rise in defence spending required a huge effort in coordination. It also spelt diverting resources from peacetime ends and it was doubtful whether state and local works could now be undertaken at the same time. Copland had, in fact, reached this position in April 1938, arguing that with full employment, public works expenditure by the states had to give way to the priority of defence spending.[115] There were other concerns articulated at the congress: issues such as high domestic costs, especially wages, affecting exports, the psychological fears engendered by monetary expansion and budget deficits and, finally, whether standards of living could be maintained in the face of a fall in export income and additional defence spending.[116]

111   'Extending employment: training plan in Australia', *SMH*, 13 September 1938.
112   'Rising retail prices', *SMH*, 21 September 1938.
113   C. Clark to D. B. Copland, 25 November 1938, UMA FECC, Box 200.
114   'Notes on economic position of Australia', 5 December 1938, UMA FECC, Box 200, pp. 3–4.
115   'Finance and defence; states part scaling down of public works', [by D. B. Copland], *SMH*, 1 April 1938.
116   'Notes on economic position of Australia', 5 December 1938, UMA FECC, Box 200, p. 6.

When it came to reviewing 1938/39, Copland was relieved to report that his prophecy of a recession had not materialised. It was, he found, 'something of a triumph that we lost so little ground' when other economies had fallen by the wayside.[117] Normally Australia would have suffered the same fate, especially with export prices falling, but extenuating factors, including proactive monetary policy, had averted it. Indeed the expansion in loan advances when export prices were falling was unprecedented in Australia's history.[118] It would be a 'mistake', Copland added, to ascribe too much to credit policy. There had been other factors at play. Among these were an outstanding level of import replacement and a high level of export production. These two factors, in tandem, promised to improve Australia's balance-of-payments problem. The outlook was favourable, too, for the pursuit of a liberal credit policy and, equally, for the raising of funds for defence and public works. These expenditures came at a time when private capital spending was lagging, so Copland predicted that employment would hold steady, if not rise slightly.[119]

Conclusion

There seemed little doubt that Australian economists from 1937 onwards exhibited a growing understanding of Keynes's new theoretical outlook. It allowed them to engage in policy advice that allowed Australia in 1938 to enjoy, a little fortuitously perhaps, normal full employment. Moreover, the Commonwealth Bank policy of 'insulation' or modest monetary stimulus, whether informed by Keynes or not, kept the Australian economy immune from the Roosevelt recession. The fact that it did must have caught the attention of the senior bank officials. They, and even some of the economists, still laboured under the notion that a boom–bust phenomenon was the lot of a market economy. Practice at keeping the economy buoyant, despite falling export prices, engendered confidence in monetary management. The real test of an authentic Keynesian approach to demand management, however, using the monetary and fiscal taps, lay just around the corner.

---

117   'The economic outlook strength of the Australian economy; prospects of expansion', UMA FECC, Box 65.
118   'The economic outlook', UMA FECC, Box 65.
119   Ibid., p. 8.

10. The economics of near-war

Introduction

The last year of peacetime in Australia was marked by difficult economic choices and political turbulence. The necessity to divert resources into defence as the security environment grew darker was jeopardised by the system of political federation and traditional ideas about public finance. By the end of 1939, there came, however, a moment of economic revelation. As Copland (1945:8) styled it: 'The lesson of the war is unmistakable in its demonstration that, given a clear and generally accepted objective, we can erect an economic structure far superior to that which we knew during the dark days of the thirties.'

True to Keynes's prophecy, the urgency of mobilising resources for the prosecution of war marked the light of reason for politicians.

This chapter focuses on when and how policymakers assimilated the *General Theory*'s framework of matching the country's real resources with claims on them. There were two stages to this process. The first step—the easier one—was an awareness of transferring idle resources into employment allowing defence outlays to take place that were essentially costless. The second, more involved step was a transfer problem. Once full employment was reached, policymakers would have to check civilian consumption to enable output to be transferred to the war effort. Economists played a critical part in both conceptualising and broadcasting the approach to war finance. At the official policy level, there was initially little recognition of expanding economic activity by bringing idle resources into circulation. As we shall see, this conceptual blind spot would ultimately force a policy crisis on the Lyons government. It revolved around the necessity of how quickly, and the means by which, to increase military spending.

With a deteriorating international environment, Australia faced a resource-funding problem in its desire to augment national defence even if it was modest compared with Britain or Germany. Raising taxes, issuing public loans or recourse to credit finance—that is, budget deficits—would disrupt economic activity. Falling export prices further complicated the difficulties. There was also Casey's prized piece of social legislation—a comprehensive national insurance scheme—to finance. Budgetary balance, of course, gave way to the exigencies of defence. This spelt sacrifices not just to programs but to political reputations.

Ultimately, the blinkered economic outlook led to a political crisis when Menzies resigned ostensibly over the abandonment of the National Insurance Scheme, arguing, as Copland did, that defence and national insurance could both be accommodated. The conventional view was that social welfare and defence were mutually exclusive. Indeed the Commonwealth Bank recycled a version of the UK Treasury's view—namely, that using resources for defence needs, even amid 10 per cent unemployment, would reduce the amount of consumer goods that could be produced when the economy recovered (Peden 1996).

Consequently, the budget brought down a few days after the outbreak of war adhered to the traditional pattern of fiscal rectitude. The Federal Treasury, like its British counterpart, did not enunciate any new financial doctrine or idea or show the slightest inclination to Keynesian thinking until well into the war years (Spender 1972:42–3). Australia was, in short, 'singularly innocent of war economics' (Walker 1947:110). The gaping lack of progress at the surface did, however, belie some institutional change in the backrooms of policy formulation. How Australian public authorities could resist for so long any experimentation in economic policy under circumstances that invited—indeed needed—bold initiatives needs elucidation.

The purpose of this final chapter, therefore, is to show how economists in November 1939 convinced politicians of that crucial point. It was at that juncture that a Keynesian revolution in economic policy 'arrived' in this country (Cornish 1993a). It came just as Keynes articulated how to use the conceptual apparatus of the *General Theory* to fight a war.

Casey and national insurance

It was Casey more than anyone else who got Lyons to commit to a National Insurance Scheme as an election campaign promise (Richards 1975:34). The venture has interest for our study as the scheme had obvious economic ramifications and also because it further revealed the limitations of Casey when he was placed under pressure. More importantly, it demonstrated the intellectual straitjacket Casey and the Treasury were labouring under over economic policy. Copland welcomed the legislation as it sat well with his desire to establish the provision of more social welfare. Casey's rival, Stevens, had been making noises about the desirability of such a scheme. The rest of the UAP government, including their coalition partners, the Country Party, was lukewarm to the proposal and wary of its cost. Even after the 1937 federal election, Lyons asked Treasury to draft a statement summarising the difficulties with the scheme (Richards 1975:13). The bill was introduced into Parliament in May 1938. The legislation would provide disablement, sickness and medical benefits, together with the old age and widows' pensions, based on a contribution scheme involving employees, employers and the government.

Brigden left the Queensland Bureau of Industry to become Chairman of the proposed National Insurance Commission. It was not long before opposition from the doctors and the friendly societies found expression in Parliament through the Country Party. In one debate, Brigden pleaded with the Prime Minister to urgently attend Parliament as Casey had lost control over the House. Lyons refused, telling Brigden: 'He talked us into this. I could see the difficulties. I never wanted it, and now he can get himself out of it.'[1] Parliamentary setbacks aside, Casey prepared the legislation and necessary changes to the public service to manage the scheme. After procrastinating over its introduction, Casey nominated 4 September 1939 as the scheme's first day of operation. Brigden felt the timing ideal, with the economy, buoyed by greater defence spending, likely to be at full employment.

According to W. C. Balmford, the Commonwealth Actuary, Brigden was out of his depth in the position and also had doubts about the scheme.[2] Cabinet ministers, however, regarded Brigden as an 'unqualified success' in his new position.[3] No doubt, Brigden was flustered by the fact that after initially educating the electorate on how the scheme would operate, his office later had to sabotage it (Green 1969:114–15). Had Lyons persevered with the scheme, Brigden felt it would have helped postwar economic management by having a huge consolidation of funds to distribute.[4] Greatly disappointed by its demise, Brigden later took up the post of Secretary to the Commonwealth Department of Supply—again serving under Casey (Clark 1950:3).

According to the Clerk of the Parliament, Frank Green (1969:114), Lyons abandoned national insurance because he did not want to antagonise financial circles in Melbourne. Richards (1975:75) rejects this claim, citing Menzies' support for the scheme even when its creator, Casey, had shelved it in March 1939 for the sake of military preparedness. National security came before social security (Hudson 1986:105). Apart from the ramifications stemming from the Munich crisis, Casey was taken aback at how much the scheme would cost when fully generated. He had already warned in late 1938 how the economy was under strain meeting the huge jump in defence spending. The failure of a public loan to become fully subscribed in February 1939 fed the anxiety that raising resources for defence meant that taxation would have to be considered.[5]

---

1   Irvine Douglas [Lyons' press secretary], TRC 121/31, NLA, p. 46.
2   'Notes on Lyons's Prime Ministership', Crisp Papers, Mss 5243, NLA.
3   'Canberra gossip', *Adelaide Advertiser*, 9 July 1938.
4   P. Heydon to P. R. Hart, n.d., Hart Mss 9410, NLA.
5   *The Argus*, 29 February 1939.

Casey had plainly not assimilated Hankey's point that when it came to marshalling resources for defence 'the limiting factor is not money, but the productive capacity of the country'.[6] The economists irreverently called the Treasurer's unyielding fiscal prudence 'Caseyism' (Butlin 1958:201). It was, in part, because Casey listened exclusively to his departmental advisers. They could not detect, as the economists could, that the real problem of war finance 'could only be appreciated by looking behind "the veil of money"' (Hytten 1940:66). A cursory review of federal budgets Casey had brought down shows only the merest acquaintance with central economic management. His successor, Percy Spender (1972:44), was, as we shall see, cut from different cloth.

While military spending shot up to nearly £30 million—from a figure of £4 million only a few years earlier—the new outlays still amounted to only 5 per cent of gross domestic product (GDP). Casey was concerned that the higher defence spending might, for the first time in seven years, place the budget into deficit. Apart from Brigden, it was Copland, of all the economists, who appeared the most upset at the abandonment of national insurance, arguing that it was hardly incompatible with greater defence spending. At worst, national insurance would add about £3 million annually to existing social security expenditure. Copland argued that national insurance would exert little demand on resources in its first years of operation, making the argument that it would impair the defence effort a spurious one.[7] Indeed, by creating a form of savings, the scheme would have facilitated the marshalling of resources for defence purposes. Britain had not suspended its social security scheme because of the exigency of defence spending, which amounted to 12 per cent of total government expenditure.[8] For the Lyons government to falter at the first hurdle in implementing this piece of social legislation was discouraging. Copland felt that the needs of defence could easily have been reconciled by diverting resources away from economic development. Social security needs, in any case, still had to be faced. Pension payments, as a newspaper editorial pointed out, already represented more than 25 per cent of the total provision of social security payments.[9]

The cabinet decision to postpone the scheme precipitated a political crisis for the government (Martin 1993:261–2). Menzies felt that the government reversing measures it had just placed on the statute books cast it in a dim light. It is not known if Copland's public advocacy for national insurance attracted or perhaps even reinforced Menzies' action in resigning from cabinet over the issue. Menzies was perhaps merely using it as an excuse to mount a bid for the leadership. Months earlier, Menzies had requested Copland arrange an interview

---

6   M. Hankey to R. G. Casey, 9 April 1937, Hankey Papers, Churchill College.
7   'We can afford both national insurance and defence', *The Herald*, 20 March 1939.
8   Ibid.
9   'An economist's defence of national insurance', *Brisbane Telegraph*, 6 March 1939.

for him with Keynes at King's College when he was to visit England on official business in late 1938.[10] Copland told Keynes in confidence that he held Menzies in high regard.[11] He was not the only one. The press magnate Sir Keith Murdoch withdrew his support from Lyons believing that the country needed a change in leadership to galvanise the defence effort. He told C. L. Baillieu, 'We should be forming new industry and forcing industrial development to the utmost of its capacity. Lyons sits still.'[12]

Menzies was, then, the coming man, but as one informed observer noted, finance was not his strong suit (Spender 1972). Hytten recalled Menzies saying '"I don't understand mathematics" and finance was always mathematics to him".[13] Indeed, on becoming Prime Minister, Menzies' first federal budget sent a completely inappropriate message to Australians about preparing to endure the costs of the war. This was much to the frustration of economists and Spender (1972:50). Fortunately, Menzies soon delegated the duties of treasurer to a more financially acute colleague who took a more imaginative view of war finance. It was a view provided exclusively by economists. Before their vision, however, was allowed to permeate through to higher authority constraints on funding defence spending loomed large.

The burden of defence

The rigours and pressures of how to fund even a modest defence effort drew out markedly different responses from politicians and economists. It was only when the war became more serious that economists persuaded some policymakers—not all—to adopt a physical resources perspective of economic capability.

The views of politicians

The mounting of only a modest defence effort, as we have seen, caused major political ructions at federal and state levels. In the 1938/39 Federal Budget, Casey had ordered a huge increase in defence spending, part of which was financed by new tax imposts. Defence, he insisted, 'writes its own ticket in matters of finance'.[14] Since the enlarged outlays absorbed the accumulated budget surplus, loans were arranged, meaning further Commonwealth borrowing at the expense of the states. When a public loan failed to generate the requisite funds, Casey hoped that his government would realise that defence spending could not be left

---

10   D. B. Copland to R. G. Menzies, 29 March 1938, UMA FECC, Box 60.
11   Contained in a note to Keynes in a letter by D. B. Copland to Giblin, 29 March 1938, UMA FECC, Box 220.
12   K. Murdoch to C. L. Baillieu, 4 January 1939, Murdoch Papers, NLA.
13   Hytten, autobiography, 1971, UT, p. 76.
14   Letter to *The Argus*, 26 October 1938.

strictly to the canons of orthodox finance.[15] The new circumstances—greater defence spending at a time of falling tax revenue—became acute as economic activity slipped due to drought and falling export prices. Economic activity was past its 1937/38 peak. Armed against its critics, the Commonwealth Bank continued to engage in insulating the economy from falling export prices by judicious credit expansion. It served, as we shall see, a dual function.

Greater public works especially by state and semi-governmental authorities, together with the rise of the manufacturing sector, kept unemployment about 10 per cent. The growth in semi-governmental authorities' borrowing, however, which the 'prodigal' states of Queensland and New South Wales had masterminded, impeded the Commonwealth's bid to access funds for defence.[16] Semi-governmental borrowings, especially by New South Wales, were frustrating the Loan Council in its task of providing funds for government and keeping the money market balanced. Canberra wanted the states to coordinate developmental works to give defence capacity the greatest priority. The funding of defence expenditure resulted in a renewed spat between Casey and Stevens over the conduct of monetary policy, particularly whether state loan expenditure and semi-governmental authority spending should be tapered to the needs for greater Commonwealth spending. Public spending by this stage was dedicated mostly to the pre-depression policy of development rather than employment generation.

Anticipating the economists, Stevens wanted the Loan Council to 'lay aside its habitual preoccupation' with each state's claims and focus on developing a national financial policy agreed on by the Commonwealth Bank. This would put men to work and also allow a greater defence contribution.[17] Stevens did not think that Casey should set 'arbitrary financial limits' on the amount of public spending that could be undertaken. For Stevens, the real limits were set by the number of men available and, with a pool of unemployment, that point had not been reached. For his part, Casey believed that Stevens' proposed 'policy of inflation' was disrupting Australia's defence preparedness.[18]

This dispute between the two figures meant that Australia moved gingerly in its defence preparations. The Munich crisis of September 1938 triggered a greater degree of cooperation. By March 1939, all the state premiers expected some resort to credit expansion to finance the defence spending rather than a resort to taxation. It also sparked rumours that Stevens would soon switch to Federal

---

15 *The Argus*, 25 February 1939.
16 'Flaws in the machinery of loans', *The Herald*, 8 June 1939.
17 'Loan Council's tasks', *SMH*, 30 March 1939.
18 'Attack on premier', *SMH*, 24 October 1938; 'Stevens hits back', *The Sun*, 24 October 1938.

Parliament and replace Casey as Treasurer.[19] Ironically, it was Percy Spender (1972:37), Casey's ultimate successor as Treasurer, who was being pressured to relinquish his seat in favour of Stevens.

In 1939, both Casey and Stevens were, in the space of a few months, removed from their respective positions. After Menzies became the new Prime Minister in April 1939, he dispatched Casey to the new federal Ministry of Supply. Stevens lost the premiership in August 1939 following doubts raised over his economic stewardship after his promise of a budgetary surplus for New South Wales for 1938/39 lapsed into deficit (McCarthy 1967:91). Following two years of balanced budgets, Stevens had planned for a surplus, regardless of the economic slowdown, to further his credentials for federal politics (McCarthy 1967:262). A year later, a chastened Stevens (1940:77) professed: 'The question of the balance or unbalance of the budget is, within reasonable limits, irrelevant so long as output and employment are kept at a maximum.'

Before then, Stevens' stance, as far as federal funding of defence spending was concerned, was inspired by a Keynesian understanding.

The whole issue of war economics rekindled the controversy about the possibilities of central bank credit. National credit adherents invoked Clause 504 in the report of the Royal Commission on Banking and Monetary Systems holding that the release of credits or budget deficits could pay for the war (Spender 1972). The Commonwealth Bank strove to stamp out such sentiments and solicited the help of the Treasury. The new Prime Minister also shunned the suggestion, but economists and the central bank saw a role for moderate credit expansion.

Spender (1972:61–2), the new Assistant Treasurer serving under Menzies, also dismissed the lopsided argument, circulated by Stevens and Forgan Smith, that restricting loans for public works to defray more military spending would automatically create unemployment. His superior, Menzies, alas, was beset by the same blinkers as Lyons. The Commonwealth Treasury advised Menzies that public loans and deficit finance of defence expenditure were likely to cause inflation and falling living standards even with an underemployed economy. Overall it was a muddled picture in need of a clear vision.

The views of the economists

It could be said that given their early appreciation of Keynesian economics, the economists could, quite early on, see the resource potential where politicians and office-holders could not. In 1939, as the shadows of war grew darker,

---

19   'Cabinet may be remodelled', *The Argus*, 19 October 1938.

Australia had 10 per cent unemployment. Neither political party, though, had a preconception of how to mobilise these idle resources. It could be achieved by additional expenditure on investment and consumption. Credit expansion would also, up to a point, disarm the dispute between the states and the Commonwealth about having to restrict public works. Giblin and Copland had publicly floated this approach in 1938 but without much impact (Copland 1951:24; Walker 1939a:44–5).

In London, Kershaw was as pessimistic as Australian politicians that the greater defence expenditure would exhaust her London funds. He felt Australia should restrict its public works programs and tighten its banking system.[20] He concluded that 'an economy strained by a fall in export prices and slightly inflated by governmental expenditure, will not have an easy task in meeting the financial demands of the war, even with some recovery in external balances as a result of better export prices and lower imports'.[21]

The economists, led by Copland, Giblin, Melville and Walker, were clear-headed about the circumstances confronting Australia. Copland was probably the first economist to touch on the matter. In April 1938, he wrote, with a Melbourne commerce student, a briefing on the implications of greater defence spending on the Australian economy.[22] At the time, the economy was at full employment and Copland stressed that military spending meant a diversion of resources away from civilian use. This could be achieved by taxation, borrowing or creating credit. Copland stressed that the last option was inflationary and offered much less equity than a considered plan of raising finance by taxation and loans.

In reviewing the 1938/39 Federal Budget, Copland argued that the greater amount of defence expenditure—representing about 3 per cent of national income—meant that the states would have to coordinate plans with the Commonwealth and defer spending on development.[23] In a series of newspaper articles published in 1939, Copland outlined the repercussions for the economy of a higher level of military spending and the need for economic reorganisation for defence. He reiterated that preparing for war meant Australia could no longer proceed with its normal economic development. Creating, moreover, a modernised defence capability meant more organisation than was the case in 1914, particularly in developing the industrial ability to wage war. There would also have to be a build-up of vital materials and supplies.[24] Copland welcomed, therefore, Menzies' initiative of creating a new Ministry of Supply. Copland suggested that perhaps half of Australia's public investment being diverted

---

20 'London funds of Australian banking system', 20 November 1939, PRO, T160/1041/16320/01.
21 Ibid.
22 'Defence expenditure and the Australian economy', 28 April 1938, UMA FECC, Box 144.
23 'An economist sums up on defence spending plans', SMH, 5 September 1938.
24 'Defence in the democracies', The Sydney Telegraph, 14 February 1939.

away from infrastructure towards military ends would not gravely diminish the standard of living. The suspension of Australia's normal economic progress would, however, be the 'price' of national security.[25] Copland told an Economic Society gathering that some degree of credit expansion to finance Australia's defence effort was feasible.[26] At the same forum, Giblin warned that financing the war effort could not be done by merely 'soaking the rich'. Rather it would be financed by reducing the standard of living of the population, though he wondered whether that would prove acceptable.

Concerned about the lack of coordination in official circles, a frustrated Copland warned that Australians did not seem to realise the peril they were facing and needed another annexation of territory by Hitler to get 'reasonable agreement upon the need for the vigorous pursuit of the arts of defence'.[27] He noted how Japan had been on a semi-war footing for some years.[28] There was some cause for optimism. With overseas borrowing out of reach, Australia had to rely on its own capital resources. The Commonwealth Bank was undertaking credit expansion to finance the loan program and maintain liquidity levels. It had taken this action to support the money market because there was a drain on funds due to low export prices and an adverse current account. Copland was concerned, though, whether the central bank had the mastery of control to tailor the credit injection to boost employment and activity without incurring rising cost levels, which would have a detrimental impact on Australia's external account. Second, Copland was concerned whether the Commonwealth Bank had enough control to ensure that the credit tap would be turned off as full employment was approached.[29] Reading expressed confidence to a West Australian politician that the bank would pass this test.[30] The key question was whether the Commonwealth Bank's actions were prompted by improvisation and learning from the past or, in fact, marked a new economic doctrine. It was the latter case, with the bank expressly following a Keynesian doctrine laid down by its economic advisors.

Both Copland and Melville were attracted by and responded to articles written by Keynes that appeared in *The Times* in September 1939 on how to raise defence spending without incurring rising interest rates. Both responses demonstrated a significant awareness of Keynesian precepts. Copland warned that Australia could only partially imitate Britain's cheap money policy as she had more access to funds by simply restricting capital exports.[31] Australia, in

---

25 'An economist sums up on Australia's defence plans', *SMH*, 1 May 1939.
26 'Credit expansion', *SMH*, 29 April 1939.
27 'Australian economic conditions, 1939, report no. 2', 27 March 1939, UMA FECC, Box 64, p. 2.
28 'Economics of war: position in Japan', *SMH*, 14 November 1938.
29 'Defence spending must not be allowed to send up costs', *The Sydney Telegraph*, 4 July 1939.
30 C. Reading to W. A. Nairn, 13 February 1939, Secretary's Papers: Finance—Credit Expansion, AA, A11857.
31 'Finance for defence: Britain's broad facilities; action limited in Australia', *SMH*, 18 August 1939.

contrast, had to contend with low export prices and being a debtor nation. A continuance of the central bank's modestly expansionary policy could, however, with the requisite degree of investor confidence, initiate and advance the dual achievement of a rigorous industrial program for defence and full employment. It was essential, Copland added, that Australian governments agree on the same economic strategy and that the financing method adopted had the support of the money market. A well-conceived liberal credit policy meant, therefore, that the Commonwealth Bank issued securities while export prices remained subdued and then reversed the process when export prices recovered. Too rapid a monetary injection, Copland warned, would spill over into imports, provoke inflation and impair Australia's external credit.

Melville, the President of the Economic Society, gave a lecture on Keynes's articles. Six months earlier he had written, perhaps with Giblin's help, the Commonwealth Bank's definitive brief on the canons of financing defence spending. There was a twist of irony in Melville's lecture on Keynes's views since he had earlier disparaged notions of the 'euthanasia of the rentier'.[32] Now, with the exigencies of war, Melville was supportive of the tenor of Keynes's suggestions, though he would not approve of his use of authoritarian controls to prevent British interest rates from rising. He agreed with Keynes that higher interest rates would choke off private capital formation and be injurious to the fabric of Australia's finances. There was, as Keynes suggested, a better method for finding the resources to wage war while the economy was at full employment—namely, taxation.[33] That expedient would, by suppressing consumption and relieving the external account, obviate the need for capital, price and investment controls. The advantages of low interest rates were 'obvious' to Melville but the real question was whether they could remain subdued. Melville concurred with Keynes that central banking techniques, including the postponement of funding, would keep rates low as long as taxation was stiffened once full employment was reached.[34]

Among the audience were Mills, Madgwick and Janes, who all agreed that at full employment, taxation should replace borrowing as the most responsible option. Borrowing at full employment would only reward the rich and impoverish the poor. Contra Melville, Mills and Madgwick felt more and comprehensive economic controls were the inevitable price of a war economy.

---

32 Melville, TRC 182, NLA, p. 160.
33 'Mr Keynes's views on interest rates', Economic Society of Australia, NSW Branch, Speech given on 22 September 1939, Melville Papers, NLA. Two years earlier, Melville told a meeting of actuaries that long-term interest rates would rise due to greater defence spending and the occurrence of economic booms ('Wars and booms: effect on interest rates', SMH, 31 August 1937).
34 Ibid., p. 2.

A few months before, both Copland and Wood had complained about the lassitude of the federal government in matching Britain's war preparations. 'Australia,' Copland found, 'had become the conservative country in economic policy in the world in the last six or seven years…and the last home of an almost undiluted form of capitalism.' By this Copland meant the reluctance to authorise an extensive array of state controls. He had long wanted the same array of economic controls Germany had used. It would make Australia impregnable from attack but he was pessimistic about it materialising.[35] The growing threat to Australia's security spelt a grave challenge to the 'apostles of tradition' who encompassed the current government and the Treasury.

With the outbreak of war, Copland had his wishes granted. There was, institutionally, a growing resort to direct controls. To forestall interest rate rises, for instance, the government commandeered the states' borrowing rights in the capital market since competing with these other borrowers, it was feared, might push up interest rates. In line with other developments in public finance, the Commonwealth also moved to gain greater control over the financial system (Ross 1995:98; Butlin 1958:200–1). At the outbreak of war, Copland was asked by Menzies to come to Canberra to become Commonwealth Prices Commissioner and Economic Consultant to the Prime Minister, with a status equal to that of a cabinet minister. The formation of these direct controls hardly corresponded, however, with an embrace of Keynes's new economics; that would come, appropriately enough, from the advice of an advisory committee of economists.

The Finance and Economics Committee

At the organisational level, Lyons had been astute enough to call again on the economists to help garner the defence effort. The Finance and Economics Committee was formed in late 1938. It was, under Giblin's leadership, to make an almighty contribution to the war effort. Its primary focus within the first years of operation was to integrate Keynesian ideas with traditional public finance and have it successfully incorporated into official policy. There has been considerable discussion of the role and contribution the Finance and Economics Committee made to Australia's war effort (Whitwell 1986 Maddock and Penny 1983 Cornish 1993a Walker 1947). The following discussion will attempt to visualise the formation of the Finance and Economics Committee as the mobilisation of economic expertise in the nation's lead-up to November 1939.

Coombs (1981:6) is adamant that the committee gave 'economic planning of the war' a Keynesian pedigree. The committee, chaired by Giblin with Wilson and

---

35   D. B. Copland to W. Downie Stewart, 17 October 1938, UMA FECC, Box 61.

Melville assisting, and under the ambit of the Federal Treasury, was initially charged with looking at the effect on the economy of a loss of command at sea and subsequent closing of trade routes. Lyons proposed to Giblin that it would be an aspect of national economic planning in a near-war situation.[36] The Secretary of the Defence Department, Frank Shedden, told Giblin that the committee would 'authoritatively review the strong and weak parts [of] our national income under stress, and indicate the direction in which planning could strengthen the weaknesses'.[37] The idea for the committee came from Wilson. It was the realisation of his 'central thinking agency' that he had spoken of in 1934 (Duncan 1934). Wilson had in mind a 'small thinking committee to which all sorts of problems could be submitted for general advice' (Whitwell 1986:2). The committee's primary task would be to advise the Treasurer and his department. Eventually this would amount to the committee challenging the Treasury's orthodox canons of war finance. After the outbreak of hostilities, Brigden, Coombs, Mills and Copland were added to the committee.

Copland was initially omitted despite having written a comment on an official memorandum in 1938 arguing that Australia could make itself reasonably independent of overseas supplies in an emergency.[38] In that comment, Copland warned that Australia had to prepare for the likelihood of war and a trade blockade within the next three years—not the seven years mooted in an official report.[39] Copland stressed that the imperative for the federal government was not development but defence policy. Apart from addressing coastal defence and internal transport needs, Australia had to develop a greater defensive capacity in its economic development. This meant diverting resources into developing 'unproductive' and 'costly' defence industries and it would inevitably spell some incursions on the standard of living. Copland and Giblin recycled these fears at the ANZAAS meeting in January 1939 (Copland 1951:24).

The committee's main role was to find the means to wage total war. This had to be achieved without causing undue disturbance to underlying economic arrangements and also had to be done equitably and efficiently (Maddock and Penny 1983:31). Waging a war effectively, Giblin pointed out to MacFarlane, usually meant ensuring that first, the economy was at full employment. Second, there had to be a smooth transfer of resources from civilian to war needs and, lastly, this process had to be undertaken by using financial policies.[40]

---

36   J. A. Lyons to L. F. Giblin, 27 December 1938, UMA FECC, Box 216.
37   F. Shedden to L. F. Giblin, 18 January 1939, UMA FECC, Box 218.
38   D. B. Copland to R. G. Menzies, 11 October 1938, and R. G. Menzies to D. B. Copland, 12 October 1938, UMA FECC, Box 60.
39   'Comment on memorandum on financial problems of Australian defence and development', 16 October 1938, UMA FECC, Box 217.
40   L. F. Giblin to S. G. MacFarlane, 21 October 1939, Secretary's Papers: Finance—Prof. Giblin, AA, A11857.

In that regard, the expanded Finance and Economics Committee would have found the Commonwealth Bank's brief on defence spending for consideration by the members of the Loan Council more congenial than any views coming from the Treasury.[41] Melville wrote the document in March 1939, with Giblin assisting. It was distributed widely. It was a short review of the principles that should guide the central bank in deciding how much to increase or decrease the money supply in certain hypothetical cases involving the necessity to augment defence spending. The bank took the view that when there was unemployment defence spending would not be at the expense of civilian goods as it would be at full employment. When it came to creating credit or public loans from the central bank, the government could apply this method only when not at full employment. A modest loan by the central bank would go a long way in mopping up unemployed resources, meaning that it would have to be reduced 'as it does its work'.[42] The bank felt that this method would still have an inflationary bias since idle savings would quickly transform into funds seeking investment as prosperity and, in turn, confidence returned due to the injection of spending. The document stated that the 'business of the central bank' was to increase or decrease money supply according to economic activity and the level of employment. Full employment, or the approach of it, was good reason therefore to restrict credit. It pointedly concluded by stating that

> [t]he needs of defence have nothing to do with determining the proper supply of money; if a central bank loan is made for defence at a time when the money supply does not require increasing then the country will pay for it through rising prices and general dislocation more heavily than if the money were raised by taxation.[43]

After being given a copy of the document, Copland told Giblin that apart from a few quibbles, he had few reservations about it.[44]

Menzies' 'business as usual budget', brought down only a few days after the outbreak of war, was very much a Treasury-inspired one, with the modest increase in defence spending sourced from taxation and public loans (Spender 1972:50). In his budget speech, Menzies criticised those who believed that war expenditure could be financed entirely by central bank borrowing or the 'credit of the community' (Butlin 1958:197). Giblin was not so dismissive of it, perceiving that the whole matter of war finance was one of physically attracting resources to war ends. One of Casey's last actions as Treasurer had been to ask Giblin, Wilson and Brigden about their views on using credit expansion to finance defence spending. Giblin took a mechanical view that credit expansion

---

41 'Commonwealth Bank and finance for defence', 17 March 1939, UMA FECC, Box 63.
42 Ibid., p. 4.
43 Ibid., p. 6.
44 D. B. Copland to L. F. Giblin, 29 June 1939, UMA FECC, Box 63.

was justifiable when there was unemployment in the economy with the proviso that the credit be withdrawn as the slackness was taken up. Wilson, while generally supportive, worried about the effect on interest rates and also the external account when credit expansion was exercised. Brigden's (1939) reaction, later encapsulated in a short and querulous article in the *Economic Record*, noted how credit expansion would result in rising wage costs as full employment was approached. The problem was that there was 'no coordination between wages policy and finance policy' to prevent wage inflation from occurring. Consequently, Brigden concluded that if credit expansion and thus, full employment, were pursued, there would have to be controls on labour, foreign exchange and investment (Clark 1950:3).

The tendency to overexpansion and therefore the need for controls attracted the attention of MacFarlane (Cornish 2000). His department's view of credit expansion was that it would bring unmitigated inflation; there was no alternative but to raise funds by the orthodox methods of taxation and public borrowings. It was extraordinary to recall that, just two months later, the Finance and Economics Committee overturned the Treasury line of thinking. It freed the new Treasurer from MacFarlane's dour, arithmetical approach to fiscal policy (Spender 1972:42–3).

It was Giblin who led the crusade of imparting a Keynesian approach to Australia's war finance. He had a new and more receptive Federal Treasurer to work with, who acknowledged Giblin's mental vision (Spender 1972:44). Giblin was, of course, aided by the other economists, including Walker, who had just published a book on the subject. Giblin had read a draft of the book and it would have merely reinforced his disposition for adopting a Keynesian approach to defence spending. Giblin felt highly of Walker's account while Copland called it 'a first class piece of work'.[45] In another place, Copland (1939) said the 'great virtue' of Walker's book was that it got 'behind the veil of money' and stated the defence problem 'in real terms'. Melville was of the same persuasion.[46]

In January, Walker (1939a) had presented a paper at the ANZAAS conference arguing that sound finance should give way to unbalanced budgets when conditions warranted it. An expansionist policy involving an unbalanced budget was now an appropriate one for Australia. Walker had more than his work cut out for him in Tasmania, where he was economic advisor to the state government and was dealing with Premier Dwyer-Grey, a Major Douglas adherent.[47] Whitwell (1986:11–13) convincingly argues that it was Walker who provided the intellectual sustenance for the Finance and Economics Committee's

---

45   D. B. Copland to T. Hytten, 28 August 1939, UMA FECC, Box 143.
46   L. G. Melville to D. B. Copland, 14 August 1939, UMA FECC, Box 144.
47   E. R. Walker Papers, UT, 21/4.1.

Keynesian approach to war finance. This is probably correct but it must be recalled that Giblin was not long back from Cambridge, where he had been imbibing Keynes's new economic philosophy. It was Giblin, too, who now held an official position of some real influence and authority.

It was Giblin, then, who encouraged Spender to attempt more with fiscal policy. Giblin demonstrated how Australia, with 10 per cent unemployment, could painlessly increase its defence budget without facing resource pressures. Instead of a heavy-handed resort to economic controls, which would intimidate business, Giblin felt the government should increase expenditure through credit expansion. The elimination of unemployment would remove an embarrassment for the government. Convinced, Spender took up the matter with Menzies, highlighting how the financial costs of the war effort could be lightened by putting the unemployed back into work. While the unemployed had, hitherto, been a state matter, Spender believed the initiative 'would not only be good politics on our part, but sound economics, if we take the lead in this matter'.

Despite the intrinsic political appeal of this, Menzies, labouring under what Copland (1945:10) called 'the myth of insufficient finance', could not fathom how more federal spending could solve two economic problems simultaneously. After consulting with his committee colleagues, Giblin re-emerged with a new memorandum called 'War finance'. Its precepts were to muster the resources necessary for war, maintain civilian production and consumption and spread the burden fairly over society. The increase in defence spending, mooted for a supplementary budget, would come from central bank credit. Spender took Giblin's proposal to cabinet on 13 November 1939 and announced, in dramatic words, that '[o]ne of the objectives of our present policy is to restore and increase the national income. This will enable us to divert resources to defence without encroaching unnecessarily on existing standards of consumption'. Spender made it clear in a second submission to cabinet how borrowing for defence would be from the central bank thus sparing private enterprise from a greater tax burden. Once capacity and full employment were reached, however, taxation would assume its rightful duty and prevent any inflation. This 'changeover' point was projected to occur by May 1940. Cabinet accepted this revolutionary new approach to economic policy thereby giving the Finance and Economics Committee an early triumph (Maddock and Penny 1983:35). Behind the scenes, Giblin assured Spender not to be unnerved by the budget falling into deficit, as the reflationary experiment was unleashed. When the Loan Council met that same month, the states were delighted to hear that their borrowings were not cut (Walker 1947:44).

Spender brought down his supplementary budget on 30 November. This was the moment when a Keynesian revolution in economic policy truly arrived in Australia. An English newspaper hailed Spender's budget as 'the answer to an economist's prayer' (cited in Spender 1972:45). At this point, it could fairly be said that Australia led the world in macroeconomic management. In October 1940, almost ten years since giving his first address as the Ritchie Reseach Professor, Giblin gave an address entitled 'Australia 1940' at the Victorian branch of the Economic Society. Giblin posed the question how well Australia had adopted itself to financing the war effort. He mooted that the citizenry would have to forgo more consumption with one fifth of national output designated for war needs.[48]

Conclusion

Tangeroa, Clear Away the Clouds that Ru May See the Stars

— Polynesian prayer inscribed on a stone memorial to Edward Shann at the University of Western Australia

In giving the Joseph Fisher Lecture, R. G. Menzies (1942) noted that '[i]n the economic history of the last fifteen years nothing will be more notable than the rise to influence and authority of the professional economist'.

While there had been some resentment at the rise of the economists, Menzies, quoting Edmund Burke, said that society must adjust to new facts and circumstances. In his lecture, Menzies recounted how the Australian economists, led by L. F. Giblin, allowed Australia to undergo a smooth transition to a war economy by channelling idle resources into war preparations. The economists' advice was justified by the results. By May 1940, as Giblin had projected, unemployment had been absorbed and Australia reverted to the more traditional ways of financing war expenditure but equipped with a stronger, more robust economy. In his own premiership that followed in 1949, Menzies surrounded himself with economic advisers, some of whom had been involved in the events covered in this monograph.

Today one rarely hears praise for economists but rather mockery or ridicule. Australia is a society, as the Australian historian W. K. Hancock (1930) sagely noted, that upholds a collective disdain for 'scientific economists'. Today, that disdain for economics continues with students electing to bypass it and electives like economic history, macroeconomics and the history of economic doctrine. Perhaps the Global Financial Crisis of 2007-9 will restore interest and with it a change in the regimen of economics degrees towards more economic history and the history of economic thought.

---

48 'Must divert 20 per cent of our income: Prof.Gibin's views" ,*The Herald* 28/10/1940. W. Prest had addressed the same Victorian branch a few months earlier on 'The Keynes Plan' of deferred consumption for financing the war effort.

This book was written partly to counteract the mentality that economic history and macroeconomics does not matter by showing how the members of the interwar generation of Australian economists were pathfinders in devising new forms of macroeconomic management. They swept away the clouds to guide the economy using either the exchange rate or, ultimately, full employment as their compass. Their insights and analysis were informed by the analytical framework provided by Keynes's *General Theory*. Coombs referred to being under the guiding influence of the star of Keynes. For the most part, the economists in this triumph were never given any national acknowledgment, though this is often the lot of the economist. More importantly, Australian economists have not been given much coverage or comprehensively examined in the international literature on the spread of Keynesianism across nations. Yet when it comes to Australia and Keynes there was, and still is, a strong bond that carries through at the academic and advocacy level. This study explores for the first time how Keynesianism came to Australia and how it was expressed in thought, ideas and, ultimately, policy advice. In November 1939, Australian economists persuaded the Federal Treasurer to reject the orthodox Treasury line and adopt a Keynesian approach to war finance. While this action was politically expedient, Keynes knew that this means to influence in shaping world outcomes was better than irrelevance. Politicians such as Spender and Menzies saw the promise and power of economics expertise.

This book sought to make a contribution to the history of economics in Australia by examining the thought and ideas of its leading economists in the decade leading up to 1939. As Part I showed, a young Australian economics profession, formally established in 1925, was thrust into an economically turbulent decade. It was to Australia's fortune that she could call on this small nucleus of economic expertise when policymakers and politicians remained panic struck. While the economists' first act of stabilisation policy enshrined in the Premiers' Plan was deflationary, they began to adjust their settings when the longed-for rise in export prices did not materialise.

Australian economists had a difficult field to hoe. Australian policymakers were, and refused to be, guided by any coherently conceptualised view of the proper relationship between the government and the economy. Most did not assimilate a Keynesian framework of national income, aggregate demand, savings and investment until the war years. Fiscal consolidation, a conservative central bank and a complaisant government allowed a deflationary policy to become entrenched. It largely shut out the expansionary line being taken by economists. It was this propensity to cautious expansionism than set the economists apart from policymakers and office-holders, though their voices were muted somewhat by the economic recovery.

Part III focused on how the Keynesian crusade asserted itself, first at the intellectual level, then at the policy level. Economists had success in convincing monetary authorities to temper the level of economic activity. The acid test was, however, whether the same authorities would expand aggregate demand when circumstances and idle resources warranted it in 1939. This they did.

A few months after the death of Keynes in April 1946, J. C. Habersberger representing the Council of the Victorian Branch of the Economic Society of Australia and New Zealand, wrote to Lady Keynes offering condolences. He told Lady Keynes that the Council had arranged a memorial lecture celebrating the life of her late husband. Habersberger also conveyed the words the President of the Victorian Branch of the Economic Society P.D. Philips had recorded on behalf of the membership.[49] It read

> That the Council be directed to forward to Lady Keynes a message of appreciation of the great service performed by the late Lord Keynes in the field of science as a whole, and in particular to the special science of Economics and also for the outstanding contrib. to the welfare of the entire British community which he so magnificently adorned.

Lady Keynes thanked Habersberger and the Council of the Victorian Branch of the Society for their 'moving resolution'.[50] The Lecture was given by Syd Butlin after Giblin, the Victorian Branch's first choice, declined perhaps due to ill health.

In the postwar era, the Australian economics establishment for a while exhibited a distinctive Keynesian rubric making it more open to heterodox approaches than their North American counterparts. This heritage stemmed from the Keynesian–Cambridge culture sown in the mid 1930s.

The focus of this research monograph was, then, to thematically undertake an examination of how Australian economists underwent a change in their thinking and ideas about economic thought and economic policy in the 10 years leading up to 1939. As the leading players in this tale, they were well aware of their changing world view. In April 1934, Giblin took stock of his colleagues' philosophical shift since 1929:

> Dyason was the one firm and consistent inflationist. Copland went that way in waves with strong back eddies. I was inclined to sit on the fence, not sure of my ground, and opposed to whatever arguments was [sic] put forward too confidently. Brigden I think was the same, and Hytten.

---

49   J. C. Habersberger to Lady Keynes, 12/7/1946, Minutes of the Council of the Victorian Branch of the Economic Society of Australia and New Zealand, Economic Society, Papers and Correspondence, UMA.

50   Lady Keynes to J C Habersberger, 31/8/1946, Economic Society, Papers and Correspondence, UMA.

Melville was of course a strong deflationist. Melville gradually and reluctantly has moved a very long way, but with always a hankering backward, which found voice from time to time. Shann, more fitfully, has even moved further the same way, and with his regret.[51]

It was a strikingly accurate assessment of his colleagues' state of mind but certainly not of himself. By 1934, Giblin had moved leftwards from a cautious deflationist of 1930 to assume the mantle of being a leading proto-Keynesian voice. Missing from Giblin's appraisal was, of course, the younger generation of Australian economists who, unlike their predecessors, were professionally trained economists. They undertook their studies when theoretical battles were raging in economics over monetary thought and lecture halls were filled to the rafters.

This book attempted to build on Giblin's survey by carrying it forward to 1939 when, according to L. G. Melville and Richard Downing, all in the Australian economic fraternity were Keynesian at least in policy outlook. Giblin and Walker were, by 1939, respectively the most persuasive and erudite Keynesians in the land, though Giblin, like his older colleagues, would hate to be typecast.

---

51   L. F. Giblin to E. R. Walker, 19 April 1934, Giblin Papers, NLA.

Dramatis personae

Baillieu, C. L. (1889–1967): Collins Street financier; associate of Keynes.

Benham, F. G. C. (1900–1962): Economist; lecturer at the University of Sydney under R. C. Mills, 1923–29; left Australia to return to his native England.

Brigden, J. B. (1887–1950): Economist, administrator and diplomat; served on several economists' committees of inquiry; Director of the Queensland Bureau of Industry, 1931–38; key author of the *Report on the Australian Tariff*; placed in charge of national insurance scheme, 1938; served on the Finance and Economics Committee.

Bruce, S. M. (1883–1967): Viscount Bruce of Melbourne; businessman; Prime Minister, 1923–29. A visionary in terms of seeing the importance of economists in public policy formation, Bruce left the Lyons government in 1933 to become High Commissioner in London.

Bruce, Sir W. (1878–1944): Insurance broker and commission merchant; chaired the Wallace Bruce Committee that reviewed the Premiers' Plan in 1932.

Bury, L. H. E. (1913–1986): Economist, subsequent Treasurer and cabinet minister; economist with Davidson's 'kindergarten'; Cambridge graduate.

Butlin, S. J. (1910–1978): Studied at Cambridge, attended Keynes's lectures in 1933–34; Sydney University economist, 1935–71, but not overly active in economic theory or policy development; spoke out against 'uncritical Keynesianism' in postwar Australia.

Casey, Sir R. G. (1890–1976): Conservative politician and diplomat; engineer by training; Australian political liaison officer in London, 1924–31. Impressed by the role economic science could play in governance, he carried that enthusiasm over to his roles as Assistant Treasurer to Lyons during 1934–35. Federal Treasurer, October 1935 – April 1939, whereupon he became Federal Minister for Supply.

Clark, C. G. (1905–1989): Member of Economic Advisory Council, 1930–31; lecturer in statistics, Cambridge, 1931–37; visited University of Melbourne, 1936; appointed Director of Queensland Bureau of Industry, 1938.

Coombs, H. C. (1916–1997): Commonwealth Bank economist, served under Melville; one of the 'young turks' behind 'the Keynesian crusade'.

Copland, D. B. (1894–1971): Doyen of Australian economists in the interwar era; Sidney Myer Professor of Commerce, 1924–40; author and chief publicist of the Premiers' Plan; economic advisor to Premier Stevens; economic consultant to A. C. Davidson at Bank of New South Wales.

Crutchley, E. T. : British government representative on migration and other matters; correspondent and diarist on Australian economic affairs.

Dalton, E. H. (later Lord) (1887–1962): Academic economist; reader in economics at London School of Economics, 1925–36; British Labour politician; visited Australia; recommended Colin Clark for the directorship of the Queensland Bureau of Industry.

Dalton, R. W. : British government Senior Trade Commissioner in Australia; took an alarmist view of Australia's mounting economic difficulties and felt that an important financial commission from the United Kingdom should administer Australia.

Davidson, Sir A. C. (1882–1952): NSW banker; noted for his view on expansionist economics; his bank led the depreciation of the Australian pound to sterling in 1930.

Downing, R.I. (1915–1975): Young Keynesian economist at Melbourne University in 1938; Copland and Giblin were his mentors.

Dyason, E. C. E. (1886–1949): Company director, economist, mining engineer and stockbroker; served on several economists' committees; an expansionist; helped compose Melbourne school stabilisation plan but later went along with the Premiers' Plan; founding member and President of the Economic Society, 1930.

Eggleston, Sir F. W. (1875–1954): Solicitor; appointed head of the Commonwealth Grants Commission, 1933.

Firth, G. (1916–99): English economist brought to Australia by L. F. Giblin; later Professor of Economics at the University of Tasmania.

Fisher, A. G. B. (1895–1976): New Zealand-born economist; friend of Copland; Professor of Economics at the University of Western Australia after holding chair at Otago; spent one year as economic adviser to A. C. Davidson at Bank of New South Wales.

Gepp, Sir H. W. (1877–1954): Public servant, industrialist and publicist; inspired by Keynes; urged formation of an economists' committee to advise the government; Chairman of Migration and Development Commission, 1926–30.

Giblin, L. F. (1872–1951): Mathematician and economist; Tasmanian Government Statistician, 1919–28; Ritchie Professor of Economics, 1929–40; developed the export multiplier, which alerted Australians to 'spreading the loss' principle especially to sheltered industries; extremely influential in the genesis of the Premiers' Plan resolutions; Chairman of the Finance and Economics Committee.

Gibson, Sir R. G. (1864–1934): Businessman and financier; President of the Victorian Chamber of Commerce, 1922–25; Member of the Commonwealth Bank Board, 1924–34; Chairman of the Commonwealth Bank Board 1926–34; —He resisted Theodore's fiduciary issues proposal of April 1931 and stood fast for parity with sterling in the face of opposition from economists, pastoralists and other exporting interests.

Gifford, J. L. K. (1899–1987): Foundation lecturer in economics at University of Queensland; signatory to November 1930 manifesto; avowedly Keynesian economist; completed his Masters at Kiel, Germany, 1932–34.

Gregory, T. E. (1890–1970): Professor of Economics at Manchester University; visited Australia with Niemeyer in 1930 and helped in framing advice; gave the 1930 Fisher Lecture.

Hankey, Sir M. (1887–1963): British Cabinet Secretary, 1916–36; Casey's London mentor; visited Australia in 1934.

Hawker, C. A. S. (1894–1938): Pastoralist and Federal MP, 1929–38; Federal Minister for Markets and later Commerce, January–September 1932; resigned from Lyons' ministry on a matter of principle; economically liberal but ineffective personal style.

Heathershaw, J. T. (1871–1943): Public servant; Secretary of Treasury, 1926–32.

Hytten, T. M. (1890–1980): Economist at University of Tasmania, 1925–32; Professor of Economics, 1929–35; economic adviser to Tasmanian government, 1929–35; initially opposed to Keynesian economics; economic adviser to Bank of New South Wales, after Shann and Fisher, 1935–49; served on Treasury Officials Committee, February 1931.

Isles, K. S. (1902–80): Studied at Cambridge; wrote a dissertation on wages policy and the price level.

Janes, C. V. (1887–1959): University of Melbourne philosophy and economics graduate; lecturer in economics and statistics there; President of the NSW Branch of the Economic Society; 'a political economist', according to F. W. Crick of the Midland Bank.

Kershaw, R. N. (1897–1981): Australian Rhodes Scholar; liaison officer between the Bank of England and the Commonwealth and other banks of the Empire, 1927–1950s; visited Australia in 1930 and 1936.

Keynes, J. M. (later Baron) (1883–1946): King's College economist; author of *The Tract*, *The Treatise on Money* and *The General Theory*; member of the Macmillan Committee and the Economic Advisory Committee.

Lang, J. T. (1876–1970): Headstrong Premier of New South Wales, 1930–33; put forward the Lang Plan; involved in political disputes with Bruce, Scullin, Theodore, Lyons and Latham.

Latham, J. G. (1877–1964): Politician, judge and diplomat; Leader of the Commonwealth Opposition, 1929–31; Deputy Chancellor of the University of Melbourne, 1935–39.

Lyons, J. A. (1879–1939): Schoolteacher, Premier of Tasmania and Prime Minister of Australia, 1931–39; Federal Treasurer, 1931–35.

MacFarlane, S. G. (1885–1970): Secretary of the Treasury, 1938; could not readily comprehend Keynesian approaches to economic policy.

Martin, C. E. (1900–1963): NSW Legislative Assembly parliamentarian. Initially a schoolteacher, he held two degrees in economics and was well versed in the works of Keynes. He was a member of the short-lived Lang Labor government.

Massey-Greene, Sir W. (1874–1952): Politician and entrepreneur; Assistant Treasurer, 1933.

Melville, Sir L. G. (1902–2002): Foundation Professor of Economics at Adelaide University, 1930; economic advisor to the Commonwealth Bank. Despite holding opinionated views about Keynesian economics, he was hailed by Groenewegen and McFarlane (1990) as the most conscious devotee of Keynesian economics. Played a key part in the formulation of the Premiers' Plan.

Merry, D. H. (1909–2002): University of Melbourne graduate; economist with the Bank of New South Wales; studied at the London School of Economics.

Mills, R. C. (1886–1952): Sydney University Professor of Economics, 1922–45; served on the Wallace Bruce Committee, 1932; played a significant role in the Royal Commission on Banking Systems. Mills pushed the case for greater Commonwealth powers over conduct of monetary policy.

Murdoch, Sir K. (1886–1952): Newspaper proprietor of the *Herald and Weekly Times*; enthusiastic supporter of Lyons; patron of the arts and to some extent of enlightened economics.

Niemeyer, Sir O. (1883–1971): Economic adviser to the Bank of England; visited Australia in 1930 and kept a wary, negative eye on Australia.

Page, Sir E. C. G. (1880–1961): Country Party politician and surgeon; Federal Treasurer in the Bruce government, 1923–29.

Norman, Sir M. (later Lord) (1871–1950): Governor of the Bank of England, 1920–46. Held a dismissive view of Australia's politicians though Lyons and Bruce's stewardship led him to a more relaxed view of Australia's loan portfolio.

Phillips, J. (1911-1975) Secretary to the Royal Commission of Banking Systems.

Pitt, H. A. (1872–1959): Undersecretary of the Victorian Treasury; member of the Copland Committee, 1931; founding member of the Victorian Branch of the Economic Society; commissioner on the Royal Commission into Banking and Monetary Systems.

Potter, Sir I. (1904–1994): Economist to Assistant Treasurer Casey, 1933–35; had considerable contact with Labor and non-Labor politicians; Sydney University graduate under Mills's influence; served in Davidson's 'kindergarten'.

Prest, W. (1907–1985): English-born economist; senior lecturer in economics at Melbourne University, 1938.

Reading, C. (1874–1946): Banker and company director; member of Commonwealth Bank Board, then Chairman from 1934.

Reddaway, W. B. (1913–2002): Cambridge economist; research fellow at Melbourne University, 1936–37; wrote first academic journal review of the *General Theory*.

Ricketson, S. (1891–1967): Financier with access to national financial markets; member of 'The Group' that backed Lyons' bid for power; supporter of Lyons but opposed the Premiers' Plan especially the impact on monetary markets.

Rivett, D. (1885–1961): Professor of Chemistry, 1924–27; Deputy Chairman of the CSIR, 1927–45.

Robinson, W. S. (1876–1967): Anglo-Australian businessman and mining magnate; former financial editor of *The Age*; critical of orthodox thinking and monetary policy; confidant of E. G. Theodore and J. M. Keynes.

Scullin, J. H. (1876–1953): Prime Minister of Australia, 1929–31. His administration put the Premiers' Plan into operation in June 1931.

Shann, E. O. G. (1884–1935): Economist and historian; Professor of History and Economics at the University of Western Australia, 1913–31; had an intellectual influence on the shaping of Premiers' Plan with Copland and Giblin; economic adviser to the Bank of New South Wales, 1931–33.

Sheehan, Sir H. J. (1883–1941): Public servant and banker; Secretary of Treasury, 1932–38; Governor of the Commonwealth Bank; probably the true originating author of the Premiers' Plan, written as a memorandum to Lyons in October 1930.

Smith, W. F. (1887–1953): Premier of Queensland, 1932–42; queried the wisdom of the Premiers' Plan and orchestrated public works for his state.

Smithies, A. (1907–1981): Treasury economist in the mid-1930s; studied under J. A. Schumpeter at Michigan; a 'staunch Keynesian' in his later life but conservatively inclined while assistant economist to Wilson at the Federal Treasury.

Spender, Sir P. C. (1897–1985): UAP politician, 1937–51; Treasurer, 1939–40; saw the Keynesian era introduced and grasped its importance.

Stevens, Sir B. S. B. (1889–1973): NSW Premier and Treasurer, 1932–39. Like his Queensland counterpart, Premier Forgan Smith, Stevens resisted purely orthodox economic policy and experimented with expansionist expedients. According to A. W. Martin, Stevens 'knew his Keynes'.

Swan, T. (1918–1989): Australian economist who developed the internal–external balance model in post-World War II era.

Theodore, E. G. (1884–1950): Queensland Premier, 1919–25; Federal Treasurer, 1929–31; enigmatic figure; proposed proto-Keynesian economic strategy in 1931 before lapsing back into promoting more orthodox policy expedients.

Walker, E. R. (1907–1988): One of the economists who pushed the Keynesian cause; doctorate from Cambridge supervised by D. H. Robertson; lecturer in economics at University of Sydney, 1927–31 and 1933–39; Professor of Economics at University of Tasmania, 1939; close adviser to Premier Stevens; pushed for the education of parliamentarians in economic matters.

Wentworth, W. C. (1907–2001): Publicity officer and economic adviser to B. S. B. Stevens; member of the 'Coffee Club'; later became a Liberal Party politician.

Whiskard, Sir G. (1886–1957): High Commissioner for the United Kingdom, 1936–41.

Wickens, C. H. (1872–1939): Commonwealth Statistician and Actuary, 1922–32; wrote a memorandum to Acting Prime Minister Fenton urging financial stabilisation based on currency stabilisation; founder and later chairman of the Economic Society.

Wilson, R. (1904–1996): Economist at the Commonwealth Bureau of Statistics; influential force behind the establishment of the Finance and Economics Committee set up to deal with war preparations.

Wood, G. L. (1890–1953): Associate Professor in Commerce at University of Melbourne, 1931; worked with Copland, Dyason and Giblin; author of an account of Australian crises and depressions in his *Borrowing and Business in Australia* (1930); wrote review pieces in the *Sydney Morning Herald* and *The Statist*.

Young, W. J. : Adelaide-based businessman and political adviser; advised and helped South Australian Premier Hill implement the Premiers' Plan without question; confidant of Melville.

Bibliography

Adam, H. 1937, 'Review of *Economic Planning in Australia, 1929–36* by W. R. MacLaurin', *Economic Record*, vol. 13, no. 1, pp. 278–9.

Alexander, F. 1963, *Campus at Crawley; A narrative and critical appreciation of the first 50 years of the University of Western Australia*, Cheshire Press, Melbourne.

Alford, K. 1994, 'The Australian economy in the era of the 1930s' Great Depression', *National Economic Review*, no. 29 (July), pp. 1–38.

Arndt, H. W. 1971, 'Review of C. B. Schedvin's *Australia and the Great Depression*', *Australian Quarterly*, vol. 3, no. 2 (June), pp. 121–5.

Arndt, H. W. 1976, 'R. I. Downing: economist and social reformer', *Economic Record*, vol. 52, no. 139 (September), pp. 281–301.

Arndt, H. W. 1996, 'Economic research and economic policy', *Australian Quarterly*, vol. 68, no. 3, pp. 93–8.

Ashford, N. 1997, 'Politically impossible?', *Policy*, Autumn, pp. 21–5.

Attard, B. 1992, 'The Bank of England and the origins of the Niemeyer mission 1921–30', *Australian Economic History Review*, vol. XXXII, no. 1, pp. 66–83.

Attard, B. 2000, 'Financial diplomacy', in Bridge and B. Attard (eds), *Between Empire and Nation*, Australian Scholarly Publishing, Kew, Vic., pp. 111–32.

Backhouse, R. 1999, *Keynes: Contemporary responses to the* General Theory, Thoemmes Press, Bristol, UK.

Bambrick, S. 1968, Australian price indices, PhD thesis, The Australian National University, Canberra.

Bambrick, S. 1970, 'Australia's long-run terms of trade', *Economic Development and Cultural Change*, vol. 19, no. 1, p. 5.

Barber, W. 1993, 'The spread of economic ideas between academia and government: a two way street', in D. Colander and A. W. Coats (eds), *The Spread of Economic Ideas*, Cambridge University Press.

Barber, W. J. 1996, *Designs Within Disorder*, Cambridge University Press.

Battin, T. 1997, *Abandoning Keynes: Australia's capital mistake*, Macmillan Press, London.

Beaud, M. and Dostaler, G. 1995 (eds), *Economic Theory Since Keynes*, Edward Elgar, Cheltenham, UK.

Benham, F. 1928, *The Prosperity of Australia*, P. S. King and Son, London.

Blainey, G. and Hutton, G. 1983, *Gold and Paper 1858–1982: A history of the National Bank of Australasia Limited*, Macmillan, South Melbourne.

Blanche, J. 1998, *Gowrie, VC*, Self-published, Hawthorn, Victoria.

Bland, F. A. and Mills, R.C. 'Financial Reconstruction. An examination of the plan adopted at the Premiers Conference,1931', *Economic Record*, vol.7, no.2, pp.161-176.

Blaug, M. 1991, 'Second thoughts on the Keynesian revolution', *History of Political Economy*, vol. 23, no. 2, pp. 171–88.

Boehm, E. 1973, 'Australia's economic depression in the 1930s', *Economic Record*, vol. 49, no. 128, pp. 606–23.

Booth, A. 1983, 'The "Keynesian revolution" in economic policymaking', *Economic History Review*, vol. 36, pp. 103–23.

Booth, A. 1984, 'Defining a "Keynesian revolution"', *Economic History Review*, vol. 37, no. 2, pp. 263–7.

Booth, A. 1989, *British Economic Policy, 1931–49: Was there a Keynesian revolution?*, Harvester Wheatsheaf, London.

Booth, A. and Peck, M. 1985, 'Keynes's alternative economic programme', *Employment, Capital and Economic Policy*, Blackwell, UK, pp. 165–99.

Booth, M. M. 1988, The debate on Australian exchange rate policy 1929 to 1936, Sub-thesis, Department of Economic History, The Australian National University, Canberra.

Bourke, H. 1988, 'Social scientists as intellectuals: from the First World War to the Depression', in B. Head and J. Walter (eds), *Intellectual Movements and Australian Society*, Oxford University Press, Melbourne, pp. 47–69.

Bridge, C. and Attard, B. 2000 (eds), *Between Empire & Nation: Australia's external relations from federation to the Second World War*, Australian Scholarly Publishing, Kew, Vic.

Bridges, E. E. B. 1964, *The Treasury*, Allen & Unwin, London.

Brigden, J. B. 1925, 'The Australian tariff and the standard of living', *Economic Record*, vol. 1, no. 1, pp. 29–46.

Brigden, J. B. 1932a, 'The optimistic outlook', *Economic News*, vol. 1, no. 6, p. 1.

Brigden, J. B. 1932b, 'Treasury bills and the avoidance of inflation', *Economic News*, vol. 1, no. 9, p. 4.

Brigden, J. B. 1933, 'Budgets and taxation', *Economic News*, vol. 2, no. 3, p. 1.

Brigden, J. B. 1934, 'Recovery and public works', *Economic News*, vol. 3, no. 4, p. 1.

Brigden, J. B. 1935, 'On inspiring confidence', *Economic News*, vol. 4, no. 1, p. 1.

Brigden, J. B. 1936, 'Recovery in transition', *Economic News*, vol. 4, no. 4, p. 1.

Brigden, J. B. 1938, '1937', *Economic News*, vol. 7, no. 1, p. 1.

Brigden, J. B. 1939, 'The credit theory of full employment', *Economic Record*, vol. 15 (December), pp. 236–7.

Brigden, J. B., Copland, D. B., Dyason, E. C., Giblin, L. F. and Wickens, C. H. 1929, *The Australian Tariff: An economic enquiry*, Melbourne University Press.

Brigden, J. B. 1930, *Escape to Prosperity*, Macmillan: Melbourne.

Brown, N. 1994, *Governing Prosperity*, Cambridge University Press, Melbourne.

Brown, N. 1997, 'A sense of number and reality: economics and government in Australia 1920–50,' *Economy and Society*, vol. 26, no. 2, pp. 233–56.

Brown, N. 2001, *Richard Downing: Economics, advocacy and social reform in Australia*, Melbourne University Press.

Butlin, M. W. and Boyce, P. M. 1988, 'Monetary policy in depression and recovery', in R. G. Gregory and M. W. Butlin (eds), *Recovery from the Depression: Australia and the world economy in the 1930s*, Cambridge University Press.

Butlin, N. G. 1962, *Australian Domestic Product, Investment and Foreign Borrowing 1861–1938/39*, Cambridge University Press.

Butlin, N. G. 1970, 'The Depression', *The Bulletin*, 5 December.

Butlin, N. G. 1978, 'A fraternal farewell: tribute to S. J. Butlin', *Australian Economic History Review*, vol. 18, no. 2, pp. 99–118.

Butlin, N. G. and Gregory, R. G. 1989, 'Trevor Winchester Swan 1918–1989', *Economic Record*, vol. 65, no. 191, pp. 371–7.

Butlin, S. J. 1937, 'The Banking Commission's report', *Australian Quarterly*, vol. IX, pp. 40–50.

Butlin, S. J. 1946, 'John Maynard Keynes', *Economic Papers*, no. 6, pp. 1–18.

Butlin, S. J. 1948, 'Of course I know no economics...', *Australian Quarterly* 22(3), September, pp. 37-51.

Butlin, S. J. 1951, 'John Maynard Keynes', *Current Affairs Bulletin*, pp. 3–16.

Butlin, S. J. 1953, 'Richard Charles Mills', *Economic Record*, vol. 28, no. 2, pp. 177–89.

Butlin, S. J. 1958, *War Economy 1939–42*, The Australian War Memorial, Canberra.

Butlin, S. J. (1961) *Australia and New Zealand Bank: The Bank of Australasia and the Union Bank of Australia Limited 1828-1951*, Longmans: London.

Butlin, S. J. 1962, 'Frederick Benham 1900–1962', *Economic Record*, vol. 38, no. 63, pp. 386–8.

Butlin, S. J. 1966, 'The hundredth record', *Economic Record*, vol. 42, no. 100, pp. 508–19.

Bystander 1934, 'The funding of Treasury bills', *Australian Quarterly*, vol. VI (March), pp. 73–86.

Cain, N. 1973, 'Political economy and the tariff: Australia in the 1920s', *Australian Economic Papers*, vol. 12, no. 20, pp. 1–20.

Cain, N. 1974, 'The economists and Australian population strategy in the Twenties', *Australian Journal of Politics and History*, vol. 20, no. 3 (December), pp. 346–59.

Cain, N. 1980, 'Monetary thought in the Twenties and its depression legacy: an Australian illustration', *Australian Economic History Review*, vol. XX, no. 1 (March), pp. 1–27.

Cain, N. 1982, 'Recovery policy in Australia 1930–33: certain native wisdom', *Working Papers in Economic History*, no. 1, The Australian National University, Canberra.

Cain, N. 1983, 'Australian Keynesian: the writings of E. R. Walker', *Working Papers in Economic History*, no. 13, The Australian National University, Canberra.

Cain, N. 1984, 'Economics between the wars: a tall poppy as seedling', *Australian Cultural History*, no. 3, pp. 74–86.

Cain, N. 1985, 'Keynes and Australian policy in 1932', *Working Papers in Economic History*, no. 58, The Australian National University, Canberra.

Cain, N. 1987a, 'Australian economic advice in 1930: liberal and radical alternatives', *Working Papers in Economic History*, no. 78, The Australian National University, Canberra.

Cain, N. 1987b, 'The Australian economists and controversy over depression policy, 1930 – early 1931', *Working Papers in Economic History*, no. 79, The Australian National University, Canberra.

Cain, N. 1988a, 'Resistance to Keynesian initiatives: an episode in Australian policy advice 1933–36', *Working Papers in Economic History*, no. 115, The Australian National University, Canberra.

Cain, N. 1988b, 'Economists and the Monetary Commission of 1936: ideas and circumstances', *Working Papers in Economic History*, no. 120, The Australian National University, Canberra.

Cairncross, A. 1986, *Economics and Economic Policy*, Basil Blackwell, Oxford, UK.

Cairncross, A. 1996, *Economic Ideas and Government Policy: Contributions to contemporary economic history*, Routledge, London.

Cairncross, A. 1998, *Living with the Century*, Lynx Press, Fife, UK.

Calwell, A. A. 1960, 'Introduction', *Economic Record*, vol. 36, no. 73, pp. 1–4.

Calwell, A. A. 1972, *A. A. Calwell: Be just and fear not*, Rigby, Melbourne.

Campbell, D. A. S. 1933, 'Australia and economic nationalism', *Australian Quarterly*, vol. V (December), pp. 54–67.

Cannon, M. 1996 *The Human face of the Great Depression*, Mornington

Casey, R. G. 1931, *Australia's Place in the World*, Robertson and Mullins, Melbourne.

Casey, R. G. 1933, *The world in which we live: a series of lectures on current events*, Specialty Press, Melbourne.

Casey, R. G. 1933, 'Treasury bills—and all that', *Australian Quarterly*, vol. V (December), pp. 56–65.

Castles, I. 1996, 'Sir Roland Wilson', *Treasury Round-Up*, Fourth Quarter, pp. 1–4.

Castles, I. 1997, 'Scientific economics in Australia 1927–31', *Academy of Social SciencesNewsletter*, vol. 16, no. 4, pp. 26–32.

Catley, R. and B. McFarlane 1983 *Australian Capitalism in Boom and Depression*, Alternative Books collective, Sydney.

Clark, C 1940 The Conditions of Economic Progress, Macmillan London.

Clark, C. 1950, 'J. B. Brigden', *Economic News*, vol. 19, no. 12, pp. 1–4.

Clark, C. 1958, *Australian Hopes and Fears*, Hollis and Carter, London.

Clark, C. 1983, 'Recollections of Keynes', *Economic Papers*, vol. 2, no. 3 (October), pp. 33–41.

Clark, D. L. 1974a, 'The causes of the Great Depression in Australia: towards a broader perspective', *Economics*, vol. 9, no. 1 (July), pp. 17–22.

Clark, D. L. 1974b, 'The Great Depression in Australia: some controversial aspects', *Economics*, vol. 9, no. 3 (October), pp. 45–53.

Clark, D. L. 1975, 'E. G. Theodore: his economics and his influence', *Economics*, vol. 10, no. 1 (March), pp. 27–33.

Clark, D. L. 1976, 'The Keynesian revolution and the battle of the plans', *Economics*, vol. 11, no. 2 (July), pp. 22–30.

Clark, D. L. 1977, 'Was Lang right?', in H. Radi and P. Spearrett (eds), *Jack Lang*, Hale & Iremonger, Sydney, pp. 138–59.

Clark, D. L. 1981a 'A closed book?the debate on the causes of the Great Depression', in J. Mackinolty (ed) *The Wasted years?:Australia's Great Depression*, Allen and Unwin, pp.10-26.

Clark, D. L. 1981b 'Fools and madmen - Australian policies towards economic depression in their international context', in J. Mackinolty (ed) *The Wasted years?:Australia's Great Depression*, Allen and Unwin, pp.175-193.

Clarke, P. 1988, *The Keynesian Revolution in the Making 1924–1936*, Clarendon Press, Oxford, UK.

Clarke, P. 1996, 'The Keynesian consensus and its enemies: the arguments over macroeconomic policy in Britain since the Second World War', in D. Marquand and A. Seldon (eds), *The Ideas that Shaped Post-War Britain*, Fontana Press, London.

Clarke, P. 1998, *The Keynesian Revolution and its Economic Consequences*, Edward Elgar, Cheltenham, UK.

Coats, A. W. 1992, *On the History of Economic Thought: British and North American essays. Volume 1*, Routledge, London.

Colander, D. and Coats, A. W. 1993 (eds), *The Spread of Economic Ideas*, Cambridge University Press.

Colander, D. C. and Landreth, H. 1996 (eds), *The Coming of Keynesianism to America*, Edward Elgar, Cheltenham, UK.

Coleman, W. 1999, 'A brief history of the Australian Notes Issue Board 1920–24', *The Cato Journal*, vol. 19, no. 1, pp. 161–70.

Coleman, W. and Hagger, A. 2003, '"An Edinburgh in the south"? Some contributions to fundamental economic analysis by Tasmanian economists in the 1920s', *Tasmanian Historical Studies*, vol. 8, no. 2, pp. 10–27.

Coleman, W., Cornish, S. and Hagger, A. 2006, *Giblin's Platoon: The trials and triumph of the economist in Australian public life*, ANU E Press, Canberra.

Commonwealth Bureau of Census and Statistics 1950, *The Australian Balance of Payments 1928–29 to 1948–49*, Commonwealth Bureau of Census and Statistics, Canberra.

Cook, P. 1970, 'Labor and the Premiers' Plan', *Labour History*, no. 17 (June), pp. 97–110.

Cook, P. 1979, 'Frank Anstey: memoirs of the Scullin Labor government, 1929–1932', *Historical Studies*, vol. 18, no. 72 (April), pp. 365–92.

Coombs, H. C. 1981, *Trial Balance*, Sun Books, Melbourne.

Copland, D. B. 1930a, 'The Australian problem', *Economic Journal*, vol. XL (December), pp. 638–49.

Copland, D. B. 1930b, *Credit and Currency Control*, Melbourne University Press.

Copland, D. B. The Economic and financial outlook', *Australian Quarterly*, no. 7 September pp. 17-28.

Copland, D. B. 1931, 'Readjustment in Australia', *Economic Journal*, vol. XLI (December), pp. 534–49.

Copland, D. B. 1932a, 'Reflections on Australian currency policy', *Australian Quarterly*, vol. IV (September), pp. 113–21.

Copland, D. B. 1932b, 'New Zealand's economic difficulties and expert opinion', *Economic Journal*, vol. XLII (September), pp. 371–9.

Copland, D. B. 1932c, 'Australian banking policy in the crisis', *Economic Journal*, vol. XLII (December), pp. 583–7.

Copland, D. B. 1934, *Australia and the World Crisis*, Cambridge University Press.

Copland, D. B. 1935a, 'Obituary of Edward Shann', *Economic Journal*, vol. XLV, pp. 599–601.

Copland, D. B. 1935b, *W. E. Hearn: First Australian economist*, Melbourne University Press.

Copland, D. B. 1936, 'Australian recovery and government policy', *Harvard Business Review*, vol. 15, no. 1, pp. 10–18.

Copland, D. B. and Janes, C. V. 1936 (eds), *Cross Currents in Australian Finance*, Angus & Robertson, Melbourne.

Copland, D. B. 1937a, 'Australian policy in depression', in A. D. Gayer (ed.), *Lessons of Monetary Experience: Essays in honor of Irving Fisher*, Farrer and Rinehart, New York.

Copland, D. B. 1937b, 'Some problems of Australian banking', *Economic Journal*, vol. XLVII (December), pp. 686–96.

Copland, D. B. 1939, 'News and notes', *Economic Record*, vol. 15 (December), pp. 230–1.

Copland, D. B. 1945, *The Road to High Employment*, Angus & Robertson, Melbourne.

Copland, D. B. 1946, *The Australian Economy*, Angus & Robertson, Melbourne.

Copland, D. B. 1950, 'E. C. Dyason: a tribute', *Economic Record*, vol. 26, no. 50, pp. 107–10.

Copland, D. B. 1951, *Inflation and Expansion: Essays on the Australian economy*, Cheshire, Melbourne.

Copland, D. B. 1960 (ed.), *Giblin: The scholar and the man*, Cheshire, Melbourne.

Corden, M. 1968, *Australian Economic Policy Discussion: A Survey*, Melbourne University Press.

Cornish, S. 1990, 'Edward Ronald Walker', *Economic Record*, vol. 67, no. 196, pp. 59–68.

Cornish, S. 1993a, 'The Keynesian revolution in Australia: fact or fiction?', *Australian Economic History Review*, vol. 38, no. 2, pp. 43–68.

Cornish, S. 1993b, 'Sir Lesley Melville: an interview', *Working Papers in Economic History*, no. 173, The Australian National University, Canberra.

Cornish, S. 1993c, 'Sir Leslie Melville: an interview', *Economic Record*, vol. 69, no. 207, pp. 437–57.

Cornish, S. 1999, 'Sir Leslie Melville: Keynesian or pragmatist', *History of Economics Review*, no. 30 (Summer), pp. 126–50.

Cornish, S. 2000, 'Stuart G. MacFarlane', in J. Ritchie (ed.), *Australian Dictionary of Biography. Volume 15*, Melbourne University Press, pp. 210–11.

Cornish, S. 2003, Sir Roland Wilson: a biographical study, Mimeo., The Australian National University, Canberra.

Costar, B. J. 1966, The Premiership of William Forgan Smith, MA Thesis, University of Melbourne.

Crawford, S. 1960, 'Giblin and profit sharing', in D. B. Copland (ed.), *Giblin: The scholar and the man*, Cheshire, Melbourne.

Crisp, F. 1961, *Ben Chifley*, Longmans, Croydon, Vic.

Cumpston, I. M. 1989, *Lord Bruce of Melbourne*, Longman Cheshire, Melbourne.

Curtin, J. 1930, *Australia's economic crisis and the 55,000,000 interest bill* Perth, ALP state executive.

Dalton, H. 1934, *Unbalanced Budgets*, Routledge, London.

Davenport, N. 1974, *Memoirs of a City Radical*, Weidenfeld & Nicholson, London.

Davidson, F. G. 1977, 'Brigden Vernon Rattigan Jackson', in J. Nieuwenhuysen and P. Drake (eds), *Australian Economic Policy*, Longmans, Melbourne.

Davis, J. 1975, *The World Between the Wars, 1919–1939: An economist's perspective*, Johns Hopkins University Press, Baltimore, Md.

Denholm, M. 1977, 'The Lyons Tasmanian Labor government 1923–1928', *Tasmanian Historical Research Association*, vol. 24, no. 2 (June), pp. 43–65.

Denning, W. 1982, *Caucus Crisis: The rise and fall of the Scullin government*, Hale & Iremonger, Sydney.

Dow, D. 1938, *Australia Advances*, Funk & Wagnall, New York.

Downing, R. I. 1960, 'Giblin as Ritchie Professor', in D. B. Copland (ed.), *Giblin: The scholar and the man*, Cheshire, Melbourne, pp.39-48.

Downing, R. I. 1972, 'Review of M. Keynes (ed.) *Essays on John Maynard Keynes'*, *Economic Record*, vol. 52, no. 137, pp. 111–12.

Duncan, W. G. K. 1934 (ed.), *National Economic Planning*, Angus & Robertson, Melbourne.

Dyason, E. C. 1931, 'Scourging the money-changers', *Economic Record*, vol. 7, no. 13, pp. 227–38.

Dyster, B. and Meredith, D. 1990, *Australia in the International Economy in the Twentieth Century*, Cambridge University Press, Melbourne.

Eichengreen, B. 1988, 'The Australian recovery of the 1930s in international comparative perspective', in R. G. Gregory and M. Butlin (eds), *Recovery from the Depression: Australia and the world economy in the 1930s*, Cambridge University Press, Melbourne.

Etzioni-Halevy, E. 1985, *The Knowledge Elite and the Failure of Prophecy*, Allen & Unwin, London.

Fisher, A. G. B. 1934, 'Crisis and readjustment in Australia', *Journal of Political Economy*, vol. XLII, pp. 753–82.

Fitzgerald, R. 1994, *Red Ted: The life of E. G. Theodore*, University of Queensland Press, St Lucia.

Fleming, G. 1996, 'Australian economists and the "educative" ideal: a historical perspective', *Journal of Economic and Social Policy*, vol. 1, no. 2, pp. 24–34.

Forsyth, P. 1972, 'Review of C. B. Schedvin's *Australia and the Great Depression'*, *Economic History Review*, vol. 25, no. 2, pp. 375–6.

Foster, L. 1986, *High Hopes*, Melbourne University Press.

Garland, J. M. 1960, 'Giblin and John Smith', in D. B. Copland (ed.), *Giblin: The scholar and the man*, Cheshire, Melbourne.

Garnett, A. C. 1949, *Freedom and Planning in Australia*, University of Wisconsin, Madison.

Garside, W. R. 1993, 'The search for stability: economic radicalism and financial conservatism in 1930s Europe', in W. R. Garside (ed.), *Capitalism in Crisis:International responses to the Great Depression*, Pinter, London.

Gayer, A. D. 1937, *The Lessons of Monetary Experience: Essays in honor of Irving Fisher*, Farrer & Rinehart, New York.

Giblin, L. F. 1930, *Australia, 1930—An inaugural lecture*, Melbourne University Press.

Giblin, L. F. 1933a, 'Australia in the shadows', *Australian Quarterly*, vol. 5 (December), pp. 3–10.

Giblin, L. F. 1933b, 'Review of E. R. Walker's *Australia in the World Depression*', *Economic Record*, vol. IX, no. 18, pp. 298–301.

Giblin, L. F. 1951, *The Growth of a Central Bank*, Melbourne University Press.

Gifford, J. K. 1935a, 'Currency devaluation, with special reference to Australia', *Economic Record*, vol. 11, no. 2, pp. 65–77.

Gifford, J. K. 1935b, *Devaluation and the Pound*, P. S. King, London.

Gilbert, R. S. 1973, *The Australian Loan Council in Federal Fiscal Adjustments 1890–1965*, Australian National University Press, Canberra.

Goodwin, C. 1966, *Economic Enquiry in Australia*, Duke University Press.

Goodwin, C. 1974, *The Image of Australia*, Duke University Press, Durham, NC.

Green, F. C. 1960, 'Giblin in politics and war', in D. B. Copland (ed.), *Giblin: The scholar and the man*, Cheshire, Melbourne.

Green, F. C. 1969, *Servant of the House*, Heinemann, Melbourne.

Gregory, R. G. and Butlin, N. G. 1988 (eds), *Recovery from the Depression: Australia and the world economy in the 1930s*, Cambridge University Press, Melbourne.

Gregory, T. E. 1933, 'Current problems in industrial finance, Fisher Lecture in Commerce', *Gold, Unemployment and Capitalism*, King and Son, London.

Grenfell-Price, A. 1965, *The Emergency Committee of South Australia and the Origin of the Premiers' Plan*, Libraries Board of South Australia, Adelaide.

Groenewegen, P. 2003, 'The economics of R.C Mills: a semi-Centenary Assessment', in *Australian Economic policy, theory and history: R. C. Mills Memorial lectures, 1958-2003*, University of Sydney: Sydney, pp 319-335.

Groenewegen, P. 2004, 'The making of good economists', *Australian Quarterly*, Autumn, pp.7-25.

Groenewegen, P. 2009, *Education for Business, Public Service and the Social Sciences*, University of Sydney Press.

Groenewegen, P. and McFarlane, B. 1990, *A History of Australian Economic Thought*, Routledge, London.

Gunn, J. A. and Alison, C. A. 1930, *Is this Depression Necessary? A short treatise on the stability of prices by control of the exchange rate.*

Hall, P. A. 1989 (ed.), *The Political Power of Economic Ideas*, Princeton University Press, NJ.

Hall, R. L. 1938, 'Review of "Economic Planning in Australia 1929–36" by W. R. MacLaurin', *Economic Journal*, vol. 48 (March), pp. 119–21.

Hancock, K. 1972, 'Forty years on', *Australian Economic History Review*, vol. 12, no. 1 (March), pp. 71–9.

Hancock, K. 1984, 'The first half century of wage policy', in B. J. Chapman, J. E. Isaac and J. R. Niland (eds), *Australian Labour Economics Readings*, Macmillan, Melbourne.

Hancock, W. K. 1930, *Australia*, Ernest Benn, London.

Harcourt, G. C. 1987, 'Arthur Smithies', in J. Eatwell, M. Milgate and P. Newman (eds), *The New Palgrave Dictionary of Economics*, Macmillan, London.

Harcourt, T. 1986, Unemployment, the economists and the 1920s: the Australian dilemma, BEc (Hons) Sub-thesis, University of Adelaide.

Harper, M. (1984), 'Douglas Copland - Applied Economist: some issues raised by the Copland Papers', A.N.U. Seminar Paper.

Harper, M. 1986, 'Economists in the 1920s and the 1930s: the golden age of Australian economics', in A. G. L. Shaw (ed.), *Victoria's Heritage: Lectures to celebrate the 150th anniversary of European settlement in Victoria*, Melbourne University Press.

Harper, M. 1989, 'The writing of the *Brigden Report*', *Working Papers in Economic History*, no. 121, The Australian National University, Canberra.

Harrod, R. F. 1951, *The Life of John Maynard Keynes*, Macmillan, London.

Hart, P. R. 1965, J. A. Lyons and the 1931 split, Mimeo., Department of History, The Australian National University, Canberra.

Hart, P. R. 1967, J. A. Lyons: a political biography, PhD Thesis, The Australian National University, Canberra.

Hart, P. R. 1970, 'Lyons: Labor minister—leader of the UAP', *Labour History*, no. 17 (June), pp. 37–51.

Hart, P. R. 1971, 'The piper and the tune', in C. Hazlehurst (ed.), *Australian Conservatism: Essays in twentieth century political history*, Australian National University Press, Canberra.

Hasluck, P. 1997, *The Chance of Politics*, Text Publishing, Melbourne.

Hawtrey, R. 1928, *Trade and Credit*, Longman, London.

Hawtrey, R. G. 1934, 'Australian policy in the Depression', *Economic Record*, vol. 10, no. 1, pp. 1–6.

Hayek, F. A. 1936, 'Review of D. B. Copland's "W. E. Hearn: First Australian economist"', *Economica*, vol. 3, no. 1 (February), p. 101.

Heaton, H. 1926, 'Progress and problems of Australian economists', *American Economic Review*, vol. XVI, no. 2 (June), pp. 235–48.

Heilbroner, R. and Milberg, W. 1995, *The Crisis of Vision in Modern Economic Thought*, Cambridge University Press.

Higgins, C. 1989, 'Colin Clark: an interview', *Economic Record*, vol. 85, no. 190, pp. 296–310.

Hodgart, A. W. 1975, *The Faculty of Economics and Commerce: A history 1925–75*, University of Melbourne Press.

Holder, R. F. 1970, *Bank of New South Wales: A history. Volume II 1894–1970*, Angus & Robertson, Melbourne.

Howson, S. and Winch, D. 1977, *The Economic Advisory Council 1930–39*, Cambridge University Press.

Hudson, W. 1986, *Casey*, Oxford University Press, Melbourne.

Hudson, W. and North, J. 1980 (eds), *My Dear PM, R. G. Casey's letters to S. M. Bruce 1924–1929*, Australian Government Publishing Service, Canberra.

Hytten, T. 1935, 'Australian public finance since 1930', *Economic Record*, vol. 11, no. 1 (March), pp. 122–38.

Hytten, T. 1940, 'Wartime financial policy', *Australian Quarterly*, vol. 12 (March), pp. 63–72.

Hytten, T. 1960, 'Giblin as an economist', in D. B. Copland (ed.), *Giblin: The scholar and the man*, Cheshire, Melbourne.

Johnson, H. 1995, *Roy de Maistre: The English years 1930–1968*, Craftsman House, Roseville, NSW.

Johnston, R. A. 1993, 'Monetary policy: the lessons of history', in M. A. Siddique (ed.), *A Decade of Shann Memorial Lectures 1998–90 and the Australian Economy*, Academic Press International, Singapore.

Karmel, P. H. 1960, 'Giblin and the multiplier', in D. B. Copland (ed.), *Giblin: The scholar and the man*, Cheshire, Melbourne.

Kemp, C. D. 1964, *Big Businessmen*, Institute of Public Affairs, Melbourne.

Kennedy, K. H. 1988, 'E. G. Theodore', in R. T. Appleyard and C. B. Schedvin (eds), *Australian Financiers*, Macmillan, Melbourne.

Kenwood, A. G. and Lougheed, A. L. 1997, *Economics at the University of Queensland 1912–1997*, Department of Economics, University of Queensland, St Lucia.

Kenwood, G. 1988, 'The use of statistics for policy advice: Colin Clark in Queensland 1938–52', in D. Ironmonger, J. Perkins and T. Van Hoa (eds), *National Income and Economic Progress*, St Martins Press, New York.

Kerr, C. 1983, *Archie: The biography of Sir Archibald Grenfell-Price*, Macmillan, Melbourne.

Keynes, J. M. 1923, *A Tract on Monetary Reform*, Macmillan, London.

Keynes, J. M. 1930, *A Treatise on Money*, Macmillan, London.

Keynes, J. M. 1931, *Essay in Persuasion*, Macmillan, London.

Keynes, J. M. 1933 *The Means to Prosperity*, Macmillan, London.

Keynes, J. M. 1936, *The General Theory of Employment, Interest and Money*, Macmillan, London.

Keynes, J. M. 1937, 'The general theory of employment', *Quarterly Journal of Economics*, vol. 51 (February).

Keynes, J. M. 1940, *How to Pay for the War: A radical plan for the Chancellor of the Exchequer*, Macmillan, London.

Keynes, J. M. 1973, *The General Theory and After: Defence and development. Volume XIV of the Collected Works of John Maynard Keynes*, edited by D. Moggridge, Macmillan and Cambridge University Press for the Royal Economic Society, London.

Keynes, J. M. 1977, *Activities 1920–22: Treaty revision and reconstruction. Volume XVII of the Collected Works of John Maynard Keynes*, edited by D. Moggridge, Macmillan and Cambridge University Press for the Royal Economic Society, London.

Keynes, J. M. 1982a, *Activities 1924–29: The return to gold and industrial policy. Volume XIX of the Collected Works of John Maynard Keynes*, edited by D. Moggridge, Macmillan and Cambridge University Press for the Royal Economic Society, London.

Keynes, J. M. 1982b, *Activities 1931–39: World crises in Britain and America. Volume XXI of the Collected Works of John Maynard Keynes*, edited by D. Moggridge, Macmillan and Cambridge University Press for the Royal Economic Society, London.

Keynes, J. M. 1982c, *The General Theory and After: A supplement. Volume XXIX of the Collected Works of John Maynard Keynes*, edited by D. Moggridge, Macmillan and Cambridge University Press for the Royal Economic Society, London.

King, J. E. 1997, 'Notes on the history of post-Keynesian economics in Australia', in P. Arestis, G. Palma and M. Sawyer (eds), *Capital Controversy, Post Keynesian Economics and the History of Economic Thought*, Routledge, London, pp. 298–309.

Kuhn, R. 1988, 'Labour movement economic thought in the 1930s: underconsumptionism and Keynesian economics', *Australian Economic History Review*, vol. XXVIII, no. 2 (September), pp. 53–74.

La Nauze, J. 1939, 'The story of Australian history 1929–36', *Australian Journal of Science*, vol. 22, no. 6 (December).

La Nauze, J. 1977, *Walter Murdoch: A biographical memoir*, Melbourne University Press.

Lang, J. T. 1962, *The Great Bust: The Depression of the Thirties*, Angus & Robertson, Sydney.

Lang, J. T. 1970, *The Turbulent Years: The autobiography of J. T. Lang*, Alpha Books, Sydney.

Learning, W. 1934, 'Australia', in H. Dalton (ed.), *Unbalanced Budgets*, Vernon Law Book Co., Kansas City.

Leeson, R. 1996, *Keynes and the klassics: an interpretation*, Working Paper, no. 145, Department of Economics, Murdoch University, Perth.

Leith-Ross, F. 1968, *Money Talks*, Hutchinson, London.

Le Pan, D. 1979, *Bright Glass of Memory*, McGraw Hill Ryerson, Ottawa.

Little, I. M. D. 1957, 'The economist in Whitehall', *Lloyds Bank Review*, vol. 44, pp. 29–40.

Lloyd, C. J. 1984, The formation and development of the United Australia Party, 1929–37, PhD Thesis, The Australian National University, Canberra.

Louis, L. J. and Turner, I. 1968, *The Depression of the 1930s*, Cassell Australia, North Ryde, NSW.

Love, P. 1982, 'Niemeyer's Australian diary and other English records of his mission', *Historical Studies*, vol. 20, no. 79, pp. 261–77.

Love, P. 1988, 'Frank Ansley and the monetary radicals', in R. T. Appleyard and C. B. Schedvin (eds), *Australian Financiers*, Macmillan, Melbourne.

Lowenstein, W. 1978, *Weevils in the Flour*, Hyland House, Melbourne.

Lyons, J. A. 1931, 'The national plan—and after', *Australian Quarterly*, September, pp. 7–14.

McCarthy, J. 1967, 'The Stevens-Bruxner Government 1929-1939', Ph.D University of Sydney.

McCarthy, J. 1979, 'The making of a cabinet: the right in New South Wales 1932–39', in C. Hazlehurst (ed.), *Australian Conservative Essays in Twentieth Century Political History*, Australian National University Press, Canberra.

McFarlane, B. 1966, *Professor Irvine's Economics in Australian Labour History 1913–1933*, Australian Society for the Study of Labour History, Canberra.

McFarlane, B. and Healey, D. 1990, 'A conversation with Colin Clark', *Quadrant*, vol. 34, no. 3, pp. 6–12.

Macintyre, S. 1986, *The Oxford History of Australia. Volume 4*, Oxford University Press.

McKibbin, R. 1990, *The Ideologies of Class Social Relations in Britain*, Clarendon Press, Oxford.

MacLaurin, W. R. 1936, *Economic Planning in Australia 1929–1936*, P. S. King and Son, London.

McTaggart D., Findlay C. and Parkin, M.1992, *Economics*, Addison Wesley

Maddock, R. and Penny, J. 1983, 'Economists at war: the Financial and Economic Committee 1939–44', *Australian Economic History Review*, vol. 23, no. 1, pp. 28–49.

Malcolm, D. O. 1929, 'Australian loan policy', *Australian Quarterly*, vol. 1 (September).

Mandle, W. F. 1978, 'Sir Otto Niemeyer, catalyst of Australia's depression debate', *Going It Alone:Australia's national identity in the twentieth century*, Allen Lane, Ringwood, Vic., pp. 73–97.

Markwell, D. J. 1985, *Keynes and Australia*, Reserve Bank of Australia Research Department Seminar Paper, September, Reserve Bank of Australia, Sydney.

Martin, A. W. 1993 *Robert Menzies: a life, Vol 1*, 1894-1943, Melbourne University Press, Melbourne.

Marquand, D. 1996, 'Moralists and hedonists', in D. Marquand and A. Seldon (eds), *The Ideas that Shaped Post-War Britain*, Fontana Press, London.

Martin, A. 1993, *Robert Menzies: A life. Volume I*, Melbourne University Press.

Martin, A. 1999, 'The politics of the Depression', in R. Manne (ed.), *The Australian Century: Political struggle in the building of a nation*, Text Publishing, Melbourne.

Mauldon, F. R. E. 1933, 'Some implications of economic planning', *Australian Quarterly*, vol. 4 (June), pp. 92–100.

Mauldon, F. R. E. and Weller, G. A. 1960, 'Sir Douglas Copland and the foundation of the Economic Society', *Economic Record*, vol. 36, no. 73, pp. 143–5.

Melville, L. G. 1929, 'Report of the British Economic Mission', *Australian Quarterly*, vol. 1 (March), pp. 93–101.

Melville, L. G. 1930, 'Federal banking and exchange proposals', *Australian Quarterly*, vol. 2 (December), pp. 44–53.

Melville, L. G. 1934, 'Plans and planners,' *Australian Quarterly*, vol. 6 (December), pp. 96–109.

Melville, L. G. 1939, 'The place of expectation in economic theory', *Economic Record*, vol.15, no.1, pp.1-16.

Melville, L. G. 1971, 'Review of C. B. Schedvin's "Australia and the Great Depression"', *The Australian Journal of Politics and History*, vol. 17, no. 1 (April), pp. 144–5.

Melville, L. G. 1992, 'Money, interest and the dollar', in D. McTaggert, C. Findlay and M. Parkin (eds), *Economics*, Addison Wesley, Sydney.

Menzies, R. G. 1942, The Australian economy during war, Joseph Fisher Lecture in Commerce, Adelaide.

Middleton, R. (1982) 'The Treasury in the 1930s: political and administrative constraints to acceptance of the "new" economics', *Oxford EconomicPapers* 34(1), March, pp. 48-76.

Middleton, R. 1985, *Towards the Managed Economy: Keynes, the Treasury and fiscal policy debate of the 1930s*, Methuen, London.

Millmow, A. 2000, 'Revisiting Giblin: Australia's first proto Keynesian economist?', *History of Economics Review*, no. 31 (Winter), pp. 48–67.

Millmow, A. 2003a, 'The power of economic ideas: Australian economists in the Thirties', *History of Economics Review*, no. 37 (Winter), pp. 84–99.

Millmow, A. 2003b, 'W. Brian Reddaway: Keynes's envoy to Australia 1913–2002', *Economic Record*, vol. 79, no. 224, pp. 136–8.

Millmow, A. 2004, 'Niemeyer, Scullin and the Australian economists', *Australian Economic History Review*, vol. 44, no. 2, pp. 143–60.

Millmow, A. 2005, 'The search for "a first class man": filling the Ritchie Research Chair in economics', *History of Economics Review*, vol. 42 (Summer), pp. 57–66.

Millmow, A. 2006, 'The book that never was: the biography of Sir Robert Gibson', *Journal of the Royal Australian Historical Society*, vol. 92, no. 2, pp. 183–201.

Mills, R. C. 1928, 'Australian loan policy', in R. C. Mills, P. Campbell and G. V. Portus (eds), *Studies in Australian Affairs*, Macmillan, Melbourne.

Mills, R. C. 1929, 'Some economic factors in industrial relations', *Economic Record*, vol. 10 (May), pp. 34–53.

Mills, R. C. 1933, 'The Australian situation', *Harvard Business Review*, vol. 11, no. 2, pp. 217–26.

Mills, R. C. and Walker, E. R. 1952, *Money*, Angus & Robertson, Sydney.

Minsky, H. P. 1976, *John Maynard Keynes*, Macmillan, London.

Moggridge, D. 1986, 'Keynes and his revolution in historical perspective', *Eastern Economic Journal*, vol. 12, no. 4, pp. 357–66.

Moggridge, D. 1992, *Maynard Keynes: An economist's biography*, Routledge, London.

Molesworth, B. H. 1933, 'The Bureau of Industry in Queensland', *Economic Record*, vol. 9, no. 16, pp. 105–6.

Monony, T. 2000, 'James Henry Scullin', in M. Grattan (ed.), *Australian Prime Ministers*, New Holland, Sydney.

Murray, R. and White, K. 1988, 'Staniforth Ricketson', in R. T. Appleyard and C. B. Schedvin (eds), *Australian Financiers*, Macmillan, Melbourne.

Nairn, B. 1986, *Jack Lang: The 'big fella'*, Melbourne University Press.

Nairn, B. and Serle, G. (eds) 1981, *Australian Dictionary of Biography. Volumes 1–15*, Melbourne University Press.

Nicholls, P. 1992. 'Australian Protestantism and the politics of the Great Depression, 1929-31', *Journal of Religious History* 17(2), pp. 210-21.

O'Dea, C. M. 1997, *Ian Clunies Ross*, Hyland House, Melbourne.

O'Donnell, R. 1996, 'John Maynard Keynes: yesterday, today and tomorrow', *History of Economics Review*, no. 25, pp. 1–13.

Osmond, W. 1985 *Frederic Eggleston: an intellectual in Australian politics*, Allen and Unwin, Sydney.

Palmer, V. 1940, *National Portraits*, Melbourne University Press.

Peacock, A. 1989, 'Keynes and the role of the State', in D. Crabtree and A. P. Thirlwall (eds), *Keynes and the Role of the State*, St Martins Press, New York.

Pearce, G. F. 1951, *Carpenter to Cabinet: Thirty-seven years of Parliament*, Hutchinson, London.

Peden, G. C. 1988, *Keynes, the Treasury and British Economic Policy*, Macmillan, London.

Peden, G. C. 1996, 'The Treasury view in the interwar period', in B. Corry (ed.), *Unemployment and the Economists*, Edward Elgar, Cheltenham, UK.

Perlman, M. 1977, 'The editing of the *Economic Record* 1925–1975', in J. Nieuwenhuysen and P. Drake (eds), *Australian Economic Policy*, Melbourne, Longmans.

Petridis, A. 1981, 'Australia: economists in a federal system', *History of Political Economy*, vol. 13, no. 3, pp. 405–35.

Petridis, R. (1994), 'The Disappearance of Australian Economics: a review essay', *Research in the History of Economic Thought*, Vol.12, pp.175-186.

Pigou, A. C. 1927, *Industrial Fluctuations*, Macmillan, London.

Pigou, A. C. 1933, *Theory of Unemployment*, Cambridge University Press.

Pike, D. 1968, *Charles Hawker*, Oxford University Press.

Plumptre, A. F. W. 1934, 'Review of *Australia in the World Crisis 1929–1933* by D. B. Copland', *American Economic Review*, vol. 25, pp. 490–1.

Plumptre, A. F. W. 1935, 'Review of *Australia in the World Crisis 1929–33* by D. B. Copland', *Economic Journal*, vol. XLV, pp. 131–3.

Polglaze J. and C. S. Soper (eds.) *Australian Economic Policy*, Melbourne University Press.

Priestley, R. E. 2002, *The Diary of a Vice-Chancellor*, edited by R. Ridley, Melbourne University Press.

Randerson, R. 1953, 'Masters of economic theory & practice', *Australian Quarterly*, vol. 25, no. 1 (March), pp. 42–54.

Raws, L. 1931, 'Economics and politics', *Australian Quarterly*, vol. 3 (June), pp. 36–45.

Reddaway, W. B. 1936, 'The general theory of employment, interest and money', *Economic Record*, vol. 12, pp. 28–36.

Reddaway, W. B. 1938 'Australian wage policy 1929-1937', *International Labour Review* 38(4), pp. 314-38.

Reddaway, W. B. 1960, 'Giblin as author', in D. B. Copland (ed.), *Giblin: The scholar and the man*, Cheshire, Melbourne.

Reddaway, W. B. 1995, 'Recollections of a lucky economist', *Banca Nazionale del Lavoro Quarterly Review*, vol. 48, no. 192 (March), pp. 3–17.

Renshaw, P. 1999, 'Was there a Keynesian economy in the USA between 1933 and 1945?', *Journal of Contemporary History*, vol. 34, no. 3 (July), pp. 337–61.

Richards, R. 1975, National insurance, PhD Thesis, Department of History, The Australian National University, Canberra.

Richmond, W. H. 1971, 'S. M. Bruce and Australian economic policy 1923–9', *Australian Economic History Review*, vol. 23, no. 2, pp. 238–57.

Ritchie, J. (ed.) 1990, *Australian Dictionary of Biography. Volume 12*, Melbourne University Press.

Rivett, R. 1965, *Australian Citizen Herbert Brookes1867–1963*, Melbourne University Press.

Rivett, D. 1972, *David Rivett: Fighter for Australian Science*, Camberwell.

Robbins, L. 1932, *An Essay on the Nature and Significance of Economic Science*, Macmillan, London.

Robertson, D. H. 1940, *Essays in Monetary Theory*, Staples Press, London.

Robertson, J. R. 1970, 'Scullin as prime minister: seven critical decisions', *Labour History*, no. 17 (June), pp. 27–36.

Robertson, J. R. 1974, *J. H. Scullin: A political biography*, University of Western Australia Press, Nedlands.

Robinson, M. L. 1986, Economists and politicians: the influence of economic ideas upon Labor politicians and governments 1931–1949, PhD Thesis, The Australian National University, Canberra.

Robinson, W. S. 1967, *If I Remember Rightly: The memoirs of W. S. Robinson 1876–1963*, edited by G. Blainey, Cheshire, Melbourne.

Roe, M. 1984, *Nine Australian Progressives: Vitalism in bourgeoisie social thought*, University of Queensland Press, St Lucia.

Roe, M. 1994, '"The best and most practical mind": J. B. Brigden as educator and economist, 1921–30', *Journal of Australian Studies*, no. 30, pp. 72–84.

Roe, M. 1995, *Australia, Britain, and Migration, 1915–40*, Cambridge University Press, Melbourne.

Rooth, T. 2000, 'Ottawa and after', in C. Bridge and B. Attard (eds), *Between Empire & Nation*, Australian Scholarly Publishing, Kew, Vic., pp. 133–57.

Ross, A. T. 1995, *Armed and Ready; The industrial development and defence of Australia 1900–45*, Turton and Armstrong, Wahroonga, NSW.

Rowse, T. 2002, *Nugget Coombs: A reforming life*, Cambridge University Press, Melbourne.

Sandelin, B., Sarafogloo, N. and Veiderpass, A. 1997, The post-1945 development of economics and economists in Sweden, History of Economic Thought Society of Australia Conference, Perth.

Sawer, G. 1963, *Australian federal politics and law, 1929-1949*, Melbourne University Press

Schedvin, C. B. 1964, Economic policy in depression and recovery in Australia 1927–1935, PhD Thesis, University of Sydney.

Schedvin, C. B. 1970, *Australia and the Great Depression*, Sydney University Press.

Schedvin, C. B. 1978, 'Sydney James Butlin', *Economic Record*, vol. 54, pp. 143–6.

Schedvin, C. B. 1987, *Shaping Science and Industry*, Allen & Unwin, Sydney.

Schedvin, C. B. 1988, 'Sir Alfred Davidson', in R. T. Appleyard and C. B. Schedvin (eds), *Australian Financiers*, Macmillan, Melbourne.

Schedvin, C. B. 1992, *In Reserve; Central banking in Australia, 1945–75*, Allen & Unwin, Sydney.

Schedvin, C. B. and Carr, J. E. 1995, 'Edward Shann: a radical liberal before his time', in S. Macintyre and J. Thomas (eds), *The Discovery of Australian History 1890–1939*, Melbourne University Press.

Scott, R. H. 1988, *The Economic Society of Australia: Its history—1925–1985*, Economic Society, Canberra.

Scott, R. H. 1992, 'L. G. Melville: distinguished fellow', *Economic Record*, vol. 68, no. 203, pp. 313–16.

Seldon, A. 1996, 'Ideas are not enough', *The Ideas that Shaped Modern Britain*, Fontana, London.

Selleck, R. J. W. 2003, *'The Shop': The University of Melbourne 1850–1919*, Melbourne University Press.

Shann, E. O. G. 1930a, *An Economic History of Australia*, Cambridge University Press.

Shann, E. O. G. 1930b, *Bond or Free*, Angus & Robertson, Sydney.

Shann, E. O. G. 1931c, 'The *Macmillan Report* and Australian recovery', *Bank of New South Wales Circular*, vol. II, no. 1, pp. 1–5.

Shann, E. O. G. 1932, 'Monetary policy', *Australian Quarterly*, vol. 4 (March), pp. 98–101.

Shann, E. O. G. 1933, 'The dead end of deflation', *Bank of New South Wales Circular*, vol. III, no. 1, pp. 8–12.

Shann, E. O. G. and Copland, D. B. 1931a, *The Crisis in Australian Finance 1929 to 1931. Documents on budgetary and economic policy*, Angus & Robertson, Sydney.

Shann, E. O. G. and Copland, D. B. 1931b, *The Battle of the Plans: Documents relating to the premiers' conference, May 25th to June 11th, 1931*, Angus & Robertson, Sydney.

Shann, E. O. G. and Copland, D. B. (eds) 1933, *The Australian Price Structure 1932*, Angus & Robertson, Sydney.

Sinclair, W. A. 1974, 'External and internal influences in the Depression of the 1930s in Australia', *Economics*, vol. 9, no. 2 (September), pp. 55–60.

Sinclair, W. A. 1976, *The Process of Economic Development in Australia*, Cheshire, Melbourne.

Siriwardena, M. 1995, 'The causes of the Depression in Australia in the 1930s: a general equilibrium evaluation', *Explorations in Economic History*, vol. 32, no. 1, pp. 51–81.

Skidelsky, R. 1992, *The Economist as Saviour. Volume 2 of John Maynard Keynes*, Viking Penguin, New York.

Skidelsky, R. 1996, *Keynes*, Oxford University Press.

Skidelsky, R. 2000, *John Maynard Keynes: Fighting for Britain 1937–1946*, Macmillan, London.

Smithies, A. 1936, 'Wages policy in the depression', *Economic Record*, vol.11, no.2, pp. 249-268.

Smyth, P. 1994, *Australian Social Policy: The Keynesian chapter*, University of NSW Press, Sydney.

Snooks, G. D. 1991, 'In my beginning is my end: the life and work of Noel George Butlin 1921–91', *Australian Economic History Review*, vol. XXX, no. 2, pp. 3–27.

Snooks, G. D. 1993, 'Bond or free? The life, work and times of Edward Shann 1884–1935', in M. A. B. Siddique (ed.), *A Decade of Shann Memorial Lectures 1981–90*, Academic Press International, Singapore.

Snowden, P. 1934, *Autobiography*, Nicholson & Watson, London.

Solow, R. 1993, 'How economic ideas turn to mush', in D. Colander and A. W. Coats (eds), *The Spread of Economic Ideas*, Cambridge University Press.

Spearritt, P. 1981 'Mythology of the Depression', in J. Mackinolty (ed.), *The wasted years? Australia's Great Depression* George Allen and Unwin, Sydney, pp. 1-9

Spender, P. 1972, *Politics and a Man*, Collins, Sydney.

Spierings, J. 1989, 'An exacting science: the university and the beginnings of economic policy making', *Arena*, no. 86, pp. 122–35.

Stevens, B. S. B. 1940, *Planning for War and Peace: Australian policy today*, Angus & Robertson, Sydney.

Sutherlin, K. 1980, The struggle for central banking in Australia: the royal commission of 1935–37 on the monetary and banking sectors, Sub-thesis, The Australian National University, Canberra.

Swan, T. W. 1939, 'Economic interpretation of John Maynard Keynes', *Australian Quarterly*, vol. XI, no. 1 (March), pp. 62–70.

Tange, A. 1996, 'Plans for the world economy: hopes and reality in wartime Canberra, a personal memoir', *Australian Journal of International Affairs*, vol. 50, no. 3, pp. 259–67.

Tomlinson, J. D. 1984, 'A "Keynesian revolution" in economic policymaking?', *Economic History Review*, vol. 37, no. 2, pp. 258–62.

Tomlinson, J. D. 1995, 'An unfortunate alliance: Keynesianism and the conservatives 1945–64', in A. F. Cottrell and M. Lawlor (eds), *New Perspectives on Keynes: Annual supplement to history of political economy*, Duke University Press, Durham, NC.

Tribe, K. 1997, *Economic Careers: Economics and economists in Britain 1930–1970*, Routledge, London.

Tsokhas, K. 1989, 'Business, empire and the United Australia Party', *Politics*, vol. 24, no. 2 (November), pp. 39–52.

Tsokhas, K. 1992a, '"A pound of flesh": war debts and Anglo-Australian relations, 1919–1932', *Australian Journal of Politics and History*, vol. 38, pp. 12–26.

Tsokhas, K. 1992b, '"Coldly received": Australia and the London capital market in the 1930s', *Australian Journal of International Affairs*, vol. 46, pp. 61–79.

Tsokhas, K. 1993, 'Federal cartel or Commonwealth hegemony?: the Australian Loan Council 1924–1939', *Australian Journal of Public Administration*, vol. 52, no. 1, pp. 95–113.

Tsokhas, K. 1995, 'Sir Otto Niemeyer, the bankrupt state and the federal system', *Australian Journal of Political Science*, vol. 30, pp. 18–38.

Tucker, M. V. 1981, 'Edward Dyason', in B. Nairn and G. Serle (eds), *Australian Dictionary of Biography*, Melbourne University Press, pp. 391–2.

Turnell, S. 1999, Monetary reformers, amateur idealists and Keynesian crusaders: Australian economists' international advocacy 1925–1950, PhD Thesis, Macquarie University, Sydney.

Turney, C., Biggott, U. and Chippendale, P. 1991, *A History of the University of Sydney. Volume 1 1850–1939*, Hale & Iremonger, Sydney.

Valentine, T. 1987a, 'The Depression of the 1930s', in R. Maddock and I. W. McLean (eds), *The Australian Economy in the Long Run*, Cambridge University Press, Melbourne, pp. 61–77.

Valentine, T. 1987b, 'The causes of the Depression in Australia', *Explorations in Economic History*, vol. 24, no. 1, pp. 43–62.

Viner, J. 1929, 'The Australian tariff', *Economic Record*, vol. 4, no. 9, pp. 306–15.

Walker, E. R. 1930, 'Some aspects of unemployment', *Australian Quarterly*, no. 6 (June), pp. 28–36.

Walker, E. R. 1932, 'The unemployment problem in Australia', *Journal of Political Economy*, vol. 40.

Walker, E. R. 1933a, *Australia in the World Depression*, P. S. King and Son, London.

Walker, E. R. 1933b, 'Saving and investment in monetary theory', *Economic Record*, vol. 9, pp. 185–201.

Walker, E. R. 1936, *Unemployment Policy, with Special Reference to Australia*, Angus & Robertson, Sydney.

Walker, E. R. 1939a, 'Sound finance', *Economic Record*, Supplement to the Congress of the Australian and New Zealand Association for the Advancement of Science, vol. 14.

Walker, E. R. 1939b, *War-Time Economics, with Special Reference to Australia*, Melbourne University Press.

Walker, E. R. 1943, *From Economic Theory to Policy*, University of Chicago Press.

Walker, E. R. 1947, *The Australian Economy in War and Reconstruction*, Columbia University Press, New York.

Webb, B. 1936, *Beatrice Webb Diaries 1924–1932*, Longman Green, London.

Weller, P. 1975, *Caucus Minutes 1901–1949*, Melbourne University Press.

White, C. 1992, *Mastering Risk: Environment, markets and politics in Australian economic history*, Oxford University Press, Melbourne.

White, K. 1987, *A Political Love Story: Joe and Enid Lyons*, Penguin, Sydney.

Whitwell, G. 1986, *The Treasury Line*, Allen & Unwin, Sydney.

Whitwell, G. 1994, 'The political power of economic ideas', in S. Bell and B. Head (eds), *State, Economy and Public Policy in Australia*, Oxford University Press, Melbourne.

Whitwell, G. 1995, 'The social philosophy of the F and E economists', *Australian Economic History Review*, vol. 25, no. 1, pp. 1–19.

Williams, G. 1938, 'Review of "Towards Industrial Peace in Australia" by O. De R. Foenander', *Economic Journal*, no. 1 (March), pp. 118–19.

Wilson, R. 1932, 'Capitalism and the second effort', *Australian Quarterly*, vol. 4 (December), pp. 56–65.

Wilson, R. 1951, 'James Bristock Brigden', *Economic Record*, vol. 27, no. 52, pp. 1–10.

Winch, D. 1966, 'The Keynesian revolution in Sweden', *Journal of Political Economy*, vol. 74, no. 2, pp. 168–76.

Winch, P. 1969, *Economics and Policy*, Hodder & Stoughton, London.

Wood, G. 1930, *Borrowing and Business in Australia: a study of the correlation between imports of capital and changes in national prosperity*, Oxford University Press, London.

Young, I. 1963, 'J. T. Lang and the Depression', *Labour History*, no. 5 (November), pp. 3–10.

Younger, R. M. 2003, *Keith Murdoch: Founder of a media empire*, Harper Collins, Sydney.

Alexander Turnbull Library, Wellington, New Zealand

Autobiography of J. B. Condliffe.

ANZ Group Archives, Melbourne

Bank of Australasia, D/O Correspondence between G. D. Healy and E. Godward.

Australian Archives, Canberra

A786: Prime Minister's Department, Development Branch Correspondence.

CP268/3: Prime Minister's Department, Various personal files.

M104: S. M. Bruce, Folders of Annual Correspondence.

CP503/1: R. G. Casey, Papers dealing with public finance.

CP503/1: R. G. Casey, Records of Conversations, CP103/19 Prime Minister Personal.

CP103/19: Lyons Papers, Purely personal.

A1421:1-3: Correspondence, Lord Casey/Lord Bruce, 1935–38.

CP503/1: R. G. Casey, Papers dealing with Public Finance.

CP503/1: Public Finance, August–October 1935.

AA1968/391: Secretary's Papers, Treasury Bills—Policy.

A5954/1: R. G. Casey, Correspondence, 1934.

CP503/1: R. G. Casey, Papers dealing with Public Finance.

Bank of England Archives

OV9/287: Australian Mission 1930, Miscellaneous.

OV9/288: Visit to Australia 1930, Unofficial Correspondence.

OV9/289: Visit to Australia 1930, Unofficial Correspondence.

OV9/290: Visit to Australia 1930, Financial Condition.

OV9/282: Niemeyer Mission, Budgetary Papers of Commonwealth and States.

OV9/292: Visit to Australia 1930, Trade and Other Statistics.

OV9/291: Visit to Australia 1930, Financial Position.

OV13/Files 1–5: Correspondence memoranda and fortnightly letters from Governor, Commonwealth Bank of Australia, giving Australian political and financial news.

G1/286: Governor's Files, Commonwealth Bank of Australia.

G1/287: Governor's Files, Commonwealth Bank of Australia.

G1/288: Governor's Files, Commonwealth Bank of Australia.

G1/291: Governor's Files, Australia—Sir Otto Niemeyer's Visit.

G1/290: Governor's Files, Australia—Miscellaneous.

G1/295: Governor's Files, Australia—Sir Claude Reading's Visit, 1936.

Churchill College, Cambridge

M. Hankey Papers

P. J. Grigg Papers

R. Hawtrey Papers

Commonwealth government reports

Royal Commission to Inquire into the Monetary and Banking System at Present in Operation in Australia, 1937, Report and Minutes of Evidence, [two vols], Canberra.

Report of the British Economic Mission, *Commonwealth Parliamentary Paper*, February 1929, Canberra.

Conference of Commonwealth and State Ministers, 25 May – 11 June 1931: Proceedings and Decisions of Conference, CPP, no. 236 of 1929–31, Canberra.

J. B. Were & Son, Melbourne

Staniforth Ricketson Diary, 1930–34

King's College Modern Archives Centre, King's College, Cambridge

Keynes Papers, Correspondence with Australian economists.

Latrobe State Library of Victoria

Sir Robert Gibson Collection, Mss 10823.

Sir Ambrose Pratt Collection, Mss 6547, Mss 6546.

Mitchell Library of New South Wales

Papers of C. M. Martin, Mss 4947.

Recollections and impressions of William Somerville.

National Bank of Australia Archive

A selection of letters from L. J. McConnan, General Manager of the National Bank, 1935–52.

National Library of Australia

Manuscript collection

E. T. Crutchley, Microfilm collection, M. 1829-30.

K. Murdoch, Ms 2827.

L. F. Giblin, Ms 366.

L. G. Melville, Ms 8671.

J. G. Latham, Ms 1009.

J. A. Lyons, Ms 4851.

C. A. S. Hawker, Ms 4848.

E. O. G. Shann, Ms 7347.

J. B. Brigden, Ms 730.

E. G. Theodore, Ms 7222.

F. Crisp, Ms 5243.

J. La Nauze, Ms 5248.

P. R. Hart, Ms 9410.

Brookes Papers, Ms 1924.

Oral Records

D. B. Copland, TRC 574.

E. H. Cox, TRC 43.

L. G. Melville, TRC 182.

C. Clark, Tape 2103.

W. C. Wentworth, TRC 4900.

R. Wilson, TRC 1612.

L. Bury, TRC 121.

Dame Enid Lyons, TRC 121/30.

Irving Douglas, TRC 131/21.

Joseph Alexander, TRC 121/10.

Personal interviews with authors

L. G. Melville, 20 June 1997, Canberra.

W. B. Reddaway, January 1997, Cambridge.

D. H. Merry, 1999, Melbourne.

Public Records Office, Kew, London

T160 Treasury: Finance Files.

T161 Treasury: Supply Files.

T176 Treasury: Niemeyer Papers.

University of Queensland Archives

S 135: Staff File, J. K. Gifford.

University of Queensland, Fryer Library

UQRF 87: Colin Clark Papers.

University of Sydney Archives

Papers of F. A. Bland.

University of Tasmania Archives

To Australia—With Thanks: Reminiscences of an immigrant, Torleiv Hytten autobiography,1971.

E. R. Walker Papers.

Patricia and Stephen Walker, Canberra

E. R. Walker Papers.

University of Melbourne Archives

Faculty of Economics and Commerce Papers (FECC): Correspondence, lecture notes; memoranda, journals and reports relating to professors: D. B. Copland, 1928–39; L. F. Giblin, 1928–39; G. L. Wood, 1930–39.

Economic Society of Victoria Branch: Papers, addresses and correspondence. Minutes of the Council of the Victorian Branch.

101/70: W. S. Robinson Papers.

Bank of New South Wales (Westpac) Archive, Homebush, New South Wales

Alfred Davidson Papers—Keynes file.

GM 302/198: General Manager Files, Casey correspondence.

GM 302/292: Bank economists.

GM 302/289: BNSW Economics Department.

GM 302/253; GM 302/221; GM 302/220: Royal Commission on Banking.

GM 302/590: Shann–Davidson correspondence.

GM 302/574: Davidson–W. S. Robinson.

A53/456: Davidson–Hytten correspondence, 1935.

A53/447: Davidson correspondence, 1933.

A54/451: Davidson–Janes correspondence.

A53/452: Davidson–Hytten, 1932.

A54-420; A53/418; A53/414: Commonwealth Bank.

A53/413-417: Janes and Copland correspondence.

A53/411: Davidson–Lyons correspondence.

GM 302//518: Sir O. Niemeyer File.

GM 302/476: R. C. Mills.

GM 302/412: Davidson–Janes correspondence, 1938.

GM 502/385; GM 302/386: Hytten correspondence.

Reserve Bank of Australia Archives

GGM-33-1: Correspondence between Melville and Senator H. Colebatch.

GGM-35-2: Melville correspondence with E. O. G. Shann.

GGM-37-1: Royal Commission, Correspondence with J. G. Phillips.

GGM-35-1: Monetary policy and the Depression.

GJG-59-1: J. M. Garland Papers.

GLG-51-5: Giblin correspondence relating to manuscript 'The growth of a central bank'.

GLG-51-1: Giblin correspondence with his family.

GLG-51-1: Giblin Papers.

GRG-33-4: Sir Robert Gibson Papers.

GLG-43-1: Giblin Papers.

Magazines and other literature

Bank of New South Wales Circular

Economic Notes

Nation and Athenaeum

Nation and New Statesman

National Bank of Australia Circular

The Bulletin

The Economist

The Margin

Newspapers

Adelaide Advertiser

Brisbane Telegraph

Cairns Post

Daily Guardian (UK)

Financial Times (UK)

Geelong Advertiser

Melbourne Sun

Smith's Weekly

Sydney Morning Herald

The Age

The Argus

The Commercial

The Daily Telegraph

The Herald

The Hobart Mercury

The Sydney Sun

The Times (UK)

The West Australian

The Westralian Worker

The Worker

www.ingramcontent.com/pod-product-compliance
Lightning Source LLC
Chambersburg PA
CBHW050038220326

41599CB00041B/7207